# On the Digital
# Semiosphere

# On the Digital Semiosphere

Culture, Media and Science
for the Anthropocene

*John Hartley, Indrek Ibrus
and Maarja Ojamaa*

BLOOMSBURY ACADEMIC
NEW YORK • LONDON • OXFORD • NEW DELHI • SYDNEY

BLOOMSBURY ACADEMIC
Bloomsbury Publishing Plc
1385 Broadway, New York, NY 10018, USA
50 Bedford Square, London, WC1B 3DP, UK
29 Earlsfort Terrace, Dublin 2, Ireland

BLOOMSBURY, BLOOMSBURY ACADEMIC and the Diana logo
are trademarks of Bloomsbury Publishing Plc

First published in the United States of America 2021
This paperback edition published in 2022

ISBN:     HB:     978-1-5013-6924-7
          PB:     978-1-5013-6921-6
        ePDF:     978-1-5013-6922-3
       eBook:     978-1-5013-6923-0

Typeset by Integra Software Services Pvt. Ltd.

To find out more about our authors and books visit www.bloomsbury.com
and sign up for our newsletters.

# CONTENTS

*Illustrations* vii

PART ONE   Spheres and globes

1   A semiotic theory of spheres 3

2   A short history of globes 35

3   Juri Lotman and cultural semiotics 53

PART TWO   Elements of the digital semiosphere

4   'Inside thinking worlds' 67

5   Dialogue and dynamics 85

6   Cultural semiotics in a multidisciplinary environment 103

PART THREE   Micro-scale: Text

7   What does culture want? 117

8   Text, transmission, translation 127

9   Text, creation, newness 145

10 Text, preservation, memory 165

PART FOUR   Meso-scale: Institution

11 Planetary systems of culture production 177

12 Bubbles: Production of continual systems 185

13 Blows: Production of discontinuities 199

14 Foam: Production of dynamic multiplicity 211

# PART FIVE   Macro-scale: Global system

15 Globe: Production of digital distinctions 225

16 The Digital semiosphere and the technosphere 239

17 Semiosis: Regulating politics and economics 255

# PART SIX   Cultural science for the Anthropocene

18 Staged conflict: New demes and classes 271

19 Populations of rules: The constitution and coordination of media-made groups 287

20 Where to now, planet? 303

*Acknowledgements* 311
*References* 313
*Index* 340

# ILLUSTRATIONS

## Illustrations by Peeter Laurits

I  'Plant Pride' (2018) from *Coming Soon*  1
II  'Foreign Tongue' (2015) from *Codex Naturalis*  65
III  'Romeo and Juliet' (2003) from *Dining with Worms* (with Ain Mäeots)  115
IV  'Heavenly News' (2001) from *Noosphere*  175
V  'Atlas of Heavens 22' (2000), from *Atlas of Heavens*  223
VI  'Down the Stream' (2003) from *Dining with Worms*  269
Colophon (Figure 20.2): 'New Earth 2' (2010) from *Tuareg Dreams*

## Figures

1.1  Archimedes' lever moves the world  6
1.2  Juri Lotman  9
1.3  (a) V.I. Vernadsky's grave, Moscow; (b) The Ukrainian Vernadsky Antarctic research base  12
1.4  Thinking spherically: Vladimir I. Vernadsky, aged 15, 1878  14
1.5  Combining 'upward causation' from reductive science (information) with 'downward causation' from system science (semiosis)  18
2.1  The array of recording equipment for meteorological observations by sea, land, air and space – the digital semiosphere intersects with the geosphere  39
2.2  Globalization as state buccaneering: Silver Medal commemorating Sir Francis Drake's circumnavigation of the world, 1577–1580  43

2.3    On the up: Globalization of data  44
2.4    All languages are world languages. The first Welsh-
       language globe (2009)  47
3.1    Guiding tubes: Juri Lotman, scholar, author –
       sculpture  55
4.1    The participants and places of the semiosphere are like
       a nesting doll  71
5.1    Core and periphery in a semiosphere  93
7.1    Where does a text stop? Playing with expression,
       boundaries and structure  123
9.1    Memes as reflexive autocommunication (delight in
       repetition)  150
9.2    Memes as irreversible innovation (delight in
       newness)  150
9.3    Estonian president Toomas Hendrik Ilves and his
       singalong selfie  153
9.4    Dialogue in the semiosphere, structured in difference:
       (a) general model; b) interacting dialogic systems  154
12.1   Early iBooks interface  192
14.1   The Water Cube, Beijing  212
16.1   Longue-durée economic/social organization, correlated
       with communication technology  242
17.1   Public space in the ideal (Aristotelian) city: both Pnyx
       and Agora  263
18.1   Coordinating rebellion: *Fridays for Future* cuts through
       where representative politics doesn't  274
19.1   A regulator or governor  294
20.1   Greta Thunberg: instituting action  309
20.2   'Through Eden took their solitary way': Where to Now,
       Planet?  310

# PART ONE

# Spheres and globes

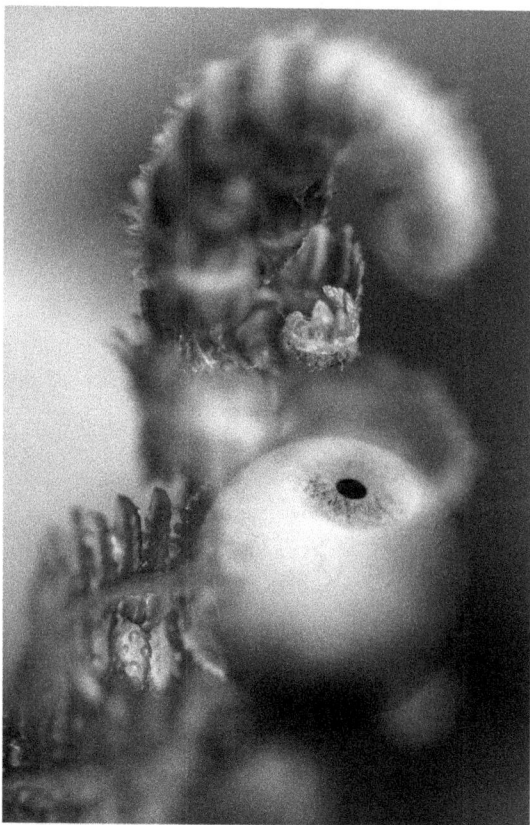

*Peeter Laurits 'Plant Pride' (2018) from* Coming Soon
https://www.peeterlaurits.com/works/coming-soon

# 1

# A semiotic theory of spheres

*The relationship between multiplicity and unity is* a fundamental
characteristic of culture. *It is here that logical and historical
reality diverge.*

(JURI LOTMAN, 2009: 3)

\* \* \*

## One world; one species

In 2016, on the eve of the Trump presidency in the United States, the
architect and commentator Michael Sorkin published an opinion-column
about the practice of architecture in the era of Trump Towers:

> Ours is not an autonomous discipline operating in a free field. Rather,
> it's ever engaged in a deepening struggle to find the terms of its own
> distinction and necessity, especially now, as the designed environment
> expands its remit to cover the whole world, and the gap between the body
> and technology grows increasingly blurry. Building always marks and
> measures space, equity, and possibility, but it's losing any clear-enough
> idea of how to perform as we race toward total urbanization on a planet
> at the point of asphyxiation.

> (Sorkin, 2016)

In the same column, Sorkin mentions that he has had to cut short a visit to
China because 'my asthma got so bad I have to come home early'. In March
2020, not in China but in New York City, he was killed by the global viral
contagion of COVID-19.[1] His words take on a portentous prescience:

---

[1]See Sorkin's obituary: https://www.architecturalrecord.com/articles/14526-obituary-michael-
sorkin-1948-2020.

Civilizations are marked by their priorities, and ours are too given over to prisons, malls, and McMansions and too little to good housing for all, complete and sustainable communities, green energy, rational mobility, structures of succor. Politics programs our architecture. The emblem of Trump's agenda is a piece of architecture – that absurd pharaonic wall he bruits for the Mexican border. His whole project trumpets control, and his mantra is shared by many an architect: just leave it to me!

(Sorkin, 2016)

Architecture is but one of many creative knowledge-based disciplines that is forced to rethink its purposes and principles in response to the globalizing dynamics of digital media, led by free-market corporate expansionism and libertarian ideologies ('just leave it to me!'). In practice, these seem to produce only their own opposite: authoritarianism and surveillance:

Trump's sensibility is deeply old-fashioned: he makes buildings, things. Far scarier than tacky, grandiose building, however, is a spatial agenda being advanced by famously liberal Silicon Valley: the 'smart' city. The phrase creeps me out. I worry that we're being sold a bill of goods by huge corporations looking to embed sensors in every sidewalk, window, and wall to create 'responsive' environments in the name of unsnarling traffic, conserving energy, and keeping megacities going, but which will be used, at best, to continue compiling consumer and behavioral profiles to sell us stuff – and, at worst, to surveille every inch of the earth to call down drone strikes on designated miscreants or raids by ICE on those 11 million 'illegals,' based on some biometric fantasy of alien-ness. Data are not neutral. Metadata can be the devil's work.

(Sorkin, 2016)

These are the issues motivating this book. It seems that humans only become aware of themselves as a single, global species when faced by a singular, globular threat. It used to be nuclear catastrophe; in the last few years, it's been global warming; now it's coronavirus. The response, however, is far from global. So far, it's nationalistic, partisan, self-interested and oftentimes stupid. It's the same as it has been since Neolithic times: 'This means war!'

That means death for some, while others prosper, careless of collateral damage while pursuing 'business as usual'. Sorkin himself was an early casualty. But his message need not be. Instead of continuing 'business as usual' by digital means, those who practice the knowledge professions, where digital globalization is most accelerated, need to work harder to understand *why* a liberal-sounding business agenda can result in a dystopian disaster for unfavoured individuals and for the planet as a whole. As Sorkin argues, those who observe and engage in the globalization of digital media and culture need to consider the terms of their own 'distinction and necessity'.

What value has each successive technological trend (from Parametricism in architecture to Blockchain in trade) if its users simply apply it to political parochialism and careless profit? Too often these bring with them no sense of shared responsibility for the species or the planet, but only deeper divisions between 'winners' and 'losers' (as US president Trump likes to put it).

Are 'we' sleepwalking into pandemics and climate catastrophe, or can we take collective action to achieve 'structures of succor' for individual selves, for social communities and the Earth system? That's the agenda for youth-led climate justice action 'on the street' (real and virtual). It's also the agenda for this book. However, we take a step back from immediate activism in the global 'designed environment' of the 'smart city' to analyse *how* culture – built and mediated – 'always marks and measures space, equity, and possibility', as Michael Sorkin put it, at micro- and macro-scale, no matter what new technological wonder is deployed to build it.

*Can* a human-designed planetary environment be both culturally humane and environmentally sustainable? It seems that the answer depends on two things:

- *Cui bono?* At the outset, who is assumed to be the beneficiary? Is this action for 'me' individual, 'we' corporate/state agency, or 'we' community/humanity?
- *Who clears up?* At the end, how is the planet assumed to recover from our destructive wastefulness, digital as well as analogue? Are our actions organized for environmental laissez-faire (conquest and exploitation), or systemic regeneration (one species; one planet)?

At the outset, for reasons we hope will become clear throughout, we assume the primacy of culture. In the end, we theorize a 'digital semiosphere', whose positive and negative heuristics need to be understood among differing intersectional knowledge systems.

'Civilisations are marked by their priorities', says Sorkin. To identify them, we need to return to first principles. This is our plan. You won't read much more below about the global pandemic, except to acknowledge that 'going viral' is a reality we ignore at our peril.

# Digital Lotman?

This book is offered as an original work that explains how communication, media and cultural studies, now and in future, can benefit from Juri Lotman's sophisticated and prescient thinking, which models a systems/dynamic approach to culture as a whole. Building out from that model gives us something to think with, an Archimedes lever (Figure 1.1), not to 'move

FIGURE 1.1 *Archimedes' lever moves the world. Illustration from* Mechanics *Magazine, 1824.*[2]

the world' but to subject globalization in the digital era to a positioned 'outside' perspective from which it can better be understood and measured. The systems approach that Lotman elaborated has a long history, going back more than a century. At the same time it poses radical new questions about the relationships among humanity, other living beings and the planet.

Our notion of the 'digital semiosphere' offers a rich and compelling framework for global digital culture and its political, economic and environmental context, at a time when popular media and local activism are increasingly focused on the unfolding climate emergency of the Anthropocene era (on this contested term, see Colebrook and Weinstein, 2015; Schneiderman, 2015; Grusin, 2017; Sperling, 2019). We situate our approach in the intersectional history of ideas but leverage the account towards a new interdisciplinary alignment that is capable of analysing both intimate personal sense-making and global 'big data'. We show how they're connected and what governs change. The book is in the Lotmanian tradition (see Chapter 3), which itself was drawn from cybernetics as well as literary theory and the semiotics of culture. But this is a future-facing account, helping readers and interdisciplinary researchers to work from an integrated, systemic-dynamic conceptualization of different levels of semiosis and their modes of interaction.

---

[2]Image by *Mechanics Magazine* (1824), Public domain, via Wikimedia Commons: https://commons.wikimedia.org/w/index.php?curid=1921693.

Thereby, cultural and media analysis can step forward with well-theorized explanatory adequacy, at a time when too much scholarship is narrowly focused, encouraging local specialization with technical detail amid a chaos of incommensurate methods, or unwittingly applying formulae derived from the spent paradigm of industrial, analogue, nation-state theorizing.

A word or two about 'digital'. The semiosphere has of course existed for centuries, and its workings have co-evolved with technologies of communication, ever since humans gained the power of speech. Human exploration and migration have accelerated throughout modernity (as we explain in Chapter 2), so that 'the global' has been understood to refer to the planetary Earth system since at least the 1500s. There is a very strong element of continuity about the 'digital semiosphere'. But we argue too that here is a step-change, irreversible and 'explosive' in Lotman's terms (2009). The shift *(colonialism, goods, industry and trade)* → *(corporate globalization of information, computation and mediated communication)* is revolutionizing the world economy, its politics and our knowledge systems, at an accelerating rate (McKinsey, 2016), with consequences going far beyond commerce and trade, provoking a new focus on the fundamentals of care, culture and community, and their prospects in a post-coronavirus world.

By 'digital' we mean the constellation of phenomena that now dominate the information or knowledge society, where converged and integrated electronics, telecommunications, broadcasting, computation, the internet, automation and artificial intelligence drive the military, the economy, politics and mediated culture at personal, corporate and international scale.

'Globalization' may not have reached all countries or industries and may still exclude the 'global poor', but digital automation may still determine how those groups are known and treated. *The Guardian* reported in 2019:

All around the world, from small-town Illinois in the US to Rochdale in England, from Perth, Australia, to Dumka in northern India, a revolution is under way in how governments treat the poor. You can't see it happening, and may have heard nothing about it. It's being planned by engineers and coders behind closed doors, in secure government locations far from public view. Only mathematicians and computer scientists fully understand the sea change, powered as it is by artificial intelligence (AI), predictive algorithms, risk modeling and biometrics. But if you are one of the millions of vulnerable people at the receiving end of the radical reshaping of welfare benefits, you know it is real and that its consequences can be serious – even deadly.[3]

---

[3]See the series on 'Automating poverty' in *The Guardian*: (https://www.theguardian.com/technology/series/automating-poverty). See especially Ed Pilkington's report on 'Digital Dystopia' (14 October 2019): https://www.theguardian.com/technology/2019/oct/14/automating-poverty-algorithms-punish-poor, quoted above.

Although digital globalization may not include everyone, it certainly governs and regulates our life chances and everyone else's. Together with what Jackie Wang (2018) calls 'carceral capitalism', the planet is entering a new phase where digital information, productivity and culture can generate untold wealth for some but unimagined 'digital dystopia' for others, under a creeping regime of digital surveillance and the militarization of policing, much of it done by corporations and partisans (Wang, 2018), backed up by 'disinformation war' in marketing and social media (Coppins, 2020).

Digital labour involves unpaid employment. It used to be called slavery but now goes by other names, from indebted bondage and prison labour to 'internships', 'influencers' and 'volunteer' work. Automation generates AI-driven uselessness among the unskilled (Harari, 2018): with a 'reserve army' of precarious, displaced and migrant labour 'outsourced' to low-GDP regions (Foster, McChesney and Jonna, 2011).

It is not just natural resources (Lampert, 2019) but also human resources that are exploited and wasted at unprecedented scale and with little accountability. Those who enjoy affluence and those who endure poverty never meet. While private wealth inequality increases, governments are poor and indebted, and public investments in poverty-reduction decrease (Alvaredo et al., 2018: 11–15).

It would be foolish to think that scholarship or even action can halt these trends simply by contesting them, although documenting the erosion of public and democratic acts, institutions and relationships is vital work. It would be far more foolish not to try to understand them. That is why we think the concept and study of the 'digital semiosphere' is of the utmost importance right now.

This is where Lotman comes in (Figure 1.2). Although communication, media and cultural studies have separately and collectively developed a distinctive object and mode of study since the 1970s, this vibrant and interdisciplinary field has borrowed more than it has returned to neighbouring fields. Economics, political, technological and social sciences all expect to influence the world, but they don't take serious account of culture and semiosis – which nevertheless (we argue) make the world go round. Lotman reminds us that 'culture' is itself a fundamental concept and powerful causal agent, side-lined in contemporary research funding but ignored at our collective peril. Thus far, however, 'culture' does not compel attention in public policy and business strategy, except as a cost to economic growth or impediment to political advantage. The result is that public policy, private enterprise and international strategies have failed to deal with the challenges of poorly regulated digital-media productivity at planetary scale, and cultural scholarship has failed to gain a seat at the table of global deliberations about the digital future.

*

FIGURE 1.2 Juri Lotman. *Photo by Malev Toom, courtesy of Juri Lotman Semiotics Repository, Tallinn University, Estonia.*

The warnings sounded in critical media studies, where scholars have developed compelling critiques of the digital semiosphere's social impact, are largely ignored by business schools, among technologists (scientists and engineers) and inside professionalized political parties, all of which groups are 'abstracted' from the social and cultural impact of their own agendas, just as a drone pilot is abstracted from the impact of their 'textual analysis' on a target on the other side of the world.

Those who think about *global digital culture* and those who analyse *global digital power* are in conflict rather than in dialogue. One camp focuses on the digital downside (and cultural identity), the other on the digital upside (and economic influence). A 'digital divide' in disciplinary knowledge systems needs to be reconnected.

Of course, critique is getting through to – and from! – many communities, citizens, students and digitally organized social movements. They have mobilized to challenge economic and political forums directly. Typically, the 'official' response to that is to treat activism as a threat, not as a source of solutions. Likewise, youth and climate activists, as well as pro-democracy and communitarian movements, see untrammelled global-digital capitalism as the main threat to their futures, not as an apparatus they can fix.

The global digital semiosphere creates and directs the global asymmetries of power that communication, media and cultural studies analyse so well.

Too often, though, such analysis proceeds in a piecemeal, uncoordinated way, with too many exceptions and not enough rules. The result is that our field's 'findings' are easy to ignore. They don't compel the attention of neighbouring disciplines (e.g. economics, political science, sociology, psychology from the sciences; history, linguistics and philosophy from the humanities), never mind the 'powers that be'.

Where to start? Our contribution suggests that a systematic approach to the creation of meaning and thence knowledge, by the whole species across the whole planet, is the analytical minimum needed to understand 'what's occurring'.[4]

# Spheres

I feel that in its present form this study is accessible to every fancier of the tale, provided they are willing to follow the writer into the labyrinth of the tale's multiformity, which in the end will become apparent to them as an amazing uniformity. (Vladimir Propp, 1968/1928: xxv)[5]

As 'fanciers of the tale', we start with the 'sphere' part of the 'digital semiosphere'. Our purpose is to establish a conceptual apparatus that is capable of theorizing the global extent of communication, and thence of digital media and networks, and from that point also capable of directing purposeful interventions and actions. The context is planetary, where culture, knowledge, politics and economics are now played out. But at the same time, the global context poses new changes and challenges in which culture – unwittingly perhaps but systematically – elaborates ever-more abstract and 'technologically equipped' (Papacharissi, 2010) modes of knowing and sharing. Our own purpose is to derive a viable and robust model of how culture works – and why it doesn't – when it competes with the complex Earth system from which it is itself evolved and which it seeks so often to govern.

A 'sphere' does not imply smooth-surfaced unity and uniformity. Indeed, it can only start where there is difference, in a 'labyrinth of multiformity', like the terrestrial sphere of the Earth system, where *different systems* encounter each other in relations of hissing and seething tectonic subduction, vulcanism, spin and spit. In social terms, we find turbulence, clash and conflict. In cultural terms, there is untranslatable incommensurability between *at least*

---

[4]See: https://www.bbc.com/news/uk-wales-south-east-wales-42738650.
[5]When Lotman first attended Leningrad State University as an undergraduate in 1939, before serving in the Second World War, Vladimir Propp was one of his most admired (and admiring) teachers (Lotman, 2014: 18–20).

*two systems* – which nevertheless meet and communicate. Our guide, Juri Lotman (who we'll introduce properly in Chapter 3),[6] observes:

> The idea that the starting point of any semiotic system is not the simple isolated sign (word), but rather the relation between at least two signs causes us to think in a different way about the fundamental basis of semiosis. The starting point occurs not with a single isolated model, but rather in semiotic space.

> (2009: 172)

'Semiotic space' is of planetary extent. We want to situate it within the larger environment of the Earth system. To do that we start where Lotman himself did: he developed the idea of the semiosphere from Vladimir Vernadsky's concept of the biosphere. We argue that this was not merely a subsidiary borrowing or metaphorical appropriation of Vernadsky's work but a radical reconceptualization that puts communication (translation between and among incommensurable codes) and culture (groups that make and share knowledge) at the heart of life processes.

* *

We follow this line of thought through from Vernadsky and Lotman to the most recent work on the 'technosphere', in order to describe an integrated approach, which has implications for the organization of scientific disciplines as well as for our understanding of globalization. We tackle these issues in Part I of the book:

**Ch1: A semiotic theory of spheres** works through the spheres first conceptualized by V. I. Vernadsky (biosphere/noosphere) and J. M. Lotman (semiosphere), to produce a 'theory of spheres' to integrate the study of Earth and culture, as well as science and the humanities, in a long-overdue synthesis for the Anthropocene era.

**Ch2: A short history of globes** and globalization, focusing on what we are tempted to call the *wrong-way-round* discovery of complexity and scale: that is, the habit of philosophy, science and human discovery more generally to work from the simple, singular and linear towards greater complexity, multiplicity and dynamism, when in reality the latter features explain the former. We must change our stories of individualistic origins (identity culture) and linear cause-effect relations (reductive science) to match the reality of global systems, which evolve *systems before specimens*.

---

[6]Lotman was a good guide. See for instance: http://jordanrussiacenter.org/event-recaps/darra-goldstein-brings-back-life-yuri-lotmans-high-society-dinners/.

(a)

(b)

FIGURE 1.3 *(a) V.I. Vernadsky's grave, Moscow (Photo by Julia&Keld, 2012); (b) The Ukrainian Vernadsky Antarctic research base (2015).*[7]

---

[7]Screen grab from: https://www.youtube.com/watch?v=kRYFvpFuXZo ('JT from www. flyingnorth.net reporting from the Ukrainian Vernadsky research base on the Antarctic peninsula').

Ch3: **Lotman and cultural semiotics**: a guide to our guide, and to some of the terms he uses, which we go on to elaborate and amplify throughout the book, in the context of global digital media.

Part II, **Elements of the digital semiosphere** (Chapters 4–6), puts on the walking boots necessary for the hike needed to catch the winds of digital globalization, and limbers up for the main sections of the book, which take us over some rugged conceptual terrain, and some beautiful ideas, as we tour three distinct but interrelated levels of semiosphere analysis in Part III, **micro/text** (Chapters 7–10); Part IV, **meso/institution** (Chapters 11–14); and Part V, **macro/planetary system** (Chapters 15–17). We arrive at a destination mapped out by our canny guide but not predicted in his own work: Part VI, **Cultural science for the Anthropocene** (Chapters 18–20), where we are able at last to pose the fundamental question relating to the semiotic Earth system: '*Where to now, Planet?*'

It seems there is much ado about spheres in this book. We discuss them not in hierarchical order but as they have arisen in scholarship – more or less in the order in which our guide Juri Lotman 'discovered' them. This means that the biggest one comes first (because we're all standing on it), but the means for *knowing* them come much later (guided by Lotman). In terms of the evolution of knowledge, then, we envelop our topic, sphere on sphere, like this:

## EVOLUTION OF BIOGEOCHEMICAL COMPLEX SYSTEMS AT PLANETARY SCALE

Summary, in order of the naming of each term in the history of scholarship (not in hierarchical order)

*Geosphere* (Vernadsky): Biogeochemical evolution, incl. *lithosphere* (crust, land), *hydrosphere* (ocean, rivers), *atmosphere* (climate, weather).

*Biosphere* (Vernadsky): All 'living matter', past and present (evolution); all living organisms, their interrelations, and conditions of existence and survival.

*Noosphere* (Vernadsky; and Ong, 2012) a term not used by Lotman, who subsumed it into the *semiosphere*: sphere of thought, including 'mediasphere' (Hartley).

*Semiosphere* (Lotman): Culture, language, communication, media: sphere of meaning; Earth-system: *semiosphere incorporates biosphere* (M. Lotman).

*Technosphere* (Herrmann-Pillath and others): Co-evolution of meaning and making; accelerationism and the digital world.

*Future-sphere* (Anthropocene): Coordinating groups (demes) and staging conflict: thinking and acting as a species, at planetary scale, without imposing centralizing rules on dynamic difference.

# Change and transformation in turbulent times

Reading Vernadsky inspired Lotman to think materially and globally – spherically – about cultural semiotics. The Russian-Ukrainian biogeochemist and geologist Vladimir I. Vernadsky (1863–1945, Figures 1.3 and 1.4) invented the concept of the *biosphere* (sphere of living matter) and, later, the *noosphere* (sphere of thought) – variously glossed by him as reason, consciousness, intelligence and not confined to humans (Vernadsky 1938a). These spheres were not intended as metaphors: Vernadsky sought to describe them as biogeochemical strata of the Earth system.

*

FIGURE 1.4 *Thinking spherically: Vladimir I. Vernadsky, aged 15, 1878.*[8]

[8]Vladimir Vernadsky, high school student of the 1st Classical Gymnasium of St. Petersburg, 1878: Владимир Вернадский, гимназист 1-й классической гимназии Петербурга. Фото 1878 г.: https://en.wikipedia.org/wiki/Vladimir_Vernadsky.

His route to a comprehensive theory of Earth-system spheres is not often followed in cultural studies or philosophy: Vernadsky went in not through 'poetics' but through *mineralogy*. In his history of Soviet science, writer Simon Ings takes up the story:

> In the summer of 1888, walking in the Alps, he had his epiphany: he saw that mineralogy, studied the right way, as a science of change and energy transfer, could connect cosmological history with the history of life itself.
> (Ings, 2106: 14)

Revolution, counter-revolution, civil war, terror and two world wars surged incessantly across the Russian empire and its successor state, the Soviet Union. In the midst of this political chaos and social conflict – 'change and energy transfer' in the social realm – Vernadsky was stimulated to *intellectual* work:

> By 1922, he had established that, of the ninety-two elements then known, over fifty were bound up in the history of living organisms. These elements comprised 99.6 by weight of the whole earth's crust, leading Vernadsky to conclude that living organisms could reshape planets as surely as any purely physical force. It was the first step on an intellectual journey that would culminate in Vernadsky's concept of the noösphere – the idea that intelligence itself was yet another planet-changing component of earth's geological system.
> (Ings: 50)

Writing in 1925, Vernadsky himself put it this way:

> There exists now on the terrestrial surface a great geological force ... This force does not seem to be a new manifestation or special form of energy, nor yet a pure and simple expression of known energy. But it exerts a profound and powerful influence on the course of energetic phenomena on the Earth's surface, and consequently has repercussions ... on the existence of the planet itself. This force is human reason, the directed and controlled will of social humanity.
> (Vernadsky, 1925: 13)

He believed that the science he wanted to pursue suited his turbulent times: indeed, that the natural phenomena he wanted to explain – change and energy transfer – were catalysed by the 'free energy' of applied thought, taken as a planetary phenomenon. Note that he did not define 'human reason' as an individualistic power but as one that is 'directed' (purposeful, even while resulting in unforeseen consequences), 'controlled' (a process of organized collective action for a purpose) and 'social' (a species phenomenon). In other words, it is the relations among thought, energy and matter that he sought to explain: this is reason at scale and at planetary extent. He wrote in 1903: 'I consider that the interests of scientific progress are closely and inextricably tied to the growth of a wide democracy and humanitarian attitudes, and vice-versa' (quoted in Ings: 19). In 1943, aged 80, he wrote:

> This new elemental geological process is taking place at a stormy time, in the epoch of a destructive world war. But the important fact is that our democratic ideals are in tune with the elemental geological processes, with the law of nature, and with the noösphere.
>
> (1943: 21)

Wishful thinking, perhaps; or – taking Zhou Enlai's famously long view of the impact of modern revolutions on 'our democratic ideals' – 'it's too early to say'![9] Either way, the betrayal of those ideals in successive political crackdowns in the Soviet Union and elsewhere does not undermine the importance of the ideals themselves, as Hans Magnus Enzensberger argued forcefully in his prescient essay on the 'Industrialization of the Mind':

> When the production of goods expands beyond the most immediate needs, the old proclamations of human rights, however watered down by the rhetoric of the establishment and however eclipsed by decades of hardship, famine, crises, forced labor, and political terror, will now unfold their potential strength. It is in their very nature that, once proclaimed, they cannot be revoked. Again and again, people will try to take them at their face value and, eventually, to fight for their realization.
>
> (Enzensberger, 1982: 10)

V. I. Vernadsky understood that, by the twentieth century, humanity had achieved consciousness of its own global extent and action, but he did not seek to appropriate 'human rights' – including intellectual freedom – as some sort of intellectual property, to be used for 'immaterial exploitation' of populations and other species. He wanted to understand the impact of 'living matter' on the planet, including the organized activities of humans (understood socially and as a totality) as part of the evolutionary life processes of the biosphere, through the cumulative action of populations, rather than individually, such that scientific thought itself could be integrated into a naturalistic model of evolutionary systems.

Where Vernadsky imagined a 'sphere' of thought, Enzensberger imagined what he called the 'consciousness industry' or the 'mind industry': the abstraction of capital from material production into the realms of 'immaterial

---

[9]See: https://www.historytoday.com/dean-nicholas/zhou-enlais-famous-saying-debunked for the story of this famous saying, which was reputed to be his opinion about the impact of the French Revolution (1789).

exploitation', via the expanding 'industrialisation of the mind'. In a list that still has analytic force, he names:

- radio, cinema, television, recording, advertising and public relations, new techniques of manipulation and propaganda, newspaper and book publishing, fashion and industrial design, the propagation of established religions and of esoteric cults, opinion polls, simulation, tourism, and the mind industry's 'most essential sphere', education. (1982: 6)

The difference between the two writers in this context is that Enzensberger is thinking historically (where thought, politics, economics and technology co-develop), while Vernadsky is thinking evolutionarily – linking such developments to the evolution of the Earth system. Like Enzensberger, Vernadsky had personally experienced the causal force of historic human power struggles, but he was focused on understanding how 'the effort of consciousness' worked at planetary scale and over evolutionary time, and not necessarily just among humans. The continuing convergence of these dynamics is what we characterize as the digital semiosphere.

# Rethinking disciplines

Vernadsky is not only important for his 'bold conjectures' (in Karl Popper's phrase) but also for his approach to the disciplinary organization of knowledge. He wanted to change *how* we know as well as *what* we know. Throughout his work, he distinguished between two types of science: 'the sciences common to *all reality* (physics, astronomy, chemistry, mathematics), and sciences related to *the Earth* (biological, geological, and humanistic sciences)' (1938a: 31).

Here, he ignores the familiar and often prejudicial disciplinary distinction that is found in university faculties, between sciences and the humanities, or between the natural and social sciences. Instead, he divides the sciences into those that study 'inert' *matter-energy*: (physics, astronomy, chemistry, mathematics) and those devoted to the Earth system's *biosphere*: (biological, geological, and 'humanistic sciences') (1943: 17). The first does not fully explain the second. Also, the biosphere has significant *impact on* the geosphere, reversing standard models of causation, because 'the matter of the biosphere' is able to convert solar energy in such a way as to create what Vernadsky calls 'free energy'. This 'free energy' was 'capable of doing work on Earth', using *collective* thought (as manifest in the systematic practical action of populations), which he dubbed the noosphere ('sphere of thought'). The noosphere includes formal science, accumulated and adjusted by thousands of hands over extended time, as well as evolved trial-and-error practices dispersed among humankind. The biosphere is conceptualized as a region of matter, energy *and 'a source of transformation of the planet'* (Vernadsky, 1998: 43–4). Therefore, causation cannot be presumed to work in a linear sequence from simple inert physics to complex living systems. Instead, each type needs its own dedicated sciences.

This is a useful model of disciplinary classification, worthy of revival, because it does not set science and culture, fact and value, molecules and meanings against each other. Indeed, among other stimuli, Vernadsky has provoked a period of mutual borrowing across humanities and sciences, which Søren Brier (2006) organizes into a 'map' showing the mutual influence of 'semiotic' and 'information' approaches (see Figure 1.5) in the development of biosemiotics.

*

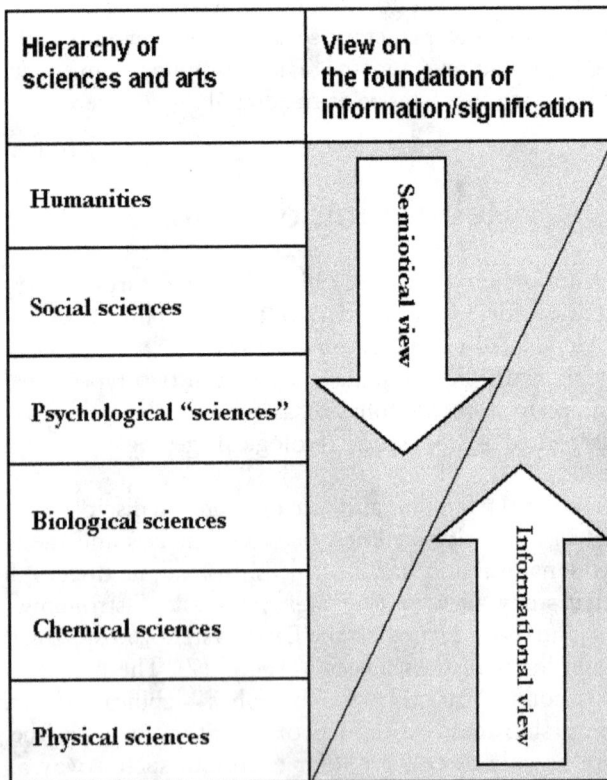

| Hierarchy of sciences and arts | View on the foundation of information/signification |
|---|---|
| Humanities | |
| Social sciences | Semiotical view |
| Psychological "sciences" | |
| Biological sciences | |
| Chemical sciences | Informational view |
| Physical sciences | |

FIGURE 1.5 *Combining 'upward causation' from reductive science (information) with 'downward causation' from system science (semiosis). The differences between humanities and the natural sciences are shown on a gradient,* not in opposition. *Source: Søren Brier (2006).*

Brier (2006) comments:

> It is interesting to see that semiotics thus has moved from the humanities
> into biology and from there even into the other natural sciences at the
> same time as the formulation of objective informational concepts has
> been used as the basis of understanding all types of cognitive processes
> in animals, machines, humans and organizations in the 'information
> processing paradigm.' Information science is thus moving from computer
> science down into nature and up into cognitive systems, human
> intelligence, consciousness and social systems and communication in
> competition with semiotics that is moving in the other direction.

Brier sees the interaction between information science and semiotics – the
'informational view' versus the 'semiotical view' – as a competition, which
may well be the case in terms of their claims over neighbouring sciences.
Once again, however, taking the long view, such competition should not be
seen in individualistic terms, requiring a winner, but in systematic terms,
requiring *synthesis*, per Julian Huxley's influential (in fact, game-changing)
'modern synthesis' of the biosciences into an evolutionary framework
(Huxley, 1942) and his less successful attempt to commence the same
synthetic transformation for the cultural sciences (Huxley, 1955). Brier
too envisages a 'total naturalism' that can only be achieved by 'uniting' the
natural, bio-, information and cultural sciences:

> My theory and philosophy of science is, then, that in a total naturalism
> we have four different approaches to the understanding of cognition,
> communication, meaning and consciousness ... which are all equally
> important and have to be united in a transdisciplinary theory of
> information, semiotics, first person consciousness and an intersubjective
> cultural social-communicative approach.
>
> (Brier, 2010: 1907–8)

We agree, although our own approach is not via Brier's use of C. S. Peirce,
but via Lotman's use of Vernadsky. Nevertheless, we share with Brier and
others the conviction that such a synthesis among the natural and humanistic
disciplines is vital and further that it must reform the sciences as well as the
humanities (but see Yudell and DeSalle, 2000).

# Geosphere to biosphere: It's not rocky science!

Vernadsky's ambition is to understand how thought influences nature. In
turn, Lotman's concept of the semiosphere offers new analytical clarity for
the era of the 'knowledge society' (Castells and Cardoso, 2005) as a global,

digital phenomenon. Lotman wrote in 1982: 'I am reading Vernadsky with fascination ... His writing is wonderful – broad and poetic. Only a geologist, who is used to thinking in segments of millions of years, is capable of writing like that' (2013: 268). In *Universe of the Mind*, Lotman quotes this early (1892) passage:

> The seeming laws of mental activity in people's lives has led many to deny the influence of the personality on history, although, throughout history, we can in fact see a constant struggle of conscious (i.e. not natural) life-formations with the unconscious order of the dead laws of nature, and in this effort of consciousness lies all the beauty of historical manifestations, the originality of their position among the other natural processes.
>
> (Vernadsky, quoted in Lotman, 1990: 125)

Here, Vernadsky is not proposing a Great Man of History notion of personal influence or a Freudian battle with the unconscious. He is locating consciousness, personality and mental activity *'among the other natural processes'*. But he distinguishes living matter from inert material on the basis of the greater transformational energy of the biosphere. Lotman quotes a further passage where Vernadsky makes clear that human activity should be understood as part of a materialist and naturalistic science:

> The biosphere has a quite definite structure which determines everything without exception that happens in it ... A human being observed in nature and all living organisms and every living being is a function of the biosphere in its particular space-time.
>
> (Vernadsky, cited in Lotman, 1990: 125)

What Vernadsky meant by the biosphere, then, is not 'life' as a metaphysical property of individual organisms, an idea harking back to the religious concept of the *soul*, but living matter as a *system* – all life, taken as a whole, together with its interconnections, both synchronic (the complex web of life) and diachronic (the evolutionary tree of life). The biosphere is made of all interrelations among all organisms at all scales (the food chain), together with their conditions of descent, existence and survival, including the environment within which they are (or are not) viable, and the extent to which they may alter that environment.

It turns out that the biosphere is pretty thin, compared with the bulk of the sphere it envelops. Life forms extend at most a few kilometres below and above sea level. Nevertheless, it is of planetary extent, enveloping the whole mass of the earth as a distinct, material but dynamic 'membrane', overlaying and interacting with the *geosphere* (the earth's crust, oceans and atmosphere). At this point it is proper to recall that much of the *inert* matter of the geosphere is itself biogenetic: the oxygen in the atmosphere, made by microorganisms and algae, and the limestones, coal, oil shale, chalk and sands, often many hundreds of feet thick, made of the shells and skeletons of marine creatures, trees and so on.

The biosphere, then, is a set of relations of planetary extent and evolutionary duration, but the 'biomass' within it, the sum of living material, is material enough to be *weighed*, or at least its load of Carbon (C) can be estimated, as has been done recently by the Aspen Global Change Institute (and see Bar-On et al., 2018): 'Estimates of the total mass of the biosphere are more than 1 trillion tons of Carbon (1TtC) and perhaps as much as 4 trillion tons of Carbon (4TtC)'.[10] However, although 4,000,000,000,000 tons is a big number, it is not the *mass* of chemical elements that impresses but the *energy* of life forms:

> Throughout the evolution of life on Earth ... all life forms have found ways to obtain energy, acquire nutrients to build organic molecules, and reproduce. Energy from the sun is captured by photosynthesizing organisms called autotrophs, or producers, that can harness solar energy to convert inorganic molecules into organic molecules – the building blocks of life. These organic molecules store energy and are consumed by other non-photosynthetic organisms called heterotrophs, or consumers. This seemingly simple process – grass being eaten by deer, for example – took billions of years to develop. (Aspen Global Change Institute)[11]

What Vernadsky called 'free energy' allows the transformation of abiotic matter (light, chemicals) into complex systems (organic molecules, organisms, biosphere):

> Living matter is the bearer for, and creator of, free energy, not existing to such a degree in any one of Earth's envelopes. This free energy – biogeochemical energy – embraces the entire biosphere and fundamentally determines its entire history. It stimulates and radically transforms the intensity of the migration of the chemical elements which compose the biosphere and determines its geological significance.

(1938a: 17)

According to Vernadsky, the biogeochemical free energy of the biosphere is geologically *significant* (it can transform rocks) but not geologically *determined* (it does not descend from rocks). If anything, the boot is on the other foot: it changes the planet. What has recently come to be called the Anthropocene era of geological time takes this insight seriously. Evidence of the commencement of the Anthropocene era has been dated to 1965:

---

[10]See: https://www.agci.org/earth-systems/biosphere.

[11]"How Does the Biosphere Work?' Aspen Global Change Institute: https://www.agci.org/earth-systems/biosphere.

ironically, from the exact moment 'when humanity invented the technology to make themselves extinct' – that is to say, nuclear weapons, the testing of which left material traces in living organisms, including trees.[12]

Not surprisingly, Vernadsky's work is enjoying a revival as a foundational theorist of this new era (e.g. Callicott, 2013: 182–99).[13] Vernadsky saw inert (physical) and living systems as separate, interacting systems; he does not subscribe to the standard story that has life emerging when simple systems evolved into complex ones (elemental atoms → complex molecules → biotic proteins).[14] There was not in Vernadsky's day and still is not evidence of when or how life started on this or any other world; nor is there direct evidence that it arose from simpler atoms, from non-life to life. As far as we know at present, all life is descended from life (*omne vivum ex vivo* or biogenesis). For Vernadsky, it is therefore *more scientific* to consider the *evolution of two systems*, inert matter-energy and living matter, both ultimately of 'cosmic' origin (relying on solar energy), coexisting and mutually transformative, but not as one system with linear causation from simple to complex.

Despite general scepticism, some scientists continue to pursue the possibilities of assigning life to cosmic rather than single-planet origins (see especially Steele et al., 2018), as explained by historian of science Stephen Fleischfresser:

> The … panspermia hypothesis posits a cosmic biology, in which, write the researchers, 'the entire galaxy (and perhaps a local group of galaxies) constitutes a single connected biosphere'. All life, both terrestrial and extra-terrestrial, is related, according to this view, as all life comes from the greater biosphere in which genetic material in the 'cosmic gene pool' is readily shared … The evidence is nonetheless provocative. Taken together it indicates, if nothing else, that there is much we don't know and that our prevailing scientific orthodoxies will undergo transformations, as all scientific theories do.[15]

Debate rages about whether, unlike all other matter, living matter can only be explained by reference to singular origins on this planet or whether its

---

[12]Based on globally distributed traces (in plants) of radioactive elements from Cold War nuclear tests: https://theconversation.com/anthropocene-began-in-1965-according-to-signs-left-in-the-worlds-loneliest-tree-91993.

[13]And see David Christian's contribution to *The Edge*'s question of 2017: 'What scientific term or concept ought to be more widely known?' His answer is 'The Noösphere': https://www.edge.org/response-detail/27068.

[14]For instance, the Max Planck Institute concedes that 'This poses a particular challenge in explaining their evolution from non-living matter': https://www.eb.tuebingen.mpg.de/protein-evolution/protein-evolution/.

[15]*Cosmos* (24 April 2018): https://cosmosmagazine.com/biology/viruses-et-and-the-octopus-from-space-the-return-of-panspermia.

origins are 'cosmic'. Be that as it may (i.e. unresolved at this date, despite the massive resources devoted to finding signs of life elsewhere, even as 'we' – the species – perpetrate mass extinctions and precipitate epochal changes in the Earth system's one and only biosphere), the furore about cosmic origins masks a different but equally fundamental insight of the systems approach: namely, that in order to explain dynamism, the object of study is not the individual particle and its behaviour but the interaction of *at least two systems*. Vernadsky contemplated the interactions of inert and living matter as two dynamic and mutually determining systems. Lotman founded his approach to meaning on this discovery. In a representative passage (from *Culture and Explosion*), Lotman writes:

> A minimally functioning structure requires the presence of at least two languages and their incapacity, each independently of the other, to embrace the world external to each of them. This incapacity is ... a condition of existence.
>
> (2009: 2)

Neither Lotman nor Vernadsky require us to choose between the standard (abiogenetic) and the alternative open (cosmic) model, because both theorists use a naturalistic, materialist, scientific imagination. Vernadsky's conceptualization of the biosphere/noosphere is not dependent on the conjectured origins of life (extra-terrestrial or otherwise) but on evidenced properties and transformative energies of living matter, taken at planetary scale, over evolutionary time. Lotman does not model semiosis on a 'single perfect universal language', rather, 'a multiplicity of languages is original and primary'. He goes so far as to claim that 'aspiration towards a single universal language (towards a single, final truth)' is 'later', a 'secondary reality created by culture' (2009: 2–3). In fact it can be dated to the earliest *imperial* (rather than autochthonous-tribal) cosmologies – that of Akhenaten (died 1335 BCE), who invented the explosively heretical idea of one god (on the model of one pharaoh) – rather late in the human evolutionary trajectory.[16] In other words, the idea of oneness – a single god, united people or final truth – belongs not to *human* or even divine but to *state* consciousness (Romer, 2012).

# Vital, or vitalist?

Perhaps in search of a 'single, final truth', some commentators have dismissed Vernadsky's distinction between inert and living matter as *vitalism* – a metaphysical and pseudoscientific folk-theory of 'vital' forces

---

[16]See: https://www.telegraph.co.uk/culture/art/10561090/Akhenaten-mad-bad-or-brilliant.html.

that defy mechanistic explanation. Long refuted in science, 'vitalism' is now used only as a pejorative term. Vernadsky was certainly unwilling to *equate* life and non-life, but he never proposed an immaterial force to explain life. On the contrary, his entire effort is to understand living matter within materialist, naturalistic and generalizable laws of thermodynamics and evolution. His own conjectures on the distinction between living and inert matter were exploring the limit of scientific knowledge in his time, and the problem is still not resolved. The crucial distinction between his thought and that of vitalism is that he never opted for a metaphysical, spiritual or immaterial explanation for living matter, harking back to the idea of the soul.[17] Instead, he sought *quantitative* evidence, such as the mass of biogenic oxygen in the atmosphere or carbon in the earth's biomass, and he focused on the material forces at work in 'scientific cognition' itself. What interested him is that living matter, taken as a whole, transforms the Earth system:

> In spite of the fact that the mass of all living organisms is negligible when compared to the biosphere [which includes the Earth's crust, for Vernadsky], since it is of the order of some tenth fractions of a percent – as a matter of fact, the living substance determines the whole chemical structure of the biosphere.
>
> (Vernadsky, 1938b: 48)

Vernadsky explains thought not by metaphysics but by pointing to collective, organized action over centuries. For instance, in a paper on 'scientific thought as a planetary phenomenon', he writes:

> The sciences concerned with the biosphere and its objects, that is, all of the humanities without exception, the natural sciences in the proper sense of the term (botany, zoology, geology, mineralogy, etc.), all the technical sciences,– applied sciences broadly understood – appear as areas of knowledge, which are the most accessible to the scientific thought of humanity. Here we have concentrated millions upon millions of continuous scientifically established and systematized facts, which are the result of organized scientific labour, and which inexorably increase with each new generation, rapidly and consciously, since the 15th to 17th centuries.
>
> (1938a: 16)

---

[17]Ironically, the term 'individual' – so much used in behavioural sciences – is derived from the concept of the soul, since Christian theology considered the soul as indivisible, and therefore any unit that was said to possess one (i.e. individuals of humankind) was considered the smallest possible unit of creation. Science knows better now but still uses the term.

Here is the crucial discovery: it is not vital force that distinguishes life; it is *semiosis*, an entirely material phenomenon (in contrast to the older philosophical meaning of 'immaterial' to refer to 'spiritual'), produced and circulated by matter-energy, albeit encountered in 'abstract' forms that have been described as 'immaterial', such as 'immaterial assets', 'non-material culture' and the long debate in semiotics about the materiality of signs and signifiers (see Chandler, 2017: 'Rematerializing the Sign'). Semiosis is an evolutionary process at population scale, albeit growing at an accelerating rate as 'organised scientific labour' and extra-somatic media have gained traction across half a millennium. What needs scientific study is not a mythical vital 'spirit' of individuals but the application of accumulated reason, consciousness and ingenuity (invention, innovation, imagination, industriousness) at species and interspecies scale, co-evolving with culture and technology over multiple generations.

# Thought transforms nature: From stromatolites to selfies

*How can* thought transform the earth? Clearly, *distributed networked intelligence*[18] does play a part in the transformation of earth materials. For instance, in Vernadsky's own example, before industrialization, native iron (naturally occurring in the metallic state) was rare.[19] It could be extracted using charcoal, but it was not until the nineteenth century that the use of coking coal in blast furnaces allowed the process to be ramped up to industrial scale. The industrial and mechanical ages are unthinkable without iron and steel, just as medieval states and empires are unthinkable without iron weapons, but neither were possible without natural inert matter being transformed by the 'free energy' of thought.

Similarly, although aluminium is the earth's most abundant crustal metal, it does not occur naturally in elemental form. First isolated in 1825, it remained a very expensive luxury item throughout the nineteenth century, being used for spectacular rather than utilitarian purposes. The pointed cap of the Washington Memorial in the United States, for example, is aluminium

---

[18]Dubbed 'the most important invention of the past two thousand years' by John Brockman, founder of *The Edge*, 'distributed networked intelligence' – DNI as opposed to DNA – is 'the collective externalized mind, the mind we all share, the infinite oscillation of our collective consciousness interacting with itself, adding a fuller, richer dimension to what it means to be human': https://www.edge.org/response-detail/11978.

[19]Rare in the Earth's crust and surface, that is. The fact that the Earth's core is mostly iron was unknown until well into the twentieth century.

(1884); 'Eros', in London's Piccadilly Circus, was the first statue to be cast in this exotic metal (1893).[20] In the meantime, a newly isolated source of energy, electricity, and a new practical invention, electrolysis, allowed it to be produced at industrial scale, just as coal (coke) had precipitated the steel industry a century before. Blast furnaces and electrolysis themselves are not products only of energy but of knowledge and artisanship. It was *thought*, processing of meaningful experiences and texts and accumulation of knowledge that transformed matter, leading to irreversible changes in the geosphere and atmosphere, some of which are now leading to further risks and uncertainties for the Anthropocene planet.

The scientific method is comfortable when dealing with linear causation, where energy (from wood, coal, oil, electricity) transforms matter, for instance by combustion. But what if matter is transformed by another process entirely? Vernadsky comments: 'Here a new riddle has arisen before us. *Thought is not a form of energy.* How then can it change material processes?' (1943: 20–1).

The answer requires the widest possible conceptualization of the noosphere: it does not confine thought to humans but extends to evolved living matter, as Juri Lotman also realized when he wrote:

> I am also convinced that thought cannot evolve from non-thought either (another thing is that, most likely, we should not deprive animals of thought, and possibly, life itself is impossible without thought). Indeed, just as life includes all forms of life activities, from anaerobic bacteria to the most complicated forms, so, too, does thought (semiosis) have simple and complex forms.
>
> (Lotman, 2013: 269)

Here is the radical potential of Lotman's approach to semiosis in a nutshell: thought is a property of *life* – from stromatolites to selfies – and *semiosis* is what distinguishes life from non-life, giving living matter its disproportionate transformational energy.

## The primacy of the semiosphere: 'A salutary correction of perspective'

Vernadsky's thought is glossed by Lotman (2013: 269) as 'semiosis'. He does not use the term 'noosphere' at all. Here we come to a further important insight and extension of the concept. Vernadsky saw the noosphere as part

---

[20]For the Washington monument, see: http://www.tms.org/pubs/journals/jom/9511/binczewski-9511.html; for 'Eros' (actually Anteros): https://londonist.com/london/history/secrets-of-the-eros-statue.

of the *biosphere*. But Lotman saw the noosphere as part of the *semiosphere*. The stakes are high, because Lotman's categorization of two interacting systems implies that the semiosphere (*including* the noosphere) may be the very system that exerts transformational force at planetary scale over the geosphere. It is not the case that 'over here' we have 'thought' (science), while 'over there' we have semiosis (meaning; culture), but rather something more fundamental and important: that all sense-making including science is part of the semiosphere ('over here'), interacting with the Earth system ('over there'), to transformational effect.

Is the semiosphere part of the biosphere? Certain critics have thought so and consequently suggested that semiotics (culture) is a branch of biology (life sciences) (M. Lotman, 2013: 271). That classification does hold a certain attraction: it would indeed be a step forward to have semiosis – the process of producing meaning – in dialogue with the evolutionary biosciences, where a behavioural-individualist notion of the (singular) mind or brain still holds sway. Currently, the study of meaningfulness is isolated in the humanities, dispersed among cultural studies, history, literature, philosophy, languages, communication, media studies and the like. It would be a step forward for all concerned to study meaning systems in dialogue with the latest insights of cybernetics, computer and web science, information theory, evolutionary economics and sociology, as well as the evolutionary biosciences themselves. Such a move is already well under way in digital media studies, but it is not reciprocated to any significant extent by the sciences. For example, in an otherwise excellent synthesizing account of *Cultural Evolution*, Alex Mesoudi (2011) makes no mention of work in the humanities, despite the long history, going back two centuries and more, of engagement with the concept of culture in that domain. The warning is clear: humanities knowledge no longer counts as science, at least among scientists. This line of thought leads not to specialization within an overall scientific domain but to speciation, division into science and non-science, where the latter is confined to questions of moral, political, ideological and subjective values, while science is exempted from such questions while pursuing an aspiration 'towards a single, final truth' – an aspiration that, as we have seen, Lotman dismisses as *cultural* (and glossed by us as *imperial*), not scientific (2009: 2–3).

In our view, an effective way to counter a trend that has resulted in unseemly and unproductive slanging matches between scientists and 'postmodernists' is to investigate knowledge as the *interaction of at least two systems*, in this case the humanities and the sciences, which is exactly what the Vernadsky-Enzensberger-Lotman line of thought models, to illuminating effect. In short, *dialogue* between the sciences and humanities is itself part of the larger semiosphere, which are not separate domains but interacting systems. It is important for science-humanities dialogue to be mutual. In fact, the need for science to learn from the semiotic approach explains Lotman's decision *not* to reduce the study of culture and meaning to the status of handmaid to the biosciences. He subsumed the noosphere into the semiosphere because *communication* underpins the workings of the biosphere more generally. And thus, by extension, the biosciences become a branch of semiotics!

Here is how David Christian, a proponent of 'big history', has put it:

> The unique precision and bandwidth of human language allowed our ancestors to share, accumulate and mobilize information at the level of the community and, eventually, of the species, and to do so at warp speed. And increasing flows of information unlocked unprecedented flows of energy and resources, until we became the first species in four billion years that could mobilize energy and resources on geological scales. 'Collective learning' made us a planet-changing species.[21]

Juri Lotman's son, Mihhail Lotman, has made this implication explicit. M. Lotman does not see semiotics 'within the field of biology' at all. He writes: 'I believe the situation to be the direct opposite: the biosphere itself is not a natural, but a semiotic object' (2013: 271). *Life is a function of communication*, not the other way around.

The scientific neglect of semiosis is a result of following linear causation, but it is mistaken, according to the Lotmans, because 'normal' (deterministic, reversible) processes are interrupted by what (Juri) Lotman (2009) calls 'explosion' (irreversible transformations), where time and causality go out of synch, because after an 'explosive' event, none of the materials involved can return to their former state. Following the work of Ilya Prigogine and Isabelle Stengers (1984), M. Lotman argues that in order to understand dynamic, discontinuous events in *semiotic* space, an analytical 'separation of time from causality' is needed:

> Causality and time now operate in the opposite direction: a situation can acquire the status of cause only after we know its effect; that is, chronologically, the effect precedes the cause. Such a concept signifies the transition to an essentially different treatment of semiotic space ... The space is not oriented toward objects and statuses but towards signs and texts, that is, toward information.
>
> (M. Lotman, 2013: 273–4)

In other words, the semiosphere is a complex, unstable, non-equilibrium system – just like global weather. Unstable systems like these can only be explained statistically, that is, in terms of probability, not exactly, in terms of mathematics (although of course probabilities must be measured and calculated accurately). It was always a mistake to try to explain the emergence and evolution of life

---

[21]David Christian (2017) 'The Noösphere': https://www.edge.org/response-detail/27068. https://www.edge.org/response-detail/27068.

by looking at individual particles, instead of whole populations, systems and relations. In short, neither the biosphere nor the semiosphere could be properly understood until the *scientific* system (the noosphere) caught up with chaos theory. As M. Lotman says, 'chicken and egg questions' are paradoxical whenever they are posed in relation to complex dynamic, unstable, indeterminate, evolutionary systems. He asks which came first: 'biologically – life or DNA, semiotically – a sign or its meaning, linguistically – a speech or its language'? (2013: 273). Wrong questions! Self-organizing systems do not work that way.

The trouble is, the story of determinate causation persists in the way that science narrates its own origin story, using a mechanical logic of simple-to-complex, primitive-to-modern, without reconsidering the narrative in the light of recent discoveries, where indeterminacy, self-organization, irreversibility, instability and probability replace the exact processes of Newtonian physics. The noosphere itself (including science, broadly understood, but also any information used for transformational processes) is just such a complex system, but it has been slow to update its own self-representation to match. Instead, it created a myth of origin (which we explore in more detail in the next chapter). Biochemist Joseph Needham, who studied the history of Chinese science, was an early critic of the ethnocentric tendencies of this origin story for science. He argued that, following the globalization effect of two world wars, the 'new universalism' of science and technology requires the recognition, not erasure, of difference:

> For better or worse, the die is now cast, the world is one. The citizen of the world has to live with his fellow-citizens ... We are living in the dawn of a new universalism, which, if humanity survives the dangers attendant on control by irresponsible men of sources of power hitherto unimaginable, will unite the working peoples of all races in a community both catholic and cooperative. The mortar of this edifice is mutual comprehension ... Certain it is that no people or group of peoples has had a monopoly in contributing to the development of Science. Their achievements should be mutually recognised and freely celebrated with the joined hands of universal brotherhood.
>
> (Needham, 1954: 9)

There is a big 'if' in there (the triumph of hope over experience, perhaps), which is just as conditional now as it was in the 1950s era of nuclear-armed Cold War, and there is a Romanticism worthy of Beethoven about 'universal brotherhood',[22] but Needham grasped that science has grown

---

[22]As in Beethoven's use of Schiller's 'Ode to Joy' in his Ninth Symphony, which proclaims that 'Alle Menschen werden Brüder, Wo dein sanfter Flügel weilt' ('All men will emerge as brothers, Where you [joy] rest your gentle wings'); and 'Seid umschlungen, Millionen! Diesen Kuss der ganzen Welt!' ('Be embracèd, all you millions, Share this kiss with all the world!'). For this translation, thanks to Michael Kay: http://saxonica.com/~mike/OdeToJoy.html.

from multifarious 'joined hands', not from a single privileged (i.e. imperial) origin. It is not descended only from those who 'contributed in a direct genetical succession to that movement in 17th-century Europe from which modern science originated'; it is a human achievement. As he remarks, 'A salutary correction of perspective is necessary'.

That correction of perspective is under way in postcolonial studies and action. At the level of performative action to call attention to the issues, for example, recent years have witnessed an international 'fallist' movement. Fallism started in South Africa, referring to the slogan 'Rhodes Must Fall', 'Fees Must Fall', 'Science Must Fall' (Roy, 2018). It quickly connected with similar calls in the United States for monuments dedicated to Confederate heroes and slavers to be removed from public places, especially civic buildings and universities. The movement touched Australia with action against statuary of invaders and settlers like James Cook amid calls to change the date of Australia Day (see Hartley, 2020: 181–97 for a fuller account). Fallism resulted in spectacular political clashes, both in the street and in the media, because far-right extremists and colonial apologists made common cause to defend offensive statues, some of which were indeed removed by local authorities or direct action, while others were defended and preserved in the name of settler heritage.

In this context, an appeal to abstract, decontextualized 'human' rights (as opposed to Indigenous rights and the rights of people of colour, women and so on) can be seen as merely 'an extension of Eurocentric thinking' (Ahmed, 2018: 16). Instead of platitudes that lend support to supremacism, some argue, radical decolonial action is needed, arising from 'the subaltern' or black body herself (e.g. Dlakavu, Ndelu and Matandela, 2017). As Rohan Deb Roy (2018) concludes:

> Unravelling the legacies of colonial science will take time. But the field needs strengthening at a time when some of the most influential countries in the world have adopted a lukewarm attitude towards scientific values and findings. Decolonisation promises to make science more appealing by integrating its findings more firmly with questions of justice, ethics and democracy. Perhaps, in the coming century, success with the microscope will depend on success in tackling the lingering effects of imperialism.

At a time when science itself is under increasing attack in populist and authoritarian discourses, and under suspicion among radical and activist movements (of both 'right' and 'left'), the distinction between science and the humanities is mutually destructive. Populist regimes – in both democratic and authoritarian systems – have made a point of undermining science as a whole, especially climate science, and so the decades-long effort by scientists to cast themselves as neutral, evidence-driven and authoritative (often in contrast to the supposedly partisan, value-ridden and relativist humanities) has come unstuck in the very executive forums they sought to influence. Science, the arts and humanities are now all in the same boat when it comes to both public debate and public funding. Each needs the other, and both have much to offer the quest for knowledge and understanding, in these posthuman and transhuman times, but they will both need to learn from marginal groups and fringe politics, rather than from corporate and state interests.

# A cultural science for the Anthropocene

Among the questions that science has not yet resolved are those concerning the origin of and distinction between living and inert matter. Cultural semiotics has drawn attention to the planetary extent and systemic nature of semiosis, focusing on its operations in the 'human-sphere', as it were. But science as a whole – that is, the natural and biosciences as well as social sciences and arts – is needed to address the larger question of how semiosis should be understood in the Earth system (and beyond!). Could it be that life itself is *defined* by semiosis within and among complex systems: that *communication* is the missing link between inert and living matter (Salthe, 2007)? This is what biosemiotics investigates (e.g. Jakob von Uexküll, Kalevi Kull, Jesper Hoffmeyer, Stanley Salthe, Søren Brier), not confining semiosis to human culture, literature and the like but extending it into the interactions of molecules, cells and organisms in general.

In this scenario, *the biosciences become a branch of semiotics*, because the 'bio' in bioscience is characterized by communication, which is the 'property' of life, and communication is a part of the semiosphere. It is a radical, marginal claim, in keeping with the planetary scope of the semiosphere concept. But what if it is right?[23] The idea is made the more plausible – and investigable – as that sphere is cumulatively overlain by a 'technosphere' (see below), whose digital and computational capabilities (i.e. tech-enabled communication that leaves physical traces, which can be recovered for analysis) begin to open up the extent to which communication, signalling, semiosis, meaning – that is, the sign, variously understood – works as a regulator or coordinator of inter-system interactions.

Technologically enhanced semiosis plays a connective role in change and energy transfer, and therefore in the transformation of matter, at global scale.

---

[23]A perennial question, famously asked by Tom Wolfe about Marshall McLuhan ('What if he is right?' Wolfe, 1968, chapter 8). Wolfe's 'New Journalism' served not only to raise that question but also to propel McLuhan into superstardom – from Canadian Catholic literary theorist to seer of the Madmen.

Scholars and citizens are now 'woke' to this, just in time to understand how the thinking species (*H. sapiens*) is messing up the planet as a whole without knowing how to regulate its own transformational energies. The potential is there for an understanding of the *digital semiosphere* – the topic of this book – to provide the evidential basis of probabilities for a 'cultural science' of the Anthropocene era, by focusing on semiosphere interaction as the driver of biosphere changes, via Lotmanian fundamentals, including the need for at least two systems to interact, the importance of boundaries, translation, asymmetry and autocommunication for the well-being of any one system (here is where autopoiesis and umwelt regulate themselves in dialogic interaction with others) and the transformational energy of meaningful or purposeful thought at population scale over evolutionary time.

In its most technical and restricted usage – in the study of language – semiotics demonstrates the relational, system-determined nature of semiosis, which cannot exist in abstract isolation but only in dynamic multiplicity. The multiplicity is the pre-condition of existence as it dictates the necessity of the Other (another person, another language, another culture) (Lotman, 2009: 2) and the dialogues with all others and their specific modes of representations and ways of seeing. Therefore, instead of a single, universal abstract truth (which is itself only an 'aspiration' or 'secondary reality created by culture'), semiotics construes languages as irreducibly diverse, interdependent and only in the aggregate capable of reflecting extra-semiotic reality, requiring:

> an open number of diverse languages, each of which is reciprocally dependent on the other, due to the incapacity of each to express the world independently ... Their mutual untranslatability (or limited translatability) represents a source of adjustment of the extra-lingual object to its reflection in the world of languages. The situation of a multiplicity of languages is original and primary.
>
> (2009: 2)

Languages and textuality have their own internal logic, but 'the space of reality cannot be represented by a single language but only by an aggregate of languages'. This applies equally to the *subject* of language – the individual speaker, or individual culture. None of them is able to make sense of the world (or anything else) on their own. The process works only at system level: *culture makes groups* (which we call '*demes*': inter-knowing groups bonded by language, culture, rules and competitive relations with other demes), while *groups make knowledge* (Hartley and Potts, 2014). It is only once the macro-space or sphere is grasped as a whole that its individual workings can be understood. However, this does not mean that the discovery of global connectedness requires a universal 'single, final truth' (Lotman, 2009: 2). On the contrary, multiplicity, dynamism and difference are the very mechanism by which a global system works. Semiosis is the means by which difference and multiplicity are mediated; translation is the process by which incommensurate codes are interoperable.

This approach relates in different ways to evolutionary and systems approaches to language, society, history, media and literature (Nick Evans, Niklas Luhmann, Peter Turchin, Daniel Dor, Brian Boyd, Carlos Scolari, Alberto Acerbi and many others). It allows multi-scalar analysis: at the micro-scale, it opens up the possibility of a science of life based on signs (not on individual behaviour or atomized information); at organism-scale, it offers new insights into the relations between individuals, cultures and environment; and at the macro–scale, it provides a way to consider how communication, meaning-making and thought (not confined to humans but common to living matter) are forming a new planetary envelope. In an accelerating process, meaning making and human thought can be seen as a catalytic mechanism, inaugurating the Anthropocene era of geological time.

The role of culture/thought as a constitutive force in such large-scale planetary changes has not been integrated into cultural, communication and media studies, at least in these terms, although of course it is a trending topic in studies of climate change, environmental waste and global conflict/inequality. The borders between semiospheres take on strategic and lethal force where cultures collide. So far, cultural studies has contributed much to the critical and affect side of such topics, but it has not until now produced an overall systems theory to account for distributed causation and thence the relationship between socialized semiosis and its planetary consequences. This is a matter of increasing urgency for the semiosphere and biosphere alike, giving further practical and political impetus to the already compelling intellectual and scientific case for integrating them into a multidisciplinary complex, focusing on *observation, calculation* and *communication* (protocols derived from meteorology, see Chapter 2) at both intimate and global scale.

# 2

# A short history of globes

*In the 20th Century, humankind,* for the first time in the history of the Earth, knew and embraced the whole biosphere, *completed the geographic map of the planet Earth, and colonized its whole surface. Humankind became a single totality in the life of the Earth.*
(VLADIMIR VERNADSKY, 1943: 19)

\* \* \*

## Finding our way around

Humans evolved in Africa, as far as we know, sometime over 200,000 years ago, possibly in response to 'explosive' (irreversible) climate change. Pretty soon, they became a scattered species, finding its way into all major land masses of the Earth system and supplanting other hominins (*H. neanderthalensis, H. floresiensis, H. sapiens subsp. 'Denisova'*). That was an unusual achievement; few species are such generalists (apart from the pests and weeds that humans take everywhere with them), able to survive in all climates and conditions. But global expansion occurred gradually, in piecemeal fashion, group by group, over the whole span of human existence, 99 per cent of which had passed before *H. sapiens* eventually girdled the world, a mere 1,500–1,000 years ago, when Māori Polynesians found Aotearoa New Zealand.

Even after this, knowledge systems, which were developed for local conflict and national or regional dominion, were not geared up to conceptualize the species in terms of the planet. It was nearly a further millennium before humanity was numerous enough and interconnected enough, with enough enabling technology, for it to *experience* itself as one global species, and we – the species – are still not very good at seeing ourselves as 'all for one and one for all' at planetary and species scale, except in imperial fantasies and pandemic panics. Bringing 200,000+ years of consciousness to bear on 200 years of population experience has not yet resulted in global consciousness at the level of collective action or 'joined hands' among humans in general. Apart from the UN, most of the agencies that have aspired to such an ambition (where 'all' means 'all humans') remain in the religious rather than political domain (MacGregor, 2018: vii), where the aspiration towards 'universal' siblinghood is necessarily, by definition, sectarian, and therefore exclusionary. Nevertheless, it can be argued that the shift from gradual (uncoordinated and untheorized, as it were: not a coherent object of thought and action) to modern global consciousness and globalization is an 'explosive' (irreversible) event, inaugurating a realizable 'right' in Enzensberger's terms (1982), even though it may be taking a few centuries for its changes to work their way through to all people in all parts.

People seem reasonably confident about identifying who 'we' are at species scale when it is a matter of distinguishing ourselves (inside) from non-human others (outside), for example animals, nature in general, diseases, AI, dead people, gods, aliens and so on. But despite the best efforts of supranational agencies like the UN, philanthropic agencies and ginger groups in science, activism and alternative politics, humanity has so far found it near-impossible to *act* as a species at macro-scale. Global *collective action* remains at meso- or institutional level, pursued by corporations (trade) and governments (power), who represent and favour limited and potentially antagonistic groups (companies; countries), even when dealing with planetary problems, like natural disasters, climate-change, environmental collapse and species extinction, or when ascribing responsibility for unforeseen effects of our collective uses of culture, technology and institutions – especially in the digital/internet era. Globalization of collective responsibility and purpose is neither fully macro (population-wide) nor fully micro (internalized at personal scale), but the signs pointing the way towards species-action are beginning to clarify. At present, for the ordinary knowing subject (the 'we' of reading), it is most evident at the level of semiosis: media, computation and entertainment. It is a meaning-led change, where stories precede experience, but that 'free energy' phase may be necessary to catalyse collective action. Until it knows it is a global group, humanity will not organize itself or its actions globally, in order to address the challenges of the Anthropocene era. 'Think global/act local' is no longer enough, where agency turns to urgency as the human turns to the posthuman, but it may be a *sequence* – thinking globally precedes collective action, which is itself granulated but synthesized in myriad 'locals'.

Such a challenge is not a call for everyone to 'bend the knee' to the 'final truth' of (Western, imperial) science but a recognition that *acting globally* is environmentally necessary – even as we work to 'localize' Western science itself (Chakrabarty, 2008), recognizing its far-from-progressive impact on colonized and 'othered' people, including those central to cultural studies, identified by gender, ethnicity or race, class, sexual orientation, age-group, dis/ability and so on. 'Thinking globally' is not a call for everyone to think the same but to adopt a Lotmanian view of the semiosphere, valorising *dialogue* across incommensurable and untranslatable boundaries between different demographics and disciplines as well as different peoples and cultures. Consequently, for science educators:

> I suggest that 'thinking globally' in science and environmental education might best be understood as a process of creating transnational 'spaces' in which scholars from different localities collaborate in reframing and decentering their own knowledge traditions and negotiate trust in each other's contributions to their collective work. For those of us who work in Western knowledge traditions, a first step must be to represent and perform our distinctive approaches to knowledge production in ways that authentically demonstrate their localness.
>
> (Gough, 2002: 1234)

# Scale

Unprompted, people seem to find it hard to think at scale. Personal experience is one thing; planetary goings-on are another, or so it seems. The sheer size of the planet, the extent, multiplicity and scale of global infrastructure, platforms, corporations and data seem to be the polar opposite of individual sense-making, even as we bury our heads in globally connected devices and screens. One of our tasks in this book is to link these apparent opposites, such that each is understood as an aspect of the other, relationally, as integral parts of the global semiosphere. Concepts at micro-scale need to be linked to their macro-scale equivalents, for example personal/planetary, self/system, individual/network, text/semiosphere, without reducing these binaries to 'we'/'they' antagonisms.

However, there is a relationship between scale and affect. Personal experience of the digital semiosphere invokes our most intimate notions of selfhood, identity, social and political allegiances, within our workaday activities of searching, monitoring and keeping up, while enjoying the manifold pleasures – and anxieties – of semiosis in real time. On the other hand, once you widen the analytical lens to look at the large-scale operations that keep these pleasures and discontents coming, the picture can seem much more bleak – not 'our' shiny uniform sphere but 'their' dark tangled web. The 'universal' human subject needs no longer to be construed as a generalized version of whichever geopolitical power is currently dominant, be that European imperialism in the nineteenth century, US-led trade in the twentieth or China's Belt and Road in the twenty-first. 'Our' affluent consumption is always also 'their' problem, not only because everything from our clothes and food to our most intricate electronic devices are made and dismantled by the cheapest skilled labour in the global South, and not only because the affluent 'haves' are outnumbered by 'have-nots' across Africa, Asia and among disadvantaged demographics everywhere, but also because the globally integrated socio-economic-political system is impacting the Earth system in uncontrolled and unsustainable ways.

For many observers, the simple act of changing scale from micro to macro changes the mood of observation, from utopia to dystopia (el-Ojeili, 2020). Over here: the emancipation of personal creativity (Jenkins et al., 2016), the growth and democratization of knowledge (Hartley, 2012) and business futures (McAfee and Brynjolfsson, 2017). Over there: global platformization (van Dijck et al., 2018), platform capitalism (Srnicek, 2016), data colonialism (Couldry and Mejias, 2019), 'the stack' (Bratton, 2016), all the way out to threatened ecological catastrophe and economic collapse of the Anthropocene (Maxwell et al., 2014; Parikka, 2014, 2015). From fun to fear in an instant; 'my' emancipation comes at the cost of 'our' planet! The young, with most to lose and to fear, duly take note, via Extinction Rebellion (https://rebellion.earth/), SS4C (https://www. schoolstrike4climate.com/), FridaysForFuture (https://fridaysforfuture. org/) and so on.

These apparent opposites can both be true at the same time, of course; indeed, some would claim that chasing the first (individual utopia) causes the second (global dystopia).[1] It is a hot topic, in both scholarly and public debate. What drives a system that can produce such polarized realities? And how does that system work at such extremes of scale?

## Selves and systems: The atmosphere

One way to hang on to both ends of global scale – the intimate with the infinite – is to have a model in mind of something that is at once personal and life-giving while at the same time being a planetary system of almost incalculable complexity and dynamism. Luckily for us all, such a model is the very medium in which we breathe and by which we speak: the atmosphere. The resting human breathes in and out between twelve and twenty times a minute, for the whole span of their lives. Speech is airborne and made of air; 'airs' are meanings carried in music, song and rhythm; speaking 'into the

---

[1]See for instance: https://thetyee.ca/Opinion/2017/11/16/humans-blind-imminent-environmental-collapse/; and https://www.theguardian.com/environment/2018/apr/26/were-doomed-mayer-hillman-on-the-climate-reality-no-one-else-will-dare-mention?CMP=Share_iOSApp_Other.

air' can also signify the *failure* of communication as people talk *past* each other (Peters, 1999).

At the same time, the atmosphere is a dauntingly big object. Meteorological science is at the cutting edge of big-data analysis (Moore, 2015), relying on a combination of:

- *Observation*, via a vast array of weather stations on land, sea, air and in space (see Figure 2.1);
- *Calculation*, using complex mathematical models and super-computation (Roulstone, 2015); and
- *Communication*, initially via the telegraph and newspapers – technologies fast enough to get observations back to head office and forecasts out to users.

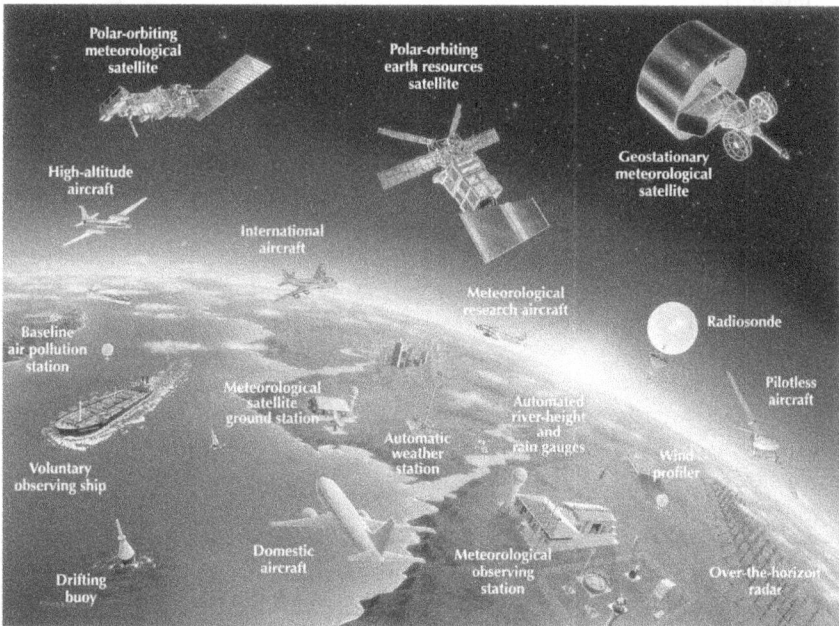

FIGURE 2.1 *The array of recording equipment for meteorological observations by sea, land, air and space – the digital semiosphere intersects with the geosphere:* Source: BOM Australia.[2]

---

[2]http://media.bom.gov.au/social/blog/1696/explainer-how-meteorologists-forecast-the-weather/

Such a modelling and sampling system, now operating transnationally, has taken over 150 years and thousands of people – working with Joseph Needham's 'joined hands' (1954) – to establish, aided by the world's most powerful supercomputers and AI machine-learning. At the outset, it could not even be imagined, let alone attempted. In the UK, Robert Fitzroy, the same man who captained the *Beagle* on Darwin's momentous voyage, pioneered probabilistic methods for what he called weather 'forecasts' – as distinct from the then prevalent magical 'prophecies and predictions'.[3] He initiated the combination of observation, calculation and communication, to initial scepticism among scientists and politicians alike:

> The belief persisted among many that weather was completely chaotic. When one MP suggested in the House of Commons in 1854 that recent advances in scientific theory might soon allow them to know the weather in London 'twenty-four hours beforehand', the House roared with laughter.
>
> (Moore, 2015)

In 1854 Fitzroy established the Met Office with a staff of three. One hundred and sixty years later it employed more than 1,500 people and had an annual budget of more than £80 million:

> Dame Julia Slingo, the Met Office's current chief scientist explains: 'FitzRoy was really ahead of his time. He was not mistaken or eccentric, he was just at the start of a very long journey, one that continues today in the Met Office.' (Moore, 2015)[4]

Meanwhile, everyone on earth continues to rely on that global system not only for their weather but also for the oxygen they breathe, which was itself released into the naturally anoxic atmosphere over billions of years by life forms long regarded as lowly, such as cyanobacteria, algae and vegetation, upon whose humble but combined efforts our individual and collective lives depend. Every organism is connected to every other, whether by direct relationship (predator/prey, for instance) or through the workings of the biosphere, itself in biogeochemical interaction with the geosphere.[5]

---

[3]Some of which can still be found in use. 'Indicators' from the US rural community include goose-bones: persimmon seeds; caterpillar behaviour; pig spleen; and the behaviour of cattle, birds and insects. See: https://www.almanac.com/topics/weather/weather-forecasts/predicting-weather.

[4]Peter Moore tells the story in a BBC magazine item related to his (2015) book: http://www.bbc.com/news/magazine-32483678.

[5]See for instance: https://en.wikipedia.org/wiki/Great_Oxygenation_Event; and https://en.wikipedia.org/wiki/Geological_history_of_oxygen.

It is appropriate that meteorology headlines our investigation into globes, because of course it was in sailing – where wind and weather were not only potential dangers but air itself provided the motive energy for sailing ships – that understanding of the atmosphere as a planetary system was a practical necessity. Accurate forecasting could be a matter of life and death; profit or loss. And although meteorology has come a long way since Fitzroy, it is still out there at the cutting edge of scientific method, being one of the disciplines most greedy for supercomputing capacity, seriously big data and complex modelling systems.[6] Nevertheless, weather forecasting remains, as it was at the outset, a *narrative art* – as much a media phenomenon as a scientific one:

> Being a meteorologist is like being a storyteller. Meteorologists take weather information – some of it highly technical – from many different sources and turn it into a digestible story that people can use to make decisions about their lives.[7]

In short, one of the first and most advanced denizens of the digital semiosphere is not the consumer but the weather. *Modelling* climate change at planetary scale has led the way towards human cooperation and understanding at the same scale. The importance of media-celebrity intermediaries in humanizing and narrativizing that model, however, is poorly recognized, regarded as a risky adjunct to the 'observation-calculation-communication' model of measurability, to date. We – scientists and publics alike – have been slow to understand that communication is a primary part of the scientific process; narrativizing natural phenomena is as important as observation and experimentation. Who cared if the world was spherical? No one, until stories circulated that promised riches, power and change. Who believed you could forecast the weather? No one did (using folk/magic belief), until everyone did, because system science worked.

## Globalization

First-hand knowledge that the planet is a single unit was gained initially by a few navigators and explorers, then by states, empires and economic interests.

---

[6]See, e.g.: https://www.zdnet.com/article/bom-gets-cray-supercomputer-for-weather-prediction/
[7]BOM Blog, 22 March 2018: http://media.bom.gov.au/social/blog/1696/explainer-how-meteorologists-forecast-the-weather/.

- At the outset of the modern era (the 1500s in parts of Europe),
  a dawning realization that the globe is a single unit linked
  adventurous buccaneers with imperial states, and both with the
  exploitation of distant resources (Figure 2.2). Globalization meant
  statecraft and colonialism.
- From about the nineteenth century onwards, where the Industrial
  Revolution kicked in, living standards rose beyond subsistence, to
  what Deirdre McCloskey calls 'the great enrichment' (2006; 2010;
  2016).[8] Global consciousness began to be shared by ordinary people,
  at first through the press, telegraph and imperial service, or through
  migration (voluntary or forced).
- Popular knowledge of the far-flung was boosted by the growing vogue
  for exhibitions of world trade, from the 1851 *Great Exhibition of the
  Works of Industry of All Nations* at the Crystal Palace in London to
  the American World Fairs (1930s–1960s) and contemporary Expos in
  emergent countries, including Expo 2010 in Shanghai.[9]
- During the twentieth century, electronic, broadcast and satellite
  communications technology extended the planetary reach of media
  content, and at the same time jets, tourism, containers and Telstar
  extended international consumer culture.[10]
- In the early part of the present century, global communication
  took the next step, when direct, instantaneous connectivity became
  possible among ordinary people across the world via the internet
  and smartphones, a change that from 2017 has included more than
  half of the world's total population as users.[11] The initial techno-
  utopianism of global-digital social media turned ugly and adversarial
  with the rise of authoritarian populism and alt-right activism, even
  as climate change and extinctions suffused global consciousness.

Doubtless much traffic is still parochial, but still, ordinary people do have global
reach for their own sense-making practices and can maintain dialogic relations
of activism and movement – from Steve Bannon to Greta Thunberg – as readily
as intimate contact with family and friends, markets and suppliers, celebrities
and topics as never before, which of course 'opens' them to conflict, surveillance,
hacking, ideological and commercial manipulation on the same terms.

---

[8]'For the term 'great enrichment' see: https://www.nationalreview.com/2015/11/bourgeoisie-economic-development/.

[9]See Wikipedia: https://en.wikipedia.org/wiki/List_of_world%27s_fairs; https://en.wikipedia.org/wiki/List_of_world_expositions.

[10]Telstar – the satellite that enabled the first live transatlantic TV broadcast – was launched in 1962. Containers were invented – as 'Trailer Vans' – in 1956; their first transatlantic shipment was made in 1966: https://en.wikipedia.org/wiki/Malcom_McLean.

[11]Source: https://thenextweb.com/contributors/2017/04/11/current-global-state-internet/.

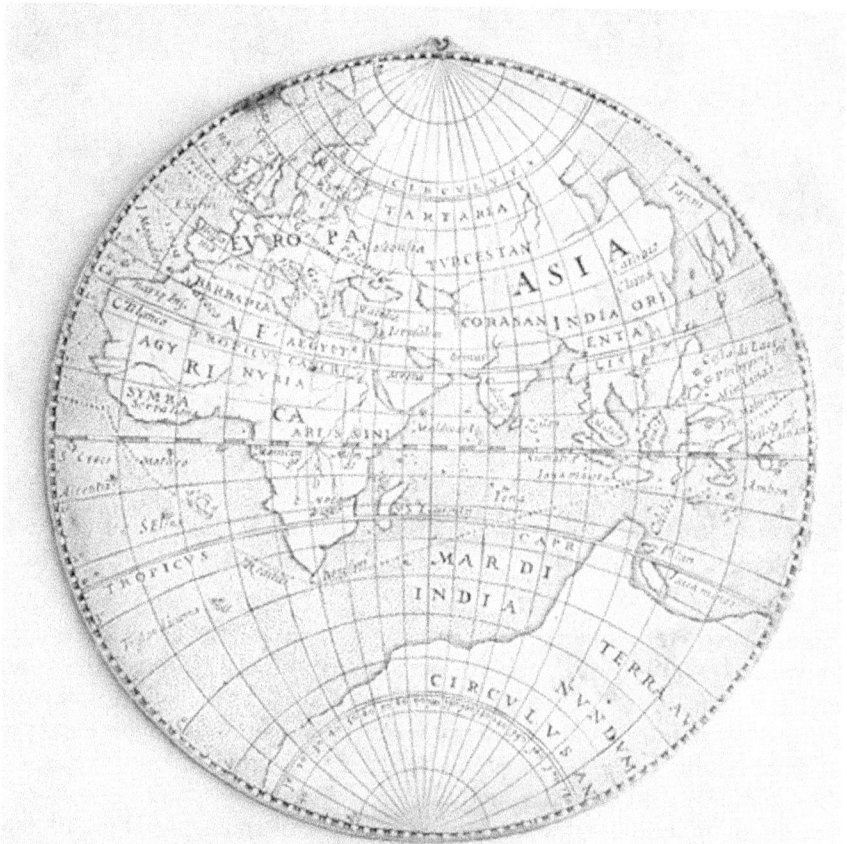

FIGURE 2.2 *Globalization as state buccaneering: Silver Medal commemorating Sir Francis Drake's circumnavigation of the world, 1577–1580. State Library of NSW, Australia.*[12]

Global *consciousness* remains, however, an incomplete project, because the semiosphere is internally bounded, with hostile borders snaking around the planet like a tectonic ring of fire, keeping nations and people apart, presenting a picture of world culture not as a single unit but as a continuing patchwork of conflict, borders and mutual distrust. It is quite possible for capital (finance), goods (trade) and data (information) to cross borders at the speed of light (McKinsey, 2016) (Figure 2.3), but people (migrants) and meanings (culture, knowledge, identity) are decidedly a different matter.

Signs and symbols are traded internationally, but we cannot yet say the same for culture or knowledge at population scale. Instead, we find strong

---

[12]Source: http://www.sl.nsw.gov.au/blogs/item-1144a-medal-commemorating-sir-francis-drakes-voyage-around. The medallion's maker was Michael Mercator, grandson of cartographer Gerard Mercator the elder. See also: https://www.youtube.com/watch?v=EB8EZYzOKgs.

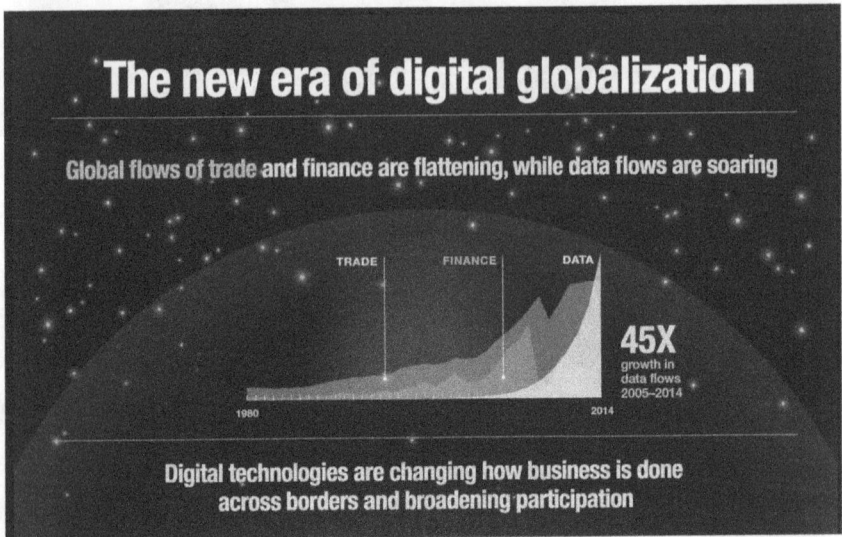

FIGURE 2.3 *On the up: globalization of data: McKinsey Global Institute (2016).*[13]

resistance to globalizing either of them. It is *conflict* (staged adversarial opposition) that is global, not one particular meaning. Although the same digital technologies carry both scholarly and popular knowledge systems, neither wants to be contaminated by the other. What one semiosphere accepts as true remains *in opposition* to truths accepted in other semiospheres, be these national (United States v. China) or sectional (science v. pop culture). Instead of universal knowledge, we observe contending versions of the real. The resurgence of what many call tribalism seems to threaten rational civilization – witness the reactionary right, Trump, Brexit, xenophobia, online misogyny, fake news and post-truth journalism. Here, it is a battle – not a meeting of minds – between expert and populist knowledge, emblematized by the politicization of climate change and science (Björnberg et al., 2017) and by systematic resistance to progressive global thinking, especially the reaction against feminism online (Jane, 2017).

Geopolitically, the trend among governments is not towards smoother international flows but towards economic and political nationalism, accompanied by aggressively parochial rhetoric (America First, hate-speech, xenophobia), anti-cosmopolitanism and the globalization of *restrictions* on the movement of migrants and refugees (see Ai Wei Wei's 2017 film *Human Flow*).[14] Countries as varied as the United States, UK, China, Russia, Turkey, Austria, Hungary and North Korea have opted for stronger boundaries, not more porous ones.

---

[13]Source: https://www.mckinsey.com/business-functions/digital-mckinsey/our-insights/digital-globalization-the-new-era-of-global-flows.
[14]http://www.cinemanova.com.au/films/human-flow.

National regulations and culture/location-specific network externalities mean that even the most international of organizations – corporate tech giants – cannot operate on a truly global scale, since they are divided between American firms (Facebook, Amazon, Google, Apple, Microsoft) and Chinese firms (Baidu, Alibaba, Tencent, Huawei). The internet is increasingly territorialized, shifting from the early global universalism of Tim Berners-Lee's World Wide Web to the current internet-of-shopping configuration, where consumers must deal with local variants (and prices) of companies that respect no such borders themselves, distributing their own infrastructure, workforce, HQ and taxation status across countries to their own advantage but not allowing consumers that scope.

How many actual humans feel themselves to be part of a unified global community is doubtful (it is in no agency's interest to ask), but such people seem more likely to be clustered around the dystopian pole, concerned about the environment, climate-change and waste, than at the utopian pole, where they are likely to be dismissed as *un*worldly. Global citizenship is a minority, alternative project, pursued by activists, NGOs and community organizations. Others who may yearn for humanity-wide communication are encouraged to achieve it through tourism (not just mindless euphoria but also edutourism, orphanage tourism, dark tourism, etc.) or to experience it in mediated form (world music and performing arts, screen media and social media): that is, as consumers who are themselves farmed by less scrupulous international players. Those who set off independently to explore the planet as 'world citizens' are often viewed with suspicion; 'cosmopolitans' may be admired for their breadth of horizon, but equally that term has a long history as racist code for 'outsiders' who are seen as a threat to white supremacy.

# Experiencing globes

It was not until the semiosphere went digital that it could be experienced as global from within, as it were, by user populations as part of their everyday activities. This possibility followed 'media convergence', integrating telecommunications, broadcast media and computing, which had been three separate industries in the analogue era (Jenkins, 2006). Previously, individual use of media, whether as reader (audience eyeballs) or as writer (participatory and social media), was very hard to identify. But once users could treat the same device as a phone, a TV and a computer, it became possible to track what they were up to. The corporate mining of user data for their own purposes has since become a major bone of contention between private users and corporate platforms, further extending the politics of scale in the study of the digital semiosphere.

So fast do things change that it is easy to forget that in terms of human history, digital media and networks are very recent innovations, despite their ubiquitous familiarity in affluent countries. There was – and for many in developing countries, there still is – a time when the agent of globalization was not personal at all, but confined to meso-level institutions and organizations, transnational firms and colonizing state forces in particular. Individuals did not communicate with the other side of the planet unless a family member emigrated, and they did not travel much beyond national borders except in warfare. Now, kids routinely chat, like and comment on each other's lives and looks in social media that deliberately foreshorten geographical distance, such that it is not always clear what country your interlocutor is in, especially if she is a celebrity or influencer (Abidin, 2018). This is not so much an abstraction of meaning from the local context (although it is that too) as the achievement of *global consciousness* at population level.[15]

Part of the retail experience of globalization is at the level of the sign: terrestrial spheres have taken on a semiotic function as a sign of modernity in streetscapes, advertising and art. Among the earliest such celebratory representations was the medal struck in 1580 to commemorate Sir Francis Drake's circumnavigation of the world (Figure 2.2), featuring a world map engraved by Mercator's own grandson. Shakespeare's theatre (built in 1599) was called The Globe; a 'wooden O' that symbolically encompassed the stage, where all that is human –love, laughter, marriage, tyranny, torture, death – is played out. Owning a globe was once the monopoly of monarchs and imperialists, who were routinely painted with their hand resting possessively on a terrestrial sphere. But now, globes have become signs of 'democratic equivalence' (Laclau and Mouffe, 1991). They are *educational*; every school and parent should have one. They proclaim that knowledge is democratized.

But at the same time they remind us that our language is bounded: many place-names are untranslatable. Like the globalization of trade, the

---

[15]Globalization has been dubbed 'globaloney' by statistician Pankaj Ghenawat (2012). According to *The Economist*, he observes that 'only 2% of students are at universities outside their home countries; and only 3% of people live outside their country of birth. Only 7% of rice is traded across borders. Only 7% of directors of S&P 500 companies are foreigners … less than 1% of all American companies have any foreign operations. Exports are equivalent to only 20% of global GDP. Some of the most vital arteries of globalisation are badly clogged: air travel is restricted by bilateral treaties and ocean shipping is dominated by cartels'. https:// www.economist.com/node/18584204. One comment on his figures criticized Ghenawat's 'carefully curated statistical sophistry' but is clear that 'globalization' is not 'global'! Also, it has benefits for some and costs for others: the globalization of both commodities (coffee, cotton, coal) and manufactured goods (TV sets, computers, cars) has had the double effect of reducing unit prices while decimating local production economies.

globalization of globes is patchy and uneven, bespeaking the asymmetry of power among different languages. Democratization extends to purchasers but not to languages, many of which still do not have their own globe. Most retail globes are made in the United States (by Replogle), with a restricted number of language versions.[16] Minority languages have been slow to globalize. For instance, the first Welsh-language Bible was published in 1588, but the first Welsh-language globe was not produced until 2009, and then only as an inflatable beach-ball type for schools, which soon sold out.[17] However, its production – supported by the National Assembly of Wales – is a strong reminder that in the semiosphere, *all languages are world languages* (Figure 2.4). Understanding the world through the eyes and languages of First Peoples would result in a very different mapping exercise from what is communicated by the ubiquitously marketed English-only version.

FIGURE 2.4 *All languages are world languages. The first Welsh-language globe (2009).*[18]

---

[16]One of the present authors bought a Mandarin-language globe in the Beijing store of the official Chinese news agency Xinhua, only to discover it was made in the United States by Replogle.
[17]See: https://www.walesonline.co.uk/news/wales-news/first-globe-welsh-sells-out-2112817.
[18]Source: https://www.walesonline.co.uk/news/wales-news/first-globe-welsh-sells-out-2112817.

This history of globalization from the Renaissance onwards has resulted in habits of thought that retain the same sequence, from energy and resources (wealth, power) to meanings and experience in steps that seem to follow a causal sequence, from geo- to bio- to semio-. However, counterintuitively, in order to understand the system as a whole, you need to entertain the possibility that causal sequence is in reality the other way round. The Earth system is best understood first as a semiotic object, because only this explains how 'we' the species act at planetary scale and the impact of that on the bio- and geo-spheres:

## 'WRONG-WAY-ROUND' DISCOVERY – 500 YEARS OF CUMULATIVE CAPITALIZATION OF THE PLANET

*1. Geopolitics*

| | |
|---|---|
| – European exploration (navigation) | sixteenth century |
| – Empires, exploitation | seventeenth century |
| – Geological resources (metals, fuel) | eighteenth century |

*2. Geoeconomics*

| | |
|---|---|
| – Biological productivity (food, fabric) | nineteenth century |
| ∘ Trade, war, manufacture | |

*3. The Semiosphere*

| | |
|---|---|
| – Communications, media-culture | twentieth century |
| – Global science and technology | twentieth–twenty-first centuries |
| – Everyday life, internet | twenty-first century |
| ∘ Authoritarian populism, alt-right activism | Now |
| ∘ Posthumanism, the Anthropocene | Next |

# Fictions – humanity's defining characteristic as a species

Communication, culture, meaningfulness, language, identity, media and the arts or entertainment are generally placed *outside* the knowledge commons encompassed by the sciences. Media and cultural studies tend to seek explanations for meaning based on the experience of those involved, using qualitative rather than quantitative methods. The effect is that in relation to contemporary media and popular culture scholarship remains a pre-evolutionary science or an interpretative field interested in values rather than facts. Mutual suspicion between sciences and humanities remains, depriving both of a critical-friend interlocutor and delaying possible consilience between them.

Until now, there has been no integrated method for *combining* systems thinking with cultural participation and meaning-making, although direct borrowings and applications of computational methods are gaining ground in the study of culture. This synthesis is what we attempt here, in the belief that both sides benefit from the insights of the other. A start must be made, if we are to understand meaning at scale without reducing culture to behaviour, to link the rich scholarship on culture with the systems approaches of the biosciences, where indeterminacy, relativistic relations and downward causation from system to specimen are no longer taboo.

First, not least to make a clear connection between digital media (imagination of humans) and planetary reality (independent of humans) – between the semiosphere and the geosphere – we point to the recent revival of scientific interest in *fictions*, as reconceptualized by Yuval Harari at species scale: fictions such as gods, nations, law, money, firms and, more recently, human rights (Harari, 2015).

Harari is a historian – a class of scholar noted for their aversion to fiction. But, he writes:

> Any large-scale human cooperation – whether a modern state, a medieval church, an ancient city or an archaic tribe – is rooted in common myths that exist only in people's collective imagination ... Yet none of these things exists outside the stories that people invent and tell one another. There are no gods in the universe, no nations, no money, no human rights, no laws, and no justice outside the common imagination of human beings.
>
> (2104: 8)

For Harari, such things do not exist in nature ('in the universe'), or at least they did not before *H. sapiens* invented and realized them as its own distinctive feature. It should be noted that ethologists might disagree that 'fiction' is a human invention, pointing to play among animals as evidence that they too indulge in make-believe and abstraction. However, that does not detract from Harari's main point, which is that these large-scale fictions do organize, connect and direct human cultures, by forming cooperative groups, using technologies of communication that have co-evolved with culture at an accelerating rate over the whole span of the human species' timeline (a unit that is now thought to be much longer than was previously estimated).

The impact of that cumulative human activity on the planet is now such that the very idea of the *primacy* of physical reality (real), over and above *secondary* mediated communication (artificial or 'immaterial'), is no longer tenable. It is human imagination and communication – meaning and making in the semiosphere – that drive the current transformation of the earth's physical systems, even though these 'fictions' (cooperative groups of strangers) and the myths that bind them (religion, nation, capitalism, science) cannot be found 'in nature'. That does not mean they are illusory (as Plato's 'shadows in the cave' parable asserts) but, on the contrary, that *mediation is just as real as rock*. In short, semiosis is a causal force in – and on – nature.

# The meaning of the sphere:
# 'The point however is to change it'

Globes have a long history as objects of knowledge and speculation, going back at least to the Ancient Greeks (Sloterdijk, 2014). For the Ancients, a representation of a sphere (and its derivatives, the vault and the dome) meant the celestial not the terrestrial globe, constellations not continents. The celestial was divine; the terrestrial or 'sublunary' sphere was literally 'mundane' – worldly as opposed to heavenly. The globe on Atlas's back at this time shows the constellations of the heavens; philosophers were practising cosmology rather than navigation.

Despite ancient interest among philosophers, there's a popular myth that 'we' thought the Earth was flat up until modern times (and beyond).[19] Modernity commenced when the revealed truth of religion was overturned by the observed truths of science. Among the latter was the discovery that the 'wide world' was not flat but a sphere. Although global navigation had been accelerating since the 1490s (when Columbus sailed west and thought he had found India) and globes were a vital tool of expansionist statecraft, the *popularization* of the idea of a round Earth took longer. It contradicted both plain sight and religious belief. Nevertheless, the idea had dawned sufficiently by about 1600 (Shakespeare is in his heyday at the Globe Theatre; the Americas are being 'planted' by European settlers; Australasia is unknown to them), to permit the priest and metaphysical poet John Donne to put the

---

[19]It is not impossible that more people alive today believe the earth is flat than the total number who did so in Ancient times. See: https://en.wikipedia.org/wiki/Modern_flat_Earth_societies.

Bible straight on the matter. Where the Bible's Book of Revelations (7:1) has: 'I saw four angels standing in *the four corners of the earth*', Donne has:

*At the round earth's imagin'd corners*, blow
Your trumpets, angels, and arise, arise
From death, you numberless infinities
Of souls, and to your scatter'd bodies go.[20]

It is a justly famous imaginative (i.e. fictional) resolution, using poetic licence to have a bet each way. People have long persisted in this rhetorical tradition. For example, although it deals in a rather more secular kind of *revelation* than the version attributed to St. John, Australia's long-running current-affairs flagship programme on ABC-TV is called *Four Corners*.

The geometric miracle, where flat becomes round, and a sphere has corners, was not merely a metaphysical conceit of the early modern period; it was a cartographical innovation. European exploration, expansionism and trade required that 'the round earth' indeed be reduced to flat planes with corners, an achievement conventionally credited to Gerardus Mercator's World Map of 1569.[21] Mercator took the globe out of philosophy and used it to change the world, just as Marx urged practical people to do, later in the story of modernity.[22]

Mercator's map had the cultural-political impact of an irreversible 'explosion', in Lotman's (2009) terms. He put global knowledge in the hands of non-experts, whose *uses* of that knowledge proved transformational at system and epoch level, accelerating European exploration and the expansion of colonization, empires and commodity trading. Modern astronomy emerged at the same time; the celestial sphere was dethroned, reduced to mundane service as an aid to navigation.

---

[20]See: http://www.bartleby.com/357/97.html; and https://rpo.library.utoronto.ca/poems/holy-sonnets-round-earths-imagind-corners-blow#0. The King James or Authorised Version of the English-language Bible was published in 1611, probably after this poem was written but before it was published.

[21]Mercator's 1569 map, see: https://en.wikipedia.org/wiki/Mercator_1569_world_map. It inaugurated a new era in mapping, partly because straight lines on the (flat) map corresponded to constant-bearing sailing on the (curved) ocean: navigators could more accurately track their course on a map.

[22]'Philosophers have only interpreted the world in various ways; the point however is to change it' (Marx's 11th Thesis on Feuerbach, 1845). In 1953, the *Sozialistische Einheitspartei Deutschlands* (Socialist Unity Party of [East] Germany) saw fit to have this thesis inscribed in letters of gold at the entrance of Humboldt University in Berlin: https://www.hu-berlin.de/de/pr/medien/publikationen/pdf/feuerbach_en.

# Terrestrial spheres

In line with Marx's thesis, attention turned to the sublunary Earth, newly understood as a single object – a sphere with its own history, resolving into sharper focus as the cumulative efforts of thousands of people over decades, running into centuries, bit-by-bit and through trial and error slowly developed naturalistic explanatory frameworks to understand this giant object. The only knowledge system capable of grasping the detail as well as the scope of such an effort proved to be empirical science; its evolving methods of observation, comparison, experiment, test and auto-correction, bold conjecture and falsification, conducted as a collective enterprise (the so-called invisible college) needed quite a few generations to dispel the myths (which persist still). Given the problems involved in cutting through the accumulated tangle of religiosity, magical thinking and fiction to get at causal processes in material objects, it was not surprising that the rift between poetic and scientific realities continued to widen. In the end, in institutionalized disciplinary knowledge systems, meaning-related frameworks of explanation were expelled altogether from the domain of science.

That could be seen as a progressive move while science inched towards a first approximation of causal phenomena in natural processes. But it has left scars on both sides – the sciences are suspicious of the humanities, and vice versa. That in turn has made it much more difficult to understand and integrate the role of semiosis in planetary processes. Is meaning merely a secondary phenomenon? Or has science been missing something? Is the terrestrial sphere just inert rock, water and air; or are life and meaning an autonomous system?

This is where the Vernadsky-Lotman theory of spheres comes into its own as an explanatory framework. The co-evolution of culture, communication and technology has brought our species to the point of *digital* impact on the planet, conceptualized as a sphere of contested semiosis, dynamic change and incommensurate meanings, a seething mix of interactive, contradictory, sometimes clashing systems (some geological, some biological, some digital), with multiple causation distributed throughout and interacting systemic dynamics producing transformational change at an accelerating rate. And now, they are automating it.

The task for analysis is to understand the stage on which both utopian and dystopian outcomes are always emergent. As in all drama, conflict is itself a relationship (not a breakdown in relations) in a larger network of connections. Recognizing that the (micro) personal and individual are part of both the (meso) institutional and (macro) global and that each level exerts influence, structure, agency and causation on the others will help to analyse the system as a whole, without prejudging it.

# 3

# Juri Lotman and cultural semiotics

*The unit of semiosis, the smallest functioning mechanism,
is not a separate language but* the whole semiotic
space of the culture *in question.*
*This is the space we term the semiosphere.*
(JURI LOTMAN, *UNIVERSE OF THE MIND*, 1990: 125)

\*\*\*

It is only since global media and digital communications became accessible to ordinary populations – with TV satellites, jumbo jets, the PC and mobile devices – that humans have been able to experience their own world as planetary in extent. For thousands of years what counted as 'culture' was confined to a communication system of 'ours' – limited by the bounds of tribe or clan, village, nation or empire up to the limit of a religion-based 'civilisation', as Huntington (1996) has contended. Those who were not part of 'our' communications system were the Others, still known by Ancient Greek terminology as 'barbarians', non-speakers (with connotations of enmity, derision or mere incomprehensible babble). Yet, over the centuries, awareness of Others has been growing, and knowledge increasing through that contact. In the process, the scope of 'us-ness' or 'Wedom' (Hartley, 1992: 206–23) has also been expanding. Rarely nowadays are cultures in other parts of the world brushed off as worthless non-cultures. Increasingly, there is at least minimal awareness and appreciation of different cultures around the world – of 'us' as co-humans even in our diversity. This awareness may be stereotyped and simplified, and it is sometimes marked by conflict and hostility, but there are also immediate and constant exchanges, flows and remixes among different cultures, groups and systems. There is increasingly greater hybridity among them and the emergence of convergent forms.

All these developments have happened using technological advances in mediation and communication. We (humans) travel more than ever before, as migrants, tourists or workers, but most of our awareness of distant others and their cultures is mediated. Furthermore, migration, mixing and the increasing integration of global businesses, workforces and markets means that 'distant others' may live next door, even as we maintain friends, family and relationships on the other side of the planet. Our awareness of ourselves as planetary species is not accidental; it has evolved because we have built over many decades the technical infrastructures and institutions of immediate mediation and communication. As a result, we now live in an era when culture is mediated and experienced globally through digital technologies.

As Roger Silverstone (2007) put it, a global 'mediapolis' has taken shape. It is a city-of-meetings, with organized encounters-of-difference in story, drama, information games and sport. The global mediapolis is built mostly by institutions (media and tech giants, and their interlocutors in government, lobbyists and business), but it is occupied, driven and used by everybody, whose collective actions and choices gradually shape and re-shape this polis as any other. In this space of relationships what is shared is the recognition of differences as well as 'like-usness', of pluralism among human cultures as well as the necessity to establish a 'proper distance' from others. The latter must build on the ability to adopt the position of the other but also to see them in their wider contexts (an accomplishment that most media fail to reach, at present, although they may value the morality of making the attempt).

The fact that the *intentions* of media institutions matter should remind us that mediation is never transparent, even if some of the global mediators insist that they (tech giants and digital platforms) are not 'the media' (broadcasters and content-makers) and, therefore, that they should be relieved of the expectations that societies have for media industries. Nevertheless, all mediation depends on the structuration, methods and agenda of mediator organizations, not just on technological affordances. And as the psycholinguist Michael Tomasello (2014) has convincingly argued, human distinctiveness derives from an ability to read the intentions of others, so as to be able to trust them for cooperative social action. Tomasello's 'shared intentionality' hypothesis applies to the institutions with which we interact as much as it does to individuals, because *'reading' trustworthy intentionality across difference* is deeply encoded in language, culture and knowledge, in order to identify 'our' group (and not just 'my' psychological aptitude). Can we trust institutions? If not, how far should we seek to build some sort of trustworthy common ground, in order for each side to derive use and value from the encounter? It does seem that many ordinary users give organizations – public, commercial and media – the benefit of the doubt, which in turn means that the resources people carry around with them to test the intentions of others are cultural, and must be learned, not behavioural or innate.

However, culture itself is increasingly technological, digital, mediated and institutionalized, and at increasing scale (we treat the 'global village' as a village). As has been systematically evidenced, contemporary global cultural exchange processes depend increasingly on 'platformisation' (van Dijck et al., 2018) and 'datafication' (van Dijck, 2014) of cultural production and consumption. And it has for long depended on the nature of *the protocol* (Galloway, 2004). As cultural content, identity and meaningfulness are digitized into corporate algorithms and mineable data, there is, therefore, a greater need than ever for broader system-level models of culture, to explain how it works as both a global abstraction and an intimate component of our daily lives.

## Lotman and cultural semiotics

Fortunately, such a model was elaborated in detail in the work of cultural semiotician Juri Lotman (1922–93) and at the Tartu-Moscow School of Semiotics he founded (Figure 3.1). Our book elaborates and updates his

FIGURE 3.1 *Guiding tubes: Juri Lotman, scholar, author – sculpture.*[1]

[1]Sculpture at Tartu University. Photo of the opening ceremony by Sille Annuk © Postimees. Used with permission.

model as a prescient tool for conceptualizing global digital cultures and communications media. It needs to be acknowledged at the outset that this may seem forlorn or quixotic undertaking: when we have climate change, authoritarian populism and 'carceral capitalism' (Wang, 2018) to worry about, why Lotman? Artur Blaim (1992a, 1992b, 1998) seeks to account for 'Lotman's virtual non-existence in the critical consciousness of English-speaking countries' (1998: 329). Blaim mentions various possibilities: Lotman's work was not 'ideological' enough (for Marxist, feminist and identity critique); it was too 'scientific' (for postmodern critical theory and continental philosophy); or it had simply missed the structuralist wave, because by the time Lotman's work was translated, the theoretical canon was established (via French readings of Saussure and Russian Formalists, stiffened with New Left Marxist theory and feminist critique). In short, the 'Lotman-Tartu' position in the cultural firmament has been determined by its own semiotic history (how it was produced, disseminated, received, processed), rather than because of any serious engagement with the work itself, positive or negative.

It has to be admitted that this situation has only become more fixed in the intervening years. But as Blaim observes in passing, the Tartu-Moscow School and Lotman's own work remain unusual in that while cultural and literary theory changed rapidly over the years, in response to intellectual fashion and its politicization in both West (identity politics, Marxist theory) and East (resistance to Sovietism), the Tartu-Moscow School maintained a focus on the problems it was founded to study, using the scholarly and conceptual apparatus it developed under Lotman's leadership. To that extent it avoided direct engagement with the political hotspots of the day, which made it less interesting to activist academics on both sides of the crumbling Iron Curtin, while modelling a properly scientific approach to its 'object domain' of culture – where, for Lotman, 'science consists in the correct posing of questions' (Blaim, 1992a: 19). However, this is not the individualist-positivist science of the STEM realism and the military-industrial complex but what Blaim calls 'constructivist' science. He traces this to Humberto Maturana and to Heinz von Foerster (1992: 17–18), among the founders of 'autopoietic' (self-organizing) bioscience and of cybernetic (systems) theory respectively.

In other words, Lotman and the Tartu-Moscow School present a well-constructed and robust *bridge* between the critical humanities and system sciences, and between 'Western' and 'Eastern' intellectual traditions:

> Estonian semiotics was a multicultural and international phenomenon both in terms of its external relations and internal social structure ... The research of these relations is topical today, because it can clarify the underestimated role of this phenomenon as a synthesis between 'Western' and 'Eastern' intellectual traditions. The problem of their interrelation

(peaceful and productive or antagonistic and destructive) has far more than a purely theoretical significance, as the recent events in Ukraine have demonstrated. (Pilshchikov and Trunin, 2016: 373)

In short, we do not seek to resurrect a forgotten 'structuralism' but to introduce global scholarship to a theory and to a body of work that can – we think should – have an explosive effect on contemporary cultural, communication and media studies (in which the present authors have our own professional formation). While this constellation of interdisciplinary studies is burgeoning in terms of new studies of new media by new talents from new places, it has not combusted into an irreversible new scientific or critical paradigm (à la Thomas Kuhn), as structuralism itself did in the 1960s. The reason why Lotman's time has now come is the 'object domain' of this book: the emergence and elaboration of global and digital but contested culture and media, in which the Tartu-Moscow School's previously more narrowly focused concern with the relations between text and society, meaning and its use, identity and system, can be extended to the global-digital semiosphere as a whole, synthesizing cultural, biological and socio-political processes into a coherent model of the world we are entering – and making – in the era of the Anthropocene.

# Juri Lotman

Juri Mikhailovich Lotman (Russian: Юрий Михайлович Лотман, transliteration from Cyrillic: Yuri Lotman, Estonian: Juri Lotman)[2] was born and educated in Saint Petersburg, which bore the names Petrograd and Leningrad during his lifetime. After graduating from the Leningrad State University with a diploma in philology, he could not get an academic position there, owing to his Jewish origin. This was despite the fact that he had been drafted and served in the Soviet army as a radio operator during the Second World War and received an excellent testimonial thereafter. However, one of Lotman's coursemates had been directed to Estonia – a peripheral place within the Soviet Union – and invited him there. In 1950 Lotman relocated to Tartu, where he worked, raised a family with literary scholar Zara Mints and lived until the end of his life in 1993.

Together with Mints, Boriss Jegorov and Igor Černov, Lotman formed an active academic circle in the department of Russian literature at the University of Tartu, concentrating on the problems of arts and artistic

---

[2]Lotman's forename is often transliterated from the Russian, Юрий Ло́тман, as *Yuri* Lotman, but we adopt the Estonian spelling – *Juri* Lotman – not only because two of us are Estonian but also because Lotman himself favoured that spelling when using Roman script.

texts (Lotman, 1977). Motivated by the concurrent interest in machine translation and cybernetics, and thus in the signifying functions of complex systems, they made contact with linguists at the Moscow State University in the early 1960s. From then on, the seed of the Tartu-Moscow school of semiotics started to grow. The scholarly domain they created gradually became known as the semiotics of culture or cultural semiotics.

Theoretically and methodologically, the school was founded on Soviet structural linguistics and literary science. In the wider picture, their thought was shaped by the heritage of Russian Formalism (esp. the Moscow linguistic circle) and the Prague linguistic circle (with both of which the linguistic and literary theorist Roman Jakobson had been involved) as well as by authors such as Vladimir Propp, Viktor Žirmunskij, Pavel Florenski, later Mikhail Bakhtin, Louis Hjelmslev, Noam Chomsky, Norbert Wiener, Bronislaw Malinowski, Claude Lévi-Strauss, Lev Vygotsky, Sergei Eisenstein, Victor Erlich (1981) and many others from continually diversifying spheres of theory (see Hawkes, 1977).

The Tartu-Moscow school of semiotics never existed as an official institution; instead, it functioned via meetings and co-publications, as an 'invisible college' (Salupere, Torop and Kull, 2013: 15). The evolutionary dynamics of cultural semiotic thought are mirrored in the topics treated at the series of summer schools held near Tartu since August 1964 and in the world's first periodical journal dedicated to semiotics *Труды по знаковым системам – Σημειωτική* (*Sign Systems Studies*), established the same year. Both have continued until today – as a biannual international conference and an annual international journal.

One of the foundational texts for semiotics of culture as a disciplinary framework was *Theses on the Semiotic Study of Cultures* (as applied to Slavic texts), co-authored by key members of the school – Lotman, Vjacheslav Ivanov, Vladimir Toporov, Aleksandr Pjatigorskij and Boris Uspenskij (Lotman et al., [1973] 2013). This work, and subsequent publications by these members, establishes culture as a complex mechanism of the collective mind/memory of humanity. That is, while in his early work, Lotman positioned himself as a structuralist, in the course of the 1970s and early 1980s, he started to move step-by-step towards a new poststructuralist, systemic and dynamic approach to culture, language and meaningfulness.

During the same period, Lotman and his colleagues started to describe culture as a collective mechanism as operating in/as *space*. That is, they developed a topological meta-language that conceptualized texts and cultural systems as structured spaces and demonstrated that *semiosis* – 'a process in which something functions as a sign to an organism'[3] – needs

---

[3] The definition given above is dated to 1907 and is a marvel of succinct accuracy. See: *The Merriam-Webster.com Dictionary*, https://www.merriam-webster.com/dictionary/semiosis. However, *Merriam-Webster* doesn't list 'semiosphere'.

an environment to emerge; the space of culture or *semiosphere*. All this work culminated, first, in his essay 'On the Semiosphere' ([1984] 2005) and, later, in other works.[4] It is often said that his translations into English came too late – when semiotics in general had started to go out of fashion in cultural and media studies. Yet, three collections of the key works from his poststructuralist period have been translated into English and have gained a steadily growing readership: *Universe of the Mind* (1990), *Culture and Explosion* ([1992] 2009) and *The Unpredictable Workings of Culture* ([2010] 2013). In recognition of Lotman's unique and, in our view, compelling approach to semiosis, we introduce here Lotman's holistic yet multi-layered approach to the cultural semiosphere, before moving on to consider the *digital semiosphere* in more detail.

# Why a book on 'digital semiosphere'?

We offer a unique account of the world-scale mechanisms that shape creative practices and forms of human communication and organization, exploring how meanings are made and distributed at population scale. We show how culture generates difference as well as identity, conflict as well as agreement. Following Lotman, we offer a cutting-edge, systematic model to link culture, meaning, media and the operations of cultural institutions (the semiosphere) to other living systems (the biosphere) and to environmental change (the Anthropocene).

Within cultural semiotics it is sometimes disputed if it is necessary to theorize digital semiosphere as distinct from the rest of the semiosphere. There is one global semiosphere after all. We see it as necessary and for three reasons.

1.  First, its physical extension around the world has enabled ordinary people, for the first time in history, to be conscious of planetary culture and communication in real time, and to participate in it directly. It is no longer weird (or dangerous) to know what is happening on the other side of the world as it unfolds; it is easy (i.e. cheap and commonplace) for those with access to a mobile device to be in peer-to-peer communication across multiple cultures and groups, and many individual humans are all-too aware of the human species as a unit – one that may be impacting the planet in unsustainable ways, to its own peril. So, instead of a patchwork of separate cultures, *the digital semiosphere* demonstrates the extent to which there is now one self-knowing human culture of global extent, albeit one that actually works by means of difference creating as well as translations between these often incommensurable systems.

---

[4]An English translation of this foundational article, by Wilma Clark, can be accessed here: http://citeseerx.ist.psu.edu/viewdoc/download?doi=10.1.1.693.9961&rep=rep1&type=pdf.

2. Second, *digital* culture and communication leave traces (conversations, clicks, bits, metadata, etc.) which can be recovered for observation and analysed in ways that spoken language and situated cultural meaningfulness cannot. Hence, the digital semiosphere may be easier to *study* than its 'natural' counterpart, but it may offer a 'proxy' indicator for larger (also non-digital) cultural phenomena. Yet, researchers need to also approach the 'data-layer' critically as it mediates and 'lies' as any other semiotic language (in terms of Umberto Eco, 1977).

3. The digital semiosphere belongs to a 'machine age' – many of the meaning-making processes are made happen by billions of computational devices connected to each other in complex ways, enabling them to produce much of the texts we are consuming for understanding our life. Here we need to address not only 'enframing' but the automation of cultural production, the functions of AI, also network-based AI, modelling and re-modelling by computers of networked activities.

## Levels of analysis/structure of the book

The distinct affordance of the semiosphere model is that it enables to distinguish between 'levels' within it – starting from individual texts, continuing with the cultural subsystems and social institutions they condition and ending with the broadest system integrating them all – the planetary semiosphere. Subsequent chapters of this book are structured in a similar way: micro → meso → macro → Earth system.

- Part III discusses the dynamics on what we see as the 'micro-level', the level of digital texts; those that are read for meaning by wider populations.
- Part IV investigates the 'meso-level' (meso simply means 'middle'): how textual dynamics shape the co-organization of contemporary institutions and their constellations – industries, sectors, markets – that produce the texts of the micro-level.
- Part V discusses how textual dynamics on the planetary scale interact with the living environment. How does the *digital* semiosphere (also called the 'technosphere' by some writers) shape the biosphere, and what does that mean for the human condition on Earth, that is for the further evolution of the Anthropocene.
- Part VI draws the hierarchies and dynamics together to complete the model of the digital semiosphere and to indicate some implications

and possibilities arising from studying it this way, illuminating the interconnectedness of micro-, meso- and macro-levels in action as well as analysis, thereby linking 'production-object-user' and 'text-institution-system' together – in a new conceptualization of class antagonism and activism in both political and market environments.

Here, let us address how we see the dynamics on these levels.

# Micro-level

The semiospheric understanding of text is especially relevant for making sense of the contemporary digital texts, featuring growingly elusive boundaries. When reception practices are described by the concept of produsage (Bruns, 2008) and take place within the context of participatory culture, then remixes, remediations, inter- and transtextual links and so on are an inherent part of the text's interpretative and meaning-making practices. They determine the way that the source text exists in culture, which is simultaneously as a whole – an integrated collection of individual signs – and a part of a larger system – its extra-textual context. Text is one of the fundamental notions of the Tartu-Moscow school and functions as a model for conceptualizing cultural phenomena as well as culture as a whole. The process of textualization – explaining something as a text – is applicable to phenomena regardless their material. That is, the framework allows for textualizing not only novels and literary texts but also tweets, films, video games, computer code, everyday behaviour and rituals, and their collections. The main merit of this conceptualization is, however, not the broadening of the 'semiotic domain' but a new understanding of text's semiotic functions.

It occurred to Lotman that interpreting the functions of artistic texts/artworks within the framework of information theory could provide new insights. Namely, such texts not only transfer information but are capable of creating new information as well as memorizing previously created information. These functionalities emerge due to texts' immersion in the semiosphere (as opposed to existing as separate structures connected only through intertextual links). Related to this is an understanding of the activity of reading as a process of dialogue with the text (as an intellectual partner in the process) rather than linear and exhaustive decoding of the text. This leads to an understanding that creativity is sourced within culture – not in an individual author – taking effect through constant translations in the situation of untranslatability as explained above.

As indicated above, the spatial dimensions of the semiosphere are accompanied by a diachronic dimension – a complex memory system – which allows for explaining the text's mnemonic functions and the mechanisms of coherence and continuities in culture. One of the keys here is understanding memory in terms of constant recreation instead of preservation. On the one hand, texts are indeed structured entities but at the same time decisively possess a dynamic dimension, realized in the process of being interpreted by different readers at different times in different intertextual and intermedial networks. Acknowledging both static and dynamic aspects of texts and the simultaneous homogeneity and heterogeneity of cultures allows for explaining the ways that cultures and their components maintain their identity throughout creative transformations. In other words, the semiosphere offers us analytical tools for the holistic treatment of dynamic processes in culture.

## Meso-level

Semiosphere theory helps us also to interpret the social and cultural dynamics, the ways people and institutions organize and reorganize themselves to produce and distribute the texts of the 'micro' level. We call this level of analysis the 'meso' (or middle) level of semiospheric analytics. What this refers to is that the semiosphere concept enables us not only to interpret the dynamics on the level of culture's individual texts, such as films, video games or novels, but also on the level of social organization of their production and consumption. One of the distinctive features of the semiosphere concept is the analytic focus on how various kinds of communities are forming in the society and culture, how are they creating self-referential discourses and sign-systems that distinguish them from others – be it other ethnicities or nations, other industries, professions or practitioner communities, other arts, other genres, other styles, other religions or other political ideologies. We argue that the creation of such binary distinctions – 'us' versus 'them' – is one of the constitutive forces in all cultures and related meaning-making processes functionally precede or condition dynamics in many other systems, be they economic, political or social.

When it comes to analysing the dynamics in contemporary digital, networked and global cultural and media industries, this meso-level analytic focus means focusing on how culture's creative communities auto-communicate, create their own means of signification or self-descriptive meta-languages to establish their difference from others. But it enables us also to look at how are they in dialogue, how they exchange and translate specified knowledge in order to reach new combinatory ideas, innovative forms of culture, related new forms of social organization and new kinds of cultural identities. When these new discourses, forms, organizations or identities are more responsive to the existing cultural milieus, they tend to replace the formerly dominant ones. That is, this level of analysis enables us to also look at the power asymmetries among existing formations and the dynamic change of these asymmetries. The fact that these processes are increasingly mediated by the digital networks, and various services built on top of those, means that they are also increasingly international, new, creative and productive communities, institutions and industries can be globally dispersed, but still immediate in their everyday communications and operations. The meso-level analysis, therefore, looks at the new forms of organizing creative and cultural institutions and the industries they form internationally.

# Macro-level

The digital semiosphere is a global phenomenon, a system of systems, not an object of 'reductive' science, where the 'smallest unit' is studied – for example the atom, or the phoneme. This means that the whole of the global semiosphere conditions its elements, such that their definition, characteristics, behaviour and interactions are *outcomes* of system-level relations. And, somewhat paradoxically, semiosphere itself results from those complex and dynamically changing interactions. As Lotman put it: 'The semiosphere is the result and the condition for the development of culture' (1990: 125).

The *digital* semiosphere is not separate from 'the' semiosphere (human culture). However, because digital communication leaves physical traces unlike speech (*verba volant scripta manent*), it does offer us an evidence base through which to study it. The *digital* semiosphere properly belongs to the 'noosphere' or sphere of thought or knowledge (Vernadsky); it is the extra-somatic trace left by human sense-making and communication and can therefore be studied as primary evidence for humanity as a cultural species.

The Earth is enveloped in signification, but what it means, for whom and what actions follow are not uniform everywhere, or over time. The semiosphere is like the *meteorological* sphere (world weather), where local turbulence and randomness nevertheless resolve into larger patterns at macro-scale, such that any given observer may be able to experience a relatively stable *climate* despite unpredictable differences in the *weather*. That same observer can breathe in and out their micro-scale component of the *atmosphere*, which is nevertheless simultaneously global in extent. The semiosphere also shares an important attribute with the *geosphere*, where structures are (at least in the short term) more stable. Both the semiosphere and the geosphere are characterized by *borders between* these structures, where *new material* is generated in intense interactions; for the geosphere, it is the dynamics of the Earth's tectonic plates; for the semiosphere, it is the border zones between two or more cultures, however defined. Finally, the semiosphere shares a characteristic with the *biosphere*. This term describes not only all living matter but also the *relations among* those organisms, which are doubly interconnected, each with all: all of the branches of life (Archaea, Bacteria and Eukarya) are linked by evolution (all life, so far as we know at present, has a common origin); and they are linked as well as by environment, because each species lives in conditions not of its own making, where it must interact with other organisms to feed and reproduce, itself deal with predation (where the existence of *predator* may both repel and stimulate *prey*).

The semiosphere is *not* like other spheres in that it does not seem to be a *source* of energy (unlike the geosphere and biosphere), which is why the sphere of meaning, thought and culture is often said to be 'immaterial'. Nevertheless, it needs to be considered in the same terms as the material sphere, because it is increasingly clear that the semiosphere has a transformative impact on both bio- and geological matter-energy, as humans use knowledge and cultural practices to transform both matter and life into resources or energy so much so that the present time appears to be a tipping point between geological periods, where the Holocene is giving way to the *Anthropocene Epoch*, where human activity is a – perhaps *the* – transformative agent of the biogeochemical make-up of the planet, a new outmost stratum of the Earth's crust, changing climate and ecosystems while leaving new 'sediments' in the form of never-before synthesized elements (e.g. aluminium), agricultural and urban landscapes and 'strata'.

But the semiosphere *is* like other planetary spheres, because it operates at the most minute micro-scale while remaining, at the same time, a global phenomenon at macro-scale, with intermediate structures (institutions, 'populations of rules') at intermediate 'meso-scale'. As explained above, we will take our cue from this remarkable property, to examine the digital semiosphere at micro-, meso-, and macro-scale respectively.

As Sir Tim Berners-Lee, the unsuspecting inventor of the World Wide Web, has concluded after due reflection, we must remember – and understand – that an 'open platform' of such scale requires regulation to prevent the web 'being weaponised at scale': 'We have to grit our teeth and ... not take it for granted that the web will lead us to wonderful things.'[5]

---

[5]*The Guardian*, 12 March 2018: https://www.theguardian.com/technology/2018/mar/11/tim-berners-lee-tech-companies-regulations.

# PART TWO

# Elements of the digital semiosphere

*Peeter Laurits 'Foreign Tongue' (2015) from* Codex Naturalis
https://www.peeterlaurits.com/works/codex-naturalis

# 4

# 'Inside thinking worlds'

Play captures a lot of what goes on in the world. *There is a kind of raw opportunism in biology and chemistry,* where things work stochastically to form emergent systematicities. *It's not a matter of direct functionality. We need to develop practices for thinking about those forms of activity that are not caught by functionality, those which propose the possible-but-not-yet, or that which is not-yet but still open.*

(DONNA HARAWAY)[1]

\*\*\*

Juri Lotman's best-known book in English is *Universe of the Mind* (1990), but the literal translation of that book's original Russian title would be *Inside Thinking Worlds.* There is an analytical value in this seeming mismatch (and see Salupere, 2015, for an illuminating discussion of differential translations of Lotman's concepts). Where 'universe' seems to point to the outside world, 'thinking worlds' are approached from the inside. This is a clue to the value of Lotman's concept of the semiosphere as an evolutionary elaboration of human engagement with the world, indeed the 'universe' (although we follow Lotman in confining that term to the Earth system rather than considering the cosmos as a whole, since humanity can only experience the cosmic universe via the noosphere, thus far at least).

To understand what's going on, it is necessary to look 'inside thinking worlds', not directly at that universe or even 'the mind', which is an abstract, individualized construction of the psychological, rather than cultural, sciences.

---

[1]From an interview in *The Guardian*, June 2019: https://www.theguardian.com/world/2019/jun/20/donna-haraway-interview-cyborg-manifesto-post-truth.

'Thinking worlds', in contrast, describes a system of internal relations and processes. As it can be a challenge to get one's head around how important these differences are, a short example may help. Think of food. Obviously, what humans eat is directly related to 'the universe' in the sense that edible material must exist separately from thinking and from the linguistic signs for food. But food is the most intimate of all material: it 'becomes' the human that eats it. And it is easy to see that the outside world plays almost no role in determining what humans eat, what they prefer and how they turn whatever comes from 'out there' into what can be put – safely, agreeably or riskily – 'in here'. The relation between infants and food is mediated by their carers, not by the availability or edibility of food. It is entirely determined by culture: the type of food, the way it is prepared, what counts as edible, how feeding is accommodated into daily routines and what is desired, preferred, avoided or forbidden are all the result of 'thinking', not 'the world'. The type of food obviously depends on geography, but place is always overdetermined by culture, so people grow up eating regional cuisine (Chinese, Indian, etc.) or 'fast' food, not the native produce of their own location. What counts as edible depends on how the continuum of nature is cut into discrete and meaningful units by culture, such that edible creatures like dogs, insects and dolphins are inedible in some cultures but not others, and 'staple' foods differ across the world – wheat, rice, millet, taro, maize – such that the contemporary dominance of meat, especially beef, is the result of prestige and agribusiness, not of direct experience of the edible environment. Humans occupy 'thinking worlds' first, and this interacts with 'the universe'; they learn, remember, act and share through the semiosphere, not by 'hunting and gathering' or even 'working and shopping', which are but executions of choices made in culture.

Lotman's unique approach supports analysis on very different levels: individual (micro) texts, institutional (meso) discursive systems of cultural production, planetary (macro) environment of communication. Simultaneously it shows us where to pinpoint the interconnectedness of these levels. Lotman's model of 'the semiosphere' allows for *many semiospheres* of different kinds, interacting with one another, while at the same time allowing for a much larger-scale semiospheres, with essentially the same rules of combination and relation as those of smaller scale.

Among others, there can be said to be national semiospheres, often based on language and historically shifted senses of ethno-territorial identity. Lotman himself was interested in the relations between national semiospheres across European history (Italian, French, Russian, etc.). Not only did they exhibit a spatial dimension but also a temporal dynamic. Each national semiosphere changed and adapted by taking dialogic turns: now as the transmitting culture for new ideas and meanings, then as the receiving culture for translations into their national semiosphere. Italian culture influenced the whole of Europe in the Renaissance (1400s–1500s); French culture did the same during the Revolutionary period (1750s–1810);

Russian culture became a semiotic hot spot during its Revolutionary period (early twentieth century). At other times, each of the Italian, French and Russian semiospheres was relatively quiescent, a receiving culture, changing according to ideas imported and translated from elsewhere.

But semiospheres do not have to be national: they can be generated and organized around any coherent, language-bound social group, all the way from 'small-world' social networks (e.g. gangs, 'insider' groups of professionals, or year-groups in school) up to globally significant groups (e.g. religions; the Anglosphere; users of digital media). Finally, these many semiospheres and their interconnections are all part of 'the' semiosphere, which is all of human cultural communication, across the planet and throughout time, which is a big unit!

It follows that any individual person or text may 'belong' to many semiospheres at once, shifting and translating between them according to context, interlocutor or intention, for example switching from family member to worker, from citizen to fan, from public to audience, from 'free intellectual' to 'gendered, raced, colonial subject', each using its own linguistic register, mode of utterance and assumed knowledge.

Lotman's model of semiosis (and hence of language and culture) is systems-based, dynamic, interactive, multi-level and evolutionary. It allows for both structure and agency, both identity and interpellation, both network and assemblage: Lotman's approach to semiosis and the semiosphere is *translational* between 'at least two systems', not an 'either/or' stretch for objective essence. It is multi-scaled, from micro- to macro, showing not only isomorphic or homological repetition of rules from micro- to macro-scale but also how both identity and difference are propagated and transformed across those boundaries.

In this chapter, let us work through some central concepts and elements of a semiosphere, as suggested by Lotman and his colleagues and followers to this day. As we go along, we will link the concepts to contemporary digital culture.

# Semiosphere

The semiosphere is the space, or more accurately space-time, of *semiosis*, a process in which something functions as a sign to an organism, outside of which meaning-generation cannot happen. According to this view, culture is not a product; it is not just a collection of individual languages and texts or of media and their products but rather a self-regulating *process of dialogue* among the texts, languages, their users and the communities that these users may constitute. As the space for communication, the semiosphere allows for conceptualizing culture as a holistic yet internally extremely heterogeneous system. Its heterogeneity stems from the fact that human communication systems may be used for modelling very different realities; that is 'semiosphere is the region of multiple realities' (Kull, 2005: 181). The realities for Saami in Finland, Noongar Indigenous people in Western Australia, slam poets in New York, dons in Oxford or Frankfurt's investment bankers require different means of expression to model the realities in their everyday. They may also need different modes of expression – communication systems in use are composed of diverse modalities and follow different compositional rules, develop at different speeds, are positioned on different levels of cultural hierarchies and each possesses complex memory systems. Programming languages, for instance, tend to evolve more slowly than the languages of fashion. Yet, both are used to communicate meaning and to organize cultural life in complex ways, building on their either shorter or longer histories of use and reuse.

Being mutually different, sometimes incompatible (incommensurable, one to the other; or *mutually untranslatable* even though they are in communication), none of the subsystems of the semiosphere could exist in isolation from others. In order to function (to mediate and create meaning), they need to be immersed in a higher-order semiotic formation. Such a 'semiotic continuum' is exemplified at different scales: the 'filters' and other conventions in use in Instagram photos or the puns in Twitter presume a wider semiotic context in order to be meaningful. So, any individual act of communication – a *text* – is functionally preceded by a more complex sphere of meaning-generation, while, at the same time, each of these texts could be understood as *isomorphic* (having the same structure/dynamics) in relation to the most general semiosphere. Archaeologists who reconstruct certain features of entire ancient cultures based on pieces of pottery are, in effect, building on exactly such isomorphic (and metonymic) relationships between an element and a whole of the semiosphere. That is, any act of communication or a text is simultaneously *a part* (of a larger intellectual whole) and *a whole* (in relation to its own constitutive parts). In Lotman's words:

> All levels of the semiosphere – from human personality to the individual text to global semiotic unity – are a seemingly interconnected group of semiospheres, each of them is simultaneously both participant in the dialogue (as part of the semiosphere) and the space of dialogue (the semiosphere as a whole).
>
> (2005 [1984]: 225)

In this aspect, 'the' semiosphere can be characterized as a Russian nesting doll, comprising similar (but differentiated) forms at different scales, each doll dependent for its own meaning on the existence and meanings of the others, and the whole adding up to more meaningfulness than the sum of the parts (Figure 4.1). Each doll is both 'participant' in dialogue with its

FIGURE 4.1 *The participants and places of the semiosphere are like a nesting doll. Each is separately meaningful, nesting within a larger part, which as a complete system adds up to more and different meanings than would be created by the parts alone or the sum of the parts.* Photo J. Hartley.[2]

others and 'space' within which such dialogue can occur. The meaning of 'Gorbachev' is modified by the dolls nesting within him – Soviet Brezhnev, Khrushchev, Stalin, Lenin; Czars Nicholas II, Catherine the Great, Peter the Great, Ivan the Terrible – and yet each doll is also the space within which those once formidable figures gain humorous but also political meaning – Gorbachev being much 'larger than life', for the time being, while little Stalin and Lenin and their tsarist forebears are 'cut down to size', rendering dictatorship, tyranny and absolutism literally ludicrous, until fierce little Ivan can barely stand up for himself.

---

[2]This version shows, in descending order, Gorbachev, Brezhnev, Khrushchev, Stalin, Lenin, Nicholas II, Catherine the Great, Peter the Great, Ivan the Terrible. A more recent 'Putin-doll' can be seen here: https://russian-crafts.com/nesting-dolls/political/putin-and-russian-political-leaders.html.

The concept of the semiosphere offers a spatial model for the interpretation of culture. Winfried Nöth (2015) has suggested that as such it also anticipated the spatial turn in contemporary cultural studies and the social sciences. Yet, despite the model being spatial, it needs to be emphasized that the semiosphere is both *synchronic* and *diachronic*. That is, as well as extending spatially, where it can be described as the structure, rule-system and meaningful utterances or texts that are possible in action at any one time (synchrony), it is also temporal: an evolving, adaptive and dynamic system over time (diachrony). All the Russian/Soviet leaders are represented as one 'system', while at the same time each occupies a rule-governed place in historical sequence (which seems to link them causally, even though many of the Romanovs and some Soviet leaders are omitted). In principle, synchrony and diachrony are interdependent (you cannot have one without the other), even if it may be reasonable, for analytical purposes, to focus on one dimension at a time.

The capability for multi-dimensional analysis of culture is a unique strength of the semiosphere model. Our aim is not only to study the 'discourse networks' (Kittler, 1990) of techno-cultural settings of different periods, to understand the historical preconditions for contemporary techno-cultures, but also to interpret the dialogues and translations among culture's different subsystems that have enabled their emergence over time. Both synchronic (network) and diachronic (causal) forces are at work at once.

The characteristics of *inside* and *outside* of a sphere, and thus of *boundary* across which *translation* can happen, as well as *central* and *peripheral* areas within a bounded system, are found in all semiospheres. However, their content is subject to powerful dynamics, caused by the determining (diachronic) *memory* mechanisms and the constant (synchronic) *exchange* of information or signification between a semiosphere's subsystems. It follows that the concept of the semiosphere is *hierarchical*. These hierarchies are both objective and subjective. They are objective because some of the semiosphere's subsystems are better positioned – that is have more power to define the circumstances for themselves and others. But they are also subjective, because these hierarchies depend on the *observer*'s perspective. Which subsystems actually matter in establishing the rules for others depends on the position and interests of perception. For a musician, Spotify or YouTube may come across as the dominant systems of the global internet. To a manager of a boutique hotel, these may instead be Trivago or Tripadvisor. A *user-based* perspective (Tomasello, 2000) is quite different from a *unit-based* one such as Saussure's (1974) 'smallest-signifying-unit' approach to semiotic science. As Michael Tomasello put it:

> Since it is obvious to all empirically oriented students of language acquisition that children operate with different psycholinguistic units

than adults, this theoretical freedom to identify these units on the basis of actual language use, rather than adult-based linguistic theory, is truly liberating.

(2000: 62)

What's more, both users and observers form intentions with respect to the signifying systems they use, and as Tomasello makes clear in his distinction between children and adults, their purposes and practices change over time. The actual process of semiosis requires users, not just rules (grammar) and units (vocabulary), and 'users' include analytical bystanders as well as direct interlocutors. The crucial role of the observer for cultural analysis is underlined in Peeter Torop's proposition:

The phrase 'semiosphere is studied by means of semiosphere' is not a paradox but points to the dialogue between the research object and its description language.

(2005: 164–5)

Any observers are part of the culture they are describing, just as any culture is replete with texts that perform an analytical, reflexive or self-critical function; they all need to use the means of that culture in the process. The semiosphere is both an *object* itself and a *meta-concept* (used to explain or account for an object). The semiosphere is in itself a research object by which we can study *semiosis*. At the same time, it is a useful model for understanding *digital culture*, with that domain's multimedia, intermedia, transmedia, hypermedia (etc.) ways of meaning-making.

In this systems model of meaning-making, the minimal unit or irreducible object of study appears to be 'the whole semiotic space of culture' (Lotman, 1990: 125) instead of a single sign. Here, Lotman's semiotics differs quite profoundly from the more familiar version (in the West at least) associated with the linguist Ferdinand de Saussure, whose 'science' that 'studies the life of signs in society' was modelled on the reductive physical sciences of the nineteenth century, which sought to build universal laws and relations from the smallest unit of matter, which was thought (at that time) to be the atom. Saussure (1974) sought to identify the 'smallest signifying unit' of language, which he dubbed 'the signifier'. When combined with a 'signified' (concept), the result is a 'sign' (see Chandler, 2017). Saussure saw his linguistic-conceptual approach as a branch of *psychology* (as does Tomasello, quoted above).

Lotman, on the other hand, started not from language (a system of utterances) but from literature (a system of texts), and he saw semiotics as a 'theory of *culture*'. The distinction yielded an approach that at first sight is quite mind-boggling: 'the whole semiotic space of culture' is the condition of existence for any one text, utterance or meaningful act, which 'itself' only exists in dialogic relation to other(s). Anything new in culture, be it a novel EDM (electronic dance music) genre or simply a Facebook post, can only be born and be 'new' in relation to everything else in culture.

Indeed, even though Lotman used the model for describing human culture, let us not forget its source of inspiration, which in fact allows for a much more inclusive, posthuman account of meaning-generation as a characteristic of all living organisms and possibly also of artificial intelligence (AI). As we showed in Chapter 1, Lotman drew the concept of 'the semiosphere' from V. I. Vernadsky's biogeochemical concept of the *biosphere*, which he understood to be 'situated on the surface of our planet and including within itself the totality of living things' (2005: 207). By analogy, Lotman created an approach to describe the totality of human culture. We may say that Lotman's approach is *ecological*, rather than reductive; and it is very far from the individualism of a psychological approach such as Saussure's, which confines language to individual intentional utterance, and to behaviour rather than systemic space-time relations.

The boundaries between (and interrelations among) the semiosphere and other contenders for a spheric or systems conceptualization, such as Vernadsky's *biosphere*, the *ecosphere* (Kull, 2005: 184), *noosphere* (Ivanov, 1998: 792), Uexküll's *umwelt* (Kull, 1998b: 305), Bakhin's *logosphere* and so on, are, however, ambiguous and deserve further clarification, which we will attempt throughout this book, especially in the light of the transformative force embodied in *digitality* (*technosphere*).

# Text (and its functions)

Text is the main analytic 'unit' of Lotmanian semiotics. However, it must be stressed that Lotman carried his user-based or cultural approach as opposed to a unit-based or Saussurian approach over to the concept of text. He made the distinction between 'striving for precise modelling procedures' of text-generation, where 'the object of study becomes not texts as such, but models of texts, models of models, etc.', on the one hand, and concentrating attention on 'the semiotic functioning of a real text', on the other:

> Using Saussurean terminology, we might say that in the first case it is language that interests the investigator as a materialization of the structural laws of a langue; in the second case it is those semiotic aspects of a text that diverge from the linguistic structure that are the object of attention. Whereas the first tendency is materialized in metasemiotics, the second by nature gives birth to the semiotics of culture.
>
> (Lotman, 1988a: 52)

Lotman pointed out (again in 1988) that 'text' designates not only a concept requiring precision of definition but a site or location for observers to concentrate on a new scientific problem:

> Today [text] is undoubtedly one of the most commonly used terms in the human sciences ... [Such words] do not so much designate a scientific concept with terminological accuracy as emphasize the timeliness of a problem and indicate an area in which new scientific ideas are being born.
>
> (1988b: 32)

'Text' is understood to be both analytical (scientific) and real (cultural), determined by how it is used (not by precise definition), while at the same time attracting extra attention at a significant moment in intellectual history (the moment of structuralism).

In Lotman's usage, a 'text' displays the following characteristics:

1. being expressed through a *sign system* (e.g. verbal, visual),

2. being *bounded* (e.g. by a compositional frame, beginning and ending) and

3. being *structured* (i.e. having hierarchical relations between its compositional elements) (Lotman, 1977: 51–3).

The concept is neutral in relation to any particular signifying system: even though Lotman's primary focus lay on literary works, we can *textualize* any communicational object in order to render it empirically analysable, including a single YouTube video, an entirety of a YouTube channel or the whole YouTube platform as a textual totality that may be expressed as a specific combination of audiovisual, visual and verbal sign-systems (see Burgess and Green, 2018). The whole-part logics that are fundamental for the semiosphere apply also to texts that may appear in culture simultaneously as a sequence/collection of signs, or as one sign with an integral meaning and integral function (Lotman et al., 1973).

The characteristics of *boundedness* and internal *hierarchy* emphasize the *structural* aspects of text. Focusing on these aspects may make texts appear as static and not to differ that much from, for instance, the structuralist take on texts. Yet, the semiospheric approach is distinct because it highlights the *functions* of texts in *culture* and the *dynamics* these tend to bring about (including the effects of reflexive and meta-discursive analysis). These functions largely coincide with those that Lotman attributes to the intelligence/thinking mechanism. He lists three functions as primary: *transmission*, *creation* and *memory* (1990: 2, 11–19; and see Part III). Which one of these dominates in any given text depends foremost on a reader's dialogue with the text. For instance, a digitized Van Gogh painting in an online catalogue can be:

- a transmitter of information about late nineteenth-century France and the Netherlands,
- a recorder of visual cultural continuities that underlie the formation of European identity,
- the creator of new information, when interrelated with other texts in the online catalogue and an instance of remix culture.

Such a text may appear as both a *transmission* of (historic post-impressionist) language and a *creation* of new language that equips the text with new meanings, themselves deriving from the new semiosphere and textual relationships into which it has been injected, even while it invokes *memory* of European high-art cultural tropes. The meanings the text is expected to communicate emerge out of the tensions between these functions.

That is also the reason why Lotman conceptualizes the reading process in terms of *communication* rather than '*decoding*' (as became familiar through the work of Stuart Hall, 1980). Decoding is made less straightforward by the fact that any text is always, at a minimum, *dually coded*, created in a minimum of two languages – a stance that resonates well with Mitchell's position that 'all media are mixed media' (Mitchell, 2005). A poem operates both in verbal language and by using metaphors that include paradigmatic replacements – that is they model the world visually. A YouTube video is a message in audiovisual language, but it is also over-coded by the codifying system guarding the functioning of videos on YouTube's pages (video length, ratio, positioning on screen in relation to other videos, included interactive features, etc.). A text's meaning-generation potential derives from such multiple over-coding – from the tensions between these codes that may be of different modalities and derive from different cultural contexts. As such, in Lotman's terms, *every text is a meaning generation mechanism*. And an artistic text may have an *explosive* potential (Lotman, 2009). While featuring specific mechanisms, artistic meaning-making is not an isolated or exclusive sphere of human communication, opposed to factual texts and physical matters. On the contrary:

> The factual judgement draws, perceptively or intellectually, the disturbing data from the exterior of language. The metaphor, on the other hand, draws the idea of a possible connection from the interior of the circle itself in its structuring connections./-/The factual judgement is born from a physical mutation of the world and only afterwards is transformed into semiotic knowledge. The metaphor is born from an internal disturbance of semiosis. If it succeeds in its game, it produces knowledge because it produces new semiotic judgements and, in the final outcome, obtains results which do not differ from factual judgements.
>
> (Eco, 1984: 86)

By this, Eco draws our attention to the potential of artistic metaphors in anticipating what could once be enunciated as facts.

# Languages and modelling systems

The semiosphere is the *sum of languages* and simultaneously *their precondition*, because 'Without semiosphere a language not only does not work, but does not even exist' (Lotman, 1984: 16). In many ways, in cultural semiotics, 'language' can be regarded as a synonym of 'sign system' or 'medium': a collection of signs and rules for their combination to form communicative utterances. There are, however, some further specifications that reveal the notion's analytic potential. Together with text, language appears as an elementary instrument of cultural semiosis, yet, it is always necessarily immersed in a larger/more complex semiotic sphere. A *semiotic monad* is formed when two languages (with cultural communities that use them), at once similar and different, step into dialogue. In this case a new unity between them may emerge – they may at least partially integrate, may start functioning as a new semiotic whole. That is, they may partially *converge* (see our discussion of this concept below). Such dialogue and convergence processes are a cultural constant, since all texts integrate at least two languages that, therefore, are forced into dialogue. All cultural communities are also forced to observe and translate other cultures/languages in order to make sense of them. Krippendorff (1995a), for instance, has shown how the vocabulary of modern design discourse stems from several sources, which can be thought of as the convergent but incommensurable 'languages' that go into the performance of the given design-object or 'text' – the arts, engineering, ergonomics, advertising, popular culture, software manufacturing, and so on. As such the meta-discourse of the design sub-domain has taken shape through observations and in dialogue among these external/convergent subsystems.

The convergence of subsystems into a new whole can be traced along the diachronic as well as the synchronic dimension. For example:

- Diachronically, Wikipedia 'remediates' (Bolter and Grusin, 1998) a print encyclopaedia, by which it is clear that 'remediation' is really 'reinvention' – using convergent subsystems to create something new.
- Synchronically, transmedia storytelling involves 'a process where integral elements of a fiction get dispersed systematically across multiple delivery channels for the purpose of creating a unified and coordinated entertainment experience' (Jenkins, 2011).

At the time when Lotman and other members of the Tartu-Moscow school were developing their approach to culture, *semiotics* was seen by the Soviet authorities as an ideologically suspicious area of study. Terms and concepts deriving from *cybernetics* were ideologically a safer choice. Some of their concepts, including 'modelling system', originate from cybernetics. A language functions as a modelling system. It is not only a means for expressing an object but it also models the object in accordance with its specific affordances (compare 'modal affordances' in Kress 2010) and the rules of analogy established between its elements and the object of perception, cognition or organization (Lotman, 2011[1967]: 250). The affordances of vectoral graphics, Excel spreadsheets or podcasts are notably different from one another, and while they all aim to establish analogy to their object, they still generate mode-specific models of the external world.

To elaborate the modelling concept and adapt it better to their understanding of the mechanisms of culture, Lotman and his colleagues developed the notion of 'secondary modelling system', referring to systems that 'have natural language as their basis and accumulate additional superstructures'. Together with the 'semiosphere', 'secondary modelling system' appears as an emblematic term of the Tartu-Moscow semiotic school. In fact, it was previously used as a euphemism for 'semiotics' itself: the Tartu-Moscow school's 1964 summer school – the first in the legendary series – was titled the *Summer School on Secondary Modelling Systems*.

To relate this term to Western scholarship, Roland Barthes's works are most relevant. Barthes developed an analogous typology of sign-systems, in which 'a system of second-order meanings' (2010 [1964]: 30) distinguished primary 'denotation' from cultural or ideological 'connotation'. However, Barthes focuses on the hegemonic discourses of modern (consumer) culture in contrast to Lotman's interest in the unpredictable mechanism of meaning-creation in general. Monticelli (2016) has foregrounded the complementarity between the semiological critique of ideology and the semiotic analysis of culture. While the context of Barthes's second-order systems is set within 'highly homogeneous ideological frames', the concept of 'secondary modelling system' is much more general, that is 'provided by the cultural system of systems with its heterogeneity and polyglotism' (Monticelli, 2016: 444).

Cultural semioticians have used the concept to explain the relationship between natural language and arts (as secondary modelling languages). Peircian theorists have developed broader models, where verbal language is not primary but secondary (see Sebeok and Danesi, 2000; Nöth, 2006). We follow the suggestion by Nöth (2006: 259) that the importance of Lotman's theory is his *hierarchy of levels* that makes up a system of *relational stratifications*. Higher levels are conceived as semiotic spaces with more dimensions in relation to the spaces of the lower levels that they embrace. In this sense 'secondary modelling languages' are effectively super-codes that integrate other subsidiary codes. For instance, any transmedia story-world is such a super-code: it integrates multiple modally different languages to communicate its message. And a semiosphere is the 'playroom' for secondary modelling. While Lotman emphasized the importance of art as a secondary modelling system, we can include here all kinds of digital media systems that integrate multiple media and modalities.

When all languages operate as modelling systems, we appear to be surrounded by multiple models of reality that are in constant conflict and dialogue. Semiotic reality is by definition multiple/diverse: semiosis multiplies reality, while a more uniform understanding of reality could result from further semiosis – that is from the potential to apply integrative secondary modelling to those different existing models and modelling systems, ranging from scientific to artistic to mythological to gamified and so on. Such is culture: the generative mechanism for all these realities and for their apprehension in a single semiosphere using what might be called 'world-building' modelling systems.

# Autocommunication – meta-texts – memory

As suggested earlier, the concept of semiosphere is a *model* of relational stratification. It enables us to study the connections and unities that culture creates on different 'levels' – higher-level models organize lower-level texts and codes, and so on. Perhaps the highest-level *model* we can think of is scholarly generalization and visualization of large-scale creative practices such as, for instance, Lev Manovich's (2017a) book on globally practiced photography in Instagram (and see Leaver et al., 2020). Manovich's method enables us to analyse the relationship of a single photo to all photos taken worldwide and posted in Instagram. Such an affordance for scale-free analysis of the semiosphere model – the ability to move between these different levels (micro-text to macro-system) and look for their isomorphic relationships – allows for another methodological innovation deriving from Lotman: the concept of cultural *autocommunication*. This means that every act of communication between any sender and any receiver can, at a higher level, be regarded as an act wherein a culture or its subsystem communicates to itself about itself (hence 'auto' – Gk. 'self'). When such communicating partners, say members of specific 'massively multiplayer online role-playing game' (MMORPG) communities (*World of Warcraft, Final Fantasy, Guild Wars* and many others), communicate with each other or about the game, then a certain 'us-ness' is established and meta-communicated. The more such communication happens in different modalities and the more the resultant self-descriptive texts exist in culture, the more there has been systemic autocommunication in Lotman's terms and the more the particular subsystem is fixed in a culture with regard to its characteristics, its identity, affordances and functions.

The capability of self-interpretation and production of self-descriptive meta-texts is a defining characteristic of meaning-generating systems (Lotman, 1997: 10). This works on all levels – starting from the smallest of groups and ending up on the level planetary culture. Lotman pointed out that culture itself may be regarded as a single message sent by the collective 'I' of humanity to itself. In this sense the culture of humanity is a colossal example of autocommunication (Epstein, 2018).

At all levels the function of autocommunication is to reduce the system's inherent heterogeneity, to create unity and establish difference from the external environment. And it does that across time. Broms and Gahmberg (1983) suggest that autocommunication turns into an organizing process through which a communicator calls forth and enhances its own values and the repeated use of the same textual material produces the mythologies of the communicating structure. Yet, the texts that are used for autocommunication may over time acquire new meanings, even as the communicating system may be reorganizing itself – so that re-interpretations of these texts may not only have a path-*fixing* function but rather create contingencies for *change*. At the level of 'Western culture' in general, the *adaptation* of canonical texts can be seen as an example. Take *The Most Excellent and Lamentable Tragedy of Romeo and Juliet* (1599), by up-and-coming showrunner William Shakespeare. Here are some movie adaptations of this much-altered play:

10. *Rome and Juliet* (2006) (Dir. Connie Macatuno)
    – lesbian, the Philippines
 9. *Chicken Rice War* (2000) (Dir. Chee Kong Cheah)
    – hawkers, Singapore
 8. *Romeo and Juliet* (2013) (Dir. Carlos Carlei)
    – teens, Verona
 7. *Private Romeo* (2012) (Dir. Alan Brown)
    – gays, military cadets
 6. *Gnomeo and Juliet* (2011) (Dir. Kelly Asbury)
    – gnomes, animated garden
 5. *William Shakespeare's Romeo + Juliet* (1996) (Dir. Baz. Luhrmann)
    – gangs, 'Verona Beach'
 4. *Warm Bodies* (2013) (Dir. Jonathan Levine)
    – zombies, apocalypse
 3. *Shakespeare in Love* (1998) (Dir. John Madden)
    – Shakespeare, 'himself'
 2. *West Side Story* (1961) (Dir. Robert Wise & Jerome Robbins)
    – gangs, New York

1. *Romeo and Juliet* (1968) (Dir. Franco Zeffirelli)
– teens, Anglo-Italian.[3]

Such variations of *Romeo and Juliet* in cinema, in abridged forms on YouTube, in experimental dance theatre or transformed in Japanese manga, can be seen as repetitions of already familiar stories in new languages. We can say that the more languages and meta-languages there are for mediating the same text, to ensure its 'transmedial recursivity', the stronger is its inclusion in what Rigney calls the 'working memory' of cultural space (Rigney, 2005: 20–1), shaping a culture's contemporary identity.

Because 'everything contained in culture's diachrony is part of its synchrony' (Lotman, 1990: 127), the mechanism of memory largely determines culture's identity, even as the present reworks the past. Everything we could possibly know and remember about the past is the result of continuing mediation and is expressed in texts. Memory studies use the term 'mediality' to draw attention to the *process* of mediation, locating its 'in-between' function in an environment of history and relationships, such that to use the term 'mediality' is to:

> criticize the idea that the function of media consists in mediating, mediatizing, negotiating, transmitting, or transducing. Media are not methods of communication; media are, making a concession to McLuhan in a figurative language: Environments for communication. Thinking of mediality as information-production, and consequently, of communication media as a major game-changer in socio-cultural evolution, implies rethinking time and temporality offering new insights into communication media history and media archaeology.
>
> (Blanco Rivero, 2019: 19/23)

Here, 'mediality represents ... the very condition for the emergence of cultural memory' (Erll, 2011: 114). Texts are *agents* in communication processes. As communication and reception practices change over time, so do the meanings 'in' texts and their position in networks of cultural memory. Digital media are especially potent in exploiting the palimpsest (written-over) nature of cultural memory – texts are deleted, modified, rewritten and recombined at an accelerating pace, while the infinite perfection of digital copying (in contrast to analogue) ensures that texts don't decay and die, although they may be modded, mistreated and lost; extinction is not an option (at least until the operating system is updated), and so 'extinct' cultural texts, unlike species in the biosphere, can be revived and reused by later cultures in

---

[3]Pop-culture sites abound with lists. This one from 2013 is for the 'top 10' Romeo/Juliet movie adaptations: https://www.spot.ph/entertainment/54878/top-10-romeo-and-juliet-film-adaptations.

ways not previously warranted, even though both the originating coding language and the culture within which a text or system was immersed are both lost (Lotman, 1990, 2005 [1984]: 212). Here, memory is not a cultural determinant; instead, one semiosphere learns from another but adapts what it finds to suit its own internal systems, not to maintain or preserve the meanings of the past. Contact with 'cultural memory' provokes newness, innovation and change – a good example being the European Renaissance, which 'rediscovered' Classical (Graeco-Roman) texts, but ascribed entirely postmedieval European meanings to them. The *border between* the Ancients and Moderns proved to be a semiotic hot spot, but 'memory' of the Ancients did not dictate the meaning of modernity.

# Border

This brings us to one of the most fundamental principles of semiosphere that 'neither a sign, an organism, a text, or a culture can exist alone, singly – it always requires another sign, other organisms, texts, cultures, in order to exist, to live' (Kull, 2005: 178). The concept of *boundary* or *border* is not a barrier but an agent of mediality. Every semiosphere or subsystem is first of all an enclosed space that is bounded off from what, according to an insider's perspective, is perceived as extra-semiotic sphere, that is the sphere of a different language, which must appear as meaningless and unorganized. This is why the Classical Ancients treated all outsider cultures as 'the same' – barbarians – whatever their internal differences or comparative elaboration. The boundary ensures that 'we' know who we are; and what's different about 'them'. Once across that border – when, for instance, a Roman army crosses the Imperial border – the soldiers are not only confronted with meaningless cultures but also their own hierarchies no longer apply. What counts in Rome as correct or incorrect, good or bad, doesn't operate in the external space. Not only can you get away with actions that would be unthinkable in the home culture – the enslavement, rape, pillage and murder of entire populations – but, like Caesar, be lauded and feted for doing it. Indeed, Rome's imperial might depends on that.

Any semiosphere, especially a large-scale one like a nation or empire, is criss-crossed with internal boundaries that distinguish its subsystems. This means that it is full of semi-autonomous systems that also function autocommunicatively, using special language, codes and customs to establish their own identity and order, and to distinguish each group from their environment. Yet, multiple texts employ multiple languages and coding, and because individual people belong to multiple social or cultural formations, these subsystems are always part of each other; they are each other's 'material', the semiotic environment for all.

Therefore, systems are always intertwined and their boundaries are areas where they overlap, are part of each other. A single website of a daily newspaper could be understood as a boundary area where the semiotic subsystems such as 'interaction-design' and 'journalism' (and also many others) meet and adapt to each other – that is where they engage in dialogic interactions that eventually shape the further evolution of both of them. Lotman suggests that such border-areas between semiospheres is where the most intense semiotic activity happens, where new meanings and formations can emerge and where systems become responsive to their semiotic milieu – that is to each other.

Relatedly, the importance of border areas for Lotman was that these are also sites of relative freedom – domains of culture that are less regulated and standardized and where, therefore, new dialogue, dynamic responses and innovations become possible. For example, the website for a newspaper like *The New York Times* can be expected to be much less experimental and responsive to change in web design trends than one occupying a more marginal position in the journalistic semiosphere. This is because *The New York Times* lies not at the flexible boundary of that semiosphere but at its core. It is regarded by others as important and influential, which inevitably imposes a highly autocommunicative and self-regulating limit to its room for manoeuvre, which is too rigid to be the source of semiotic dynamism in the wider cultural scene. In contrast, new journalistic endeavours, such as Buzzfeed, Vice or others, initially peripheral, have been able to respond flexibly to changing circumstances, to carve out new forms and operational models that are better adjusted to the changed cultural milieu.

# 5

# Dialogue and dynamics

*I think I am a writer and an actor and an artist.*
But I haven't believed the purity of my own intentions
ever since I became my own salesperson, *too.*
(TAVI GEVINSON, 2019)

\*\*\*

Semiospheres and their subsystems are unavoidably in dialogue with each other across their different boundaries, facilitating innovations elsewhere but also ensuring that each sphere maintains a coherent identity even as it adapts to changes among environmental subsystems. One special kind of dialogue – *translation* – is treated as especially important in Lotman's semiotics, because it explains how communication occurs across boundaries, in a situation of *untranslatability*. However, translation in this context does not simply refer to a mechanical switch from one language to another but a fundamental characteristic of language, which has to accomplish the impossible: to enable at least two *incommensurable* and *untranslatable* systems at any scale to communicate with one another. The meaning that each derives from the encounter differs for each interlocutor, but nevertheless meaning does emerge and communication does take place. There is as a result simply no such thing as a determinate, precise, exact or true meaning, only more or less equivalent translations, of any and all utterances, among persons, texts or languages. Nor is it possible to go back to an authentic source – an individual brain, text or culture – to fix on a true or original meaning, since it only emerges situationally in dialogue. Formally, there is a systematic lack of exact equivalents between the signifying elements of different languages, so an exact translation from one to the other is in principle impossible. This applies to modally different signifying systems such as 'visual images' and 'verbal languages'. They are untranslatable systems. Nevertheless, translation is still attempted at every turn. Dialogue still occurs. Meaning is established.

Meaning is established *across boundaries*. The greater the differences between a source language and target language, the more creative and potentially fruitful are the results of a translation operation. As Lotman puts it, 'translation of the non-translatable carries the information of highest value' (2009: 15). Hence, for example, data-visualization, the quickly evolving craft of visualizing vast corpuses of discrete data, works by the same means as does the use of metaphor in poetry: the production of new, otherwise unattainable information out of untranslatable systems. Data (information) and narrative (story/drama) are not mutually 'translatable' without 'data-visualization' or some other recoding operation. *Transmedia storytelling* practice is important for the similar reason. It requires translation between modally contrasting sign-systems (different media forms), and in the process, it enforces the production of new and socially pertinent cultural forms, meanings and ideas (Ibrus and Ojamaa, 2014; see also Scolari, Bertetti and Freeman, 2014).

In principle, languages and other semiotic systems of the semiosphere relate to each other on a scale ranging from total mutual translatability to total mutual untranslatability, except that neither extreme exists in real life. Languages can be clustered in 'families', but these are rarely mutually intelligible.[1] Even within a single tongue there are notorious differences of region, accent, class or specialism. Nor are native speakers in control of language evolution, even of their own language. English was shaped by those who had to learn it, as conquerors, traders or subjugated populations, including Celtic-speaking Britons, Norse-speaking Vikings and French-speaking Norman conquerors. Its 'founding' speakers came to English with another mother tongue in their heads because most of those dwelling in the British Isles spoke another language: a situation that persists to this day because of English's global status – most speakers use it as a second language. Along the way, English itself evolved not only lexically, with borrowed words, but also grammatically. Compared with its own linguistic neighbours, English is 'weird'.[2] Linguistic propinquity is no guarantee of intelligibility. Establishing any sort of commonality requires translation across numerous boundaries, linguistic, demographic, regional and hostile.

One of the characteristics of translation between differently organized languages is irreversibility. A translated text cannot readily be translated

---

[1] Language families can be browsed here: https://www.ethnologue.com/browse/families. Just as an example, the *North* Germanic languages (Danish, Norwegian and Swedish) are said to be mutually intelligible, but the *West* Germanic languages (English, German, Dutch) are not.

[2] See John McWhorter (2015) 'English is not normal: No, English isn't uniquely vibrant or mighty or adaptable. But it really is weirder than pretty much every other language': https://aeon.co/essays/why-is-english-so-weirdly-different-from-other-languages.

back to the original. A film or TV adaptation could never be 'translated' back into the literary form of the original books (as many a frustrated fan has complained). But the irreversibility of the process doesn't mean that it is inadequate or erroneous; rather, it signals that the semiotic systems in play are a source of creativity. It is noteworthy that early attempts to automate translation made slow progress until they embraced uncertainty and adopted an emergent 'deep learning' neural network model. The improvement of apps like Google Translate suggests that unexpected novelty in translation has migrated out of the human domain to become part of the repertoire of artificial intelligence.

The fundamental process underlying digitization is translation from continuous (analogue) codifying systems to a discrete (digital) system, which is in principle similar to translating a visual text into a text in verbal language. Continuous iconic systems – like a photograph with infinite gradations of tone – are characterized by the primacy of *text* (whole picture) over individual *signs* (individual pixel), because analogue texts cannot easily be deconstructed into elementary units. In digital systems, texts are coded as sequences of individual signs (many pixels) and, therefore, signs can be regarded as primary. A result from Lotman's perspective is that it is *impossible* to translate one to the other, as Winfried Nöth points out:

> Lotman emphasizes the essential difference between discrete and non-discrete texts and postulates the impossibility of their mutual translatability, since 'the equivalent to the discrete and precisely demarcated semantic unit of one text is, in the other, a kind of semantic blur with indistinct boundaries and gradual shadings into other meanings'.
> (Lotman, 1990: 36–7, cited in Nöth, 2006: 251)

In the process of digitization, the movement is in the opposite direction, towards clearer demarcation of individual elements. This has brought along a shift in the analysability of continually coded texts with computer technology. Lotman's original suggestion was that discrete and continuous systems appear as an incommensurable semiotic binary and that any meaning-generating system needs to contain at least two codifying subsystems, one of which is discrete and the other continuous. The impossibility of exact translation between them is the source and condition of meaning-generation (which is simultaneously inexact and nontrivial). Relatedly, two opposing, yet simultaneous processes may be traced within a semiosphere: decomposing signs into opposing (sub)units on the one hand and integrating opposing signs into textual unity on the other.

These processes are traceable, for example, in contemporary digital archives and online databases. In order to make their content, for instance films or music, findable/searchable, they are indexed: tags or other kinds of metadata are assigned to these texts. Then, based on the particular metadata categories used, new textual wholes are created, comprising all the texts in a particular category (like keywords or hashtags). As a result, formerly separate texts appear as variations of an invariant element. The songs someone would have on their personal Spotify's Discover Weekly playlist end up being assigned there algorithmically, based on the listener's previous listening. Spotify's algorithms and automated processing look for similar songs using three methods:

- based on the 'collaborative filtering' method (users having similar listening patterns),
- by analysing a song's musical structures, and
- by searching for social buzz and discourses that model new genres and semantic connections between songs from all kinds of music blogs and message boards in the web.

Analytically generated discrete data then interlinks songs that may never have been seen as close, yet the new musical constellations end up positively surprising Spotify's users.

For our purposes, we can see in this process that initially continuous wholes of music (songs) were translated into discrete digital denotators (metadata; tags) and then again into continuous wholes (playlists), using the organizational affordances of these digital semantic systems. The *automated but creative* process affecting the choices and experiences of millions of users around the globe is, therefore, enabled by *translations between untranslatable systems* – in this case, continuous and discontinuous modes of textual representation.

Consequently, it is no surprise to find that for Lotman, *thinking* itself is essentially a *dialogic* process, occurring between at least two systems. As he put it, 'the elementary act of thinking is translation [and] the elementary mechanism of translation is dialogue' (1990: 143). Hence, concepts originating in translation studies, especially Roman Jakobson's notion of 'intersemiotic translation' (1971 [1959]), appear as fruitful tools for analysing how the semiosphere interacts with its subsystems, as well as the dialogue among subsystems. In this context, translation is the mechanism for introducing change into the semiosphere. What from the internal viewpoint appears to be meaningless matter or noninformation is semiotized by the translating filters that constitute the boundary of the system.

This is also how new applications and services typically enter the semiosphere, by being translated into its existing languages. Apple Lisa was the first ever operating system with a graphical user interface (GUI). All its visual composite metaphors were modelled on the then typical office space (think of 'folders', 'clipboard', 'wastebasket', etc.). Analogous processes of translation, first into the terms of familiar environments or cultural forms, are observable in the early stages of any new medium or platform. Marshall

McLuhan called this 'rearviewmirrorism', arguing that each new medium copies and contains its predecessor: 'The content of writing is speech, just as the written word is the content of print, and print is the content of telegraph' (McLuhan, 1964: 8). It may be said to apply to any technological innovation, where novel inventions do not first appear in their mature guise, be they railway carriages (horse-drawn coaches) or concrete buildings (Tudor half-timbering).[3] For change to happen, such new ideas, languages and other cultural or built forms need to be translated into the host system's existing terms, in order to allow their own radical potential to emerge.

Therefore, dialogic contact with extra-semiotic space is vital for any semiosphere to maintain its status as a meaning-generating mechanism and thus to ensure its dynamics. Evolution is dialogic in nature, requiring a dialogue partner that is at the same time both similar and different – a text from another system translated to the language of the semiosphere, where it might start functioning as a catalyst for change.

The requirement for dialogic systems to be both similar and different is another paradox. In the hypothetical situation where two systems are absolutely different, communication would be impossible, whereas in the case of complete similarity, communication would be redundant as the systems would have no new information to share with each other. However, in the process of communication between asymmetric systems (where information can be exchanged), similarity between them increases. This means that diversity can be both created and destroyed by dialogue. Kalevi Kull infers therefore that 'too much communication can be described as a general reason for many ecological problems that lead to homogenization of the world and loss of diversity. This is the case both in biological communities and in cultures' (2005: 186). At the same time, this threat is acute only in the hypothetical situation when two systems communicate only with each other, whereas in reality, most systems are in dialogic relations with multiple others.

# Explosion, unpredictability, innovation

Juri Lotman's notion of cultural 'explosion' refers to sudden irreversible change, rather than gradual or evolutionary change. The idea of 'explosion' served more than one purpose for Lotman. First, it allowed him to introduce an obviously dynamic, transformational process into semiotic analysis, which had concentrated on static structuralist description of synchronic relations in a system. Second, Lotman wanted

---

[3]Carriages: https://railwaywondersoftheworld.com/railway-carriage.html and http://www.victorianweb.org/technology/railways/p2.html; Tudoresque timbering: http://www.gregynog.org/ (Gregynog Hall, Wales); and see Ballantyne and Law (2011: 151–7).

to incorporate chance, uncertainty and hazard into his model. An explosion produces unpredictable effects; the only certainty being that nothing stays the same afterwards, and so 'the moment of explosion is also the place where a sharp increase in the informativity of the entire system takes place' (Lotman, 2009: 28). And third, 'explosion' allowed him to connect textual with extra-textual (a.k.a. real life) elements, where 'the future' interacts with the present, such that cause and effect are reversed (fear or desire for some unrealized future causes action in the present, so effects precede causes). 'The future', which by definition does not yet exist and is necessarily both extra-textual and uncertain, generates new information, particularly in the form of what economists call 'exogenous shocks', such as Revolution, where all the rules are broken. Mikhail Epstein (2018) offers an illuminating example of how Lotman used the concept to analyse the 'interaction between textual and extratextual reality' and 'the interaction between the present and the future':

> The evolutionary manner of reform attempted by Mikhail Gorbachev in the late 1980s degraded into a drawn-out series of palliatives and bureaucratic prescriptions, with no contact with reality; whereas the revolutionary means employed by Boris Yeltsin, including his method of shock therapy and the instantaneous launching of marketization and privatization, endangered the very goal of evolutionism, and brought the country, at the time of Lotman's writing, to the brink of civil war.

According to Epstein, Lotman preferred evolutionary development and the middle ground, urging post-Soviet Russia to forego its historic preference for binary extremes and a destructive explosion that would destroy 'the old world to its very foundations' before 'constructing a new one on its ruins'. Lotman preferred 'ternary' systems of the West – systems with more institutions and more subsystems that have therefore always also more alternative ideas circulating, where the new systems can emerge more gradually and the social/cultural system as a whole is more ready to absorb external shocks. Epstein comments that 'as a rigorous scholar of Russian history, Lotman understood, better than many politicians, the near-impossibility of this evolutionary change of cultural paradigms' in Russia, citing his remark that 'even when we are talking of gradual development, we [Russians] want to accomplish this through explosive techniques' (Lotman, 2009: 174).

A semiotic system's ability to generate new meanings via translations with unpredictable results is a sign of its ability to *innovate*. At certain times floods of new texts enter the system, before it has evolved a meta-language for describing them. This was the case with the first instances of transmedia storytelling. As Henry Jenkins (2006) explains, audiences of *The Matrix* struggled to make sense of the whole idea of mediating a story via a network of subtexts, which appear simultaneously as parts and wholes, in different media. After the initial *explosion*, efforts to define the practice were made by both academics and industry representatives on blogs, conferences, individual papers and monographs and finally also in handbooks and encyclopaedias that aim at stabilizing the field with autocommunicative meta-descriptions. In the history of the overall semiosphere system, periods of stable and linear evolution alternate with instances of explosion that generate qualitative discontinuities and change the whole system.

At a time of rapid change, future trajectories always seem unpredictable. The phase of unpredictability is usually followed by intense attempts at self-description and dialogue with the system's memory. These autocommunicative efforts are aimed at explaining and therefore fixing the system, establishing rules (after the event) to make the future more predictable (with probabilities if not precision), while linking it meaningfully to previous evolutionary phases of the system. From the viewpoint of the meta-texts thereby created, the 'legitimacy' of the new order and power asymmetries are established by hindsight. The path that was eventually taken seems self-evident. The opposite case – failure to generate an adequate meta-language – would dissolve the explosion's creative potential into chaos. Unfortunately, the institutional desire for order is thwarted by explosive or revolutionary cultural transformations, so any scientific model of evolutionary continuity needs to allow for unpredictable disruption (see under 'asymmetry/power', below).

# Convergence and divergence

*Convergence* is often glossed as a technological process, when previously separate platforms and their associated industries are integrated following technological developments. The classic example is the convergence of *telecommunications* (phone networks), *broadcasting* (content supply) and *computation* (digital interactivity) (Jenkins, 2006). At the same time, convergence is a semiotic phenomenon. It happens when previously unconnected systems end up in a dialogue. That is, they start overlapping and intertwining, when they become part of each other – when texts, individuals and their cultural identities or institutions emerge that are part of both systems.

For instance, when the online content services industry started to combine their operational models with the film and TV content production and distribution industries, a new convergent system emerged out of that combination: the 'video-on-demand' (VOD) industry. Of these services, Netflix, YouTube, Vimeo, Hulu, Amazon Prime and Stan are prime examples. This new domain soon started to work autocommunicatively: it got a name and with that an industrial identity; it created its own meta-language, carved out distinct operational models to be copied, adopted and adapted around the world. VOD is no longer only a distinct form of content delivery but also a cultural genre and an institution. The VOD model has quickly evolved from having a peripheral role in the audiovisual production and distribution system to become its driving core. It is not only that YouTube and Netflix, among others, have become the most significant global distributors of audiovisual content but also that they have facilitated the emergence of entirely new genres, new kinds of players and (semi-) professional identities in productive systems, new subcultures that use audiovisual expression for communication and identification, new forms of usage. In short, new semiospheres.

The dialogic zone where online and audiovisual cultures once met and where they converged has not only *emerged* as a distinct system of its own but generated a broader audiovisual culture subsystem. That is, it has *diverged* as a subsystem – created its own evolutionary path affecting others. One of the suggestions we have, therefore, is that from the perspective of semiosphere theory, *convergence, emergence* and *divergence* constitute the same process.

When a new system emerges, it does not mean that the old systems disappear. Typically, once-dominant media forms (writing, print, cinema, broadcasting, digital, mobile) are *supplemented* not *supplanted* by their technological successors, over the extreme long term. They continue to be part of each other and in this way are also forced into dialogue. Film and TV production industries, their semi-autonomous processes, their conventions and convictions, continue to affect the operations of, for instance, Netflix, and vice versa. For example, the binge-watching format, introduced by Netflix, has affected the TV-series genre by these needing to have storylines that evolve across episodes and not needing to use elements such as the cliff-hanger. Netflix's user data analytics and metadata schemas have also opened up formerly established genre categories, with filmmakers given a freer hand to address a larger variety of niche audiences. Yet, next to these developments we see, as recognized by Vonderau (2016), for instance, how YouTube's focus has changed over the years from a community to a commercial service: from facilitating sharing by individuals and servicing interactions within networked communities to streamlining the consumption processes. Its interface increasingly resembles that of Netflix, trying to remediate television's programmed flow rather than imitating the interaction on a dating website, as YouTube did, at least in its infancy.

# Asymmetry/power

Lotman suggested that every semiosphere is constituted by the centre-periphery dichotomy. The distinction between core and periphery is constituted by the relative capacity of its subsystems to establish descriptive meta-languages for the whole system. A subsystem with such a capacity is understood as the system's core. The subsystems without similar capacities constitute its periphery (Figure 5.1).

The core's capacity, however, involves a seeming paradox. Sooner or later its order-creating, law-forming and autocommunicative subsystems become

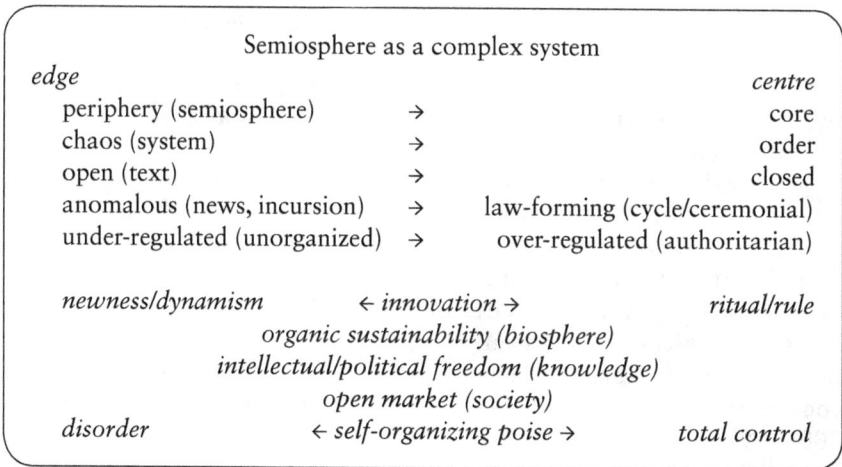

```
            Semiosphere as a complex system
  edge                                            centre
     periphery (semiosphere)       →                core
     chaos (system)               →                order
     open (text)                  →               closed
     anomalous (news, incursion)   →    law-forming (cycle/ceremonial)
     under-regulated (unorganized) →   over-regulated (authoritarian)

  newness/dynamism            ← innovation →          ritual/rule
                     organic sustainability (biosphere)
                  intellectual/political freedom (knowledge)
                          open market (society)
     disorder              ← self-organizing poise →    total control
```

FIGURE 5.1 *Core and periphery in a semiosphere. Note: The relation between core and periphery should be seen as a gradient, not a binary. Freedom, innovation, sustainability and openness are achieved somewhere along the gradient, with a 'poised system' (Kauffman, 1991). Here, stable complexity can be maintained, between order and chaos, at a point that must be found and adjusted by continuing collective trial and error under conditions of uncertainty*

rigid or closed. As Andrews (2003: 68) explains, meta-description as an activity always gives rise to higher entropy. As the core of a system increases in self-regulation, it becomes more rigidly organized and loses dynamism. Having exhausted their reserve of indeterminacy, central subsystems become inflexible and incapable of further development. On the periphery, in dialogue with the external environment and with other semiospheres, the idealized or reified norms of the core will come to contradict changing semiotic reality. The closer to the periphery, the more the power of the core diminishes and the rules of the core become illegitimate. Therefore, the relationships between semiotic practice and the norms imposed on it become increasingly strained.

Lotman points out that it is in such conditions – relatively unregulated dialogic spaces – where innovation happens and new social and cultural formations emerge. Here we could think of the different avant-garde movements and progressive cultures that are relatively independent of existing power structures. These might include avant-garde arts and other creative pursuits (e.g. fashion and music), academic cultures (Castells, 2001), open source movements (Weber, 2004; Mansell and Berdou, 2009) or communities of creatively engaged users who organize themselves as informal 'fringe groups' (Sawhney and Lee, 2005). All these include agents that break the rules, innovate and, in this way, secure pluralism and renewal in systems. Over time, however, as the new formations prove their worth, establish themselves and overtake the dominant roles, what happens in Lotman's terms is the 'maturing' of the periphery – the process in which the peripheral disruptions become the dominant norms for the whole semiosphere.

It is for this reason that Schönle (2001, 2003) has attributed to Lotman himself the status of innovator of Western cultural studies. While Lotman shared the poststructuralist view that discourse has a primary role in founding reality, his theory suggested that the unavoidable heterogeneity of a semiotic environment starts mitigating the subject's dependence on any specific discourse. 'Thus subjects act on their impulse to autonomy by playing discourses against each other, recording them in an act of auto-communication that generates novelty in the process' (Schönle and Shine, 2006: 24).

In this context we need to recognize, however, that questions of autonomy and questions about who can create discourses, or regulate and establish rules for others, are questions of agency and power. Therefore, we also need to address the semiospheric theory of power. While Lotman could not develop an explicit theory of power (owing to circumstances in the Soviet Union at the time), the conceptual grounding of his theory connects with those of Niklas Luhmann and Michel Foucault. Let us quote Luhmann to draw the parallels:

There may be hierarchies, asymmetries, or differences in influence, but no part of the system can control others without itself being subject to control. Under such circumstances it is possible – indeed, in meaning-oriented systems highly probable – that any control must be exercised in anticipation of counter-control. Securing an asymmetrical structure in spite of this (e.g. in power relationships internal to the system) therefore always requires special precautions.

(Luhmann, 1995: 36)

Here Luhmann criticizes the classical or 'juridical-political' concept of power, which makes three main assumptions (see Foucault, 1990: 94–6). First, it asserts *possession* – power is conceptualized as a substance that can be possessed or exchanged, which implies an idea of power as a zero-sum game, because if I 'take' power, you 'lose' it. Second, it assumes *repression* – to exercise power is to curb freedom. Finally, it assumes *a location* – power is imagined to be concentrated in a centre from which it flows to the rest of society. Foucault and systems theorists like Luhmann have demonstrated how contemporary societies are no longer organized around a monarchical apex or centre; instead, they continue dispersing into operationally (semi-) autonomous (decentralized) subsystems, associated with administrative bureaucracy, not the command-and-control power (on pain of death) of a feudal overlord.

Instead of *sovereignty*, Foucault conceptualizes power as *governmentality* (Rose, 1999; Foucault, 2002a: 201–22). Power is the process of taking 'action upon action'. To exercise power is to structure the possible field of action of others, of all the actors in a shared environment. All the systems present in a particular environment face contingency. In order to reproduce themselves, on the basis of their own autonomous principles of replication, they must influence each other. As Pottage (1998: 22) puts it, each of the actors is dependent on the autonomy of the other. 'The art of the game is not to dominate the opposing actor, but to anticipate and exploit its interventions, and to make one's own interventions dependent upon an opponent's restless invention of (counter-)strategies'. Understood in this way, power is relational and emerges from situated oppositions among autonomous and discontinuous processes: it is nonsubjective, emergent and contingent (Ibrus, 2015b).

At this point, the inherent heterogeneity of any semiosphere becomes relevant to the question of power. Systems and semiospheres are overlapping and intertwined in complex ways, such that it would be a mistake to locate 'power' at the centre and 'lack of power' at the periphery. A semiosphere's elements can be both active and receptive at the same time: in one system the centre, in another the periphery. A distributed model of power is therefore appropriate. For instance, the Amazon bookstore is a trendsetting core when it comes to international book sales, but it is at the receiving end when it comes to cultural subsystems such as the form of the printed book or how natural languages work and evolve, how payment technologies such as credit cards operate or again how postage systems establish, define and redefine themselves, although it may seek to develop a new core there, for instance using automated factories and drones. And so on. These and all other subsystems have their own power asymmetries, but also a semi-autonomous evolutionary logic, conditioned by both autocommunicative and dialogic processes. The fact that such communication always uses some sort of language or code puts the semiospheric model in the box seat for understanding the complexities of power dynamics – which Foucault calls 'biopower' – in modern society.

For Luhmann, power could be understood as 'communication coded in a certain way'. For Mandoki, a cultural semiotician (2004: 100), power is an effect of meaning for a specific subject in a specific situation according to a specific code. Krippendorff (1995b) argues that power is dialogically embodied, emergent in 'burdensome languaging' with the Other. Hence, from the cultural semiotic perspective, existing power relations are constantly redefined in the languages and codes of the semiosphere, thereby enabling mutual adaptation and co-evolution: 'actions upon actions'. For Lotman, every system could be incorporated into different autonomous super-systems (Lotman, 1997). It follows that every system participates in multiple language systems and also in a variety of power relations that are to some extent independent of each other. In some of these a system can be active and in others passive, in one context governing and in another being governed by others.

From the perspective of semiosphere theory, digital culture can be viewed as a heterogeneous mesh of texts of different levels, modes and materiality. The evolution of this mesh suggests an immensely complex power dynamic, made of multileveled mechanisms of control and countercontrol between diverse nets of actors and subsystems (Krippendorff, 2008), where the degree of freedom or constraint varies (Mansell and Silverstone, 1996: 6). The term 'dialogic control' has been suggested (Ibrus, 2015b) for understanding and describing such relationships, in order to avoid a too-simplistic use of the centre-periphery metaphor. 'Dialogic control' refers to co-evolution of autocommunicatively operating intertwined systems that are conditioned to absorb new information from other systems as well as to accommodate the changes effected by these other systems – resulting in an evolutionary process conditioned and controlled by multiple agents, all in dialogic contact.

Linking the concept of power to Lotman's notion of dialogue emphasizes a balanced take on power that does not deny its generative role in meaning-making. As Schönle and Shine (2006: 24–8) point out, Lotman's theory provides resolution to a long-standing contradiction in cultural studies, between hegemonic unity and decentred power. They argue that for Lotman, culture is essentially both, 'for it evidences both centrifugal and centripetal forces, which play themselves out on various, coexisting layers'. It is a significant paradox of digital media evolution that media convergence does not result in an apocalyptic one-way flow into semantic implosion, as Baudrillard once suggested (1983), but also generates emergent languages, borders, distinctions and functionalities: new discontinuities within new continuities.

# Evolution

As part of a recent focus on the evolution of novel systems, commentators have concluded that the theory of the semiosphere is really about the *evolutionary dynamics* of culture (see especially Ibrus, 2010). If that is the case, then it is not just culture that needs to be rethought in the light of evolution but evolution that needs to be rethought in the light of culture. We can start with the dichotomy of continuity and discontinuity, which is a crucial intrinsic characteristic of most of the existing evolutionary theories, including Lotman's. Every semiotic system autocommunicatively self-defines its boundaries in space and/or time. But a cultural system also identifies 'the other' and its characteristics – it has to observe, interpret and translate external or environmental features for itself (Kotov, 2002). Or, as Luhmann puts it, boundaries cannot be conceived without something 'beyond' – presupposing the reality of a beyond and a possibility for transcendence (Luhmann, 1995: 28): a problem that has preoccupied philosophers since Rousseau, as Jacques Derrida taught in his discussion of Rousseau's Mediterranean-centric distinction between 'polar' opposites, where South (origin, warmth, passion) and North (death, chill, need) are in a 'supplementary' relation (Derrida, 1967: 216–18). Derrida is critiquing Rousseau's designation of *language* as primary (closer to animality, nature, childhood, nonlanguage) and *writing* as supplementary (distant, less pure, less alive), pointing out that the distinction is itself a product of writing, which makes the boundary a *relation* where 'difference' is produced, not a polar or binary opposition such as that between north and south (prompting the paradoxical question, when you're at the pole, of 'what is South of the South?'). When translation across such a boundary is conducted, then the communicative act has found a place, and through this, new information enters the cultural space. Such an act of communication decreases entropy locally; that is, it produces change within the system. It is *communication between* society's different subsystems or semiotic spaces (different disciplines, industries, professions, firms, countries, etc.) that enables the production of new information and innovation.

But it could also have an opposite effect. In Lotman's terms, if information is translated from one of culture's subsystems to another, then this might have an effect of an 'explosion' (Lotman, 2009), rather than a mere incremental accretion of meanings. The moment of explosion causes an extreme information expansion for the broader system. That explosive expansion, in turn, (re-)establishes some unity within it. This takes us to the paradoxical essence of such 'explosions' – they yield succession and continuity within the broader of the system, while the continuous independent evolution of different subsystems facilitates discontinuity (see Andrews, 2003). We suggest, therefore, that communication within the system and translation-acts across its boundaries facilitate the preservation functions of a culture as well as its drive for change.

This is also where Lotman's theory relates economic approaches to innovation, especially evolutionary economics. Take, for instance, the proposition by Freeman and Louçã (2001: 123–35) that the long-term economic growth of societies and its broader waves of development are brought about by the dynamic that presumes, on the one hand, semi-independent and asynchronic development of subsystems such as culture, technology or economy and, on the other, their occasional 'synchronisation' – ultimate information change among them that disrupts the society, effects innovations, establishes the ground for new technological regimes (Freeman and Perez, 1988) and new stages of growth. Zylko (2001: 405) has pointed out in this context that on the societal macro-level, Lotman's 'explosions' manifest themselves in epoch-making inventions and discoveries that change society's direction of development and prompt transitions from one historic phase to another. The sequence of events does need to be analysed carefully, however. To take the most-studied example, the Industrial Revolution witnessed an irreversible 'explosion' with the invention of steam power, but the 'Revolution' itself occurred over numerous decades in myriad acts of uptake, amendment and application that were undertaken by shed-level anonymous artisans who wanted to solve local, micro problems (how to spin, thresh, pump, move or hammer objects), using the new resource/technology/know-how, developing new meso-institutions (firms, infrastructure) and delivering system-wide transformation across an entire national culture, including its politics and economy, starting in Britain (Mokyr, 2009) and eventually globalizing through imperial colonialism. Immanuel Wallerstein's 'world system analysis' makes powerful use of the core/periphery aspect of systems theory, which is also prominent in Lotman's semiosphere theory, to explain how capitalism and imperial colonialism form a necessary circuit (Wallerstein, 2004).

Broad societal evolution happens via mutual effects of dialogic information exchange and the capacity of existing and new system autocommunicatively to create order and select what parts of the available information they can use in creating that order. This puts also a focus on the concept of 'selection'. It is not used by Lotman; it has a central place in other evolutionary theories. Chris Freeman, the evolutionary economist, has suggested (1992: 122) that despite all the problems with applying the biological metaphor of 'evolution' to societal processes, the principle of 'selection' is still a useful stimulus of thinking. As he puts it, evolutionary selection is at work at all possible 'levels' – that of R&D project or a programme in the R&D system, the individual innovation within the firm or the firm itself, the industrial branch, the nation or a wider social system on a global level – and in the interplay of these and similar 'levels'. This matters because there is no abstract formula for change, even when all the necessary ingredients are in place. This is why the Industrial Revolution took place in Britain but not in Germany or the United States (which might claim to being more advanced technologically and scientifically than the UK). The set of selections that brought artisans, experimentation and industry together were unique to Britain, which also had a flexible 'environment' for change (e.g. laissez-faire government, imperial-scale marketplace and skilled workforce). We can link this to Lotman's theory and propose alike that all semiotic systems, as they autocommunicate, also 'select' – more or less consciously or purposefully – and the aggregate outcome of all these selections is the cultural and societal order of an era.

Yet, when it comes to the term 'evolution' itself, Lotman agreed with Joseph Schumpeter that the use of the biological metaphor in social and cultural analysis may sometimes be misleading. Lotman (1990: 127) argued that while biological evolution involves species dying out (irreversible extinction), this is not what happens in culture. Works or genres that come down to us from remote cultural periods continue to play a part in cultural development as living factors. 'A work of art may "die" and come alive again; once thought to be out of date, it may become modern and even prophetic for what it tells of the future' (Lotman, 1990: 127). He proposed that what 'works' at any point in time is not only the most recent synchronic system of meanings but the whole diachronic history of cultural texts: everything contained in the memory of culture is directly or indirectly part of culture's every contemporary moment, as either resource or text. For Lotman, therefore, behind evolutionary change is not linear development but what Bolter and Grusin (1998) identify as 'remediation' of material from the 'history' or 'periphery' of culture into its current mainstream, where what is remediated, despite being 'old', may appear as an innovative disruption.

Both Lotman and Schumpeter have emphasized the cyclical dynamics that underlie evolution. For Russian Formalists as well as for Lotman, cultural forms as well as ideas move constantly between the cultural centre and periphery according to the pace with which they 'defamiliarise' (Shklovsky's term) themselves and/or acquire new innovative potential. And different languages evolve at their own pace: 'fashion in clothes changes at a speed which cannot be compared with the rate of change of the literary language' (Lotman, 1990: 126).

How, then, to understand the term – 'evolution' – as it will be used throughout this book? We suggest linking Lotman's approach to that of Schumpeter, the parent of evolutionary economics. Evolutionism for him was simply a consideration of organic evolution in real time, or of historical and irreversible processes of change. This is also how evolution should be understood here: referring to dynamic, irreversible change in the digital semiosphere across its systemic entirety, that is inherently interconnected among heterogeneous organic, textual, institutional elements, on the diachronic axis of real time.

# Open/closed systems

Autocommunicative and dialogic processes need to be balanced within semiotic systems in order to ensure both identity preservation and evolution, along a closed/open gradient where a sweet spot will be found that sustains this balance as a 'poised system' (Kauffman, 1991). However, in reality most systems are not so much poised as tilted towards one or the other pole. Consequently it is possible to describe a system as either open and dialogic or closed and oriented towards autocommunication and self-organization. However, a system's status – open, poised, closed – depends on its position in the semiosphere and, relatedly, on its relative powers to autocommunicate. Those systems that constitute the cores of the semiosphere are relatively more inward looking; they work on self-regulation and rule-making. But these activities reduce their readiness to observe and interact with their environment, to translate texts from their extra-semiotic environment. Instead, they close themselves to the uncontrolled influx of such texts, as these may undermine their internal order. For instance, Vladimir Putin's administration in Russia decided to control the distribution of English-language newspapers in the summer of 2019.

In contrast, the relatively unregulated peripheral systems of the semiosphere are by definition open systems. In Lotman's terms, they are at the 'receiving stage' of dialogue. They observe their environment, welcome the inflow of new texts, search for new solutions and react to existing gaps and apparent necessities. This is what Russia and all of the rest of Eastern Europe were like at in the 1990s – relatively powerless, unregulated, but thirsty for new ideas, new meaning systems, new forms of content and of organization. Uniquely, cultural semiotics understands the cyclical shifting between open and closed states of systems. This seems to relate to their relative power in the larger intercultural semiosphere – are they rule-makers or takers; are they in the 'sending stage' or 'receiving stage'?

Lotman (1990: 146–7) described five distinct phases that take a system from a receiving stage to a sending stage of cultural communication. As we discuss later on (Chapters 9 and 15), this turn-taking process and each of its five stages are homologous across at least three different types of cultural interaction: the reception of foreign *texts*, translation across *languages* and *institutional* trade across international borders. In each case there's a to-

and-fro process – not just linear transmission – for receiving, internalizing, indigenizing, remixing and resending semiosis and its organized agents. Lotman explained how systems (1) internalize texts whose initial value is their foreignness, (2) start copying and adapting them by translation, (3) remix them with their own local cultural traditions, canons and cultural systems, (4) arrive in this way to entirely new types of texts that they may then start codifying and (5) 'exporting' out to other systems, thence to become gradually new cores of the broader semiosphere. Hartley (2020: 111–13) summarized the five stages as: (1) *strangeness*, (2) *transformation*, (3) *abstraction*, (4) *productivity* and (5) *transmission*. For example, take the emergence of Nordic Noir as TV genre. For decades, Scandinavian countries were peripheral to the global production of television drama, but they absorbed its influences, mixed these with ideas from the popular and evolving local crime-novel scene, and the outcome was a new form and expertise that became salient and was copied worldwide.

A telling but unintended consequence was the stimulus that Nordic Noir's success provided to regions that had previously been neglected as peripheral, but which suddenly flowered into gloomy, anxious and foreboding life. In the UK, series like *Shetland* and *Vera* foregrounded the Scottish Isles and Northumbria, but perhaps the most remarkable innovation was 'Welsh Noir'. The opening move was the unexpected success of *Y Gwyll* (*Hinterland*) (2013), which was made as a Welsh-language series, seeking to explore a specifically Welsh landscape and mindscape. Its English-language version ran successfully for three seasons on UK-networked TV. This innovation generated a new format: series that were shot in both languages, bringing new quality drama to Welsh-language television and a new TV experience to the Anglosphere. These included *Un Bore Mercher* ('One Wednesday Morning'), renamed as *Keeping Faith* in English (2017), which aired a second season in 2019, and *Craith* (*Hidden*) (2018). *The Guardian*'s critic made much of this show's link to Nordic Noir (including the same BBC timeslot and lead character's hairdo) but concluded: 'The Welsh crime drama ticks a lot of the Scandi-noir boxes, but with its bilingual edge and familiar scenery, it is weirdly wonderful in its own way.'[4]

# Closure

But systems do not always have to start exporting new forms. They may become exhausted from the need constantly to absorb novelties from outside. Then they need time for synthesis and for organizing their internal space. They are motivated towards at least temporary closure. This is

---

[4]Graeme Vertue, 2 July 2018: https://www.theguardian.com/tv-and-radio/2018/jul/02/missing-the-bridge-already-hidden-could-be-the-perfect-replacement.

something that may be observed among many Western and former East European countries in the 2010s, when they elected radical right parties into government: parties that promised the closure of borders, both literal and cultural.

In the digital domain, the question of how to maintain a poised balance between the openness and closure of systems has become an increasingly acute one. It is typically understood that, in the era of market saturation and the attention economy, both the production and consumption of cultural products and services need to be inclusive and participatory, so as to build loyal communities of collaborators and fans and to exploit the resulting 'network effects' and economies of scale. It is for this reason that in the digital development domain, open source production has emerged as a significant phenomenon, and in consumer markets, various kinds of 'freemium' and 'user-created' business models have been experimented with since the emergence of the web, marked by the contrasting fortunes of those who provided content (broadcasters) and those who trade in traffic (YouTube).

On the other side of the coin, however, is the risk that participation is messy and may take systems in a direction that their cores do not see as fit. Think here of why, after having been purchased by Disney and preparing for the new *Star Wars* sequel trilogy, Lucasfilm disregarded their fan-created but previously semi-official 'Expanded Universe' (including most *Star Wars books*, comic books, video games, spin-off films, television series, etc.) as 'Star Wars Legends' – officially disconnected from the canon of the storyworld. Similar concern has been voiced by media professionals even in the smallest of projects, seeking to control strictly and to 'protect' transmedia storyworlds from too active fans (see Ibrus, 2012). Of the perceived advantages of closed systems, one could think also of the Apple iOS platform for mobile devices. In contrast to the competing Android operating system, Apple does not allow any third parties to have a controlling role over it. This approach has been generally touted as successful – consumers appreciate the sleek but also predictable design. Jonathan Zittrain (2008), however, criticizes such one-sided control over digital platforms for curbing creativity. From the perspective of cultural semiotics, this is to say that closed systems are not dialogic and therefore not apt to facilitate innovation. The paradox that becomes apparent in case of Apple's iOS, however, is that large and powerful digital systems still attract innovations owing to the (economic) power they muster. It's just that the power of innovation is appropriated by for-the-time-being dominant corporations, narrowing the range of consumer participation and choice as well as competing entrepreneurial systems (start-up firms), whose business plan may not be to trade directly in the market but to be bought out by one of the tech giants, reducing innovation to a tech service industry.

# 6

# Cultural semiotics in a multidisciplinary environment

*We argue for the value of* recovering an understanding of class as culture, *rather than as simply socio-economic categories or abstracted relations of production.*

(TONY MOORE, MARK GIBSON AND CATHARINE LUMBY, 2017: 218)

\* \* \*

Cultural semiotics is itself positioned and shifting in dialogic relation to other scholarly approaches. These include numerous more or less distinct disciplinary or interdisciplinary fields, such as cultural studies, general semiotics, media archaeology, media ecology, mediatization theory, cybernetics, evolutionary economics, cultural science and other approaches to innovation studies. The interdisciplinary range is necessarily wide because specialist techniques developed in very different scientific fields may yield insights not yet discovered or realized in others. Let us in the following discuss briefly the ways the semiosphere theory has been in dialogue with, has learned from and could contribute to the advancement of some these theoretical domains mentioned.

## Cultural studies

Cultural studies in its current form dates from the 1960s and 1970s (Hartley, 2002). Semiotics played a central role in that formation, not only because the study of signs extended literary and social studies of culture into new media and forms but also because semiotics promised a systematic method and conceptual apparatus to bind an open interdisciplinary field into some sort of disciplinary order. Socially, cultural studies was prompted by the post-war attempt to broaden the social base of higher education that brought women, people of colour and previously under-represented classes and minorities into the university system. Youth culture provided a creative crucible for new consciousness and a growing market for new ideas, as the baby-boomers sought new ways to express identity and subjectivity through culture (music, fashion, dance, media, festivals – and ideas), not least as an alternative to the post-war/Cold War politics of the Vietnam era in the United States and decolonization in Europe.

Cultural studies emerged as an amalgam of these forces. On one side was a commitment to 'opening' knowledge systems and a willingness to rethink how meaning is created and communicated, using insights from pop culture, protest politics, experimental and drug cultures and the democratization of everyday life. On the other side were the 'closed' disciplines of the nineteenth-century 'imperial archive' of formal knowledge, resistant to change and bristling with disciplinary border patrols, such that the admission of new ideas and methods felt like a break to the whole system. Because of its systematic purpose as the 'science that studies the life of signs within society' (Saussure, 1974), semiotics proved to be a handy crowbar (an Archimedes lever) to prise open the methodological toolbox of different disciplinary discourses, including philosophy (Jacques Derrida, Michel Foucault), ethnography/anthropology (Claude Lévi-Strauss), literature (Roland Barthes, Umberto Eco), linguistics, psychoanalysis (Anthony Wilden) and as-yet unsystematized new fields like cinema studies (especially in the journals *Screen* and *Screen Education*) and media studies.

But, at the same time, the formalist tendencies in Saussurian linguistics quickly dominated Euro-American semiotics (Chandler, 2017), despite the competing claims of Russian Formalism (Shklovsky, Tynianov, Bakhtin), pragmatist semiotic theories (Peirce, Sebeok) and a strongly social or dialogic version of semiotics derived from Vološinov (1973), Jakobson and others including Lotman and the Tartu-Moscow School.

This marked an important parting of the ways between text-based and social-based approaches, part of a larger 'division of labour', as it were, between critical humanities and behavioural social sciences. Formalist semiotics and cultural studies thrived in the text-based humanities, while linguistics migrated towards the behavioural and evolutionary sciences. Semiotics was modelled on 'reductive' or objective science, seeking the elementary particle (Saussure's 'smallest signifying unit') and building a model of the system (langue) from that. Even so, its most prominent proponents, like Roland Barthes and Umberto Eco, used it for *critical* rather than *cumulative* purposes, its 'scientific' ambitions proving to be of rhetorical rather than methodological value. Philosopher Jacques Derrida used Saussure to 'deconstruct' modernist rationality and its discursive representation. For its part, cultural studies used semiotics to underpin what was from the start a highly politicized intellectual enterprise, concerned with identity, power and radical opposition to existing power/knowledge arrangements. Its scientific and systematic claims were not used to build a new discipline but were sampled and remixed as one strand of thought among many others that preoccupied cultural studies at the time – ranging from 'high theory' (deconstruction, poststructuralism, postmodernism) to ideological critique, media analysis to identity politics.

Saussurian semiotics was highly abstract, its object of study being language-in-general (langue), rather than this language (say, French) in the here and now (parole). Its methodology was focused on elements and relations within a system of difference, seeming to presume equally abstract individual enunciation (a single speaker or author producing a linear stream of signs). As a result, once cultural studies had moved from texts, discourses and their ideologies to practices, audiences and their uses, formal semiotics began to lose its appeal. Institutionally, cultural studies became established as a scholarly lingua franca across the humanities and social sciences, not a distinct discipline in its own right (Chandler, 2016), so developing one method (to the exclusion of others) in order to establish a distinct institutional-disciplinary identity was not seen as appropriate. Searching for the philosophical foundations of meaning ('language speaks us'), or the scientific process of causation in cultural systems, was no longer a priority, compared with the struggle to reform the existing disciplinary array ('knowledge speaks us'), to participate in cultural politics 'out there' ('patriarchy speaks us *no longer*') and to synthesize the two in an attempt to align 'power/knowledge' with 'culture/identity' through 'discourse' (Hall, 2001), where oppression is understood as a 'cooperative achievement' through the workings of hegemony (Hall, 2006).

Meanwhile, alternative approaches to semiosis remained unexamined or were consigned to the 'been-there-done-that' pile, as leftover structuralism, needing no further critical exploration, since a comprehensive discipline of semiotics was not the goal. Juri Lotman's work was caught up by these intellectual trends and splits, at least in the Anglosphere. Lotman's own work was slow to be translated into English: His literature-centric *Structure of the Artistic Text* was published in the 1970s, but it was not until 1990 – after cultural studies had been widely institutionalized in the Anglosphere – that *Universe of the Mind* appeared, introducing the concept of the semiosphere. This book had an important but unsystematic influence in cultural and film studies. For example, Tom O'Regan uses Lotman's notion of 'cultural transfers' (which we would gloss as translation across semiospheres) to make sense of Australian national cinema (1996: 195–207). Beyond that, Lotman's direct influence was piecemeal, more likely to be felt in European (Southern, Eastern and Northern) than American cultural studies. More recently, as cultural studies has taken the global and digital turn, it has 'discovered' big data, algorithms, platform capitalism and complex systems. The relationships between culture and cybernetics, culture and the biosphere are back into focus. Consequently, Lotman began to be 'rediscovered', via biosemiotics and data analytics – which had of course continued all the while in the Tartu-Moscow semiotic school work and journal. This book is an attempt to recentre Lotman from the anomalous periphery of cultural studies to its rule-making core. Whether 'cultural studies' will survive that change is an open question; 'cultural science' may be an alternative, but see also the series 'What Is Cultural Studies?' in the *International Journal of Cultural Studies* (2020), with contributions by Johan Fornäs, Ien Ang, Nick Couldry and Benjamin Woo.

# Media archaeology

A unique affordance of semiosphere theory is its ability to highlight how the past settings of culture and existing constellations of cultural memory shape contemporary cultural dynamics. Media archaeology is similarly focused on how the past conditions the future, making it a natural dialogue partner for cultural semiotics. Yet, the archaeological focus remains firmly on the material record and technologies of media and not on the 'semiotic layer'. There are significant differences between the two approaches, but these could also be seen as a useful complementarity. One attempts to understand the role of machines (technology) in the evolution of digitized culture, while the other uses a systemic/holistic take, focusing on how various communication, translation and mediation processes (including those facilitated by digital apparatuses) facilitate the emergence of novelties and shape the evolution of culture. Two of us (Ibrus and Ojamaa, 2020) have previously pursued a dialogue between these approaches in order to discuss their methodological complementarity.

Media archaeology has been based on Foucault's criticism of 'old' historicism. With his *Archaeology of Knowledge* (2002b: [1969]), instead of looking for objectivist genealogies in historical narratives, Foucault focuses on the dichotomy of continuity/discontinuity, identifying discursive dispersion within existing diachronic continuities. Foucault suggests that archaeology is in fact a rationale for a methodology: it offers a catalogue of analytical-strategic questions by which to study 'documents' and invoke historically situated discourses (Foucault, 2002b: 7; Andersen, 2003: 8). Following on from this, Erkki Huhtamo (1995) proposes that 'media archaeology' has two main objectives: first, the study of *cyclically recurring* elements and motives underlying and guiding the development of media culture; second, the search for ways that these discursive formations *have been 'imprinted'* in specific media machines and systems in different historical contexts.

Huhtamo (1994) argues that cyclical phenomena are not random or an accident of specific circumstances. Instead, he claims, they 'contain' certain common elements or cultural motives that have been encountered in earlier cultural processes. He proposes that such motives could be treated as *topoi*, using a term from classical rhetoric. *Topoi* can be considered as formulae that make up the 'building blocks' of cultural traditions, providing a 'pre-fabricated' mould for experience. This offers a dialogic link between media archaeology and cultural semiotics: the *recurrence* of cultural formations refers to the logic of *defamiliarisation*, which Lotman borrowed from Russian Formalist Viktor Shklovsky (Hawkes, 1977: 62–7), where a form borrowed from the history of culture (as another periphery) may sometimes generate novel meaning-potential in a new context – it may be *re-familiarised* as new and intriguing. Recurring fashion trends are a prime example here. Typically, the novelty and meaning-potential of the recurrent form is exhausted over time, when it is likely to fall back to the inactive reservoir of cultural memory. Hence, the dynamics of the recurrence of cultural forms across the span of time is a research area that could benefit from a dialogue between semiosphere theory and media archaeology.

The second research direction within media archaeology, the study how dominant discursive formations of any era are *imprinted* in the media machines of that era, has broadly been built on the works of Friedrich Kittler (1990, 1999, 2009). Kittler set out to look for inscriptions that tell us how the materiality, the technology 'underneath', uniquely limits a medium, predisposing a move towards certain cultural forms and certain discourses at the expense of others (Bender and Wellbery, 1990: xii). This focus on the unique contingencies that change historically according to the material and technical resources at their disposal led Kittler to a form of radical historicism that questions the universality of concepts such as 'media'. Yet, it needs to be noted that despite its original contribution to media history, media archaeology is not a theory of evolution, although it does suggest that media dynamics may have led to the formation of 'discourse networks' (Kittler, 1990: 369) in certain eras. In its modern form, media archaeology is largely a rationale for an unconfined set of methods that can be gathered under the general title of 'materialist discourse analysis'. It was not its ambition to make claims about the evolutionary dynamics of media and society. Instead, in line with a general Foucauldian agenda (Atterton, 1994), Kittler opposes any connection with social evolution theory and has expressed strong criticism of Niklas Luhmann for instance (see Winthrop-Young, 2000: 411).

We argue that their differences are methodological. Media archaeology investigates structural materiality, based on media technologies and the discourses and texts these technologies have conditioned in a given period, and it examines the differences between different periods on a diachronic axis. It is especially interested in the process of technical mediation – to think through algorithmic calculation (Parikka, 2013: 9). The strength of cultural semiotics at the same time lies in the analysis of the contingent dynamics on a synchronic axis and of dialogic communication between (and autocommunication within) different domains and systems, including memory systems (i.e. texts from preceding times that may be actualized anew), showing how the accumulation of knowledge and the emergence of new relationships, identities and systems across different periods affect the examination of dependencies on the diachronic axis (Ibrus and Ojamaa, 2020). Therefore, the media archaeological gaze is focused on the materiality of digital media, their technologies and how cultural forms are calculated from that. Cultural semiotics looks at systemic processes before and after that technical calculation – how the technological forms that mediate come about, resulting from the mesh of communications among a culture's different subsystems; and how mediated texts are re-used, re-interpreted and shaped.

The complementarity of these approaches for enriching the contemporary cultural analysis is apparent. Furthermore, this potential is even more timely given the aim of the present book – to investigate the interactions between the semiosphere and the planet, its biosphere and its material forms. Media archaeology itself has moved in this direction, especially through the work of Jussi Parikka (2014, 2015). After all, the core rationale of cultural semiotics is that any cultural language, including analytic meta-language, is necessary as long as it reveals new facets of cultural realities. Especially desirable, however, is the occasional dialogue between such languages, as these create opportunities for the emergence of convergent or 'creolised' a language that again opens up novel viewpoints.

# Mediatization

While media archaeology is just a research vehicle for studying media change as an historical process, 'mediatization' makes rather grander claims about broader societal change in the contemporary era. The idea here is that media are part of that change: constituting, conditioning and shaping it. Media are seen to have become part of all relationships, mediating and constructing our 'social worlds' (Krotz and Hepp, 2013; Hepp and Krotz, 2014). As such, mediatization is one of the ongoing meta-processes (Krotz, 2007): a part of broader modernization and equal to processes like urbanization, individualization, globalization, commercialization and so on. This notion relates to our claim about the evolution of the global semiosphere through the development of media technologies that connect the population of the entire planet and thereby intervene in everyone's meaning-making practices. This is why we need to address the relationships between these two approaches.

It needs to be recognized, first, that mediatization theory is in the broadest sense a sociological one. It is interested in social change, in the development of new social institutions and in the mediation and construction of 'social worlds'. It builds on several traditions of sociological thought, notably those of Norbert Elias, Pierre Bourdieu, Berger and Luckmann and others, and its main proponents are media sociologists such as Andreas Hepp, Nick Couldry, Knut Lundby, Stig Hjarvard and others. It seeks to explain how mediation and communication are done by various institutions or other kinds of social formations and how these emerge and evolve (Hjarvard, 2013: 4; Hepp and Hasebrink, 2018: 30). Its purpose is to explain and illuminate the *meso*-level of social and cultural change. In comparison, cultural semiotics is derived from the humanities. It focuses on interpreting textual expression at different scales of culture – from single texts (*micro*-scale) to the entirety of planetary culture and its communication flows (*macro*-scale) – and is explicitly interested in moving between and linking these levels.

Perhaps the central difference between the two approaches, however, is the extent to which they are interested in *generativity*. This is what cultural semiotics is all about – how novel meanings and ideas emerge from interactions among the semiosphere's subsystems. In contrast mediatization theory seems to have settled for a zero-sum game, since most accounts discuss the extent to which other fields are mediatized or not. Realizing this, Ibrus (2019) has integrated mediatization theory, especially that of Winfried Schulz (2004), with the innovation systems approaches of Potts et al. (2008) and Lundvall (2010), together with ideas and concepts derived from Lotmanian cultural semiotics.

There are, nevertheless, several places where cultural semiotics and mediatization theory are complementary and where their further dialogues could indeed produce new insights. What would ease the dialogue is for mediatization scholarship to admit (as they do) that the concept is really only a 'sensitising' one (Jensen, 2013). That is, it is supposed to give the user a general sense of reference in approaching empirical instances of 'mediatization' and to suggest directions to follow. As such it provides a general tool for denoting the phenomena under review but is not really supposed to limit the analysis. When it comes to more concrete areas of complementarity and dialogue, still with a focus on generativity, then Roger Silverstone's 'mediation theory' (1999) – a predecessor to mediatization theory – puts a firm emphasis on how meanings change as they are mediated by different media, by genres and modalities, between different usage and interpretation contexts and so on. To understand further how translation and mediation processes interact, and how sociological and humanities approaches are not alternatives but dialogic partners in the production of new insights, dialogue between these approaches are in place and are also addressed in this book.

A concept within mediatization research that relates more directly to semiosphere theory is that of 'communicative figurations' (see Hepp and Hasebrink, 2014, 2018). This concept was originally built on the 'figurations' concept of Norbert Elias (1978: 30), which he developed to address how structural transformations happen in societies. For Elias, figurations were dynamically shifting networks of individuals and other actors – organizations, institutions and so on. Mediatization researchers added to this the realization that such figurations are increasingly facilitated not only by communicative *practices* but by various modally and technologically heterogeneous constellations of *media*. Some figurations may be entirely constituted by specific media and their affordances – such as mobile phones and WhatsApp groups. Some may use variety of media, for instance *Star Wars* fandom communities, which operate transmedially (Jenkins, 2019).

The idea of mediated, mediatized and self-aware cultural communities is not distant from how the semiosphere theory understands the way that culture's subsystems emerge, endure and change. That is, they autocommunicate by exchanging texts – in other words, mediated communications. Depending on the autocommunicative activity, these communities may be strictly or more loosely defined; emergent or fading. The contrasting theories are also similar in understanding that figurations/subsystems may be larger or smaller, but the whole of society consists of an indefinitely intertwined mesh of such systems. Mediatization researchers have undertaken empirical research into how such figurations emerge; how they come together, enable or disable participation, limit or open up communicative freedoms; and how the affordances of different media affect the figurations. These findings are also valuable explanatory evidence for cultural semiotic investigations into the dynamics of contemporary digital culture. In exchange, as we demonstrate in Part III, the tools of the cultural semiotic approach provide detailed analysis of the textual matter used for mediated communications, which is necessary not only to interpret the functioning of specific figurations/subsystems but also to understand the broadest phenomena in the planetary semiosphere.

Mediatization theory also discusses globalization and differentiation in ways that are congruent with our work in this book: for example to account for the emergence of new specialized services or technologies, or of media forms for small groups of users only. Indeed, it is notable how Stig Hjarvard (2013) uses nearly the same vocabulary and conceptual categories that we use in Parts IV and V. These were originally developed by Bakhtin and Lotman: homogenization versus differentiation, centripetal forces versus centrifugal forces. Yet there are important differences in how these terms are used in each approach. For Hjarvard, 'centrifugal force' means that national media spaces are opened up and connected to the global sphere of media flows. 'Centripetal force' refers to processes where media spaces become more 'introverted', mediating the immediate environments, as in case of local newspapers or community radio. According to Hjarvard's account, these forces are parallel but do not seem to interact. But from the perspective of cultural semiotics and semiosphere theory, these forces *condition each other*: too-narrow or limited representations condition the need for the broadening of perspectives, while too-general representations in turn condition the need for texts and modes of representation to provide meanings that are detailed enough. According to Lotman, there are phases when one dominates, but because of this dominance, the need for the other emerges. As we discuss in Chapter 15 (Globe), it could have been because of the exhaustion of internet-driven globalization and platformization that the newest phase of global digital media evolution evidences regionally or nationally driven resistance to the homogeneity of the global internet. Yet, we also show how the locally autocommunicating cultural spaces may create differentiation and uniqueness, which may attract global interest and hence also new global flows of culture: as for instance in case of the Korean K-pop wave. That is, we propose that semiosphere theory and its tools may offer necessary insights to mediatization theory.

# Posthumanism

A question that could be asked is whether Lotman's cultural semiotics and the semiosphere concept are, in effect, 'posthumanist'. This question has gone broadly unaddressed in the specialist literature until now. The core group of posthumanist thinkers have certainly not used Lotman's work; nor have contemporary cultural semioticians explicated their relationship with posthumanist thought. Nevertheless, we see this not as 'incommensurability' (except in the sense of Lotmanian difference) but rather as an opportunity for new insights. We propose instead that similarities and interrelations between the two domains not only exist but also evolve and grow. We argue that the semiosphere concept is in essence posthuman and the theory of posthumanism would gain from incorporating the cultural semiotic toolset.

Posthumanism as an approach is inherently highly heterogeneous. But most of its substreams build on various combinations of critique of the traditional Western humanist ideal of 'Man' – humanity – as the universal measure and end purpose for nature. Posthumanism rejects the idea of the ability of humans to control the formation of autonomous subjectivity, as well as species hierarchies and human exceptionalism (Braidotti, 2018). Posthumanists argue that, in terms of biology and cognitive processes, the distinction of humans from other organisms is overstated, and the lines between human and nonhuman are difficult to draw definitely. As Cary Wolfe (2018: 358) has put it, 'human' is the product of processes that are inhuman and ahuman. What is human is understood to co-evolve with other organisms, and with broader semiotic and technological systems.

The co-evolutionary process and the idea of humans being only semi-autonomous parts of larger systems are core principles linking the semiosphere concept to posthuman thinking. As we have argued, Lotman's theory is about co-evolutionary change wherein no individual system, including those of some specific human systems of meaning, cannot dominate, because meaning and change in general assume at minimum two interacting systems. Grosz (2011) argued that Darwin's original evolutionary theory was one of the first to deflate humanist pretensions and was a precursor of the crisis of human exceptionalism. We would understand that insight to be extended by all other evolutionary theories, including Lotman's.

To address the co-evolution of cultural semiotics and posthuman thought, we need to start with their shared roots. There are many. The first of these is the work of Jakob von Uexküll (1909 and, in English, 1957) and more specifically his concept of *umwelt* – the world created by an organism's cognitive affordances (senses) and interpretative abilities: not 'the environment' as it is, but only as a given creature perceives, interacts with and is shaped by it. Owing to these differences in affordances and abilities, the umwelt of different organisms can be very different despite the fact that they may share the same environment. Thus, some mammals see red but others don't; many creatures have evolved eyes but few can navigate the planet as migratory birds and insects do; humans can taste, smell and touch, but octopuses can do all that with their tentacles (and so on!). Such species difference can be extended to individual difference ('I' see this pond differently from the way that 'you' do), but also it can be communicated among individuals via their interactions ('we' see the pond this way). Translations between umwelts emerge and may become shared, and in this way, a semiosphere can emerge and evolve. This logic is very similar to the way that Gilles Deleuze and Felix Guattari (1987) interpret Uexküll's ethology and their proposals about life and subjectivation in *A Thousand Plateaus*. According to their approach, human and in-human agencies participate in a common ecology made of rhythmical and melodic cycles of perception-action. This work has become one of the main bases for contemporary posthuman critical theory.

Uexküll (who grew up and studied in Estonia) is also one of the foundational sources for contemporary Tartu semiotics (Kull, 1998b, 1999: Kull and M. Lotman, 2012). This work, integration of cultural semiotics with the works of Uexküll, has been ongoing since the 1970s and has by now evolved into a distinctive approach called biosemiotics, where theories and concepts deriving from Uexküll (umwelt), Vernadsky (biosphere) and Lotman (semiosphere) have been well integrated. This has been relatively easy as these different inputs have been harmonious (Andrews, 2003; Kull and M. Lotman, 2012, and as we explain throughout this book). Not only do the biosphere and umwelt concepts share many features, but the semiosphere as an inclusive concept is modelled on both of them. Further, for both Uexküll and Lotman, autocommunication is where communication starts (Torop, 2008; Kull and Lotman, 2012). For Lotman, autocommunication, the ability of a system to communicate about itself in an environment, underlies the ability to translate what is external into the own system/code. For Uexküll, similarly, modelling of all meaning and the structure of the umwelt is created through translation.

An important precondition for posthuman thinking to emerge has been the evolution of cybernetics. As recalled by Wolfe (2010: xii), the genealogy of posthumanism starts (among other sources) with the Macy conferences on cybernetics from 1946 to 1953 (Pias, 2016) and with the invention of systems theory via Gregory Bateson, Norbert Wiener, John von Neumann and others. It was this work that produced a new theoretical model for biological, mechanical and communicational processes, which removed the human from any privileged position in relation to matters of meaning, information and cognition. It is also widely known that Ludwig von Bertalanfy was strongly influenced by the work of Uexküll when he developed his 'general systems theory'. At the same time the works of Norbert Wiener and Ross Ashby were crucial for Lotman to articulate his theory and, to an extent, to detach it from linguistics and thence to generalize and apply it to all communications and forms of information and meaning-processing. Most evident of this was his development of the 'modelling systems' concept. His development of the semiosphere concept was also inspired by Ilya Prigogine's work on dissipative structures, self-organization and irreversibility.

The outcome of Lotman's dialogue with cybernetics and with theoretical biology was his eventual focus on the heterogeneity of modelling process by all systems – especially their ways of self-modelling/autocommunication. We suggest that, in addition to the synergies with umwelt-theory, it is this focus on self-organization of semiotic systems, their dialogues/translations and the resultant production of complexity in adaptive but rule-based systems that make semiosphere theory by definition posthumanist. Posthumanist thought, as Wolfe (2018: 359) puts it, is both *index* and *agent* of such complexity-making.

With the focus on autocommunication and self-organization ('autopoiesis' or self-creation), the production of 'meaning' becomes untethered from its moorings in the individual (Cartesian) consciousness and becomes a process of translation among autocommunicating systems within the semiosphere/biosphere/technosphere. As Lotman put it, the smallest unit of analysis needs to be the semiosphere itself. The semiosphere *precedes* any act or process of semiosis. This relates to Wolfe's view that posthumanism comes before humanism. He writes:

[posthumanism] names the embodiment and embeddedness of the human being in not just its biological but also its technological world, the prosthetic coevolution of the human animal with the technicity of tools and external archival mechanisms (such as language and culture) [...] all of which comes before that historically specific thing called 'the human'.

(Wolfe, 2010: xv)

In the rest of this book we aim to address the conditioning of the human by the co-evolutionary processes among the biosphere, semiosphere and technosphere, such that the 'umwelt' of cultural humanities can never be the same again! That is why we are proponents of a new interdisciplinary enterprise we call 'cultural science' (Hartley and Potts, 2014; Ibrus, 2019; Hartley, 2020), which is intended to synthesize humanities and science approaches in a new, posthuman and perhaps also postdisciplinary constellation of analysis suited to the era of 'big data', global textualization and the digital semiosphere.

# PART THREE

# Micro-scale: Text

*Peeter Laurits, 'Romeo and Juliet' (2003) from* Dining with Worms *(with Ain Mäeots)*
https://www.peeterlaurits.com/archive/dining-with-worms

# 7

# What does culture want?

*It's a set of laws! And it's global! It extends all over the Earth,
there's no escaping it, we're all in it, and no matter what you do,
the system rules!...* The laws are codes! *And they exist in computers
and in the cloud. There are sixteen laws running the whole world!*

(KIM STANLEY ROBINSON, *NEW YORK 2140*. LONDON,
ORBIT, 2017: 5)

\* \* \*

While reflecting upon the *raison d'être* of human culture, Juri Lotman and
Boris Uspenskij came to the very same conclusion as did another great
cultural semiotician, Umberto Eco. Eco's internal dialogue went:

> What does culture want? To make infinity comprehensible. It also wants
> to create order – not always, but often.
>
> (Eco in an interview to Beyer and Gorris, 2009)

Lotman and Uspenskij argued that the fundamental 'task' of culture is in:

> structurally organizing the world around humanity. Culture is the
> generator of structuredness, and in this way it creates a social sphere
> around humanity which, like the biosphere, makes life possible; that is,
> not organic life, but social life.
>
> (Lotman and Uspenskij, 1978: 213)

This is the 'social sphere' that Lotman later dubbed the semiosphere. That
concept is in principle an elaboration of his dynamic understanding of *the
text* (see Salupere, 2015; Torop, 2017). Text is treated as the 'micro' unit of
the semiosphere, although it is not an 'element' in a complex structure but

is itself semiospheric in a scale-free systems of systems. It is characterized by internal heterogeneity and a simultaneous capability to serve the functions of transmission, creation and memorization of information, as we elaborate in the ensuing chapters. Understanding the text as a structure is therefore balanced by understanding the text as a process, the ontology of which is conditioned by its dialogue with the extra-textual.

In the present global context, the connection and overlap between understanding the mechanisms of organic life and of social life can be further elaborated (see Part IV of this book). In dialogue with Thomas Sebeok's (2001) proposal that the definition of life may coincide with the definition of semiosis, Kalevi Kull has developed the notion that organisms function as self-reading texts (Kull, 1998a) and argued that Lotmanian 'semiotic terminology of text and dialogue, recognition and translation may be … suited for the description of isomorphisms between biological and cultural phenomena' (Kull, 1998b: 302). It is for this reason – the universality of the 'text' as a concept – that we focus on its natures and function in a variety of contexts.

# Pulverization

In this part of the book we attempt the application of the Lotmanian notion of the text to global digital culture. What appears to complicate the analysis of *digitally mediated* culture most is the pulverization of textual creation and fragmentation of reception practices. Simply copying and pasting information from one context to another is now possible on scale unimaginable in the 'papyrocentric' paradigm, instilling a sense of constant movement and instability into the textual environment. In addition, analytic challenges are posed by the very poetics of digital communication (see Frosh, 2018), characterized by Eu Jin Chua on the example of YouTube videos by 'pensive reverie, hypermnesic longing, interiorism, embeddedness, fragmentation, reparative patchworking, in-built obsolescence, and frayed imperfection' (Chua, 2011).

The classical notion of text that communicated structural unity and homogeneity is obviously unsuitable for making sense of the situation. At the same time, this pulverization is not totally random and regarding it like this would only take us to schizophrenia and the collapse of identities – a 'condition' that some hostile modernist critics did indeed ascribe to postmodernity (Harvey, 1991). We need terminological apparatus that allows for balancing statics and dynamics, homo- and heterogeneity, fragments and holistic dimension and so on. A Lotmanian isomorphic treatment of the text and the semiosphere offers just that. As the text need not be a physically bounded object but is an analytic unit, a textualized object of analysis, it facilitates making sense of the situation that dominates all sorts of digital databases.

Traditional single texts are as if slipping from our hands as they are simultaneously positioned in a myriad of configurations and series, which, however, can in this framework be conceptualized as higher-level texts themselves. Such conceptualization is supported by the realization that uni-functional and secluded textual units cannot exist in reality anyway and the minimal semiotic monad capable of textual generation consists in an interrelation of *at least two* previously existing texts immersed in a contextual space, that is, a semiosphere. Arguably, this fundamental analytic triad, of two self-contained and mutually untranslatable systems and a semiotic meta-system, facilitates addressing open and collaborative database practices, while still retaining a graspable human scale to the processes.

# Technological and semiotic agency

Another binary that needs to be addressed in a complex manner is the one between *technological* and *semiotic* agencies within the cultural changes currently underway. It is clear that the way digital technology mediates culture, for example in the form of algorithmic curation of content on platforms such as YouTube, Netflix or Spotify, has its effect on the ways that users perceive and make sense of the content as well as of the wider semiosphere in which the subsystems of traditional music, film and other criticism are fading. It is equally evident that within the digital environment several traditional cultural categories are completely reorganized owing to technological affordances. A central example is the eclipse of the boundaries between words, images and other modalities as they have been translated into bits and bytes and organized in networks, resulting in the rise of multimodal textualities and a general diversification of creative, distributive, curatorial and receptive practices. From the viewpoint of digital technology, there is no difference between live action footage obtained through photographic lens, synthetic 3D graphics and manually created imagery – all of them exist as easily reconfigurable pixels. Besides the blurring of the indexical and non-indexical in visual texts as in case of computer-generated or -enhanced imagery, a similar process is mixing fictional and nonfictional environments of entertainment as the story-worlds created by global conglomerates expand into street-life and everyday life in more immersive modes of engagement, as never before in the entertainment industries.

At the same time, any semiotic system is characterized by autocommunication. Therefore, attempts to overcome the chaos that surrounds human cultures remain a human cultural constant, regardless of the formats and technologies of communication, by generating meta-languages for self-descriptions and stabilization of identities that also facilitate anticipation and learning. This stabilization can take place by mnemonic logic – repetition of what is already memorized in another sign-system – and by creative logic – establishing new networks between the contents of memory. Creative logic can be initiated by introducing a new text into the system that will not just be an addition to what is previously there but reconfigure what already exists. Such dynamics, taken together, result in a paradoxical recognition that:

> the internal space of a semiosphere is at the same time unequal yet unified, asymmetrical yet uniform. Composed as it is of conflicting structures, it none the less is also marked by individuation.
>
> (Lotman, 1990: 131)

A vivid example of this semiospheric principle on the level of text is *transmedial stories*. These comprise a number of subparts expressed in different media, which make up a whole that is not explainable as the sum of its individual parts but only by interpreting dialogues and inter-semiotic translations, in a situation of untranslatability. Isomorphically, the semiosphere is also built as a multilayered synchronic space consisting of mutually untranslatable languages and meta-languages, texts and fragments of texts in these languages.

# Asymmetry makes sense

The asymmetry of the semiosphere is first conditioned by mutually untranslatable languages, ranging from rigid artificial sign-systems to poetic/artistic languages, which feature fundamentally distinct affordances and constraints for transmitting information as well as for describing and modelling the world we live in. Furthermore, languages also develop at different speeds, and at any given instance, some might be undergoing explosive changes while others are characterized by gradual processes of succession. Yet, via the processes of translation between languages, significant changes in one language system condition changes also in others – facilitating the development of distinct cultural epochs. At the same time, texts in the semiosphere are not only expressed in these languages but also generate languages. Texts do not function as static structures but exist via reading, as partners of dialogic processes. The codes harnessed in these dialogues are subject to changes and often radically so in cultural diachrony. The codes of the Gutenberg print era are obsolete in the age of social media (despite our residual attachment to the nomenclature of 'papers', 'journals' and 'books' that only exist in e-forms). Yet, new media and new texts do not simply and completely substitute the old ones but alter the interpretive strategies and practices – as is exemplified by a popular wave of Instapoetry.

Texts from previous epochs should in principle become incomprehensible (as extinct species are irrecoverable) but in fact are only reconstructed in accordance to new codes (in culture, the 'evolutionary past' remains productive), which determine systemic and nonsystemic elements of the text. That is, they shift meaningful (core) and meaningless (peripheral) layers, whereby elements and meanings once located around the peripheral areas inevitably become the dominants and vice versa. Texts exist in culture through selected fragments, which generate recollections of the whole. This is simultaneously a mechanism of continuity and of innovation, facilitating the semiotic system to develop while still retaining its identity (Lotman, 2009: 1).

# Culture as artificial intelligence

From this it follows that semiotic systems are characterized by the capability of learning while being simultaneously aware of the (paradoxically growing) incompleteness of one's knowledge. The incompleteness of the individual viewpoint is compensated by the stereoscopic nature of the collective. This is the ground on which Lotman built the argument of culture as collective intellect or a 'thinking *ustrojstvo* or intellectual apparatus/artificial intelligence' (on this notion see Salupere, 2015). The latter can operate only under the condition of being immersed in the semiosphere. Therefore, creativity cannot be located in an individual mind let alone in intellectual property but can analogously function only within dialogic culture, which is in turn immersed in the semiosphere and is dependent on the mechanism of (collective cultural) memory. The balance between algorithmic progression based on simple transfers of information and unpredictable selective recursivity (i.e. creation and preservation) results from inter-semiotic translation.

# Text in the digital semiosphere

The 'textual practice' of making sense of the surrounding world includes increasing numbers of participants: now everybody can produce such texts, and the unbounded freedom of interpreting texts has become a given. In parallel, media and their modalities (especially the fact-fiction boundary) are becoming increasingly varied, and content is more fragmented and unstable. All of these shifts have something to do with digital technology and the internet. These have rendered creating, sharing, commenting, rating and other ways of reacting to written posts, photos, videos, their mashups and remixes (text) so ubiquitous, for so many, that scholars have called for conceptualizing new types of literacies, including digital literacy (Gilster, 1997; Bawden, 2008; Hartley, 2009) and transmedia literacy (Scolari et al.,

2018). The need for these (re)conceptualizations stems from a divide that appears to have opened up between the technical skills of production and the competencies in critical reading of content. One of the key authors in the sphere of media literacy, Sonia Livingstone, has insisted on formulating the emergent creative and receptive practices 'in textual terms' (2004: 9).

'The text' might seem a counterintuitive concept for discussing contemporary online communication. Lev Manovich (2017b), for example, has announced an end to the time of the text in the face of massive archives and big data, shifting our attention from single textual artefacts to infinite series of textual material. Such a statement, however, proceeds from a notion of the text that differs from the one we implement below. It is not uncommon that commentators establish equivalency between the concept of the text and an account of structuralism characterized by tracing self-contained cultural phenomena. As we explain in this part (Part II) of the book, the core of the cultural semiotic concept of the text lies elsewhere – on the positions and dynamic functions of texts within broader cultural entireties. Besides this, Manovich's claim is only partially convincing, because we are already witnessing a prevalent tendency to delimit digital infinity by means of data-visualization as well as curation of (play)lists, (mood)boards and other collections of one's own, which can likewise be conceptualized as practices of textualization.

The text is a unit that has a human dimension and that also resonates with recent calls for balancing quantitative approaches to data with qualitative ones (Wildfeuer et al., 2018) as well as with the motto that Divina Frau-Meigs has proposed for media literacy: 'No Coding Without Decoding!' (no production of digital text without an understanding of the context and modes of reception), which is to say that literacy is a social practice not a technical skill. In addition, acquisition of the language of digital culture resembles the process of learning one's mother tongue. It happens by means of texts on the basis of which a language system is reconstructed. In the case of acquiring a foreign language, the system (i.e. vocabulary, grammar rules, etc.) comes first and the ability to read and construct texts follows.

What makes the Lotmanian understanding of the text's function in culture clearly applicable in the present context is the explicit integration of long-divided 'high' culture and 'popular' culture, which are obviously indispensable for both the dynamic and sustainable functioning of the semiosphere, notwithstanding the judgemental bias that routinely labels one valuable and the other worthless. Congenially but independently, both Lotman (1977) and Roland Barthes (1977) proposed the text as a tool for raising the analysability of culture. They framed 'text' as a *methodological unit* for studying cultural creation neutrally in relation to its material or to the sign-system in which it is codified. In this framework, for example, each of the four compositions titled *The Scream of Nature* by Edvard Munch, as well as the series as a whole, and also parodic memes and other remixes of the famous image, are equally textualizable for studying their respective means and mechanisms of meaning-making.

In *The Structure of the Artistic Text* (1977: 51–3), Lotman brings out three defining parameters of the text:

- *Expression* – e.g. in verbal, visual or any other sign-system, including a synthesis of different sign-systems;
- *Boundary* – i.e. a frame that demarcates it as an autonomous whole with an integral meaning and function in culture;
- *Structure* – i.e. the text is not just a sequence or collection of signs but features an internal organization or hierarchy.

In our example of digital remixes of *The Scream* (Figure 7.1), these parameters manifest themselves in *expression* in the visual or audiovisual sign-system; being *bounded* by the margins of the image or the beginning and ending of the video; and *structured* through the dominant position of

FIGURE 7.1 *Where does a text stop? Playing with expression, boundaries and structure.*[1]

---

[1]Source: see image 17 of 18 here: https://www.wmagazine.com/gallery/banksy-self-destructing-art-meme. Image courtesy of drift.r, Instagram (9 October 2018): https://www.instagram.com/p/BorqKTDgDlw/.

the facial expression of the depicted figure, which is often substituted by that of another subject for comical effect. The latter's dominance can be compared, for example, to the colours around the figure, which on Munch's compositions contribute significantly to the overall impression of anxiety.

In addition to discussing texts with clear material boundaries, Lotman's notion allows for the textualization of research objects that are usually regarded as too diffused or blurred. These can include individual behaviour, a city or a nation, or the whole oeuvre of one author or one epoch, as well as the adaptations of all these 'texts' into different media, forming a transmedial system. The streetscapes of Paris (the city) and all their representations – a Google map of them, its representations in Instagram or Richard Linklater's film *Before Sunrise* (filmed in Paris) – together with all other representations of Paris could be seen forming such a transmedial system. Textualization as a methodological tool does not, however, consist in random drawing of boundaries but is always guided by the creation of a holistic notion of the research object, which ensures an integral meaning and a function for that object in culture. The latter is pertinent from the viewpoint of digital displays in which the border of the screen constitutes one boundary (but see Figure 7.1, where this border becomes a point of contestation in art politics), which may or may not coincide with the outline of the initial textual whole. The ability to zoom and consequently to change scale (fractally) is immanent to digital artefacts. That is why digitalization of analogue visual objects is an especially interesting case. For example, the physical dimensions of large paintings remain concealed on screen, and their minute details may become visible only through zooming, which is as if cutting them out from the whole and creating a new text. The easiness of creating copy-paste collages is entrenched not only in the technological but also in the conceptual logic of the digital semiosphere.

The thematic division of the next three chapters springs from the typology of functions that Lotman attributed to texts in culture. More precisely, he proposed three analogous functions in different publications, attributing them (1) to a thinking object (1978: 3), (2) to a semiotic system (Ivanov et al., 1987: 14–15) and then (3) both to language and text (1990: 11–19). The seeming incompatibility among these three types does not result from an unsystematic approach but from the structural-functional isomorphism (= 'same structure') within Lotmanian semiotics, linking cultural phenomena at different scales: (1) *thinking mind* (micro), (2) *artistic text* (meso) and (3) *culture – the semiosphere* (macro). Note that in this schema, which also structures the present book's succession of parts, 'text' corresponds to the 'meso' or institutional level of evolutionary economics: a text is a coherent, organized and action-oriented group of system attributes, much like a firm is one way to produce a coherent, organized and action-oriented group of economic agents at meso-scale. Both are *actualizations* of system-level *rules* (Dopfer et al., 2004), and both texts and firms are *agents* in the sense that they wreak *changes* in those systems. Just as a firm is not really explicable by asking what it 'is' – only what it 'does' will work – so a text is not a 'thing' so much as a 'population of actualisations' among those who make, encounter, use and modify it. However, because we are concerned here with 'textual functions' but in the book as a whole with 'isomorphic systems' we are not confining text to the 'meso-level' of analysis, but taking it as our 'micro-level' unit, in order to focus on the 'individual' text and its components, rules and functions, before going on to consider the agencies (meso) and systems (macro) within which each text circulates, in Parts II and III respectively.

The three key cultural functions of text include:

- **transmission** of existing information;
- **creation** of new information, which cannot be deduced algorithmically from the existing; and
- **preservation** of information from previous textual communication.

These functions are distinguishable for analytical purposes; in actual practice, they overlap and intertwine. The functions elaborate the immanent analysability of the text and explain the necessary immersion of every text in a semiosphere.

By contrast, Roman Jakobson's model of communication consists of six fundamental factors and their corresponding functions (Jakobson, 1985:113):

- *The referential function*: refers to something, for some organism.
- *The poetic function*: plays with the code.
- *The emotive function*: communicates the addresser's state.
- *The conative function*: gives orders (seeks to change the addressee's state).
- *The phatic function*: keeps the channel open between communicative participants.
- *The meta-lingual (reflexive) function*: refers to the use of language-about-language.

Compared to this, Lotman's typology appears scant. Unsurprisingly, the reason lies in the two approaches' different focus of interest. Jakobson's six functions abstract an act of communication from the rest of communication processes. This appears to imply constancy of the information exchanged between the sender and the receiver. Indeed, accurate transmission of information is classically considered as the core problem of communicative systems (Shannon and Weaver, 1949). Lotman, however, was interested in what else can happen to information in communication processes. He proposes that in principle two things occur: the *generation* of new information and *preservation* of information generated in previous communication acts. Jakobson's functions can all be seen as subfunctions of the *transmission* of messages, saying little about their reception, processing and meaning in context.

The phatic function is indeed prominent in digital communication, cemented by 'connected presence' (Licoppe, 2004), where *connection* between users may be more important than the *content* of any one message. Besides, in the current age of distraction, content that could be considered peripheral dominates many internet users' daily lives, because these short flicks are all we have time for amidst the information excess and, indeed, successful business plans rely on enforced rules of brevity (e.g. number of characters on Twitter, length of video on TikTok, limit on photos-per-post on Instagram). The phatic function is not only manifest in micro-formats such as emoticons, tweets and other forms of microblogging and social media updates, which Miller (2008) has termed as 'phatic culture', but also observable in longer forms such as in far-right polarized communication (Madisson and Ventsel, 2016). The underlying characteristic of both short and long forms is that the content of the messages is in principle already known and accepted; the messages themselves serve the establishment and maintenance of social ties.

This is to affirm that the *transmission*, *creation* and *preservation* of 'information' are not all there is to say about the functions of communication. We select them in what follows to guide our path through a Lotmanian contribution to understanding the textual aspects of digital culture.

# 8

# Text, transmission, translation

*Now this is the Law of the Jungle – as old and as true as the sky; ...*
*As the creeper that girdles the tree-trunk the*
*Law runneth forward and back –*
For the strength of the Pack is the Wolf, and the strength of the
Wolf is the Pack.

(RUDYARD KIPLING, 'THE LAW OF THE JUNGLE,' 1895)[1]

***

According to Lotman's three-part model of the text's functions, *transmission* prevails in cases where the message is transformed in accordance to strict rules of codification, ensuring the reversibility of its results; that is, when in the case of computer-mediated communication the direction of some algorithmic operation is reversed, the result would be the source text. At the same time, the sign-systems that humans use for communication range from artificial languages – that indeed allow for the reversibility of transfer operations – to languages of arts, which are basically hopeless at mediating constant or fixed meanings.

For example, in the case of traffic lights, red signifies stop and green signifies go, and we can talk of exact equivalences. At the same time, the colour palette of the film *Amélie* by Jean-Pierre Jeunet is also built upon the complementarity of red and green, while they lack exact equivalences in verbal language as was the case with traffic lights. If we were to describe the meanings we've attached to the colours in the film and ask someone to create a movie palette on the basis of our verbal account, it would never result in the return of *Amélie*. Returning to the artificial code of red/green

[1]http://www.poetryloverspage.com/poets/kipling/law_of_jungle.html.

traffic signals, it turns out that this simple system results from a *social* rather than technical history. It originates in the regulation of shipping, where red/green signifies not 'stop/go' but 'port (left)/starboard (right)' (Gollop, 2016). Indeed, technically, the red/green opposition is not optimum, because those with colour blindness find this pairing of colours hard to distinguish. Hence, we will have to broaden our focus as we touch upon some general principles of digital transmission of 'information' in both artificial languages and artistic ones, where the aspect of creativity cannot be escaped, before we even get to that function (see next chapter).

## An 'open number' of systems and levels

When discussing the Lotmanian notion of the text, one of the first specifications that needs to be made concerns the expression of the text. We refer to the somewhat misleading notion that a text is expressed in one language. In fact, the cultural semiotic view holds that a text must be at least dually coded (Lotman, 1988: 53), that is, bilingual; in other words, 'realised in the space of, at minimum, two semiotic systems' (2012: 10). For instance a novel is simultaneously expressed in written verbal language and in literary language, so the command of Estonian language does not automatically bring with it an understanding of all the novels written in Estonian.

Henry Jenkins opens his influential chapter on transmedia storytelling ('Searching for the Origami Unicorn', in Jenkins, 2006: 95–6) with the example of a comic strip by Peter Bagge, which depicts people divided between those who are completely fascinated by *The Matrix* and those who are struggling even to comprehend it. He used this example to suggest that the narrative strategies of the groundbreaking transmedia project (i.e. its means of message transmission) were so new and demanding that spectators who tried to decode it in accordance with the existing rules or language of movies failed to grasp it, because it uses a new codifying system, where, for example, some elements of the film make sense only after playing the computer game and/or watching the animated shorts and so on.

Understanding the conventions of audiovisual storytelling is not enough to understand transmedia storytelling. Similarly, many people who understand the system of online video found it very hard to grasp the concept of Snapchat, because they miss the system of codes underlying *connected* presence. Snaps are published for only twenty-four hours on Snapchat and disappear once the given contact has seen them, whereas the fact that the users are almost constantly online renders obsolete anxiety about missing some content. However, once users were familiar with the new rule, others sought to exploit it too, notably

Facebook's 'Stories' feature, which was introduced across its platforms (Instagram and WhatsApp as well as Facebook), in order to 'squash' Snapchat.[2]

To explicate further the multiple levels of codification of every text, one can differentiate between the levels of a text's material (words, images and their configurations – i.e. a collection of elements), its internal composition (the hierarchical relations between the elements within textual boundaries – i.e. a certain unified whole) and its extra-textual relations (including genre conventions, intertextual relations, knowledge about author's biography, etc.) (see Lotman, 1977: 73–7; Torop, 2017: 321). Thereby, in the case of a novel we can distinguish and mutually relate meanings of the words in natural language (e.g. the noun 'arms' in English), meanings of the words within the given novel (e.g. the way the word 'arms' is framed in Hemingway's *A Farewell to Arms*) and the semantic associations of the words that stem from the text's relations with other texts (what we know of Hemingway's experience of war and loss, the homonymous poem by George Peele and the way weapons and embraces are represented in its later cinematic adaptations, etc.).

In artistic languages, the scope of a meaningful unit (e.g. a word or an image) can be narrowed or widened simply by its placement in a text, without direct reference to the nondiegetic world. Think of the equivalences established by rhymes in poetry, where two different words acquire similarity as the second rhyming word revives the previous one, or by cinematic variation, a good example being first and the final frames or shots in movies, which are often deliberately (and poetically) matched or contrasted by directors, as the side-by-side compilation videos by Jacob T. Swinney illustrate very neatly.[3]

While more clearly related to the creative and mnemonic functions of the text, plurality of codes is fundamental for any semiosis, which means that it should be kept in mind from the outset. *Code plurality* can be attributed to the ontology of living systems (Hoffmeyer and Emmeche, 1991; Kull, 2015: 258), making semiosis 'the process that occurs in the situation of incompatibility between codes' (Kull, 2015: 259), while polyglot transmission of meaning can be regarded as an evolutionary step towards complexity in human culture:

> The idea of the possibility for a single ideal language to serve as an optimal mechanism for the representation of reality is illusion … The idea of an optimal model, consisting of a single perfect universal language, is replaced by the image of a structure equipped with *a minimum of two* or, rather, by *an open number* of diverse languages, each of which is reciprocally dependent on the other, due to the incapacity of each to express the world independently.
>
> (Lotman, 2009 [1992]: 2)

---

[2]See: https://www.wired.com/story/copycat-how-facebook-tried-to-squash-snapchat/.
[3]See: https://vimeo.com/jacobtswinney; and https://twitter.com/firstfinalframe.

Plurality of codes or languages alone is not enough, though. What facilitates the birth of semiosis is mutual untranslatability or incompatibility of these codes. Both a single text and an entire culture are internally polyglot; text and culture can be described as isomorphic. Thence we can conceptualize culture as one text (Lotman, 1979a: 507). The capability to differentiate the codes according to which a text is encoded needs to be coupled with a capability to understand their hierarchy and the meaning-generating tensions and dynamics among them.

## Discrete and continual sign-systems – visual/verbal, digital/analogue … entertainment/education

While the digital shift has clearly brought along diversification in the forms of self-expression and ways of synthesizing words, sounds and images, it has become a truism that the present era is dominated by the visual in contrast to the era of print (and partially similarly to the era of broadcasting). Think of the quantitative jump in images, permeating not only digital but also physical streetscapes, and of the global spread of the language of emoji, punctuating and many times substituting written communication (see Danesi, 2016). When a verbal text is located on computer screen, it is immersed in a visual field, which clearly influences (arguably more so than a book page would) its interpretation and increases the meaningfulness of its visual aspects, such as composition and layout, colour, size and typeface and so on. While browsing databases of texts that combine verbal and visual information (e.g. an online bookshop), the choice of which text to look more closely at is mostly motivated by its visual characteristics, and this understanding is something that underpins interface design, also privileging the visual. This is especially evident when the goal is to reach a wider category of visitors, many of whom can be described as 'culture snackers' to use a term generated in the context of heritage sites for 'users with a casual interest' (Brinkerink, 2014: 10).

After the launch of the digital platform of the Rijksmuseum in Amsterdam – the *Rijksstudio*[4] – its head of publishing, Martijn Pronk, generalized the term 'culture snacker' to describe 'the typical Internet user of today, pinning on Pinterest, watching videos, sharing photos. Interested in art, design, travel, but not an art lover per se. Rijksstudio is the "translation" of a museum website for this group' (Gullström, n.d.). Besides echoing the visualization of the overall experience of culture, this characterization also testifies to the democratization of art production, curation and consumption, and its translation from objective modernist *thing* to active postmodern *process*.

---

[4]https://www.rijksmuseum.nl/en/rijksstudio.

Whereas artworks used to imply a pilgrimage to specified locations – spaces that were often designed and built specifically for displaying art and even particular pieces – they are now displayed in ever more heterogeneous contexts, among the clutter of everyday life. Already on the screen itself, a digital reproduction of an artwork is surrounded by other divergent images, whose content, configuration and succession are very often marked by serendipity or even pure arbitrariness. At the same time, the screen itself is surrounded by visual, aural and tactile stimuli that can be very uncharacteristic of the places where the original works were once displayed. In the digital semiosphere, the expert discourse, historiographic sequences and gilded frames that previously anchored the texts are juxtaposed with a variety of ways for making sense of them in one's own terms, up to the limit of tolerance of copyright law.

Needless to say, at the same time, critical voices do not keep quiet, as exemplified by Viola Rühse's bitter verdict in accord with other concerns over the 'Disneyfication' and 'McDonaldisation' of cultural heritage: 'Rijksstudio is more a cautionary tale of the commodification of culture in neoliberal times than a positive example of open content and democratic culture enabled by digital technologies' (2017: 38–9). Rühse contrasts Rijksstudio to the Rijksmuseum's former website, which featured more explicitly educational content, most of it mediated in verbal form.

National museums everywhere – along with scholarship in general – face the dilemma at the heart of this challenge, not only between verbal and visual modality but also the evaluative asymmetry implied between them, and the contrasting cultural commitments of scholars and 'snackers'. National museums 'of the people' must act in the name of whole populations, not only those in the know. This is how the Palace Museum in Beijing has sought to reconcile the polarities for the Forbidden City's 600th anniversary in 2020:

> The year 2020 will mark the sixth centennial of the construction of the Forbidden City and the ninety-fifth anniversary of the establishment of the Palace Museum, an historic cultural occasion deserving society-wide celebration. The Palace Museum has the mission to promote the legacy of China's outstanding traditional culture, diligently advance the protection, research, and preservation of the world cultural heritage it encompasses, and develop innovative ways to propagate the excellence of traditional Chinese culture.[5]

'Society-wide celebration' means not only finding ways to 'translate' the Forbidden City and its collections into the current vernacular but also to

---

[5]This and the following quotations are from a museum news release (30 December 2019): https://en.dpm.org.cn/about/news/2019-12-30/3125.html.

take the Museum beyond the City and out to the people via multimedia, including a TV series *Glory of the Forbidden City (Gugong rumeng)*, TV documentary *The Forbidden City,* TV series *There's Something New in the Palace Museum (Shangxinle Gugong)* and a 'large-scale epic drama', *The Forbidden City (Zijin cheng)*, thereby:

> sharing the fascination of traditional Chinese culture with the younger generation, broadening their horizons, igniting patriotic feelings, and strengthening cultural confidence ... which all serve to usher the culture embodied in the Palace Museum into daily life and benefit the general public.

All this, while at the same time holding a series of academic conferences to show how the museum is 'performing its role in efficiently cultivating core Socialist values and putting them into practice all while laying a solid foundation for protecting and safeguarding the legacies of the Forbidden City for the next 600 years'.

For Lotman, as well as for contemporary museum directors, the cultural pessimism that underlies notions of commodification, 'Disneyfication' and 'McDonaldisation' – in *opposition* to yesterday's values expressed in yesterday's media – was an alien characteristic, simply because his semiospheric understanding of culture as a self-balancing system (Lotman, 1990: 134) sees that opposition as a *relation*. Thereby, new languages for holding dialogue with cultural texts do not necessarily substitute the old ones but can exist simultaneously in different parts of the semiosphere. Hence, Rijksstudio and the Palace Museum are both exploring possible ways for communicating with art and not as a superficial substitute for classical art education and visits to the museum. In other words, Rembrandt on coffee mugs or 'a commemorative logo ... and release commemorative banknotes, coins, and stamps' for the Forbidden City are not *a priori* profanation but function as nodes within the semiosphere and potential links to Old Masters or the Ming Dynasty.

Another way to make sense of Rühse's confrontation, which is essentially a tension between verbal and visual systems of meaning-making, is a 'neutral' distinction proposed by Kress (2003: 1) between the world as told and the world as shown. Both these modalities have their own affordances and constraints for mediating the world. In his work on the transmedial literacy of teenagers, Koskimaa (2018: 37) has observed among his respondents a growing tendency to use YouTube as a search engine alternative to Google. We could here apply Kress's distinction to YouTube (shown) and Google (told) respectively and in that case Koskimaa's observation, together with data on YouTube's expansion (Burgess and Green, 2018) in general, testifies to the domination of the 'world shown' over the 'world told', extending visualization to forms of textuality that were hitherto not considered to be visual: such as Schich and colleagues' attempt to chart the hotspots of 2,000 years of cultural history in a five-minute-long animation (Schich et al., 2014); Brodbeck's animated 'fingerprints' and posters visualizing quantitative data on editing structures, speech, motion and other characteristics of movies (Brodbeck, 2011); Lev Manovich's Cultural Analytics Lab's visualisations of large image and video collections, including, for example, MoMA Photography collection and Instagram. Yet another example of this is contained in the way that 'Instagrammability' directs users' pathways in physical locations and governs their choices at stores.

At the same time, in the digital semiosphere, the statement that visual languages are closer to our contemporary cultural core than verbal ones are is also not enough on its own, because *digital visuality* appears different from analogue visuality. Ravelli and van Leeuwen (2018) have adapted Kress and van Leeuwen's highly operable framework for describing modality in visual texts to the digital era. They demonstrate the clear reconfiguration of modality markers in online environments and explicate how 35mm photography has lost its throne as the criterion of analogue 'naturalism' or truth of perception (a position established in the 1930s and 1940s with the ascendancy of the great pictorial weeklies such as *Picture Post, Life, Vue, Berliner Illustrirte Zeitung, Pix*), owing to proliferating forms of user control over image modification such as Photoshop or filters for images on every smartphone. Therefore, a shift should be noticed in modal variables (e.g. in degrees of colour saturation, inclusion of movement), coding orientations (e.g. in what constitute as markers of 'historical authenticity') as well as in other aspects of visual modality.

In addition to the prevalence of images, other nonlinear modes of transmitting information have emerged in the digital semiosphere. Fascination with mapping and the spread of map-based applications are a case in point. The British Film Institute has experienced unprecedented success in popularizing their archival content by curating it on the basis of shooting locations – as based on a digital online map. A related example is the looming emergence of topotheques[6] – digital collections of privately owned material relevant to local communities. Linking content to physical locations is a way of converging the digital and analogue realms, in order to represent complex topics through familiar spatial frames and to reduce the contemporary overflow of information to a human scale, mimicking the human experience of the world. The latter is inescapably situated in a spatial location, perceived by five senses, such that the richest experiences are those that offer material for sense-making for all five.

This is why screen media try to compensate for the missing modalities through alternative ways of sense-making. Ted Nelson's 1963 concept of

---

[6]https://www.topothek.at/en/principle/.

*hypertext* (1965: 96) referred to a nonlinear and multidimensional system of establishing connections between different textual elements. Its operating principles were supposedly more similar to the way human mind makes connections when compared to linear writings, promising creative and educational merits. As such, hypertext indicates the potential inherent in topology, topography and other disciplines related to spatiality as a conceptualizing principle for digital networked realms.

Whichever modality we happen to have at hand, a fundamental principle to consider when discussing a digital text is the 'discrete' nature of digital representation, that is being encoded in binary code. This recalls Lotman's distinction between *discrete* and *continual* sign-systems as 'two essentially different ways of reflecting the world' (1990: 36). The epitome of a discrete sign-system is written verbal (and mathematical) language, consisting in conventional signs, while images with their iconic spatial logic correspond to continual sign-systems. In a discrete system, texts are formed like 'linear chains of linked segments', for example letters (or symbols) per word (or algorithm), *a la* block chain, which makes the *segment* (the sign) the primary bearer of meaning, while the meaning of the whole text is derived from these. In the continuous system, in contrast, the primary bearer of meaning is the *text* itself, as the segments or individual signs are not (easily or naturally) distinguishable. The meaning of the whole is 'washed over' the n-dimension semantic space of the given text, whether that is the canvas of a painting, the granularity of a photograph, the space of a stage, a screen, a ritual, social behaviour or a dream.

It is fruitful to remember that the human desire to understand the surrounding world is itself linked to 'the segmentation of non-discrete space' (Leach, 1976: 34; Lotman, 2009: 161). In this framework it is interesting to consider digitized paintings displayed in digital databases. While in the analogue form it is difficult to isolate the component elements of a painting, a transfer into digital sign-system is describable as 'discretization', or decomposition into individual segments/bits (which are signals rather than signs). While from the viewpoint of the *represented* (i.e. the objects depicted), an attempt to make a comprehensive list of all constitutive elements 'smacks of artificiality' (Lotman, 1990: 36), on the level of the *form of representation*, exact description (pixel by pixel) appears the most natural thing. Computer vision technologies allow visual characteristics of a painting to be described in a way that is not realizable in the analogue system by means of natural language. A human being can see and make meaning from differences between subtle changes of hue in the same colour, but in most cases, words for naming these are missing from human languages. In sharp contrast, with the aid of computer technology, all the paintings in a collection are describable and relatable with significant precision from the viewpoint of colour gradients, and from other visual characteristics too, including textures, degree of sharpness and blur on images, speed of movement in videos, etc. (Manovich, 2017a: 11). This facilitates new kinds of automatic indexing of visual texts in large collections, and it has huge potential in developing visual literacies.

# Secondary modelling systems

Indexes in databases are also known as 'metadata' – data about other data, data that models and organizes these other data, that makes claims about them, usually about their potential information value, but also about their affordances and uses. In the digital semiosphere and its infrastructures, metadata is everywhere. Digital data exist always in organized layers – there have to be meta-layers explaining the contents and afforded uses of data to algorithms that are designed to operate with them. Such layered-ness takes us to a key concept that Lotman's semiotics offers for making sense of the digital semiosphere: that of a *secondary modelling system*. As the name suggests, secondary modelling systems are based on a primary system – natural language – and they 'accumulate additional superstructures' (2011: 250), either 'directly (the supralinguistic system of literature) or in the shape parallel to it (music, painting)' (Lotman et al., 2013[1973]: 72).

We can propose that especially the schemas of 'descriptive metadata', which are used to describe and summarize the content in digital systems, could be understood from the semiotic perspective as reductive meta-languages. Thereby, a description of a database object (its metadata profile) appears as a meta-text. And the language of its expression – the metadata schema – appears as a meta-language, where 'the modelling influence of the meta-language on its object is inevitable' (Lotman, 1977: 21). We can conceptualize a metadata schema as a modelling system defined as 'a structure of elements and rules of their combination, existing in a state of fixed analogy to the whole sphere of the object of perception, cognition, or organization' (Lotman, 2011: 250). This seems to imply that the metadata profile of a text in a digital archive or database is not only a signpost pointing towards the text or a simple means via which we automatically get to the text but also a model of the text itself, the extra-textual reality that the text mediates, as well as the text's potential and real uses and positions in dynamically changing contemporary cultural networks (Ibrus, Ojamaa, 2018, 2020). This in turn suggests the *creation* of information in addition to its mere transfer, underscoring once more the interrelatedness of the functions of the text.

Application of the notion of a modelling system implies that any text is the result of *modelling* processes and consists in a (dynamic) model of the extra-textual world – the 'real' world outside of texts. The premise that there is one extra-textual world, but that multiple models of it are realized in multiple modelling systems in culture – as if mirroring one object from different angles – attaches to culture the characteristic of *stereoscopy* (Lotman, 1974). Lotman proposed that the evolution of modelling systems is headed towards growing individuality – more and more specialized languages emerge in complex societies as a response to a perceived gap between the (insufficient) models of the world and actual extra-textual reality. He also suggested that, in the process, all users of those modelling systems, for instance media institutions that both send and receive texts, need to grow in complexity as the number of semiotic systems that are used by the organization, its employees, customers or other partners is also destined to grow.

This means that there is no such thing as a single or univocal meaning and hence any universal understanding of texts (although abstract mathematical and scientific notation seek to minimize equivocal meaning). This in turn complicates mutual understanding and shared identities among speakers and users. As a result, attempts to generate grammars, unified descriptions, artificial meta-languages or standardized and interoperable metadata schemas for aggregate platforms become commonplace. These are designed to balance the environment of communication and insert a sense of universality. Individuality and fragmentation are indeed characteristics associated with the digital sphere and culture's attempt to balance it can perhaps be seen in the explosive rise of the topic of media and information literacy as well as in initiatives of digital archives and aggregate platforms for collecting and organizing cultural heritage and other content as a basis for shared cultural identities.

At the same time, contemporary digital archives are themselves an example of bidirectional logic: on the one hand, their aim is to systematize content and through this create coherence, on the other, to provide material for repurposing content in creative ways and hence facilitate multiplicity – new remixes and constellations, new forms and secondary modelling systems emerging from these new constellations. In practice, both of these directions depend on appropriate metadata schemas, allowing the modelling of archived texts both as source material for creation and as a part of a curated collection for preservation. This is especially acute in the context of multimodal aggregate archives (such as *Europeana* or *Google Arts & Culture*),[7] which include texts that have traditionally been located in separate, medium-specific collections within which they are described and contextualized in medium-specific meta-languages. *Europeana* in particular is designed to facilitate interlinking (and therefore systematizing and standardizing) Europe's very heterogeneous pool of heritage, stored in hundreds of different specialized museums or archives;

---

[7]See: https://www.europeana.eu/portal/en; https://artsandculture.google.com/.

and also, responding to the EU's related policy goals, to facilitate the new uses of this heritage in the digital domain. That is, *Europeana* facilitates two mutually incommensurable developments: first, *centripetal* movement – the integration of all of European cultural heritage; second, *centrifugal* movement – the further dissemination of heritage, to be used in new contexts and by new target groups, and interlinked with alternative realities.

## Boundaries and part/whole relations

The growing elusiveness of textual boundaries exemplified by this case is another central characteristic of digital communication and culture. Textual analysis is complicated by the fact that texts appear simultaneously as a source out of which some fragments are chosen for reuse and also as small fragments of larger thematic collections or of a seemingly infinite flow curated by recommendation algorithms – say, of YouTube or Spotify. That is, all texts are constituted as bounded wholes of their fragments but also as fragments of again larger wholes. Members of the Tartu-Moscow school described this tendency as a cultural universal in their *Theses on the Semiotic Study of Cultures*: 'on different levels the same message may appear as a text, part of a text, or an entire set of texts' (Lotman et al., 2013[1973]: 58). Later, Lotman has generalized this discovery in semiospheric terms, explaining how:

> [c]ertain parts of the semiosphere may at different levels of self-description form either a semiotic unity, a semiotic continuum, demarcated by a single boundary; or a group of enclosed spaces, marked off as discrete areas by the boundaries between them; or, finally, part of a more general space, one side of which is demarcated by a fragment of a boundary, while the other is open.
>
> (2005[1984]: 138)

Upon 'entering' culture, a text is often accompanied by paratexts in various media (Gray, 2010), which are not confined to marketing purposes. A text's existence in culture continues via adaptations, remixes, fan creations and so on that are based on either the whole or a fragment. Also, the practice of creating and curating collections and lists, both by professionals at archives and other institutions as well as by users, has become characteristic of the digital environment.

It is exactly here that the Lotmanian dynamic notion of text proves most useful, as it allows the research object to be determined within a seemingly indeterminate flood of data. By understanding text this way (1977: 51–3), we can conceptualize for example one photo uploaded to Instagram as a text, but also all the photos of one user as a text, as well as Instagram *in toto* as a text. The parameter of *boundary* is then defined by the frame of the user account in the first case and the application or the platform in the second and third. This allows the means of expression as well as the internal hierarchy of the object to be described and analysed. A textual 'boundary' seems strongly to suggest a static nature of the object, but a text is also bounded by its duration. In the case of Snapchat or Instagram 'stories', for example, duration is technically controlled (from a few seconds to twenty-four hours), while for any one user the duration of their own photo archive partakes of both 'preservation' (a store of memories for that user) and 'creation' (a continuing source for other users who might comment or like items within one's feed over an extended period). Like Twitter and Facebook, Instagram operates as a kind of semiotic fire hose (Bruns and Burgess, 2012), with a massive flow in the here and now, which means that in practice most of the single texts last as long as the user community's attention span.

## Part/whole

The cultural semiotic concept of a boundary is dynamic not only in a text's social use but also analytically: it depends on the analyst's chosen level of focus and consequent *part/whole relations*, and it is also dynamic from the viewpoint of this double function. Boundaries function as the space of contact and dialogue in culture: 'only with the help of the boundary is the semiosphere able to establish contact with non-semiotic and extra-semiotic spaces' (Lotman, 2005: 210). For instance, a 'Share to Facebook' button in an online newspaper constitutes a boundary or a 'bilingual translatable "filter"' (2005: 208) that sets the given website into a dialogue with Facebook as a platform and with much else on this platform. Such rhetorical interconnecting of two different semiotic systems, however, opens the door for further growth of meaning. The share button communicates potential for a widened context for a statically presented news story; it tells of potential user agency and motivates imagination on further participation in contextualizing the story. But it also tells of threat – of the story being commodified by a global surveillance platform, for the sharing act being counted and participation being measured. That is, a button next to a news story forces onto it new frames motivating new interpretations of its role and context, that is, enabling an immediate growth of meanings attached to it.

## Platforms

A social media platform, like any other sign-system, presumes immersion in a semiosphere and contact with others in order for it to function:

'none of the sign systems possesses a mechanism which would enable it to function in isolation' (Lotman et al., 2013: 53). Therefore, the conventional separation of media forms appears inadequate – it is rather their mutual interrelations than the internal logics that determine medium specificity. This claim is well supported in the diachronic view in which the position of any medium within the system of media is carved out through other media. For example, cinema relates to painting, animation, television and theatre. However, an archaeology of cinema's prehistory would add its descent from *gaming* to these (see Strauven, 2011). Cinema can be located in the context of pre-cinematic optical toys, home-entertainment-viewing apparatuses and arcade games, including the magic lantern, thaumatrope, phenakistoscope, praxinoscope and so on. These in turn have led to Nintendo's Wii device and in a way also to interactive titles on Netflix, such as Charlie Brooker's *Black Mirror: Bandersnatch* (2018). By repositioning cinema within the history of gaming, Strauven (2011) foregrounds not only the corporeality of images on screen but also an active observer, whose subjective embodied vision and hand are foregrounded over the eye, which here acts as a mediator between the observer's sense of touch and brain activity. To generalize this vantage point, the larger system determines also the ontology of the individual texts and languages.

Within the framework of dynamic part/whole relations, we can again notice a paradoxical tension between opposite drives, towards integration with other systems and towards disintegration and maximum individuality (Lotman, 1988). In the first case, what is commonly perceived as context becomes text. In the second case, we see the tendency for individual parts of a text to function as separate aesthetic units, where the previous text becomes context for them. This tension can also be exemplified by the formation of texts, such as all photos posted on Instagram by one user as one text, on the one hand and, on the other, the disintegration of a given photo into its representational components: figure, location, clothing and so on, each as separate signifying systems, which can in turn be amplified by the selection of hashtags attached to the photo. Alternatively, we can perceive a photo together with the comments as one text as well as a composite of different texts. This tension is clearly manifest in transmedia storytelling and other cross-platform practices, where an overarching story-world is simultaneously a textual whole and a context for individual stories that we may see in cinemas, on video game consoles, on Netflix, on the streets via Alternate Reality Games and so on.

# Paratext

In addition to full-scale narratives, contemporary texts are routinely preceded, surrounded and followed by adjacent texts that Jonathan Gray, borrowing from the literary scholar Gérard Genette (1997), describes as 'paratexts' (2010). His explanation of paratext, being 'both "distinct from" and alike – or intrinsically part of – the text', is compatible with Lotman's part/whole dynamics. The lion's share of paratexts typically belongs to marketing. Gray reports that major movie studios spend a third of the average film budget, and smaller companies even two thirds of it, on promotion (2010: 7), in the form of trailers, commercials, online and offline banners, posters and other promotional materials. While these texts clearly have a coherent message and function in culture, in most cases they make sense only in relation to the core text. More substantial examples include game-based releases, such as the massive gamified promotion of *The Dark Knight*. These can stand on their own feet from the audience's viewpoint. Indeed, the blockbuster trailer is now clearly a 'form' in its own right, being 'dropped' well before a film's release, often to widespread cultural discussion, and inevitably spawning its own genre of parody/homage.[8]

## Compression and expansion

Carlos Scolari (2013) has refined Gray's approach by proposing a taxonomy of the transmedia strategies of *compression* and *expansion*, employing the notion of 'paratextual nanotext' (Scolari, 2013: 48). While their textuality is evident structurally, their functional autonomy is minimal, although in some cases, they 'provide fundamental building blocks for understanding the narrative construction' (2013: 64) An example of this can be seen in the transmedial story-world of *Lost*, in which several interstitial contents serve a deeper explanation of the core text, while the threshold between the marketing and the marketed is quite evidently being crossed. Also, depending on the target audience, marketing can paratextualize quite different things to promote the same text, as demonstrated by Netflix's 'title key art' – seeking to ignite interest with algorithmically chosen still frames from the source title, which vary from one audience segment to another, based on numerical data about their viewing history (Chandrashekar et al., 2017; Riley et al., 2018).

Besides the context of promotion, the concept of paratext can also be applied to the comparably large-scale (and growing) online receptive practices of fans, including publishing written fan fiction on sites such as fanfiction.net or archiveofourown.org (AO3) (see De Kosnik et al., 2015; Jenkins, 2019), uploading audiovisual recaps of individual episodes or full shows on YouTube and so on. In Scolari's taxonomy, published fanfic would be classified as an *expansion* strategy, mostly motivated by characters:

---

[8]See: https://www.youtube.com/user/Auralnauts; this 2017 one by Auralnauts with well over 2 million views uses the trailer's generic code (citing Newton's Third Law of Motion) to send up the form: https://www.youtube.com/watch?v=KAOdjqyG37A.

'[t]he greater the number of major characters and the greater the number of potential romantic/sexual relationships and friendships (and enemy-ships) between the characters, the greater the fan production' (De Kosnik et al., 2015: 160). Fan-produced online audiovisual recaps (e.g. *Lost Seasons 1–5 Recap in 8 Minutes 40 Seconds*) and *Best of* scene selections are examples of *compression* strategy. They 'cancel the textual excesses' (Scolari, 2013: 60) with the aim of synthesizing plot or character, or even to propose an alternative reading of the text (Gray, 2010: 162), enforced by an added soundtrack or voiceover. These instances of fandom illustrate the dynamics of contemporary textual boundaries, especially the ways that adjacent texts are simultaneously individual wholes, while also determining the meaning of the core text for the given reader.

## Archives

Part/whole dynamics are evident in the practice of digital collecting and curating individual collections inside larger digital archives (see Torlasco, 2013; Baron, 2014). The possibility of creating collections in accordance with personal interests is already an inherent part of the interface of many collections of digitized heritage, as is suggesting alternative collections either by algorithms or by professional curators. Rather than being based on the logic of chronological succession, such collections are motivated by multiplicity of alternative perspectives. A good example of the relevant practices can be found on the *Google Arts & Culture* website and app, which is effectively a virtual museum, incorporating the collections of over 1,000 museums worldwide. The user can virtually tour museums or explore thematic exhibitions, stories and experiments with machine learning, which combine works from different museums or curate subcollections of one's own favourites. Digitized data can also be browsed by artist, medium, art movement, historical figures and events and places as well as by popularity, chronology and colour.

For example, one of the thematic subcollections features a virtual counterpart to the British Library's Exhibition *Harry Potter: A History of Magic*, framing one prominent theme of the book series as a part of a text that concurrently includes visual and verbal overviews of objects related to witchcraft and magic in the British Library's extensive collection, including manuscripts on potions from Medieval Europe, Chinese oracle bones from 1600–1050 BCE, instructions on how to protect oneself from dark forces from eighteenth-century Ethiopia and so on. One of the characteristic features of the audiovisual text is an automatic zoom that directs the user's attention to topically relevant details on manuscripts, drawings, paintings, figures and so on. Overviews are accompanied by Q&As with the creators, videos of The Super Carlin Brothers (a popular YouTuber duo whose channel is dedicated to trivia about *Harry Potter*, *Star Wars* and Pixar, Disney, Marvel productions) exploring the exhibits and so on.

The simultaneous inclusion of texts and text-parts into thematically different, sometimes even inherently controversial digital wholes, can be conceptualized by the notion of 'dynarchive' proposed by media archaeologist Wolfgang Ernst (2013: 81). According to Ernst, the essence of the digital archive is less the archived material *per se* than a dynamic conception of the *idea* of the archive (Hartley, 2012), because the archival process no longer focuses on the content of individual archived materials but rather on creating meaningful links among them, not on the objective essence of collected *objects* but on the probability of finding meaningful *signs* in the plenitude of 'logistical interlinking' (Hartley, 2012: 155–75, Ernst, 2013: 84–5).

Revealing intertextual systems is theoretically and methodologically an old idea, but digital technology allows for implementing it on a new scale. Evidencing this are *culturegraphy*[9] and other forms of network studies and visualisation methods within digital humanities (see IRMA, 2019, Chapter 13, Bruns and Moon, 2019). Two principles are evident here. One is balancing the different structural wholes within which a text can belong. The other is balancing the discreteness of textual representation with the continuity of perception of the world. Former ways of organizing and distinguishing cultural texts into discrete sections, which were based on the immanent characteristic of the texts (e.g. the covers of books), have now given way to organizing the texts in accordance with the changing interest of the user. Texts in different media and discourses from different historical epochs are not necessarily an archival mess but an alternative whole, organized according to new principles. And in accordance with semiospheric logic, this new whole determines the meaning of its individual parts in the given context, not vice versa.

The observation that file-oriented practices have yielded to use-oriented ones (Ernst, 2013: 81; see also Hartley, 2004) has led Hartley to employ the notion of a 'network or probability archive' (2012: 155–75). Probability archives are founded 'on the principle of uncertainty, where meanings may vary according to their position, momentum, and a version of the "observer effect"' (2012: 161). In contrast to modernist or 'essence' archives, which are organized around 'the coherent object', the new archives that appeared with internet affordances like YouTube are organized around 'found objects' (found by search engines) of a certain class, formed on the basis of metadata, which are unstable or unreliable (they can be deleted, modified or removed by platform moderators). How these objects, say YouTube music videos, are

---

[9]A concept developed by Kim Albrecht (see, e.g., https://www.kimalbrecht.com/vis/#culturegraphy).

then interlinked, for instance, into continuous streams of video content, may often appear as unpredictable, motivating discussion on the 'creativity' of archives (Ibrus and Ojamaa, 2020).

On archives, within part/whole systems, then, we may state that in culture the text is never exhausted within its material limits. Digitization practice itself makes it clear that materiality can be considered only a stage of existence, not the text as it exists. What has been more important for us here is the growing importance of extra-textual space in the digital semiosphere. It is easy to resituate textual fragments into new contexts, which oftentimes includes transfer across media boundaries. This clearly demonstrates the inherent dynamics of the text. Texts as well as cultural languages are not closed systems but are to a large extent conditioned from the 'outside', the context in which they are situated. To give an example in marketing terms, Bilton (2017: 71) has observed a shift in datafied creative industries, from the logic of 'content is king' to that of 'context is king'. In other words, where we consume, how and with whom, is more important than what we consume. To generalize, the extra-semiospheric is already 'written into' the existence of the semiosphere. This is the source of evolution of the system and creation of new meanings within it.

Therefore, instead of an objective and stable artefact, given once and for all and carrying constant meanings inserted into it, we need to come to terms with the text as a generator, that is, a device (*ustrojstvo*) for meaning-generation. The text is not only expressed in a language but *generates* a language of its own (that emerges out of the combination of previous codes in a specific new context), and this characteristic was also what forced the members of the Tartu-Moscow school to develop the 'cultural semiotic' concept of the text and textual communication beyond the cybernetics in which their earlier works were mostly sourced. As Salupere (2015: 80) has explained in relation to the modelling systems concept, 'For Lotman, cybernetic metalanguage was a common language that enabled treating extremely dissimilar phenomena as homogenous'. This was instrumental in developing the holistic theory of culture. However, the exact methods offered by cybernetics and information theory were not well-enough equipped to explain the mechanism of radical growth of information characteristic of the creative functioning of artistic texts in culture and thence the source of value for the creative industries, and the mechanism for the growth of knowledge in knowledge-based economies. Lotmanian cultural semiotics fixes that deficiency.

# 9

# Text, creation, newness

*Today, the status of science in society is increasingly contested ...*
*I argue that in these contexts, 'art' becomes an epistemic mode on*
*equal status with 'science' conventionally understood:* Art is the
epistemic mode of co-creation.

(CARSTEN HERRMANN-PILLATH, 2020)

\* \* \*

The mechanism for the creation of new information belonged to the core of
Juri Lotman's scientific interests. This explains also his pull towards the arts
and poetics, where the creative function appears in its purest form. What
could be regarded as noise and error from the viewpoint of transmission is
regarded valuable and enriching in arts by offering unpredictable models
and modelling systems for making sense of the surrounding world.

The mechanism of creativity is based on *translation*, because 'the
elementary act of thinking is translation' (Lotman, 1990: 143). We have
in mind here a process compatible with Roman Jakobson's (1971) notion
of 'intersemiotic translation'. This is a situation in which the material – the
signs – as well as the syntagmatic logic and rules of the source language
are different from those of the target language. There is a lack of exact
equivalents among the elements of the languages between which translation
takes place. This lack, that is the asymmetry of the semiotic structures
involved, causes the need for choice in the process of translating and thereby
renders it creative.

On even more fundamental level, though, we will see that 'the elementary
mechanism of translating is dialogue' (Lotman, 1990: 143). Dialogue
presumes simultaneous difference and similarity of dialogue partners.
Therefore, the greater the internal heterogeneity of the semiosphere, the
more fruitful is its soil for creativity. Digital cultural archives, which we

discussed in the previous chapter in relation to *transmission*, can also serve as a case in point for *creation*, offering various descriptive metadata systems for exploring archived objects. If for example a collection of paintings is annotated and searchable not only chronologically and by names but also by colours, brushwork, shapes, compositional logics, motives and objects depicted and so on,[1] then the number of potential dialogues within it also rises accordingly. Furthermore, this type of machine-readable information about the expression level of artworks is often the type that users who are interested in creative reuse of the works search for.

The premise that the semiosphere is not only an externally bounded whole but also criss-crossed with internal boundaries and internally heterogeneous, such that a culture is characterized by *difference*, ensures its creativity. Semiospheric boundaries are *spaces of dialogue* between adjacent sign-systems as they simultaneously belong to internal and to external space. The boundary constitutes 'a bilingual mechanism, translating external communications into the internal language' (Lotman, 2005: 210), thereby establishing the possibility of growth via contacts with extra-semiotic spaces. While for example the 'Share in…' features of some media platforms function in accordance with exact linear algorithms, the differences between the internal languages of platforms will alter a post, sometimes significantly so. Examples include the shift in dominance of the illustrative photo of a newspaper article shared on Facebook, or the further shift in significance for the first 280 characters of a post shared on Twitter, not to mention the context of the given feed into which the post is immersed on another platform. The asymmetry of different semiotic systems and the problems of translation related to this reflect the difference of word and image that together constitute a fundamental binary of any meaning-making system. This is related to the distinction between discrete and continuous sign-systems (see previous chapter). When attempting to translate a verbal text into a visual one, the translator is confronted with a situation where '[t]he equivalent to the discrete and precisely demarcated semantic unit of one text is, in the other, a kind of semantic blur with indistinct boundaries and gradual shadings into other meanings' (Lotman, 1990: 37). This is basically a situation of *untranslatability*, which in the semiotics of culture does not imply the total impossibility of dialogic communication but, on the contrary, its necessity. It reminds us that translation is always *transformation* (from one code and context to another), with significant alterations of meaning, which render the process simultaneously nonexact and nontrivial, with a creative, innovative potential (Lotman, 1990, 137).

---

[1]See for instance: https://courses.lumenlearning.com/boundless-arthistory/chapter/visual-elements/ (and, for Lumen Learning: https://www.geekwire.com/2018/edtech-startup-lumen-learning-raises-cash-aims-replace-textbooks-digital-open-educational-resources/).

In the situation of incomplete or partial translatability, where the mechanical logic of *transfer* is not applicable, the *abductive* logic of creativity necessarily steps in.[2] Whereas the logic of transfer presumes a linear sequence of events (if $x$, then $y$), creative logic implies the existence of a number of nonlinear alternatives, among which an algorithmically unpredictable choice will be made – one where 'abducting' a meaning is 'an act of insight ... putting together what we had never before dreamed of putting together', and so creating newness from existing elements (Peirce, 1988: 227). This, in turn, means that attempts to reverse the process and to translate the results back to the source language are doomed to fail: 'new texts are the texts that emerge as results of irreversible processes (in Ilya Prigogine's sense)' (quoted in Torop, 2005: 169).[3] The degree of creativity is determined by the number of possible alternatives for establishing equivalence between units of translation in the source and target languages.

# Memes

One example of an abundance of alternatives is the realm of 'viral' digital memes. Memes are a significant phenomenon of digital user culture, even though the term itself is inappropriate, from the cultural semiotic perspective. 'Meme' derives from Dawkins's theory (2006 [1976]) of the 'selfish gene'. Dawkins conjectured that a mechanism for replicating meanings in culture might follow the logic of genes, hence 'memes'. Memes are etymologically related to *sameness* and thought to operate in accordance with the logic of copying atomistic units. This is why Dawkins's approach to cultural creativity is incompatible with cultural semiotic approach, based as that is on translation within a semiosphere. The Grumpy Cat meme, as a prominent example, first entered the semiosphere via photos of a snowshoe cat with a grumpy-looking face posted to Reddit. It has since been expressed as image-macros with added verbal statements (from the cat's perspective), juxtaposed with images and videos of fictional and nonfictional characters with equally stern facial expressions, commercialized for the marketing of a wide range of consumer products and so on. Grumpy Cat is an instance, not of *replicating* a discrete atomistic unit but of what could happen when a

---

[2]For present purposes, we can adopt CS Peirce's explanation of abduction as 'an act of insight, although extremely fallible insight. It is true that the different elements of the hypothesis were in our minds before; but it is the idea of putting together what we had never before dreamed of putting together which flashes the new suggestion before our contemplation' (Peirce, 1988: 227).
[3]For Prigogine's 'irreversible processes', see e.g. https://www.nobelprize.org/uploads/2018/06/prigogine-lecture.pdf.

text *propagates* within the creative continuity of a semiosphere, its meaning growing through recontextualizations and interpretations in different sign-systems. The functioning of decontextualized discrete memes as described by Dawkins would not allow for the growth of meaning apparent in online memes. We can substitute the definition of memes with a semiotic notion of 'a system of signs with the tendency to take new translational habits' (Cannizzaro, 2016: 576). Grumpy Cat herself died a global celebrity in 2019, but of course the meme lives on.

Yet, if we follow Lotman, the question remains: Do memes function in the same way as arts? According to Lotman (2009), the way an artistic text *concentrates* information and its potential *explosivity* brings about its capacity for triggering irreversible change. Memes spring from the 'vernacular creativity' that Burgess (2006) attributes to online communities. The abundance of alternatives characteristic of individual digital memes could be seen as an instance of what Kull has described as 'amplification of random mutations' (Favareau et al., 2017: 17) rather than to the generation of an unpredictable new language (although such a distinction may itself just be another way of reproducing evaluative distinction between popular culture and art). While this quality does characterize the phenomenon of digital memes as a whole, individual instances are created within a limited set of determinants (i.e. the rules of the code) and then realized in a number of less predictable variations, which is an instance of 'the conversion of the text into an avalanche of texts' (Lotman, 2005: 216), that is, the quantitative growth of communications in culture, 'filling the various nodes of the culture's hierarchic system with various texts' (Lotman, Uspensky 1978: 215). Grumpy Cat memes are determined by a specific facial expression, especially when contrasted with a statement or an image expressing untrammelled joy, but what that face *signifies* is *group-making*, not 'selfish' – it 'spoke for all of us in our darkest moments', as Grumpy Cat's *New York Times* 'obit' put it.[4]

An interesting example from the viewpoint of the randomness of mutations is the so-called Cigar Guy meme. A photograph of the golfer Tiger Woods at the 2010 Ryder Cup, whose golf ball is flying directly towards the camera, was inadvertently photobombed by a spectator sporting a turban, fake moustache and cigar. Via Photoshopping, the meme spread to other iconic historic photographs, to amusing effect.[5] One of them was Nick Ut's legendary photograph, *Accidental Napalm Attack*, on which the head of the face of the fleeing girl was replaced by that of the Cigar Guy. In their

---

[4] See, e.g., https://www.nytimes.com/2019/05/17/business/media/grumpy-cat-dead.html.
[5] See https://knowyourmeme.com/memes/cigar-guy. Several years later, 'cigar guy' still featured as #1 in a list of 'the best sports memes of all time': https://bleacherreport.com/articles/1777316-the-best-sports-memes-of-all-time#slide15 (2013).

analysis of the remixes of Ut's photograph in digital culture, particularly in relation to Cigar Guy, Boudana et al. (2017) argue that memes can both enhance and degrade democratic public culture. It is enhanced where the source texts as wholes are meaningfully and interrelatedly reframed (e.g. Banksy's appropriation of the same photograph); it is degraded where a fragment of one text is simply inserted into another text to see whether or not a comical effect unfolds.

The distinction between vernacular and artistic creativity is itself unstable and therefore productive. It is not enough to categorize one side as valuable (Banksy, art, enhance) and the other as worthless (memes, joke, degrade). According to Lotman, 'if there were no elements of individuality in a collective work and no elements of the collective in an individual work, they could not form contrasting oppositions or interconnected pairs' (2013: 177). The value of vernacular creativity and the creation of what Lotman called, using the language of his day, 'pseudo-novelty' or 'pseudo-new' (174–198), through copying (fans re-enacting movie scenes and music videos) and quoting (e.g. GIFs punctuating blog posts), lies in acquiring literacy and an understanding of the mechanisms of creation, which potentially support cultural coherence.

From this perspective the value of the digital means of self-expression and self-publication is substantial, because they render some universal strategies of culture's creativity and memory explicit and widely acquirable. They enable the learning of culture's plurality of codes and how to combine them in order to make new meanings. For instance, Figure 9.1 builds on the intertextual reference to a film (in this case the Estonian film *Supernova*) to make a commentary on memes themselves in contemporary culture. As Wiggins (2019) eloquently demonstrates, memes should be analysed as a discourse, as effective multimodal means for ideological practice, especially by those less empowered to use other, more established and formal means.

Can internet memes facilitate the emergence of entirely new meaning systems and, in effect, irreversible change in cultures? This question is about the observational distance to the object. While individual memes as remixes rarely update culture's meaning-making reservoir substantially, their small variations (as 'incremental innovations') may accumulate in cultures producing entire cultural subdomains, facilitating further intertextual dynamics and the generation of yet more new layers of textual material. While consisting of small changes, in aggregate they facilitate the emergence of new complex systems and as such irreversible change in the semiosphere. Not surprisingly, there are memes out there to illustrate this phenomenon (see Figure 9.2).

In fact, widespread *literacy* in the 'memetic context' of digital culture now has legal force. An oil refinery worker was sacked by BP Western Australia for using the much-parodied bunker scene from Oliver Hirschbiegel's *Downfall* (2004, with Bruno Ganz as Hitler) to satirize his employer. He was reinstated on appeal to the Fair Work Commission, which found that:

Me trying to explain the complexities of memes to someone who doesn't affiliate themselves with such culture:

FIGURE 9.1 *Memes as reflexive autocommunication (delight in repetition).*[6]

when you laugh at a dumb meme and ur partner, who is not an internet person, asks what's funny but it's like a tier 3 meme and you gotta explain about 7 years of internet for them to understand the nuances

FIGURE 9.2 *Memes as irreversible innovation (delight in newness).* Photo Peter Griffin (public domain).

---

[6]Still from *Supernova* (Tallinnfilm, 1965). © Estonian Film Institute/Estonian Film Archives. Used with permission.

That the clip has been used thousands of times over a period of more than a decade ... has had the result of culturally dissociating it from the import of the historical events portrayed in the film. After this period, any interest which remains in the clip will usually reside in the degree of inventiveness involved in successfully adapting the scene to fit some new situation. Anyone with knowledge of the meme could not seriously consider that the use of the clip was to make some point involving Hitler or Nazis.[7]

It needs to be emphasized from the perspective of cultural semiotics that such combinations of different modalities, cultural conventions or textual materials, derived from different contexts or historical periods, are anything but new. In principle, the strategies of remix, mash-up, collage, mimicry and so on are not characteristic of the digital age, nor of postmodernism, nor even traceable merely to the succession of Ancient Greece by Ancient Rome and antique sculptures and frescoes by Renaissance paintings (e.g. Botticelli's treatment of Venus), or indeed the long career of the artistic nude within that tradition, which is itself an extended remix or mash-up of the 'same' idea from the Venus of Willendorf to Lucien Freud and, despite its modern colonial history, by no means restricted to Western art (Nelson, 2010). Remixing is a characteristic of culture in general, from the creative uses of found objects that Claude Lévi-Strauss called 'bricolage' to the creative mixing of found 'intellectual dimensions' (accounting, modelling, storytelling, speculating) to achieve what Yves Citton (2012) calls a 'cheerful mix of theory and bricolage' that he dubs 'theoricolage' – an *in*disciplinary (not inter-) bonding of incommensurable interpretive strategies that take the place of a dethroned and 'unsustainable pretention to truth and authority', recognising that art, science and premodern thinking all share the work of making sense and making new.

The domination of certain heritage aesthetics in cultural creation fluctuates periodically, but it is clear that any creation of new always includes repetition of the old, or re-reading old texts and their fragments by applying new codes in the situation where the previous codes have become missing or have lost their relevance. Oftentimes what is in fact the creation of new codes is subjectively understood as the reconstruction or recollection of previous ones (Lotman, 2005: 215; see also McLuhan's notion of 'rearviewmirrorism', discussed above, Chapter 5). Instances of this can be seen in the framing of selfie or vlogging phenomena as logical successors to oil-painted self-portraits and handwritten diaries from centuries ago and so on. These Lotman's

---

[7]For the Fair Work decision, see: https://www.theguardian.com/australia-news/2020/feb/28/downfall-bp-worker-sacked-over-hitler-parody-wins-his-job-back#maincontent. For *Downfall*, see: https://www.theguardian.com/film/filmblog/2013/may/16/downfall-final-days-adolf-hitler#maincontent. For the *Downfall* parody meme, see: Voigts (2017).

insights – applying new era-specific codes in order to recycle, reinterpret and accommodate certain cultural forms – explain more thoroughly the phenomenon that media archaeologist Erkki Huhtamo (1995) has called the circular re-emergence of rhetorical *topoi* throughout different eras.

# Selfie?

Areas of enhanced creativity of the semiosphere lie close to the cultural periphery or border zones. These are the less-described and incomplete areas that may be represented by only some fragments of a language or separate texts, which might start acting as 'a catalyst in the whole mechanism of the semiosphere' (2005: 214). A perfect instance of this is the journey of the word and practice of 'selfie' (Senft and Baym, 2015), from its first written documentation in an Australian online forum,[8] to a state of ubiquity that motivated – among billions – Toomas Hendrik Ilves, president of Estonia, to take one as a culmination of his speech at the traditional Song Celebration Festival, the most famous regular public event of that nation and, despite the size of the Estonian population, one of the largest amateur choral singing events in the world (see Figure 9.3).

The case of videoblogging follows a very similar road, from individual peripheral instances (a site of 'mundane expression, cultural innovation and social hope') to an aesthetics manifest in the content and form of mainstream media and cultural production (Bjørkmann Berry, 2015, 2018). The functioning and occasional creative impact of such online communities as Dr. Karl's Self Service Science internet forum in Australia refers to the multiplication of peripheral areas, and consequently also of cores of textual production, characteristic of the digital semiosphere.

These examples confirm that the *source* of creativity is located in group-forming culture instead of being the property, intellectual or otherwise, of an individual creator (cf. Legg, 2013 on a similar idea in C.S. Peirce, in the context of developing the Semantic Web). The text in culture emerges from a dialogue of in-textual and extra-textual levels (Torop, 2017). The latter can be regarded as context of reception, which is subject to constant change. The extra-textual context determines which are the most important elements within the text, framing its overall meaning, and also the intertextual networks in which the text can be actualized. The elements that a contemporary viewer notices on Botticelli's *Birth of Venus* and the other texts he or she relates it with are decisively different from the ones that were available to a

---

[8]See this good account by recovering lexicographer Ben Zimmer: https://slate.com/human-interest/2013/11/selfie-etymology-an-australian-man-takes-a-photo-of-his-lip-after-falling-down-drunk-but-he-didn-t-coin-the-word.html.

FIGURE 9.3 *Estonian president Toomas Hendrik Ilves and his singalong selfie* *Photo of the president* by *Erik Prozes* © *Postimees Grupp. Selfie by the President* © *Toomas Hendrik Ilves. Used with permission.*

fifteenth-century viewer. Hence, it is an impossibility of semiosis for a text to be sequestered from its context; it can have no meaning; and because the context changes meaning is dynamic. The appropriation of texts as the property of just one individual is a legal fiction, not a cultural fact.

# Dialogue

Consequently, Juri Lotman conceptualized the reader's activity as Bakhtinian dialogue *with* a text instead of decoding or deciphering *of* it (Lotman, 1988: 58). This represents reading as well as writing as a creative practice. In the process of reading a text 'non-comprehension ... reveals itself to be just as valuable a meaning-making mechanism as comprehension' (2009: 6). Lotman's paradoxical claim is explained by his model of dialogue, which can be graphically depicted as a Venn diagram (Figure 9.4), where the circles represent the respective lingual spaces of the dialogue partners.

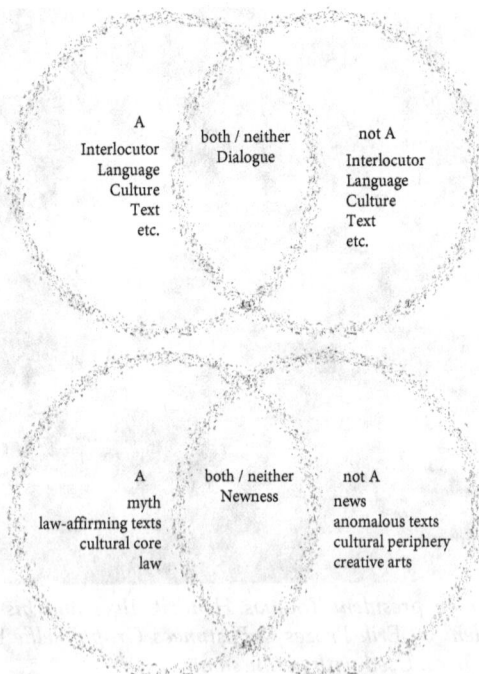

FIGURE 9.4 *Dialogue in the semiosphere, structured in difference (see Leach, 1976): (a) general model; (b) interacting dialogic systems, where each type consists in being what its opposite is not, a 'Saussurian' binary that cannot occur in practice, because dialogue overlaps, producing new semiosis.*

If the 'circles' do not intersect at all, communication would be impossible as there would be no means for establishing or holding it. In the reverse case, if the spaces completely overlap, communication would be trivial and rigid as the communication partners would have nothing new to say. Therefore, the process of communication incorporates a tension between 'the struggle to facilitate understanding, which will always attempt to extend the area of the intersection [overlap, in the diagram], and the struggle to amplify the value of the communication, which is linked to the tendency of maximally amplifying the difference between [dialogue partners]' (Lotman, 2009: 5). The tendency to amplify difference means that dialogic acts between systems are irregular and in tension. Systems autocommunicate internally to maintain and amplify that difference. For instance, this can be observed when a subcultural community around an emergent electronic music avoids contact with the music industry and the press as well as with other genres, in order to keep their alternative approach. But at the same time, the very 'difference' is itself a form of dialogue with the mainstream interlocutor from which the emergent community seeks to set itself apart.

This is also related to how texts are read. As codes organize texts into hierarchical layers, unmarked and peripheral elements for one code might turn into dominants from the viewpoint of another. This is well demonstrated by the reframing of US Confederate monuments, and the US Declaration of Independence, as 'hate speech',[9] or feminist readings of fairy tales, in which motives that once appeared almost transparent can attract criticism later (Haase, 2000). In these examples, the readership community seeks to separate itself completely from a given class of text, altering that category's meaning for all.

There are cases where maximum similarity, where the interlocutors seem to be unified into one, is considered desirable – notably the law, where the creation of new information (in the zone of both/neither ambiguity) is undesirable. In situations of creative communication, however, it is vice versa: difference and non-[exact]-understanding become valuable. Indeed, there is an element of core/periphery structuration in this formal distinction between law and creativity, where what Lotman calls 'law affirming' texts (1990: 151–3) are distinguished from 'anomalous' ones, as myth is distinguished from – but related to – news (Hartley, 2008: 88) (see Figure 9.4 (b)).

---

[9]Monuments, see: https://www.curbed.com/2017/8/15/16150826/charlottesville-confederate-monuments-historic-preservation. Declaration: When a local US newspaper posted sections of the Declaration on their Facebook page in 2018, Facebook's monitor-bots removed it, because it contains the words 'merciless Indian Savages', which constitute hate speech and violate FB's Community Standards. Facebook later restored the post: https://www.theregister.co.uk/2018/07/05/us_declaration_of_independence_labeled_hate_speech_by_facebook_bots/.

The unfolding dialogic process presumes willingness to hold dialogue and to participate in a dialogic situation. But this is exactly what some have claimed to be missing in internet forums (Colleoni et al., 2014; Georgakopoulou, 2014; Bouvier, 2015), where discussion threads often disintegrate as they are treated by some users as boards for expressing already-existing views, with no sign of receptivity towards alternative ones, or willingness to translate ideas between different lingual spaces. A likewise common practice is conscious destabilization of discussions using irony and ambiguity as tools (see Phillips and Milner, 2017). This refusal of dialogue has given rise to the idea of 'echo chambers' or 'filter bubbles' that replace communication online, although their existence has been challenged by Axel Bruns (2019), who concludes, 'these concepts are very suggestive metaphors, but ultimately they're myths'.

The dialogic model can also be applied to reader's communication with the text, shifting the understanding of the text as a finished product, to be (linearly) used up by the consumer, towards a concept of the text as a partner in the continuous process of dialogue. The text acquires traits of an *intellect* and its social-communicative function becomes more complex. It begins to 'act' like the agent of an untranslatable language:

Lotman (1988) enumerates five different aspects of this function:

1. Communication between sender and receiver in which the text serves as a carrier of *information* transferred between the dialogue partners;

2. Communication between audience and cultural tradition in which the text serves the function of *cultural memory* that is capable of accumulating information and periodically actuates certain meaningful layers and de-actuates others. Examples of this can be derived from the prolonged life of many canonical texts in culture, like the way the text of *Hamlet* has been invested with both existential and social-revolutionary ideas. The music video by the Carters (Beyoncé and Jay Z) for *Apeshit* anchors Da Vinci's 'Mona Lisa' (previously representing ideas of feminine mystique, the epitome of high or bourgeois art, etc.) in a critique of white dominance.

3. The reader's *autocommunication* (dialogue with oneself, in the process of self-description), in which the text helps to restructure the reader's personality. Clear examples here include the proliferating self-help texts and platforms that curate texts into collections of inspiration (#tripspiration, #thinspiration, #archspiration, #mindspiration, etc.). Yet, in principle, any text can be read in this way, to actuate certain aspects of the reader. Product placement marketing strategy makes a lot of use of it.

4. Communication between reader and the text in which the text offers the reader the kind of information that the reader is prepared to receive. Transmedia storytelling projects often manifest this aspect, by delivering 'hidden messages' and initially concealed narrative layers to dedicated fans, while the general audience is also able to follow a coherent story without drilling into these hidden layers.

5. Communication between the *text and cultural context* in which the text is itself either source or receiver of information. Comparative examples of such contextual dynamics can be provided by looking at the practice of adapting Western media programmes to some Asian media markets, where several factors related to the content, production and audience's cultural capital can create lacunae of understanding and appreciation and impose barriers to the program's cross-cultural success (Rohn, 2011). Another example stems from the attempts to translate a story successful in, say, film to video games, which fail to account for the *ethos, mythos* and/ or *topos* of the original story, as was the case with *The Lord of the Rings: The Fellowship of the Ring* game (Klastrup and Tosca, 2004).

All five of these aspects can be manifest in a single text. Which one dominates depends on the reading strategy adopted by the reader. In his foreword to *Culture and Explosion*, Torop, (2009: xxxv) frames Lotman's five socio-communicative processes, and his understanding of reading as communication instead of decoding, as a crucial '*semiospherical turn*' in his work, developed before the concept itself emerged later on. It allows for the explication both of the holistic and bordered dimension of the text – including a whole culture as a text – and of culture's internal heterogeneity, realized in continuous dialogues among its subsystems.

Current digital archives and databases contribute to the eclipse of a linear understanding of reading as mere decoding or deciphering – although this model persists most strongly in instrumental discourses, in industry, economics, policy and so on. Instead, *linking texts*, by means of selected characteristics (often realized by algorithms that follow usage metadata instead of inherent traits of the texts themselves) and *exploratory browsing*, appear as the key reading practices. This means that texts appear much less firmly contextualized in their era or in other works of the author, the artistic wave, a previous collection or even their medium and so on. Instead, the reader creates new open-ended wholes of recontextualized parts, on the basis of their own interests. For instance, one and the same allegorical artwork can properly be included in a set of seventeenth-century Dutch paintings and in a multimedia collection of pretty ladies and cute pets on Pinterest. Such practices have also given ground for the concept of *participatory culture* (Jenkins, 2006b, Jenkins et al., 2013; Burgess and Green, 2018, etc.), observing the ways that textual creation, publication and reflection that were previously firmly located in the professional sphere of expertise are now open to anyone via platforms like SoundCloud, WordPress and Vimeo.

The aspect of reflection is especially noteworthy for its crucial role in explicating the dynamic character of text, for which many traditional conceptualizations do not leave room. So, a text's creativity does not end with the author, who inserts (as it were) meaning into the text. Instead, it is dependent on realization in the creative process of reading that in the online digital sphere often converges with further writing and curating (remixing, recontextualizing, annotating/tagging, recommending and sharing, not to mention commenting that could range from an emoji or even a mere timecode for a video or audio track to mark a funny/surprising/pleasure evoking instant to full analyses on personal blogs, etc.). The digital semiosphere possess a '"reflexive" architecture' (Papacharissi, 2009: 244), which significantly increases the malleability of the text.

# Artificial intelligence

The translational logic that underlies creativity is relevant also in the context of artificial intelligence, the development of which was of interest to Lotman. His basic premise in this matter was that 'an essential condition of any intellectual structure is its internal heterogeneity' (Lotman, 1978: 6). So, the structure of artificial intelligence needs to include mutually untranslatable semiotic formations, one based on the linear-discrete principle and another on the continual-homomorphic principle. Without such diversity, 'the apparatus would be without internal dynamics and capable only of information transmission, but not of creation' (1978: 8). Lotman characterizes a *thinking* object as necessarily characterized by partial and selective knowledge, which concurrently implies a certain semiotic freedom to establish new equivalences between the object domain and the meta-language. Therefore, the growth of knowledge causes a *growth of unawareness* instead of diminishing it. This perceived lack of knowledge ('known unknowns') can be compensated by the stereoscopic or triangulation approach – the possibility of acquiring different and new projections of one and the same reality and its translation into different but integrated codes/meta-languages (1978: 16). Based on this, Lotman relates artificial intelligence to poetic text (1981: 17) upon its entering into a circle of communication, where it is capable of creating new meanings depending on the codes put to use. Semiosis precludes isolation and is fundamentally dialogic: 'To function, a consciousness requires another consciousness – the text within the text, the culture within the culture' (1994: 378).

As we noted earlier, a word-for-word translation of the original Russian title of Lotman's work *Universe of the Mind* would be *Inside Thinking*

*Worlds*. In the first part of the book, 'Text as a Meaning-generating Mechanism', Lotman stresses the centrality of making a choice between the elements of interpreting language while establishing a conditional, previously indeterminate equivalency between the elements of source and target languages (1990: 14). So, *intelligence* – which is 'always an interlocutor' – is contained in the act of selection at certain bifurcation points.

However, what is important is that selection is exercised as a purposeful and goal-directed decision in the given context, to move in one rather than in another direction. The result is not governed by randomness but by a freedom of choice *within* a certain artistic concept or another system that appears integrated from the internal viewpoint, and that is also what distinguishes a *thinking dialogue partner* from an *automatic unconscious mechanism*. In other words, a structure that has risen to the level of intelligence 'transforms randomness to freedom' (2000 [1989]: 645). The result of the impossibility of a singular scenario is the potential existence of many different but in principle equally correct translations as the output of the mechanism's operation. Then, in the case of self-equilibrating systems, a mechanism of correction, likewise based on selection, starts up to determine the most relevant results in relation to the hierarchy of codes within the system (1981: 10). This hierarchy changes over time as well, and that is why the predictability of culture remains very low (culture can be analysed in terms of probabilities not predictability). The semiospheric logic that a heterogeneous whole *precedes* its individual subparts, which acquire meaning and function only contextually, is characteristic of living systems and the opposite of the mechanical logic of discrete succession (as exemplified by the logic of image recognition algorithms, etc.).

Broadly, all this means that for Lotman only an autonomous and self-aware consciousness, deeply immersed in culture, can be 'creative' in the strict sense – striving purposefully to create new meanings. This means that as long as an autonomous machine has not passed both the Turing Test and The Lovelace Test, there does not seem to be a ground for arguing that AI agents would be able to affect dynamics and heterogeneity in the semiosphere.

Or could they? Marcus du Sautoy argues in *The Creativity Code* (2019) that there are three types of creativity. Machines can be programmed to achieve all of them.

– First, a type that he borrowed from Margaret Boden (1990, 2016), is the *exploratory creativity* that involves experimentations within the boundaries of a certain genre, using all its inherent structural opportunities until possible extremes.

– Second is *combinatorial creativity* – the logics of different genres or other modes of expression combined in a new way. This appears

> to be closest to Lotman's understanding of dialogue as the core mechanism of creativity, and it links semiospheric creativity with the 'combinatorial evolution' of technology described by W. Brian Arthur (2009).
> – Third is what Boden defines as *transformational creativity* – resulting in entirely unexpected phenomena such as Picasso's cubism or James Joyce's modernist literature.

The emergence of *transformational* forms may appear as entirely unexpected, bending existing rules and presuming significant 'out-of-the-box thinking' (du Sautoy 2019). Yet, using the case of how computer program 'AlphaGo' (made by Google DeepMind) beat Lee Sedol, eighteen-time international title winner of Go, the Chinese strategy board game in 2016, du Sautoy demonstrates in detail how a machine was taught to be strategically irrational, designed to break the rules and was, as such, perceived to be 'creative'. Du Sautoy shows similarly how *exploratory creativity* as well as *combinatorial creativity* could be programmed, yet in a limited way – for instance, making neural networks integrate two pre-defined genres or modes of expression. This leads him to conclude, as we have argued based on Lotman, that as long as there is no free will in the agent, it will not be able to pass the Lovelace Test – a machine creating something truly novel and valuable, which it was not originally designed to make. The difficulties that machine learning algorithms continue to have with artistic texts are their inability to interpret and place those texts.

It is well known that in our digital lives the choices we make and our phatic online communications are readily traceable and countable – our data are mined, systematized and as consumers we all get profiled (see Miller, 2008). We are functional tools in the hands of online marketers. Yet, the ungraspable complexity of poetic texts for AI is also apparent – for instance in the generally poor recommendations by Netflix or YouTube for content you can watch, based on our previous choices, or the social-media presentation of ads for goods we've just bought. Artistic texts are the 'dark matter' of datafied societies as existing metadata schemas cannot really catch their positions in the semiosphere and, therefore, most attempts to systematize them appear as flawed or irrelevant. As Wendy Chun has put it, 'the problem is not access [to content databases] but rather larger epistemological frameworks', as access does not equal understanding and AI alone is incapable of 'turning an *information* explosion into a *knowledge* explosion' (2008: 159, italics original).

Nevertheless, du Sautoy (2019) does demonstrate how the various AI-based tools can enhance human creativity. For instance, the Continuator app analyses the music that a jazz musician plays, learns the patterns and then plays that music for the musician – providing tips on how to vary his or her style.[10] There

---

[10]https://www.francoispachet.fr/continuator/

are similar projects emerging in relation to other art forms. However, while such affordances create new opportunities for expression, they also frame and limit or channel creative work in specific ways (see Lesage, 2016, 2017).

From the perspective of the semiosphere theory, we should recognize an important difference between understanding the creativity of autonomous agents and the unpredictable effects of accumulating incremental changes. In the case of AI, cascading selections by semi-autonomous algorithms may be purpose-built, but with purposes that may be rather different from each other. As they react to each other's selections, the end result may be unpredictable and unexpected and, as such, can be understood as creative. We might think here of different image-recognition algorithms in different databases, being designed to identify different elements in photos. Other algorithms, with different purposes, may link those elements and texts across databases and recommend their constellations to human users, who have been identified by yet another algorithm, based on their chosen interests. With the emergence of the Semantic Web and increasingly interlinked cultural databases, we will see more of such cascading selections by autonomously operating single-purpose algorithms. They operate in relation to humans, their designs and actions, but the cascade of their selections may lead to unintended and unpredictable changes in the semiosphere.

# Explosion

*Explosion* is another central concept in Lotman's treatment of creativity that could be used to explain the *transformative* type of creativity. The occurrence of an explosion is caused by the collision of mutually untranslatable codes/languages within one text or semiosphere. The new language that has entered into the semiosphere's organized sphere from the disorganized outside is initially received in the form of a continuous and unified (sub)text. But it is perceived as highly useful for meaning-making, is copied and imitated, discussed and modified – with its mutations, it diffuses across the semiosphere explosively, changing it for good. After developing a suitable meta-language (similar to the mechanism of correction) that initial whole can be seen to comprise different discrete parts (2009: 133–7). This is the second phase of explosion. As a result of the collision of two different languages, a third, new and unpredictable structure might appear. For example, it transpires that AI has changed human chess-playing in the period since grandmaster Garry Kasparov first lost to IBM's Deep Blue in 1997: defensive strategies have been seen in a better light than they used to be (because a computer is not emotionally affected by being in a weak position); and the way training process now benefits from a computer's capability of explicating every single mistake made in a game (see Kasparov, 2017; Follett, 2019). The same may be expected of the aftermath of AlphaGo's victory in 2016, discussed earlier:

> AlphaGo is already starting to teach humans new ways to play their own game, even starting with a human education. What if it were entirely self-taught? What kinds of alien game play would emerge? Would it take humans a long time to adapt to this new style of play to be able to win again? How much of the technique honed by humans over a millennium is really optimal, and how much will have to be reconsidered in the wake of this new, growing intelligence?[11]

In sum, the moment of explosion is a moment of *unpredictability*. It implies 'a collection of equally probable possibilities', which appear as 'indistinguishable synonyms' (2009: 123) within a given text, each potentially meaningful and correct. For a textual example, *Hamlet* has been interpreted as a political figure in the context of protest against the Soviet regime (Grigori Kozintsev's *Hamlet*, 1964), and as a modern day high-school girl's love object in the framework of contemporary young adult fiction (Michelle Ray's *Falling for Hamlet*, 2011) (among myriad others). Such a collection can be huge, but not unlimited: 'Pragmatic links can materialise in peripheral or automatic structures but cannot introduce into a text codes that are principally absent from it' (Lotman, 1994: 378). A story featuring a Hamlet character who is at all times decisive and confident, or even merely in favour of the current regime, would fail to form a poetically logical whole. Out of all the possible alternatives for new language or cultural form, however, only one will achieve dominance at any given time, while the others become dispersed in the semantic space. After this, the second phase follows, where a meta-language for describing and explaining the change in the system is developed. This is 'the moment in which the explosion is exhausted' (2009: 15), the chosen form appears as inevitable and the only possible choice, while others acquire semantic difference.

A further key feature of cultural explosion, besides unpredictability, is its being based on *memory*. This is because:

> Semiosis always requires a previous semiosis which produced the translator. Since the translator already recognizes, i.e. matches with something, the form of which has been stored, i.e. which has previously been matched, it follows that the current translation process is preceded

---

[11]Michael Dougherty, writing in *Medium* (2016): https://medium.com/@maackle/learning-from-alphago-artificial-wisdom-77ac14f12844.

by some previous translation process. Also, the text used for translation is the product of a previous semiosis.

(Kull, 1998b: 302)

The logic here is that explosions are usually followed by self-descriptions, which fix the positions and meaningful links among the most important texts. At the same time, the texts are in active use, not as wholes but via fragments that recollect the whole, while different fragments set different dominance for recollections. Hence, the *creativity* of memory, a function to which we now turn.

# 10

# Text, preservation, memory

*Nothing seems so adequate as to think of steampunk as a cultural*
*text: computers emitting smoke, flying steam trains ... Lotman*
*adds that artistic texts expand the space of unpredictability. And, if*
*memory is the genesis, when creating an explosive text, it produces*
*the future: unknown, expected in dreams and in the imagination –*
*unpredictable ...*
*Inventive memory ... is visionary and made of bricolage, either*
*through narrative actions or the use of second-hand, obsolete,*
*recycled material – and even changed on purpose to look old.*
Steampunk productions are also memories of the future.

(MÔNICA REBECCA FERRARI NUNES, 2019)

\* \* \*

As any new text is located within a semiosphere, which itself is the result
of previous semiosis, it acquires memory in the cultural process, that is, a
capacity to condense information on its complex intertextual contexts in a
compressed form (Lotman, 1988). It is impossible to study a text in isolation
from previous meanings stored in it or to study culture in isolation from
its history. This is to condition the past, not to destroy it so that it passes
into extinction, as is often feared on the emergence of new technology, but
to subject the past to the mechanisms of choice and complex re-coding.
Memory is preserved to re-emerge under certain conditions (Lotman, 2000
[1986]: 615). Culture and memory are functionally uniform – Lotman and
Uspenskij (1978: 213) define culture itself as 'the nonhereditary memory of
the community'.

In practice, new texts are created by means of selected memory-bearing symbols and vocabulary, the meanings of which will be re-actualized in new contexts. The selection of the most relevant textual layers inevitably leads to forgetting or de-actualizing others. Therefore, texts are vehicles not only of preservation but also of forgetting. At the same time, recontextualizing and remediating a text also functions as a mnemonic device or memory aid, as it may help to reveal aspects that seemed forgotten in another context. From this perspective, the technological capability for perfect copying of digital texts, which creates a vision of complete memory because nothing is lost in the transmission process, is unachievable at the level of culture and in the textual practice of meaning-making. Meaning is not reducible to an automatic process but results from a dialogue with/by the text. Memory of meanings is not automatically stored together with the copies of texts stored in archives. Cultural memory is never complete. What digital collections offer, rather, is a potential for more active actualization of chosen meaningful layers, compressed within the texts (together with other layers that will remain hidden for possible later actualizations). Preservation is as much a 'search' function, in which memory is made, as it is a curation or conservation one (Reading, 2011).

Taking the digital *Mona Lisa* as an example, the website *megamonalisa. com* is an open gallery of remixes of the painting, from parodic to porno. The opening page features fifty of the most popular images, displaying re-codings of the appearance of the original model into different codifying systems: optical illusion; cultural icons from previous epochs; distinct artistic style (e.g. of Picasso); actual artworks (statue of Manneken Pis); stars of entertainment, both fictional (e.g. Darth Vader) and factual (e.g. Amy Winehouse); as a symbol of femininity (juxtaposition with images of naked or half-naked women); playing with the composition, conventions of paintings, clothing, hairstyle, her ordinariness; her status as the most famous/expensive/elitist painting; cultural symbols such 'Mona selfie'.

The translational nature of these simple examples underlines the mechanism of *variation* as the core of *preservation* in cultural memory. In other words:

> texts form compressed mnemonic programs..., gravitate towards symbolisation and transform into cohesive symbols. These symbols attain a high degree of independence from their own cultural contexts and function not only on the synchronic level of culture but also in its diachronic dimensions.
>
> (Lotman, 2012: 13)

The compressed repository of meanings contained within the text is realized upon contact with other texts and new contexts that trigger for readers new complex correlations with the current synchronic level. Intersemiotic translations are also culture's way of creating understanding, because the translation of old texts into the languages of new culture is concurrently a search for descriptive languages and models for explaining these texts and understanding oneself. Translation of verbal texts into audiovisual ones or visual texts into virtual-reality ones are simultaneously part of culture's *autocommunicative* self-description.

# Database narratives

The mnemonic function of texts has certain peculiarities in the era of access to digitized heritage. Recontextualizing texts from the past into one's own synchrony is easy, and that may promote the practice of 'de-symbolising reading' (Lotman, 1990: 105), which 'turns symbols into simple messages'. At a time of digitized texts and proliferating metadata fields, formerly established contexts may be eroded. Texts can be anchored in new, ahistorical collections by means of occasional keywords pertaining either to the content (e.g. bird), expression level (e.g. aerial shot), technical qualities (e.g. 4K resolution) or administrative aspects (e.g. copyright ownership). Today it is common to encounter a visual image, on one's wall, on a T-shirt or on Pinterest, without anchorage to its origins, in contrast to times when art was 'read' in museums, books, courseware and other institutional formats. While some see such unanchored traditions as accelerating postmodernism, eroding the last remaining connections between the *representation* and the *real* (Baron, 2014: 143), the cultural semiotic view suggests that culture as a self-stabilizing mechanism. It balances huge variation in cultural languages, subsystems, forms and media with a diachronically stable set of symbols that resist disintegration. De-symbolizing the reading of symbols in a given time-space does not render them extinct. In any case:

> The semantic potentials of the symbol are always greater than any realization of them: the links which, with the help of its expression, a symbol establishes with a particular semiotic context, never exhausts all its semantic valency. This is the semantic reserve thanks to which a symbol can enter into unexpected relationships, altering its essence and deforming its textual context in unpredictable ways.
>
> (Lotman, 1990: 104)

This cultural logic, combined with the technological affordances of online databases, has among other things brought about an eclipse of previously dominant narratives. The linear (verbal/print-based/diachronic) logic of, say, mediating the past or conceptualizing cultural evolution is balanced by a diagrammatic (visual/iconic/synchronic) one. Both of these logics are present in any culture, and the dominance of one is a question of asymmetry rather than replacement, as Manovich (2001: 225) suggests with the growing visibility of 'database' as a format of cultural expression, alongside narrative. A good example of this tendency is manifest in Andre Silva's (2005) video *spam letter + google image search = video entertainment*. The work combines a generic 'Nigerian' spam letter with the first result of Google Image search for each word in the letter. The letter is read out loud by a computer voice-generator over a corresponding image on the screen. Choosing a single word as the unit of intersemiotic translation into an image deprives the written/spoken sequence of its meaning. The narrative of the letter has been side-lined, and there appears no difference to where the video starts or ends. This experiment confirms the way that content in digital archives rejects the linear sequencing of natural language and makes sense rather as an incomplete paradigm with blurry boundaries. In place of a single overarching narrative, a number of individual narratives – possibly incompatible and contradictory – can emerge from it. A related concept is that of 'database narratives', proposed by Marsha Kinder, who explains that 'database and narrative [are] not alternative ways of organizing images but rather two sides of the same process' (Kinder, 2003: 22). By exposing 'the dual processes of selection and combination that lie at the heart of all stories and that are crucial to language', database narratives reveal the ideological bias or 'arbitrariness of the particular choices made and the possibility of making other combinations, which would create alternative stories' (Kinder, 2002: 127).

Such variance clearly calls into question any idea of culture's memory (including its institutions, media and texts) as a stable container or storehouse. Instead, memory is understood as a mechanism of variation. Memory entails not only preservation of information but also its simultaneous generation. One of the merits of such a reconceptualization is a more inclusive approach to remembrance, as digital platforms allow for the publication of histories that include untold stories of hitherto un(der) represented agents such as *Everyman* (Hoskins, 2001; van Dijck, 2007), animals (Kean and Howell, 2018), children (Cunningham, 2005) not to mention women (Morgan, 2006). Memory is one of the mainsprings of the digital storytelling movement (Garde-Hansen et al., 2009; Hartley, 2015b).

# Digital storytelling

*Digital storytelling* (Lundby, 2008; Hartley and McWilliam, 2009; Lambert, 2013, and see https://www.storycenter.org/) makes it possible to imagine a radically decentralized mode of memory-work: 'one different story told *by* each person' (online, with the help of facilitated workshops and community organizations), as opposed to 'the same story told *to* every person' (via popular media). Digital storytelling and participatory online archives, where these popular nonanonymous memories are shared, make the selective actualization of cultural layers especially apparent. Aspects of the past that were considered unimportant or accidental, scattered around the semiospheric boundary, are semiotized and (re)attributed meaningfulness.

It is open to discussion to what extent these personal accounts are in fact (unwittingly) reproducing already institutionalized ways of mediating the past and are not as radically and democratically innovative as might seem at first sight (Thumim, 2012). This raises the politics of *authenticity* between the creative and reproductive aspects, but the cultural-semiotic concept of *text-code* was proposed by Lotman instead. Text-code balances, on the one hand, control the environment for digital storytelling that supports the remediation of previously established formats of mediation, with, on the other, the agency of the user. Text-code functions as an intermediate link between language and text. It is a syntagmatically organized code of organization of the particular type of text. From the viewpoint of textual transmission, text-code 'serves an interpretive and prescriptive' role (Lotman, 1994: 377), while it is also realized via the generation of textual variants on the lower hierarchical levels of the system. Simple examples include reenactment videos of movie scenes shared on YouTube or TikTok, and the avalanche of photos posted on social media, which more or less consciously mimic the posts of social media celebrities and influencers – who in turn might be reproducing the text-codes generated by marketing companies. Text-code is also an organizer of memory, able to streamline contradictions, and it establishes the limits of a text's possible variation (1994: 378). One's own narratives are formulated on the model of previously institutionalized ones (see Jane and Fleming, 2014; Madisson, 2014). Lotman characterizes these as the audience's co-creativity or participation in textual generation (Lotman and Mints, 1981), which is typically realized via text-codes drawn from cultural memory.

Relatedly, variation in memory appears to be a general way that chosen texts are preserved in culture. The actualization of texts 'takes place within the framework of a certain invariant allowing us to say that despite the variance of interpretations, the text preserves identity with itself in the context of a new era' (Lotman, 2000 [1985]: 673). Changes in interpretation and diversity in re-actualization do not amount to complete exchange or substitution but include *repetition* of a 'certain invariant' that renders a new text recognisable as the equivalent of old text.

The preservation of variation in culture is to a large extent caused by the irregularity of the semiosphere's layers and the fact that 'the hierarchy of the languages and texts, as a rule, is disturbed' (Lotman, 2005: 213). For instance, while once a city's or region's literary scene was coordinated and codified by literary magazines, much of this activity is now overtaken by specialized portals like Goodreads or social media platforms as the new dominant layer. They do this, however, based on their own rules of organization and affordances. Even more so, as the main social media platforms are designed to favour video content, the mode of short explanatory videos and trailers are increasingly used to meta-communicate about literature among other forms of culture.

# Mental text

As a result, the elements of the semiosphere collide and texts 'appear to be immersed in languages which do not correspond to them, and codes for deciphering them may be completely absent' (Lotman, 2005: 213). Effectively, new codes are developed for investing them with meaningfulness lost in line with evanescence of the previous codes. Estonia, where two of us come from, has been a borderland between Eastern and Western Europe for centuries and has periodically seen turbulent times. As such it is a wellspring of examples for such 'recollections'. Immediately preceding and following the liberation from the Soviet Union (1988–91), there were many attempts to establish continuities with local cultural roots. One of its manifestations was *maausk*, the literal translation of which would be 'the faith of the land' – presented as the ancient religion that was practiced before the arrival of Christianity in the thirteenth century While people practicing *maausk* firmly support the authenticity of their belief, it is easily describable as what Raymond Williams (1961) called the 'culture of the selective tradition': in this case drawn from previous religious movements and ideas, folklore archives and – crucially – modern nationalist discourse (Västrik, 2015). In principle, the mechanism behind this upsurge is similar to the way that yoga has been translated into Western lifestyle, fitness and commodity industries, while still being surrounded with an aura of an ancient tradition. In some cases, the codes are directly adapted from an existing system to compensate for a lack of them in the repertoire of an older one, as has been the case with literary trailers. Culture's continuity consists in a gleaming of its previous epochs through the overlay of contemporary texts and languages. The less complex a unit, for example a symbol, the more adaptable it is to new contexts.

When a text is simultaneously interpreted by the codes of different systems in culture, for example a narrative is adapted into different media, various versions are memorized as a certain mnemonic collection, which is describable as a *mental text* (Torop, 2004: 327). Later versions of that text will influence the memorization of earlier ones, because although the 'mental text' possesses the characteristics of boundedness and structure, it is built in accordance with the current hierarchy of sign-systems in the semiosphere. In our collective memory of a well-documented historical period like the Second World War, visual versions influence the memorization of verbal or aural ones – we 'recall' the look more than the sound (for a corrective history of 'noise' in this period, see Mansell, 2017), but both may be supplied by much later semiosis (e.g. print sources, documentary films, movies). In such cases linear chronological logic collapses: the 'mental text' of an era belongs to the era that remembers it.

The notion of 'mental text' has been established mainly in folkloristics (Honko, 2000) for describing the storytelling practices of oral communities. Instead of a single physical original, there are multiple performative versions – from historical re-enactment societies (like Sealed Knot) to fantasy cosplay – that make up a mental whole only in the memory of the storyteller and the community participating in the performative narration. From the cultural semiotic perspective and in relation to the semiosphere, Torop has explained the notion of mental text as:

> an abstract whole the structure of which depends on the amount and types of textual transformations [including transformations of text's parts] in a given culture or, more narrowly, in a given cultural situation.
>
> (2004: 327)

# Hypertext

In comparison to the digital environment, the logic of writing – the 'prison of paper, enforcing sequence and rectangularity' (Nelson, 2010: 120) – does not support explication and representation of such wholes (Ong, 2012). The connective restrictions imposed by paper on ideas and creation led Ted Nelson to propose that the benefit of his vision of a global hypertext system – Xanadu – would be 'psychological, not technical' (Nelson, 1965: 98). This is based on observation of the increasing fragmentation of the world of information, while, on a deeper level, fragments of information are still intertwined. Nelson's illuminating ideas have led Barnet to conclude that 'the dream of a universal digital archive and publishing system originated with Nelson' (2013: 75). The hypertext system was based on bidirectional links between bits of texts; that is, authors could 'transclude' fragments of earlier texts that point back at the source text in their own hypertext creations. The links would be tied to the content itself, not to the location of the document, which is the structural logic of the Web that also causes gaps in the form of '404 errors' and thereby appears to cement the feeling of a proliferating mess of data.

# Organizing digital memory; clusters and lists

Attempts to organize the messy myriad of data – that is *digital memory* – are inherent to web usage, as demonstrated by users' individual efforts and by algorithms designed to trace patterns and concurrences initially hidden from the human eye and thereby to cluster fragments of different texts into new wholes. Baron (2014: 154–5) and Torlasco (2013, chapter 2) have proposed that the practice of creating sequences of objects simultaneously similar and different has emerged owing to the need to introduce patterns, to reveal recursivity. YouTube is flooded with compilation videos, while listings have become a format often used by bloggers. Umberto Eco associated lists with times of insecure identities (Eco, 2009), because lists help people to balance infinity and boundedness. Lists are a graspable cut-out of infinity and bring order into what is perceived as chaos and/or as incomprehensibly vast. Listing similarities of objects from different epochs – as selfies are represented in the same row with similar self-portraits by canonical painters on Google Arts – also demonstrates a crucial cultural semiotic notion that culture's *diachrony* is part of its *synchrony*:

> Creative memory is not governed by the formula 'the newest is the most valuable'. It is opposed to time, preserving what once was as what currently is. From the viewpoint of memory as a mechanism that works through its whole depth, the past is not the past.
>
> (Lotman, 2000 [1985]: 674)

Such a panchronic vision of culture is possible due to the mechanism of cultural autocommunication, that is, culture's communication to oneself about oneself. When Roman Jakobson employed a comparable notion of 'intrapersonal communication', he specified too that '[w]hile interpersonal communication bridges space, intrapersonal communication proves to be the chief vehicle for bridging time' (Jakobson, 1985: 98).

## Culture as a autocommunicative text

Lotman proposes that it is possible to perceive human culture as 'one message transmitted by the collective "I" of humanity to itself' (1990: 33); that is, on the most general level, human culture appears not only as a vast collection of most diverse communicative acts but as *one* vast instance of autocommunication. From this perspective, the preservation function of intersemiotic translations of texts into new languages becomes especially clear. The reason why canonical literature cannot remain only literary texts, but become also audiovisual texts, is because culture is constantly looking for ways to describe them as part of its current living culture, to make sense of them in accordance with contemporary meta-languages and modelling systems. The more languages are involved in this process, the stronger is the past's attachment to the synchrony of culture, sometimes exploiting the possibilities of 'hypermediacy' (Bolter and Grusin, 1998), where the act of seeing is itself the story. At the same time, texts cannot in principle exist without meta-texts, because in order properly to receive a text into the semiosphere, culture needs to make sense of it, and the tool for the latter are texts about the text.

Among these texts about texts, self-descriptions produced at the core, but describing the whole of the semiosphere, stand out. Their function is to organize memory and to raise the coherence of the semiosphere, fixing chosen texts as belonging to the canon and firewalling others from it. The regularity modelled by self-descriptions is of course a constructed layer over 'the irregularity of a real semiotic map' (Lotman, 2005: 213) – above the semiosphere that is both synchronically and diachronically amorphous and heterogeneous. Their production is especially active when levels of unpredictability and uncertainty rise, during intensified and frequent contacts with external areas and after cultural explosions. The constitution of a boundary between 'own' and 'other' occupies a central position in cultural self-descriptions, as contacts with the other can ignite both innovation and conflict, depending on the autocommunicative state of the semiosphere, as is evident in increasing nationalistic rhetoric in many countries during times of crisis.

From the viewpoint of memory, possible conflicts may appear *inside* one mnemonic community over the exclusive distinction between a semiosphere's core and periphery. The peripheries preserve texts that have been excluded from the self-descriptions of the core. Texts born within the dynamic periphery appear opposed to the artificial norms of the static core, needing the development of alternative descriptive systems (1990: 134) to signify what's been considered insignificant. This is the situation that online digital tools and participatory projects have helped to mend, multiplying the nuclear structures producing 'legitimate' self-descriptions. At the same time, conflicts are caused via the mechanism of opposition *between* the internal and the external, whereby certain groups are excluded from the mnemonic community altogether, causing the assignment of negative values by the opposite community. The semiospheric boundaries between inside and outside cannot be erased, as the epistemic closure makes signification possible in texts and culture, as well as in organisms as described by the notions of *Umwelt* (Uexküll, 1992; Kull, 2010) and *autopoiesis* (Maturana and Varela, 1980) for all living systems.

From the perspective of identity preservation, it is important to consider the simultaneity of two processes acting as mutual incentives. On the one hand, different areas of the semiosphere are subject to growing *specialization*. On the other hand, *creolization* of their respective languages takes place via contacts among the different areas, in order to permit self-understanding across a semiospheric whole. Creolization of the languages of the semiosphere can be regarded as 'an intermediary stage at reaching a new autonomy or pure (self)description' (Torop, 2009: xxviii cf. Lotman, 1978: 9–11). These processes become evident at times when nation-based and territory-based identities are substituted by more flexible identities, based on mutual interests or affiliations and facilitated by digital communication technology. Cultural coherence among individuals and communities situated in different physical locations is increasing, while coherence between physically proximate communities is decreasing, and these textual tendencies have consequences in political, poetic and popular discourses.

In sum, texts in the semiosphere are the means by which we understand the past and via this also oneself. At the same time, the relation between the textualized object and the text itself is not static but is re-established over and over again within a dynamic space of variation. The limits of this variation also determine the system's capability for cultural evolution and change. The broader the accepted space of variation, the more probably can the text accommodate new and alien contexts and evolve meaningfully. Strict limits, on the other hand, gradually narrow down the mnemonic field, pave the way for destructive conflicts between the own and the alien and can lead to stagnation and abandonment instead of preservation.

# PART FOUR

# Meso-scale: Institution

# 11

# Planetary systems of culture production

*Humanity is in the early stages of the most significant evolution in its history:* learning to think as a species. *This is the linking of human minds, values, information and solutions at lightspeed and in real time around the planet, via the internet and social media.*

(JULIAN CRIBB)[1]

\* \* \*

The theory of semiosphere is a theory of cultural change. In Part III we looked at how the dynamics of change work on the level of texts, which are regularly read for meaning by the majority of the global population – the texts that belong to what we conventionally understand as the domain of media content, of arts and culture. Yet, everyday life includes myriad 'texts' that we may 'produce' and 'consume' in speech, language and conversation, documents and screens, cultural codes and rituals, even more ubiquitously than those of media and the arts. These are the texts that people and organizations create and use to coordinate their actions and to organize themselves, to articulate their differentiating distinctions, their unifying connections and the rationales for highlighting preferred versions of these at different moments in time. Texts of these kinds may include various kinds of laws, regulations, manifestations, marketing messages or forms of advertising, PR-texts, newsletters, emailing lists, messaging boards, chatrooms and so on. Such texts are used to build shared memories and

---

[1]Science writer and policy analyst Julian Cribb, on the RSA (Royal Society of Arts) blog, 2018: https://www.thersa.org/discover/publications-and-articles/rsa-blogs/2018/03/learning-to-think-as-a-species.

to establish new paths, to limit and regulate as well as to enable. They are used to create and organize all kinds of cultural and social groups and communities, including the formations that, in effect, 'produce' the cultural texts that we discussed in previous chapters.

In Part IV, therefore, we take a step to another level of analysis, from 'micro' (single-text) to the *meso* or *mid*-level perspective on semiospheric dynamics. Here we investigate how and why social and cultural *institutions* organize themselves, both regionally and globally, where one of their purposes and functions is to utter 'micro' texts where the enunciator is not a natural person but what's known (in copyright law for instance) as a *persona ficta* – entities such as corporations, government agencies, firms, associations and trade unions (in some jurisdictions). They are treated in law as if they were persons and can enter into contracts, be sued, own property and so on. Culture goes much further than intellectual property law in recognizing group entities as identities, where '*personae ficta*' become often 'imagined communities' (as they are known in media theory, following Benedict Anderson, 2006/1983).

Culture-made groups (demes) scale all the way up from household to neighbourhood to nation, from work-unit (e.g. the *danwei* in China) to corporation to class or industry, from friendship groups (buddies, BFFs) to affinity groups (fans, readerships, audiences) to what are called 'demes' (Hartley and Potts, 2014), which are culture-made 'we'-groups bonded by common language, custom and interaction, bounded by competing or adversarial groups, and often co-extensive with a country (where heterogeneous populations still share a sense of 'wedom'), or with a tongue (e.g. the Anglosphere) or diasporic ethnicity (Chinese, Latinx, etc.) or a medium (the largest global 'we'-groups are TV and movie audiences, consumer groups such as 'Mac vs pc or Huawei' users). All such groups are more loosely circumscribed than 'legal fictions', but nevertheless they are bonded by 'rules' (ways of doing things, codes of conduct, trust, shared meanings and formulae). In institutional economics a 'population of rules' defines *institutions* (Potts, 2011) – in this case institutions of language and culture, or semiosphere subsystems.

You can see that commercial and regulatory institutions and demes play a leading role in producing the global semiosphere as experienced by ordinary populations (as opposed to expert groups). Many such groups are organized around media, which is why the 'digital semiosphere' is so important in media studies. To exemplify and illustrate what is at stake, let us first investigate in more detail what has been perhaps one of the largest changes in the global media systems in the recent years – the emergence of mobile media, its convergence with rest of media systems and the rapid evolution of its own distinct forms and textualities.

# Case study: the early evolution of the mobile web

The established cultural practices of reading books, magazines, newspapers and work papers, taking notes or sending postcards while on the go could be seen as laying grounds for the mobile media (see Huhtamo, 2011). These evolved over a long period before the twentieth century. Parallel technological developments, especially in the area of telecommunications and electronic media, spurred the fictional imagination and popularized the idea of evolved technological device for such practices. Think of Dick Tracy, a comic-strip detective (from 1931) who in the 1960s began to feature fanciful space-age gadgets, including a wristwatch with two-way video-call capability, or the James Bond movie franchise, whose gadgets, supplied by 'Q', were a popular attraction, with audiovisual communication affordances linked to lethal powers and cool lifestyles. Such fictional fare continued a long-standing tradition of creating the horizon of popular expectations for real life developments, where fantasy is a kind of pedagogy for the technological sublime. In parallel, the emerging forms of portable screen devices (calculators, watches, handheld video games, etc.), the development of personal computers and their user interfaces, packet-switching technology and Internet networks generated other expectations that converged on mobile handsets as much more than simply devices for speech. This potential – and the demand for it – was made manifest with SMS as largely a user-driven innovation (Von Hippel, 2005).

The widespread adoption of SMS and the cultures that quickly developed around texting (a teenager-led innovation, not an engineering intention) indicated a new market for similar services and applications. This resulted in a feeling of urgency in the industry that the internet had come to stay and that, therefore, the mobile internet needed to find a way into the future (Funk, 2001: 20; Sigurdson, 2001: 11). Work towards this goal started in two different camps and followed initially different paths – one often celebrated as a success, the other, at first at least, as a failure. The first was the i-mode platform developed by Japanese operator NTT DoCoMo. The second was the Wireless Application Protocol (WAP) developed in cooperation among European and North American handset and software vendors, and deployed in several regions of the world. The adoption of i-mode in Japan was quick and wide, while in the Western markets, WAP was anything but. Reasons for this difference have been sought (Funk, 2001; Helyar, 2001: 199–203; Sharma and Nakamura, 2003: 162; Lindmark et al., 2004: 353; Tee, 2005: 151). At first, i-mode was marketed as a platform for cheap services to teens, autonomous and complementary to the 'full web'. In contrast, WAP was marketed as the exclusively priced 'internet on your phone', but in reality it was clearly inferior to the desktop web at the time. It was very slow and clunky, the minimalistic WAP-sites did not compare with the websites of the time and there were very few specific WAP services around.

The failures of WAP could be related to the slow convergence of telecommunications and online services industries, in relation to both dialogic and autocommunicative processes. While i-mode was fully controlled and designed by Japanese operator NTT DoCoMo, WAP was effectively an open standard developed in the late 1990s by WAP Forum. The latter, while initiated by handset makers and software developers, eventually consolidated hundreds of industry players, including mobile operators, who all worked in slightly different circumstances and had different ideas for the future of the mobile web. Many of the problems derived from the absence of a dominant design for handsets and services alike (Steinbock, 2003: 374). As a result the initial WAP standards had feeble 'output legitimacy' – these were deployed in a variety of ways, which resulted in WAP ending up as a designer's nightmare (Kumar et al., 2003: 82). There was a lack of shared standards and conventions that might have guided content developers as well as its users.

These problems all suggest a lack of coordination (in effect, autocommunication) in the industry. This first phase of the evolution of the mobile and ubiquitous web was therefore characterized by an unsettled convergent domain. Deficiencies in usability were conditioned by the limited dialogue among relevant stakeholders and restricted possibilities for network operators and content providers to influence the service design of the 'mobile web' of the time.

To improve such dialogue – tellingly, in the early 2000s – the WAP Forum was renamed the Open Mobile Alliance (OMA). Here, operators and service- and content-developers were both included. This 'alliance' constituted the first step towards subsequent industry consolidation along the value chain. That consolidation, however, was put on a new footing with the arrival of the 3G air interface standards, together with technically more advanced handsets. The network speed – 384 Kbps – thereby enabled users to imagine accessing the real web from a mobile device. To enable this, in 2005 ICANN approved a new top-level domain (TLD) –.mobi – to create a subdomain of the internet dedicated only for mobile content. The top-level domain was sponsored by a multistakeholder consortium including Google, Microsoft, Vodafone, T-Mobile, Samsung, Sony-Ericsson and Nokia. These were the biggest handset makers, telecom operators and online service providers of the time and their cooperation indicated a shared understanding of the need for convergence to happen. This development, however, triggered criticism from the World Wide Web consortium (W3C, the standardization body for the web), for breaking the device independence of the internet. According Tim Berners-Lee, inventor of the World Wide Web and chair of W3C, the web was designed as a universal space and it needed therefore to continue operating independently of different hardware, software or networks. So,

W3C was motivated to fight the fragmentation of the web into device-specific subspaces.

In parallel, content and services industries were already facing insurmountable trouble with developing WAP content. They called for the standardization of the mobile web, to enable content providers to 'create once and publish everywhere' with ease. The mobile industry (operators and manufacturers) took notice of this and started to look for a neutral institutional framework for standardization. The best track record in this regard belonged to W3C, and it gained quickly mobile industry support, marking a crucial step in the institutional convergence of mobile and web domains. That is, telecoms and handset vendors agreed to converge their own domain (WAP) with the real web, and they allowed W3C to lead the way as the web standardization body.

The convergence agenda emerged as the common denominator of this constellation of institutions. They worked towards this by first developing a new mobile-specific mark-up language (XHTML Basic 1.1), which was fully compatible with the full web – new websites could be accessed on any device. And they developed new guidelines on how to design websites to look good on all devices. Further, various mobile browser developers and operators also developed 'transcoders' for redesigning 'legacy' sites for mobile viewing. But these steps added up to an attempt to seize the initiative from the content providers, restricting their freedom to design websites and to decide what content is aimed at which device, which makes this phase of media evolution historically distinctive. The objective was to extend the technological continuity that enabled the Web to become a marketplace for goods and services. For this purpose, a new and ever-more homogeneous mesh of technical and institutional systems was emerging, consisting of large telecommunications and web enterprises (the 'infrastructure enablers') that saw convergence as a means to gain control over the new integrated domain, over its media forms and codes of conduct for cross-platform publishing.

After having established stable modes of dialogue, this constellation of industries started to work autocommunicatively – producing all kinds of guidelines, standards, press releases and other media texts, as well as models of the domain expressed in, for instance, convergent pricing of internet services and so on. All this modelling activity in different sign-systems was used to fix the new device-agnostic web to a specific evolutionary path (Ibrus, 2010, 2013a, b). This vision, however, did not go uncontested. Content and service providers opposed the 'generic design' for all devices, because it would have meant leaving their content effectively 'un-designed', ceding the power to design to other parties such as browser vendors. The content providers wanted to keep that power to themselves: to decide what content, in what form, to deliver in what circumstances to what media or platform. With this they were claiming the right to establish discontinuities among different access media.

The solution to achieve this emerged at the very periphery of the industry, in an online forum of independent content developers for mobile handsets. The idea was simple. As device vendors were reluctant to disclose the characteristics of their phones, which developers needed to identify and optimize their content, they decided to collect this information on their own. They created a shared document where anybody could fill in data about different phones. These data could be then used by servers to recognize the device and deliver only the relevant content with optimized designs. Hence, what we know today as the 'responsive web' originally evolved as a peripheral 'cheat' – a countercultural trick by independent content developers.

Finding wide take-up, such content adaptation evolved as a kind of conduct that favoured divergence within the web, across access platforms. Ultimately, as it gained support, W3C began to warm up for its 'One Web' principle to be defined. It fostered continuity in the technologies that would enable 'thematically same' (W3C, 2005)[2] content to be delivered to all access platforms but did not prescribe the way the content (and exactly what content) was presented to users. The dialogic process between different industry subsystems yielded web standards that then conditioned divergence in media forms. Homogeneity in the cross-media web was possible but not satisfactory to agents who saw that meaningful communications necessitated distinctions in media forms. During this phase of the multiplatform web, we can recognize the formation of two industry subsystems that both worked autocommunicatively: 'infrastructure companies' and content industries. Both tried to design the convergent domain according to their own needs and understandings. One created new continuities between convergent domains; the other wanted to enable meaningful discontinuities within the new space.

This observation recalls Lotman's view that there are concurrent *centrifugal* and *centripetal* movements in culture, that unity and plurality presume each other. We can observe the systemic convergence of industries and homogenizing normative modelling conducted by the infrastructure firms from a distance, at the industry meta-level. But at the same time we see divergence within the ubiquitous web; content producers were ready to fragment the web in order to retain the power to determine forms of the media content. But 'responsive design' and context-specific (device-based) forms of the web not only served the interests of specific industry players; they also provided more accessible, useable and meaningful experiences to users. The content adaptation solution emerged from immediate contact with the governed objects – media texts, their existing formats and genres – based on the need to model them in their contextual and circumstantial particularities.

---

[2]https://www.w3.org/2005/MWI/BPWG/techs/CategoryBpThematicConsistency.html.

The next phase in the development of the multiplatform web arrived with the development of smartphones (and, later, tablets), with touchscreen interfaces and associated 'app stores'. The format of 'native' apps that were designed for specific mobile devices was a new cultural form. It enabled content and service providers to utilize the novel affordances of advanced smartphones. The app-store platform also enabled uncomplicated ways of monetising the services and content provided.

The app-format was liked by content providers because it enabled them to overcome the uncertainties of the mobile web described above, to have better control over what content was presented and how it was displayed. At the same time some control was lost to Apple, Google and other platform owners as the new hegemons of the mobile media domain. As with the i-mode ten years earlier, the new app-sales platforms were sternly controlled by the owners – this time the American-owned tech giants. Not only did they control the content but also prices and hence the distribution of wealth. They did not agree to share most user statistics and contacts, denying content and service providers a direct contact and dialogue with their audiences. This became a source of tensions between Apple and content providers, creating new grounds for a search of an alternative.

The alternative emerged a few years later as a new set of W3C standards – HTML5 and its 'device API' (application programming interface) – allowed developers to create web applications that interact with device hardware. These new affordances quickly earned the recognition and uptake by content providers owing to the limiting conditions of the 'native' applications markets. Leading industry analysts of the time recognized that app-store fragmentation had become a mounting challenge for content and service providers (Visionmobile, 2011). The numbers of such stores had grown rapidly, and each had its own intricate regulations. Eventually the marginal cost of distributing an application through yet another app store became prohibitive. At the same time the new HTML reduced these costs by lowering barriers to entry as well as exit from native platforms. There was also growing evidence that the mobile web was becoming a preferred tool for the content and service industries as they entered the era of cross-media content distribution.

To characterize this continuing phase of the ubiquitous and cross-platform web, we should recognize that this time, unlike the previous phase, it was the content and service providers who wanted more homogeneity among media platforms. In terms of semiospheric dynamics, the *centrifugal* force of app-store fragmentation needed a balancing *centripetal* response. This time it was the content and service providers who were supportive of W3C's standardization work, which aimed to surmount the app-centric fragmentation of internet services. And it was the large technology vendors (Apple) and online service providers (Google, Facebook, etc.) – the 'infrastructure enablers' – who were now behind some of developments towards fragmenting the web space.

This case study of the evolution of the mobile web has demonstrated how media convergence tends to be complex and multilinear and involves both dialogic and autocommunicative communications as constituent forces. In the case of the cross-platform Web, convergence was shaped by dialogue between partners who were, in effect, new to each other: namely, telecommunications industries, online service providers and content providers. We saw how these dialogues, which were ineffective at first (the era of WAP), progressively through the two following phases, brought about a balanced design for the new cross-platform web. We saw how new alliances formed through dialogue and how these constellations quickly started to autocommunicate in order to model the new emergent domain according to specific favoured needs. We also saw how there were always multiple such autocommunicating subsystems, sometimes overlapping, but as a rule dynamically changing. These autocommunicative discourses were also path-dependent; they were used by the respective industries to sustain their existing operational models (Ibrus, 2014, 2015a). From this we can observe how autocommunication is also about power – power to enforce one's model in order to keep the system's core identity and to avoid disruptive and possibly ineffective change.

This case study of the mobile or cross-media web has demonstrated the rather quick undoing of the original technical fragmentation of the internet, the harmonization of technical incompatibilities in order to enable a truly cross-platform global marketplace for content and services. This could be understood as resulting from the *centrifugal* force of the global semiosphere. Yet, the story has also identified a counterforce – a *centripetal* movement towards pluralization of meaning, responding to the need to provide meaningful and distinctive experiences to people in different everyday contexts. The next three chapters aim to address the tensions between these forces, the interdependency between dialogic communication and autocommunication and the dynamics they bring about for the industries that produce the systems of meaning we operate with and live through.

# 12

# Bubbles: Production of
# continual systems

*We cannot understand the world without concepts and we cannot
communicate without some form of language ... The transmission
of information from institution to individual is impossible without a
coextensive process of enculturation, in which the individual learns
the meaning and value of the sense data that is communicated ...*
This ... suggests that the starting point of explanations cannot be
institution-free. *What is required is a theory of process, development
and learning, rather than a theory that proceeds from an original
'state of nature' that is both artificial and untenable.*
(GEOFFREY HODGSON, 2007: 12–13)

In Part III we described how cultural autocommunication works through
all kinds of artistic *texts*. Here in Part IV we can see that the same logic
facilitates the social organization of all kinds of *institutions*, industries,
countries and so on.

## Bubble-babble

We apply the term 'bubble' to relatively autonomous institutional media
systems, such as story-worlds encompassing multiple media and their
productive institutions, increasingly facilitated by the evolving practices of
transmedia storytelling. 'Bubble' does not refer to the notion of 'filter bubbles'
in media studies or 'elite bubbles' in political discourse, which are widely
discussed in social-media and journalistic circles but, as Axel Bruns (2019)

has demonstrated from Twitter and data analytics, do not in fact exist. Our usage of the term may suggest instead the work of Peter Sloterdijk, whose model of humanity's *selfhood* ('bubble'), *world* ('globe') and plurality of *communities* ('foam') is presented in his *Spheres* trilogy (2011, 2014, 2016). Sloterdijk's three-part distinction among spheres parallels our own spatial model of semiotic-economic-cultural systems: his micro-bubbles (self), meso-foam (community) and macro-globe (world) map onto our micro- (text), meso- (organization) and global (system) levels; and both models are predicted and encompassed by Lotman's semiosphere. However, we have used 'bubble' not to identify the philosophical individual or the micro-text (as Sloterdijk's three-part distinction seems to) but to identify instances of institutional (organized) semiospheres as dynamic and transient subsystems of the overall semiosphere (and see Chapter 14 for 'foam'). Our application of the concepts of 'bubble', 'foam' and 'globe' *invokes* Sloterdijk but is not the same as his model.

# Autocommunication

Numerous authors in organization studies have elaborated how all kinds of contemporary communications that organized bodies or systemic structures might produce (such as strategic plans, corporate reports, marketing communications, press releases) may eventually start to work autocommunicatively (see Broms and Gahmberg, 1983; Christensen, 1997; Cheney and Christensen, 2001; Morsing, 2006; Steedman, 2006). Even if the communicative act was originally meant not for internal use but for the outside audience, once the message feeds back to its authoring structure, an autocommunicative effect has taken place. Sometimes these messages 'return' to the structure later in time, regularly if not repeatedly. In these instances, the function of messages is to keep organizational evolution in check, close to its 'roots'. As Christensen (1997: 202) and Morsing (2006: 175) have argued, autocommunication is not primarily oriented towards sending and receiving messages but towards the production of meta-texts concerning the identity and nature of the communicating system. Broms and Gahmberg (1983) suggest that autocommunication turns into a process of organizing through which a communicator evokes and enhances its own values. The repetitive use of the same textual form produces the mythologies of the communicating structure. Yet, at different times, these returning or revisited messages may be interpreted differently, depending on the dominant cultural frameworks of the time. This allows also for the receiving structures to change, to adapt to the current cultural climate.

Autocommunication can happen in all modalities. Clearly bounded institutions (firms, agencies) produce newsletters, video tutorials, development plans, websites, corporate reports and so on, which also feed back meanings to everybody in these institutions and so have an organizing, consolidating effect. But for more abstract institutions, say, the video game industry, all sorts of communications that in some way address the us-ness of these industries could be viewed from a higher perspective as institutional autocommunication. Specialized industry publications such as *Gamesindustry.biz* or *Gamasutra.com* generally have such a function. Any discussion in a specialist message board on what defines the object-texts – video games – could also be understood as a self-description that defines the 'purpose' of the particular industry. But, as the story of the mobile web suggested, official technical standards that establish the bounds of the domain, and the rules and role of institutions within these bounds, can also be expected to work autocommunicatively.

When the subsystem that is autocommunicating is young, still emerging out of the dialogue of preceding systems, the textual matter used for autocommunication is not copious. For instance, augmented reality (AR), which is currently emerging as a media platform, has not yet produced much descriptive textual material to fix it on any evolutionary path. As we write, the evolution of this medium is still in its most dynamic phase. Its potential as a form of mobile location-based entertainment was demonstrated with Pokémon Go. Since then AR has been picked up and further facilitated by Apple. Other companies, such as Magic Leap or Microsoft, with its Hololens headset, are working towards other kinds of form and functionality that utilize head-mounted glasses, which mix the real and virtual realities in different ways. This has led to new industry discourse, proposing convergence between AR and VR as currently distinct new-media forms.[1] Dynamic experimentation that converges or diverges related subforms, technologies or genres is, indeed, typical of early phases of a medium's development. If we follow the example of previous media, the experiments will eventually lead to optimal solutions that satisfy various (but never all) industry fractions as well as user groups.

In the processes, as systems mature, the descriptive textual layers thicken, mature and start working autocommunicatively, so as to regulate the domain in increasing detail. Handbooks, textbooks, standards and guidelines emerge that fix not only the medium and its forms but also practices of their production. As Lotman suggested, every system produces self-descriptions, but as these become more granular over time, they start to regulate the system in ever-more detail and therefore also more effectively.

---

[1]Hardware is labelled as 'XR', combining augmented (AR), virtual (VR) and mixed reality (MR) devices. In January 2020, the front-runner company at the trade shows was Chinese Nreal: http://virtualrealitytimes.com/2020/01/13/the-week-in-xr-most-important-ar-vr-and-mr-news-in-the-past-week/.

The highest form and final act of a semiotic system's structural organization is when it describes itself. This is the stage when grammars are written, customs and laws codified.

(Lotman, 1990: 128)

In Lotman's terms, the stage of self-description is a necessary response to the threat of too much diversity within the semiosphere: the system might lose its unity and definition and disintegrate.

# Innovation

Innovation theory is familiar with the Abernathy and Utterback model (1978), which describes three stages of industrial innovation – a fluid phase, transitional phase and specific phase. The first is characterized by the dynamic absorption of new information and frequent major changes in product designs, while development and production processes are flexible and, as such, inefficient. In the second phase, production processes have become more rigid, and dominant product variations have already emerged, with changes occurring in major steps. In the third phase, innovation is predominantly only incremental product innovations and process innovations, with cumulative improvement in cost and quality; the product line consists of undifferentiated standard products. There is an economic rationale for optimizing production routines over time and, therefore, standardizing products. Much standardization discourse is about defining the moment to replace creative disorder with secured stability (David, 1995).

This aligns with Manovich's (2001) implicit proposition that in media development there are two universal stages: a short initial gestation period, where it evolves at a rapid pace and develops its main characteristics; and a second stage, where, having acquired its final form, it undergoes only minor changes during the rest of its existence. This analytical division of evolutionary processes into two follows both Eco (1979: 138) and Lotman (1977), who distinguish between 'grammatically oriented' and 'textually oriented' cultures. Kress and van Leeuwen (2001: 113) similarly identify 'lexically' and 'grammatically' organized semiotic resources. According to Lotman, *textual* culture generates texts directly, which constitute macro-units from which rules could eventually be inferred. Kress and van Leeuwen add that in such cultures, semiotic modes are in practice approached as a paradigm, a loose collection of signs. The paradigm functions as a more or less unordered storehouse of ideas and resources where one can browse and shop for ideas. In *grammatically* oriented cultures, texts are generated by combinations of discrete units and are judged correct or incorrect according to their conformity to the rules of the particular system:

Grammars ... use very broad, abstract classes of items, but provide fairly definite rules for combining them into an infinite number of possible utterances. They are decontextualised and abstract, but also powerful in what can be done with them. Perhaps it is no wonder that grammatically organised modes have tended to be the most powerful modes.

(Kress and van Leeuwen, 2001: 113)

The emergence of autocommunicative grammars is indicated by various kinds of handbooks. In Lotman's terms, this refers to the stage of 'grammatical orientation' of cultures – where self-descriptions result in detailed codifications of how new forms of culture should be produced, by whom, in what circumstances, with what qualifications and so on (Eco, 1977: 138; Lotman, 1977). Such handbooks work to self-describe the whole of a given productive subsystem, codifying its bounds and practices. During the web's early days, Rivett (2000) described how web design was codified by various groupings publishing their handbooks on the subject matter. The same happened with the mobile web a few years later. The same was visible again later, with the emergence of practices of cross-platform content presentation strategies or transmedia storytelling.

While forms of cross- or trans-media have always existed (Scolari et al., 2014), it was in the mid-2000s when this practice was pinpointed as a characteristic trend in contemporary convergent media industries (Jenkins, 2006). Media industries around the world picked the term up, and some of its practitioner communities used it to autocommunicate the emergence of a new professional domain. As a result, in 2010, 'Transmedia Producer' became a new addition to the professions recognized by the Producers Guild of America. This was important because it *codified* a new practice in the most dynamic entertainment market in the world. It was followed by a plethora of pioneering handbooks (e.g. Alexander, 2011; Bernardo, 2011; Pratten, 2011; Phillips, 2012; Dowd et al., 2013) and by new training courses, academic study programmes, grant systems around world, all adding further textual layers to the autocommunicating 'bubble' of transmedia storytelling practice.

What makes digital culture distinctive, however, are the technical modes that are used for autocommunication. Metadata is a descriptive device that models and fixes the forms of culture. In digital communications all data are accompanied by various forms of metadata. These metadata schemas could be understood as 'very simple languages' (Pomerantz, 2015: 30) that are used to model specific compounds of digital data, of practices or of communications. Digital cultural domains, therefore, are bounded by thick layers of autocommunicatively functioning technical languages. This in turn affects the formation of industries. During the early phase of mobile web evolution, the consortium of global companies we call the 'infrastructure enablers' developed 'mobileOK' checkers, which indicated if a website could be presented more or less the same on all devices. These checkers then added metadata that approved the sites for mobile browsers – effectively codifying their vision of the mobile web for the constellation of industry structure.

## Classification as autocommunication

In this regard an interesting current trend is the dynamic change in genre categories of forms of culture. Genre divisions and related professional identities, especially in film but also in music and performing arts, have traditionally evolved as recognition and marketing devices – one may identify as a fan or maker of, for instance, horror movies or shoegaze pop because such cultural frames and divisions have been autocommunicatively reproduced for a long time. However, the personalization algorithms of, among others, Netflix or Spotify, utilize much wider sets of musical markers than just established genre categories. Netflix's metadata schema has been reverse-engineered (Madrigal, 2014),[2] to generate no less than '76,897 unique ways to describe types of movies' – potential genres that are activated according to users' personal tastes (i.e. previous choices). Netflix's commissioning policy is based on their data analytics, visibly ignoring the existing divisions in the film and TV industry, having a knock-on effect on industry organization more widely, in the United States, especially.

A different case has been the video games industry that is native to the digital age. It was born into what Lev Manovich (2001) has called 'database culture'. The genre characteristics and divisions for video games have been more strict and less dynamically changing than in case of other forms of culture. This can be related to video games always needing to adjust to digital catalogues, categories and metadata systems of online game stores such as Steam, Nintendo Game Store or Playstation Store. On these platforms it becomes apparent that those games which do not fit the established genres are categorized as 'indie'. That is, while the 'indie' term generally refers to a mode of game production where there is no support from a game publisher, it also refers to independence of form, compared with the mainstream industry's strict categorization of game genres.

While the video games industry does organize itself into multiple subsystems, such as the producers of, for instance, AAA games, MMOs (massively multiplayer online games), casual games, social-media games, console games or mobile games and so on, its broadest distinction is between those within the actively autocommunicating, and therefore regulated, core and those who are 'independent', in the less-regulated periphery: those

---

[2]See: https://www.theatlantic.com/technology/archive/2014/01/how-netflix-reverse-engineered-hollywood/282679/.

who experiment with forms and ideas coming from other artforms. This peripheral segment has had its own distribution platforms such as *itch.io* and *Playism*, which tend to have entirely different categorization systems from the mainstream. In recent years, however, platforms like Steam have started to provide a unified environment for game distribution, where the line between AAA and indie has become blurred. There is often little to identify the 'independence' of the indie game industry other than rhetoric. For instance, *Minecraft* and *Insanely Twisted Shadow Planet* were developed by indie studios, but both are published by Microsoft. Nevertheless, the autocommunicative rhetoric of the indie games subsystem continues to emphasize creative freedom, artistry, authenticity and so on.

In case of video games, the relatively slow change in mainstream genres can be explained by their *technical* framing, but it still needs to be noted that genre categories and conventions have traditionally evolved and are reproduced for easing *consumption* decisions and interpretation processes among audiences. Media producers need to provide novel information or experiences, but they need to balance this with familiar/comfortable frames of interpretation. An innovation cannot be too radical; it has to rely to a significant extent on existing and widely recognized representational conventions or the 'horizon of expectations' (Jauss, 1982) that audiences are assumed to have. It is for this reason that, in domains of software design and HCI, a shared conviction has emerged that designs for new applications have to rely on established conventions from other media, so as to give users cues and resources for learning by using (Brown and Duguid, 1996: 71). Therefore, continuity in interpretative abilities could be seen as one of the causes of 'remediation' (Bolter and Grusin, 1998), that is the step-by-step innovation by dislocating representational conventions from earlier and current media. What Bolter and Grusin suggest relates to Lotman's distinction between 'textual' and 'grammatical' culture, discussed above. The emergence of autodescriptive grammars is evidenced, we suggest, by the emergence of *handbooks* (using that term broadly to signify any meta-level discussion of a system's rules and workings). Textual cultures, on the other hand, are the domain of *books* – whole textual units or forms are dislocated from their original context into new ones. Representational conventions of earlier media are reused in newer media in the absence of forms and grammars of their own. As an example, consider the very first graphical user interface – the one of Apple Lisa, introduced to markets in 1983. At that time computers were used almost exclusively in offices, so the first interface, which established a genre, imitated familiar office accoutrements – files, folders, WasteBasket, ClipBoard, Calculator and so on. Decades later, when it introduced its iBooks app for Apple's iOS platform, the app interface first imitated wooden bookshelves where 'books' were laid out (see Figure 12.1). When introducing innovative forms in the digital space, such imitation by metaphors tends to be the rule. Yet, a few versions later, the

FIGURE 12.1 *Early iBooks interface.*

iBooks app turned more abstract in appearance; the wooden-shelf metaphor disappeared. iOS and its core applications started to acquire their own form and grammars.

# Continuities

Another instance of using audience interpretations to create continuities in culture is what is commonly known as the personalization of online services. When they make recommendations to their users, Amazon or Netflix's algorithms base these, first, on previous choices by the same user and, second, on the choices of other users with similar interests. This has led to fears of 'filter bubbles' (Pariser, 2011), where choices built upon choices might isolate like-minded groups from different like-minded groups with different clickstream habits. In the case of news consumption, these risks may be overstated – and nothing new, since selective newspaper-buying produced the same effect, which were called not 'bubbles' but 'imagined communities' (Anderson, 2006). Only a very small minority of media consumers occupy such 'echo chambers' exclusively; others access more diverse menus and belong to overlapping demes, groups, institutions and systems, such that 'the semiosphere' is as multivalent for individuals as it is for cultures (Dutton et al., 2017; Bruns, 2019).

However, when we look at the personalization phenomenon in the broader sweep of cultural evolution, we can see how these apparently technical or marketing innovations contribute to the production of various continuities in culture and how their productive subsystems as well as audiences are organized. Not only are algorithms re-producing specific 'taste-communities' by filtering related content from their catalogues but also their platforms commission new content based on their data-mined perception of generalized user-types. Netflix has admitted to basing its investments on algorithmic user modelling, and Spotify has been shown to motivate new music production by specifically targeting their system of playlists.

A related phenomenon is the emergent *semantic web*, conceptualized and driven originally by W3C, but taken up by major search engines, online content providers and archives. The 'semantic web' refers to the utilization of W3C's Resource Description Framework (RDF) to facilitate the evolution of semantically integrated data networks, where one unit of data can function as metadata for another unit of data. The British Film Institute (BFI), for instance, has structured all data on all British feature films into such a 'linked data' format. Film and broadcasting archives across Europe are following suit.

The semantic web and linked data formats rely on *metadata schemas* as their base structure. These schemas, however, model those data in specific ways, deriving from the perceptions and ideologies of the period when they were created. Therefore, the ways that metadata and linked data networks contextualize data are just one possible pathway; there could always be alternatives. Media archaeologist Wolfgang Ernst (2013) has suggested that contemporary archives might be renamed as 'dynarchives' – referring to the way that the constant addition of new data to archives, especially usage data, causes dynamic change in the linked relationships in databases. Yet, because the creation of metadata is too expensive to carry out regularly, most metadata schemas are standardized to last. Archives weren't meant to be dynamic. The question remains, therefore: what is the role of technical models in facilitating the evolution of various kinds of cultural continuities – in texts as well as in the social and cultural communities and production systems they facilitate – and thence what is their role in structuring the textual networks that represent us our cultural past and present?

In innovation studies, questions of continuities are posed as path dependency, historical 'lock-ins' and techno-economic paradigms. For path dependency, David (2000) has offered the following definition: 'Processes that are non-ergodic, and thus unable to shake free of their history, are said to yield path-dependent outcomes'. An historical lock-in is:

the entry of a system into a trapping region – the basin of attraction that surrounds a locally (or globally) stable equilibrium. When a dynamic economic system enters such a region, it cannot escape except through the intervention of some external force, or shock, that alters the configuration or transforms the underlying structural relationships among the agents.

(David, 2000: 25–6)

David's argument is that there is a point in the diffusion of a new technology where the spontaneous decisions of individual users 'lock in' one technology and drive out the others, even though at the outset they were taken as equally good competitive solutions. This understanding relates to the economic concept of 'network externalities', which refers to an incentive for individuals to adopt a certain sort of behaviour only because a considerable number of others have already adopted it. Potts et al. (2008) call the result a 'social network market' and suggest that choices made on the basis of the choices of others are a distinguishing feature of the *creative industries*, where price is dependent on prestige, word-of-mouth, reviews and so on, not on standardization and efficiency of production.

In addition to choices of users there are also other sources of positive feedback that can lead to path dependency. According to Lundgren (1991: 70–1) these include *technological interrelatedness*, where the functioning of the parts is contingent on the functioning of the whole, which deters revolutionary changes of each part. Similarly, *industrial networks* may curb rapid development by sticking to established rules and regulations, routine transactions, relationship-specific investments and so on. And *learning as a social process* is unavoidably slow for large communities, hindering rapid changes in established systems.

David has suggested that the configurations that result from such positive feedback processes could be understood as 'self-sustaining equilibria' (the 'equilibrium' in his model owes to economic theory in the first place). According to David, a 'locked-in' equilibrium point can rely on anything, from societal or institutional hierarchies to technologies or behavioural norms (David, 2000: 29). Garrouste and Ioannides (2000: 4) use the term 'self-reinforcement' of systems. Building on Lotman's semiotics, it can be suggested that all of these – hierarchies, technologies and behaviours – are expressed in different kinds of communication and materialized textually, via machine-readable protocols, metadata schemas, workflow guides, design norms, programme formats, interaction or trading conventions, international standards documents, all of which tend to lock each other in. Such textual mutuality generally results from complex social dynamics, often from hard negotiations or enduring standardization efforts, and from power asymmetries among existing institutions. Yet, as a rule, such efforts can enjoy only limited degrees of freedom. Modifications of individual elements are contingent on the whole, on all other elements of the system. As such, particular textual, technological, economic and social constellations facilitate technocultural continuities and re-produce various kinds of subsystems in culture.

# Paradigms

Carlota Perez (2009) calls these continuities 'technoeconomic paradigms'. Building on Schumpeter (1939), Kondratieff (1984) and Dosi (1984), she has suggested that new techno-economic paradigms tend to emerge when, first, there are new inputs around that are inexhaustible, cheaper, all-pervasive in applications and capable of increasing the power and decreasing the cost of capital and labour. Second, these new inputs, most often new technologies or platforms, need to facilitate the perception of profitable opportunity spaces. Third, the new paradigm needs to incorporate criteria for better organizational practice – new principles of organization that prove superior to previous ones, to become part of a new common sense for efficiency and effectiveness. If these preconditions are fulfilled and a new, robust technology is developed and brought to market, there is a chance for it to condition a technoeconomic paradigm 'around' it. Take the arrival of television:

> A sufficiently radical innovation such as, for example, television stimulated the emergence of the industries that manufacture receiving and broadcasting equipment and of multiple specialized supplier industries. TV spurred the transformation of the producing and advertising industries as well as the film, music and other creative sectors, plus new maintenance and distribution activities and so on.
>
> (Perez, 2009: 6)

This means that when an early-stage technological innovation that fills certain opportunity space enters the world, it also generates various kinds of externalities – related opportunity spaces for ancillary technologies, practices, businesses, textual matter and forms of culture. At the outset, a particular technology may evolve dynamically; alternative trajectories are tested. Early TV experimented with mechanical as well as electronic scanning devices, and with collective audiences (in halls, town squares) as well as private ones. As more design decisions are made and more ancillary solutions established, the whole system gradually gets more locked in and alternative trajectories become impossible, even unthinkable (as mechanical TV now seems to be). As the opportunity space fills, new innovations are ever-more incremental and optimized for the existing system.– until entirely new paradigms emerge (such as digital, networked and on-demand distribution of audiovisuaal content).

Both smartphones and the web were already robust technologies at the beginning of their convergence. Therefore, the converging industries – telecoms and internet – imagined quite different possible futures for the new cross-platform mobile web. However, it took complex negotiations, multilinear power struggles and constant testing of alternative solutions to condition the eventually dominant set of techno-cultural forms: 'native apps', 'web apps', 'responsive web' and so on. The same process can be observed among a new generation of mobile content industries, starting with Snapchat or Instagram and ending with an army of 'influencers' and other content providers operating on its platform and producing various kinds of codes of conduct for their business and practices. The evolution of the mobile web/media platform is a thoroughly dialogic process involving a global legion of actors of different kinds consisting of complex forms of 'interactive learning' (Lundvall, 1992) between them. But this process is also slowing down, owing to multiple layers of technologies, codes and textual matter that have codified the medium and as such exhausted the opportunities for radical change.

A technoeconomic paradigm (Perez, 2009), then, is the result of a complex collective learning process, articulated eventually as a model of the best economic, technological and organizational practice for the particular period in which a specific technological revolution is being adopted and retained by an economic and social system. Perez argues that each technoeconomic paradigm presumes broadly shared perceptions and practices about the optimal designs and practices associated with the paradigm. In Lotman's terms this means that systems have started to autocommunicate to produce these shared perceptions and standard practices.

While shifts in technoeconomic paradigms can be traced back across the centuries, there is an important new logic that is specific to the internet economy. It contributes to the formation of new kinds of techno-economic paradigms, to their autocommunication and possibly to the production of long-term continuities in global internet industries and their inherent asymmetries. This is the logic of 'network externalities' (also: network effects).

# Network effects

The theory of network effects stems from economic theory and claims that the value of a network depends on its number of users (Katz and Shapiro, 1986; David and Greenstein, 1990; DiMaggio and Cohen, 2005), very much in the manner of a phone system, where one user is impossible and the utility of the service increases with every extra subscriber, which is why phone systems were often established as monopolies (the utility of competing systems decreases if they are not interoperable). The dominance of, for instance, Instagram, for sharing mobile photography, and the subsequent swarming of 'influencers' on this platform follow from Instagram's dominance over competitors. Instagram – and its influencers – benefit from network effects. The more members a platform has for sharing purposes, the more attractive it is for any of its users (Ahn, 2011; Cusumano, 2011; Kwon, 2011). What this means for the internet economy is the process known as platformization (van Dijck et al., 2018). Although not all members of a network may be relevant to a specific user, according to Reed's Law (Reed, 2001), the utility of a social network scales exponentially with its size, even if the direct number of contacts per individual is very small. Hence, large international platforms for sharing purposes (especially important for youth and popular culture) benefit from network effects that no national or local platform could offer.

The problem with this is that such 'value pull' also leads towards concentration in the specific markets, since the majority of consumers tend to prefer the most popular services. The logic of and efficiencies of economies of *scope* (producing a variety of related goods across various platforms, for a lower average cost per item) and *scale* (increased production of one good, for lower marginal cost per item) have traditionally conditioned media and information services markets, rewarding a company that can produce more for less across more platforms, which encourages oligopolistic corporate structures. Network effects exacerbate this tendency. Global hybrid economies in contemporary media and content sectors are increasingly under the control of monopolistic global 'tech giants' (Google, Amazon, Facebook, Apple and Microsoft from the United States; or China Mobile, Tencent, Alibaba, Baidu, Huawei and Xiaomi from China). That is, the contemporary market concentration in online cultural markets is not happening within the bounds of national markets but globally and has led to the dominance of only a handful of platforms nearly everywhere. What this means for cultural diversity or political pluralism almost everywhere remains an open question.

Centripetal (inward-pulling) force results from the autocommunicative processes in culture (Schönle and Shine, 2006). As it describes and defines, codifies and regulates, it produces continuities, it facilitates coherence and stability and it slows down dynamics. This force tends towards bringing the system together into a fixed structure, all the way from the global layers of internet protocols and web standards or highly platformized global marketplace to specific sets of digital tools that, for instance, a start-up in Estonia can use to enter global service markets. Even if it is a 'unicorn' company such as Bolt that competes internationally with Uber, it still needs to rely on online mapping services provided by Google or Apple and their specific ways of representing and standardizing spatial relationships. Therein Bolt, Uber, Lyft, Didi and only a handful of others are competing for global dominance in ridesharing or, to be more exact, in coordinating the spatial link-up of offer and demand in transport services. Drivers and customers will gravitate towards platforms with the most offer/demand traffic, trying to capitalize on the *centripetal* force of network effects. Competition among the main ridesharing companies has been driven by a tacit understanding that in the long term only one provider of such spatial representation and coordination services can win this game and become a de facto standard for such services. Current evidence, however, suggests that the network externalities of these platforms are not very strong: both drivers and users switch between different applications or use several in parallel, searching locally for either higher pay/lower cost or closest car/customer. The system is still dynamic. But the belief remains that global network externalities will emerge, based on emergent 5G networks, internet-of-things and self-driving vehicles.

In this context we propose that, on a higher level, *all* the communications that are part of the network effects of a platform – for instance the representations of spatial relations between the users of a taxi hailing app, communications between these users, their discourses on their uses and actions – could be understood as forms of autocommunication in Lotmanian terms, reproducing the network, its discourses and practices, the technological and cultural forms (the platform) they use for their coordination work. Such autocommunications produce specific technocultural 'bubbles' (as discussed at the beginning of this chapter). These bubbles are for the most part overlapping with Perez's technoeconomic paradigms, because they are produced by both communicative/cultural and technical/economic relationships. Further, these communications and relationships are often the same, as has been demonstrated by Lundvall (2010): user/producer relationships in innovation systems include interactive learning, feedback loops, interdependencies, mutual trust and hence lowered prices. Moreover, as demonstrated by Ibrus (2013b), pricing can also be used as a form of autocommunication – to signal the semiotic 'place' of what is sold. That is, striving towards the formation of 'bubbles' – semiotically homogeneous systems – could be understood as 'economical', where systems are communicatively effective (meaning is transferred). Unfortunately, in another version of 'economic' – that is, in terms of providing new value – homogeneous systems may not be effective at all. This is what we discuss in the following chapter.

# 13

# Blows: Production of discontinuities

*In the absence of* 'good institutions,' *[citizens] formed vast illicit
networks that subsumed the ordinary functions of markets
(ex. coordination, information aggregation, risk sharing, lending)
and created productive assemblages of capital, labour, and
knowledge.*
(ADAM K. FROST)[1]

\* \* \*

Homogeneity means familiarity and familiarity means lack of surprises.
Yet, there is value in surprises, in the unexpected and in difference, even
including competition, clash and conflict. Meaningful life presumes
meaningful distinctions, opportunities to denote varieties in experiences.
Searching for distinction in meaning motivates learning, creation and
discovery as well as our everyday consumption of cultural products. We
seek new films, novels or news – and links to new social-media content
– in a search for meaningful novelties, for texts that inform, and where
there is delight in surprise. Enterprises in arts and culture markets are
therefore working towards satisfying these 'needs', balancing on the fine line
separating familiar novelties and those that surprise too much, or are too
hard to interpret. Cultural industries are therefore always in the business
of small variations, of incremental innovation. Most other industries
also seek to provide distinctions in the form of unique propositions –
what Schumpeter (1939) saw is motivated by the aim to disrupt existing
market equilibria, to produce temporary monopolies, new product or
service categories that generate higher margins for their producers. That

---

[1]Paper delivered at Lund University, Sweden, May 2019 (https://www.lu.se/event/innovation-at-the-margins-illicit-entrepreneurship-in-socialist-china). Full paper accessible here: https://pdfs.semanticscholar.org/ba38/48944eec10f302c63df9a181b7975c394dff.pdf.

is, what is apparent in contemporary digital economies is that not only do they produce *homogeneity* at scale but also, and at an increasingly rapid pace, they produce *heterogeneity*, in Lotman's terms. The centripetal force discussed in the previous chapter is always countered with the centrifugal force of the semiosphere – thence producing difference.

# Centre and periphery

The core dichotomy that, for Lotman, produces these opposite-but-interdependent forces is that of *centre and periphery*. We discussed the complexity of this relation at the micro- or textual level in Part III: depending on the textual subsystem or context, texts could be understood as being part of a core or of a periphery, at the same time. This is because different subsystems may have their own core-periphery oppositions, so a text may be at the core of a subsystem and at the periphery of a larger system. The same applies at the meso-level of institutions. For instance:

- VKontakte (the Russian social network ВКонтáкте, meaning InContact) is dominant or core in the Russian online sphere, but peripheral in the context of the global social networking advertising and data-surveillance industries.
- Netflix was once a peripheral entity in relation to the global audiovisual industries but is now core in terms of financial clout and the resulting power to reshape the nature of the trade in these industries. Nevertheless, it is still quite peripheral in terms of industry's internal recognition and reward system, as its own-produced films struggle to be recognized at major film festivals.
- *Europeana* may be entirely peripheral to the digital online economy, but it functions as a core in working out and standardizing the methods and means by which heritage content is presented online.
- Google may be core platform/infrastructure for much we do online right now, but its social networking service Google+, its video-calling app Duo or its smart messaging app Allo have remained only peripheral compared to the network effects of the competing solutions such as Facebook, Skype or WhatsApp.

And so on. All cultural practices, genre systems or service types tend to have their core-periphery asymmetries. These may be interdependent as, for instance, Google tends to have enough market clout to facilitate the success of their own ancillary services. But this power is not absolute. We can therefore conclude that meso-systems of institutions, their communications, practices and texts, overlap and intertwine in complex ways. In so doing, they enforce changes on each other, but owing to the heterogeneity of interacting forces, the results are as a rule unpredictable (requiring analytics based not on linear cause-effect prediction but on nonlinear probability).

Complexity and dynamic uncertainty are increased by the contrasting asymmetry of core and periphery in any relationship. Core is the subsystem with *power*; it works to sustain that position and develops the necessary grammars and rules. It codifies forms, practices and transactions. Cores autocommunicate systematically, generating the centripetal processes and effect closures that we have discussed. At the periphery, in contrast, *dialogic* communication dominates. Dialogue (among other functions) aims both to understand the other and to explain oneself to the other. Dialogue can create a situation of mutual understanding and exchange of information that was initially alien. Knowledge is made in this way; the process facilitates more communication, more shared understanding, more adjustments to the Other, more opportunities of addressing what unites and, therefore, more chances for autocommunication – communicating about the dialogue and what emerges as a result, which is a new 'us' in dialogue, a new system. Dialogue is the first move towards the formation of new systems, towards autocommunication and thence to the growth of knowledge.

When it comes to the agents who are in dialogue, then from the perspective of meso-level analysis, our concern is with institutions. While all institutions – companies, NGOs, organizations, social movements and so on but also informal but rule-bound institutions such as markets, disciplines and what we call 'knowledge clubs' (Potts et al., 2017) – are in various dialogic relationships, dialogue tends to be a dominant form for those relatively close to the sociocultural periphery: those that are newer, less settled and searching for or proposing alternative solutions; avant-garde movements; start-up companies; subcultural groups; open-source communities and so on. They are less oriented to *autocommunication* because their internal rule-systems are tacit, informal, more readily transgressed and less vigorously enforced. They do not have settled identities to reproduce. In the context of globally intertwined systems, a 'periphery' may refer to a subsystem that is typically still emergent at the boundaries of other systems, resulting from the dialogues of those systems, and quite possibly challenging them. It has not yet arrived at the stage of strict self-regulation, autocommunication and expansion. The 'mobile web' was just such a peripheral subsystem, emerging at the time through dialogues among other systems (mobile telecommunications, online services, web infrastructure industries, media content, etc.).

More recently, Ibrus and Rajahonka (2019) have described the emergence of the EdTech industry through dialogue between the video-gaming industries, educational publishers and public education services sector in Northern Europe. The EdTech sector has been emerging as a 'dialogic industry', able to mediate between private video game industries and the public sector – parties that otherwise have found it too difficult to cooperate. The EdTech industry currently remains 'peripheral' as it is still emerging. Yet, in the English-language countries, however, their development is increasingly boosted by large platforms that seek to commodify all forms of digital and mediated learning. Although its financial and institutional clout remains insignificant compared to mainstream video games or educational publishing, its future is more promising. The COVID-19 turn to online education and working-from-home has opened new pathways, using games engines, VR, AR and Zoom.[2] There are no widely accepted rules on how to use digital technologies in education.

Such emergent industries are dialogic, as they need to be – their own knowledge systems are not settled yet; they need to seek out relevant expertise in order to work on new combinations (i.e. innovations) in a grounded way. The EdTech industries combine a varied set of expertise from pedagogy, educational policy, game design, scriptwriting and narration, service design and so on, but as Audrey Watters has pointed out, they draw equally on Silicon-Valley ideas about technological libertarianism, on individual-behavioural models of learning and on the support (and rhetoric) of both state and private agencies committed to cutting the cost of education to the public purse through automation, casualization and privatization. Watters runs a 'watch' blog called hackeducation.com, in which she presented a review of the 2010s decade at the end of 2019. While it is certainly US-centric, it is an excoriating critique of 'The 100 Worst Ed-Tech Debacles of the Decade' and should be required reading for all who work on bringing EdTech from the periphery to the mainstream of education. Here is Audrey Watters's list of 'a decade of ed-tech failures … and flawed ideas':

1. Anti-School Shooter Software
2. (Venture) Philanthropy
3. Venture Capitalism
4. 'The Year of the MOOC'
5. Gamergate
6. 'Everyone Should Learn to Code'
7. ClassDojo and the New Behaviorism
8. LA Unified School District's iPad Initiative
9. Virtual Charter Schools
10. Google for Education

---

[2]For those who don't know where to start, help is always on hand, e.g.: https://tutorful.co.uk/blog/the-82-hottest-edtech-tools-of-2017-according-to-education-experts (updated for 2020).

11. Altschool
12. The New GED
13. Blockchain Anything
14. inBloom
15. Jeffrey Epstein and the MIT Media Lab
16. Amplify
17. Test Prep
18. Bridge International Academies
19. Platforming Education
20. Predictive Analytics
21. Rocketship Education
22. Automated Essay Grading
23. OPMs and Outsourcing
24. The Secretaries of Education
25. Peter Thiel
26. Google Glass
27. Online Preschool
28. Computer-Based Testing Blunders
29. Student Loan Startups
30. 'Precision Education'
31. The Gentrification of *Sesame Street*
32. Common Core State Standards
33. Online Credit Recovery
34. *The LA Times* Rates Teachers
35. Pearson's 'Digital Transformation'
36. 'Personalized Learning' Software (and Facebook and Summit Public Schools)
37. Ed-Tech Payola
38. Coding Bootcamps
39. Knewton
40. IBM Watson
41. The K-12 Cyber Incident Map
42. 'Social Emotional Learning' Software
43. Juul

44. YouTube, the New 'Educational TV'
45. WeGrow and WeWork
46. Compulsory Fitness Trackers
47. Brainwave Headbands
48. The Hour of Code
49. Yik Yak
50. One Laptop Per Child
51. The Math Emporium(s)
52. Virtual Reality
53. The TED Talk
54. Google Reader
55. Montessori 2.0
56. Brain Training
57. TurnItIn (and the Cheating Detection Racket)
58. Deborah Quazzo and the Chicago Board of Education
59. Clayton Christensen's Predictions
60. The Death of Aaron Swartz
61. Edmodo
62. *Edsurge*
63. ConnectEDU
64. Alexa at School
65. Apple's iTextbooks
66. Slave Tetris
67. UC Berkeley Deletes Its Online Lectures
68. Instructure
69. 'Unbundling'
70. Galvanic Skin Response Bracelets
71. 'Uber for Education'
72. Chatbot Instructors
73. Pearson PARCC 'Spies' on Students
74. 'Deliverology'
75. Kno
76. Channel One (and the Unsinkable Chris Whittle)
77. Course Signals

78. The Fake Online University Sting
79. Altius Education
80. Viral School Videos
81. Interactive Whiteboards
82. 'The End of Library' Stories (and the Software that Seems to Support That)
83. Shark Tank for Schools
84. Ed-Tech Startup Accelerators
85. The Teacher Influencer Hustle
86. Badges
87. Amazon Inspire
88. Bundling Textbooks with Tuition
89. Clickers
90. 'Ban Laptops' Op-Eds
91. Unizin
92. 'The Flipped Classroom'
93. 3D Printing
94. Online Grade Portals
95. 'Roaming Autodidacts'
96. Ning
97. Textbook Publishers vs. Boundless
98. 'Rich People's Kids Don't Use Tech' (and Other Stories about the Silicon Valley Elite)
99. The Promise of 'Free'
100. The Horizon Report.[3]

This long list indicates both the unsettledness of the domain and also its inner conflicts, including academic critique, as summarized by van Dijck, Poell and de Waal (2018: 117–36). They show how the platformization and datafication of education have facilitated forms of teaching and learning that may undermine the status of education as a public good and weaken educational systems that are oriented towards facilitating equal opportunity and upward mobility. They argue that EdTech facilitates 'learnification' – learning processes divided into short-term personal missions focused on

---

[3]See: http://hackeducation.com/2019/12/31/what-a-shitshow. Some of the listed items are counterintuitive because they may not seem ed-tech related, but Watter draws lessons from them for her general theme: it is definitely worth your while to read the whole sorry tale.

acquiring specific skills and not facilitating education as *Bildung* – in bringing up enlightened and self-reflective citizens able creatively to synthesize multiple bodies of knowledge and to arrive at judgements in complex and dynamically changing environments. In the language we develop in this book, the 'foam' of learning apps is not meaningfully linked up to produce a coherent semiosphere.

However, in terms of the further evolution of EdTech, academic critique is part of the dialogic process that shapes the domain. Such dialogue includes both resistance, for instance by educators and users committed to public and cultural purposes for education, as well as failures, where innumerable experiments over a lengthy time span eventually yield those that succeed, creating a new map of the industry. This may resemble neither proponents' aspirations nor opponents' worst fears, but it can be explained by a model of innovation based on inter-institutional meso-level dialogue.

To offer a related example, Ibrus and Tafel-Viia (2019) have shown how emergent VR-health industries need to hire medical experts, often only as mediators who speak the appropriate 'medical language', in order to be credible in the 'knowledge club' (Potts et al., 2017) of the medical sector. In addition to gaming, experiments in VR technology have been applied to various health issues – to treat phobias, used in therapeutics or rehabilitation, or as simulations in medical education and so on. Startups in this area face impediments related to tech development, notably data privacy issues. Equally significant, however, is the difficulty they encounter with the 'club-like mentality' of doctors and hospital personnel. If app developers do not master medical terminology or show awareness of the culture and custom of the field, they cannot earn its trust. For this reason, in order to market their proposed services, emergent VR-health industries have needed to build their medical expertise in-house, before they establish formal contacts with hospitals. As a result of such dialogue, the epistemic VR-health community has been evolving rapidly in the last few years, as 'disruptive' tech-consciousness battles with 'knowledge-club' rules, and two semiospheres generate newness along their incommensurate edges.

If the VR-health industry does manage to carve out a feasible operational space in the market, this could result in a radical innovation in the way that health services are provided. It would also be radical in terms of the inherent dialogues, because, until recently, video gaming, audiovisual storytelling and health sector/hospitals would have seemed strange bedfellows. Yet, it is this defamiliarized strangeness that promises significant innovation – as Russian Formalist Viktor Shklovsky intuited long ago, prefiguring cultural semiotics. As de Vaan, Vedres and Stark (2015) have demonstrated in the case of US video game industries, the larger the 'cognitive distance' between included teams, the more radical tend to be the resultant innovations. When there is some tension, some untranslatability between the perceptions of teams that master different styles or techniques, this tends to translate into distinctive output in the market – into novelties. Juri Lotman (2009) offers a general rule: the more culturally distant the cultural domains that end up in a dialogue, the greater could be the cultural 'explosion' resulting from it. Unique and innovative forms of culture are born from a combination of previously distant or conflicting ideas, forms or conventions.

Clive Thompson, in *Wired* magazine (Thompson, 2019), wrote that San Francisco and Silicon Valley have produced a vast number of successful internet companies. But the engineers living there typically do not encounter people from other walks of life and therefore have focused on organizing people's everyday lives – providing apps for socializing (Facebook), ride-summoning (Uber) or work interactions (Slack). Thompson contrasts this scenario with what he sees as a telling difference on the opposite US coast:

> In contrast, consider my home of New York City. Techwise, it's an also-ran compared with San Francisco, with less than a third of the venture capital. But it benefits from a greater diversity of influences. This is a city defined, in varying degrees, by publishing, finance, art, advertising, theater, and nightlife. And it produces a different landscape of talent. The tech people may be less likely to crank heads-down on their startups until midnight – because, hey, there's an Inuit throat-singing ensemble doing a residency in Red Hook!

Thompson concludes that place and social context influence innovation:

> The ideas platform is broader and weirder. When you think of New York's mainstream startups, many were founded to solve some problem that's almost hilariously artsy. There's Tumblr (fansites for emo teens) and Etsy (sell your bespoke handmade warez) and Kickstarter (get your poetry journal funded, folks!). SF has Patreon, sure, but NYC gave birth to the 'check-in', via Dodgeball and Foursquare. Cofounder Dennis Crowley wanted to use tech partly to make barhopping more fun.

Such emergent enterprises call for what Küng has called an 'interpretive' approach to strategic management (Küng, 2017: 70–2). In her view, firms in contemporary dynamically evolving sectors cannot rely on a 'rationalist' approach to strategy development, where studies of the competitive environment are carried out and then multiyear plans are developed to pursue set goals in that environment. Instead, the interpretive approach focuses on complexity within firms. It acknowledges that in contemporary institutions, people may be participants in multiple epistemic, social or cultural communities; they may be connected to the external environment in multiple ways; they may use different kinds of channels to acquire information; and they may interpret messages that reach them in different ways. The differences bring about communicative difficulties or disagreements within organizations, but by the same token, they constitute a model for bringing alternative viewpoints and new information and they facilitate the consideration of a diversity of options. Difference and disagreement enlarge the pool of alternative trajectories – the horizon of the possible – for the firm. All this means that the firm as a 'knowledge club' becomes more capable of responding to 'the actual semiotic milieu', as Lotman put it (1990: 134). It is more flexible, agile and able to recognize new trends in the environment, emergent needs among different people, new opportunities to use and combine existing knowledge to find solutions to existing challenges.

## Dialogue as action

All this suggests that dialogues are not explicit, easily identifiable processes – say where two parties are sitting at the desk and negotiating a technological standard. According to cultural semiotics, boundaries are everywhere and, therefore, so is dialogue across them, making dialogue more ubiquitous and multiparty than is usually assumed in the model of the psychological dyad. Boundaries distinguish different kinds of enterprises, but they also occur between people within enterprises who have different kinds of competences and belong to different epistemic communities or knowledge clubs. This means that dialogue is effectively an unavoidable cultural constant. It results from existing social groups – in economic sectors or industries, professions, interest groups, subcultures – intertwining and overlapping in increasingly complex ways, which may be understood as both tangled (somewhat chaotic) and rule-bound (somewhat controlled).

To extend an example we have discussed, the early mobile web domain evolved as a meeting ground for existing industries – handset makers, browser vendors, telecommunications industries, online services, content industries and so on. Sometimes they talked to each other directly, but, for the most part, as their operations became increasingly interrelated, they could react to each other's actions, with 'actions upon other actions', according to Foucault's model of governance (Foucault, 1982: 789–92; Pottage, 1998). Via these interoperative actions, the mobile web domain eventually settled into a coherent identity, convergent with the 'desktop web'.

This example enables us to understand 'dialogue' as a reaction to the action of others, which can take place in any semiotic modality, when those actors who are part of a domain react to or interact with others also part of a domain. As Foucault makes clear, taking action upon the action of others is part of the processes of power, where 'human beings are made subjects' (1982: 777), where 'subjects' are created in and through dialogic relations: they are *objectified* (e.g. speaking subjects), *divided* (e.g. good/bad, we/they) and *self-created* (e.g. sexual identity). A 'subject' then is one whose actions and identity are determined in and by dialogic relations, where Foucault locates power.

Via such a process – effectively 'interactive learning' in Lundvall's terms (2010) – the technological, textual, institutional and metacommunicative forms of the emergent domain gradually emerge. Once this domain starts to autocommunicate, self-codifying its norms, establishing distinctions with what it is not, it also starts to reduce opportunities for dialogue with the other. It is for this reason that in the semiosphere's periphery, dialogues dominate, while in its core, autocommunication predominates.

# Endogenous/exogenous

What this suggests for the analysis of change in digital society and culture is that an 'endogenous' approach is justified. This introduces a pair of terms that are familiar in economics but less so in cultural semiotics. Endogenous change is determined within the terms, values and variables already included in an explicit model of the economy. Change occurs when one of these variables changes. Exogenous change is imposed on the model from the outside; such as from politics, culture, technology and so on. Any resulting alteration in the economy is an 'exogenous shock'. For instance, in neoclassical economics, technological innovation is an external shock to the system. Innovation comes unexpectedly, out of the creative minds of inventors. As it is introduced to the market, it temporarily disrupts the established market 'equilibrium'. An endogenous approach, including the one we are proposing here, expands the model to include what neoclassical economics keeps external (Mansell, 2012). It turns the analytic gaze towards peripheries and to complex dialogues among different social and cultural subsystems, to exchanges of knowledge and learning arising from dialogue and to their settled combinations. In this view, no innovation emerges from a single enterprise but from the interactions between them: it belongs to systems, not to abstract inventors/minds acting outside the semiosphere.

## Endogenous semiospheres

An endogenous view, therefore, requires the analyst to identify the particular semiosphere they are interested in – say, the semiosphere of Augmented Reality – and to treat all dialogues and interactions related to it as internal. The aim would be to understand how such dialogues act (and thus cause change) in response to new forms, systems and institutions of the particular semiosphere, as well as to changed core/periphery asymmetries. As endogenous change is codified and institutionalized in action, it will create its own core – its dominant structures. At the same time there will also evolve a resistant, alternative or avant-garde periphery, which continues experimentation and dialogue with 'external' systems and institutions and exerts *endogenous* pressure to change in an already-solidifying core.

When change is institutionalized and its particular solutions and novel 'rules' (Dopfer and Potts, 2008) find wider take-up, the whole semiosphere of augmented reality may grow to become dominant in the culture, to become one of the new core systems of the global digital semiosphere. This has been suggested by technologist Kevin Kelly (2019), under the label of 'Mirrorworld' – a digitally created three-dimensional 'copy' of the 'real world', which integrates both the technologies of the semantic web (everything with metadata and links, contextualized and machine readable) and the 'internet of things' (gadgets connected to the internet). As the 5G internet infrastructures and standards evolve, this Mirrorworld would then *augment* or *gamify* the real world in unexpected ways. But, in the first place, all of it would be underpinned by novel augmented reality technologies – 'the awkward newborn that will grow into giant', as Kelly has put it (2019:76).

While the potential for AR to grow significantly is certainly there, right now its evolution is still in the early 'origination' phase (Dopfer and Potts, 2008). As Ibrus and Lassur have demonstrated (2019), this new technical affordance is currently driven mainly by very large technology vendors (Microsoft, Google, Apple), and then, in localities, by public sector agencies, be it local tourism boards, museums or other cultural heritage institutions. These often invest in experimental projects partly in order to prove to local ICT and online services companies that a feasible business case in AR can be made. It remains to be seen what subsequent developments will motivate AR's wider take-up by users and how the dialogue and interactions among different of institutional stakeholders will shape its global forms.

The purpose of this chapter has been to demonstrate that, in Lotman's cultural semiotics, the centripetal evolutionary force of culture, driven to codify and standardize, to generalize, fix and rule in proven ways, is always countered by another one. This is the centrifugal force resulting from dialogue in 'powerless' peripheries. These dialogues result from dissatisfaction, from perception of new needs and new solutions, from the desire to meet the other, to learn from it and to combine formerly distinct knowledge or meaning domains. For Lotman, dialogues and their effects are cultural constants; however, in digital culture these processes have not only intensified but become also more readily traceable (via data and 'clickstreams'). They may also be more crucial: in an increasingly interconnected world the closure of distinct domains may present risks. In order to ensure that institutions and systems adjust dynamically to new realities and to cope with new challenges, of planetary scale, the 'bubbles' may need to be blown from time to time.

# 14

# Foam: Production of dynamic multiplicity

*Words matter: we need a new vocabulary for policymaking.*
*Policy is ... about shaping a different future:* co-creating
markets and value.

(MARIANA MAZZUCATO, 2018, 'WHY VALUE MATTERS')

\* \* \*

In the previous chapters we discussed how autocommunication facilitates
the emergence and further evolution of subsystems in economic sectors that
produce culture. We demonstrated how autocommunicative activities help
to organize, reorganize and constitute sectors, industries and different kinds
of institutions; how autocommunication codifies and stabilizes them. Then
we showed how fixed, stable and enduring autocommunication conditions
a counterforce – the need for interchange, for dialogue among different
industries, sectors and institutions. The interactions of these two forces –
one facilitating relative homogeneity in the whole of the semiosphere, the
other heterogeneity – result in what we might call (following Sloterdijk,
2016) social 'foam' – an inherently tightly interstructured system where
every constitutive subsystem autocommunicates but is also forced into
dialogue with others.

If you'd like to think about a visualization of such a 'foam' structure,
then the Water Cube in Beijing offers a valuable glimpse of the multiple
possibilities. First, the cube itself is an architectural challenge, creating a
structure built for Aquatics in the form of bubbles, made of ETFE (a
fluorine-based synthetic polymer) on a steel frame, designed by Australian
architecture practice PTW. According to PTW:

FIGURE 14.1 *The Water Cube, Beijing Olympic Park* (photo Aaron Zhu, Wikimedia Commons).[2]

---

[2]Source: Panoramio, Creative Commons (https://commons.wikimedia.org/wiki/File:%22Water_Cube%22,_Olympic_water_events_stadium,_Beijing,_China_-_panoramio.jpg).

The concept combines the symbolism of the square in Chinese culture and the natural structure of soap bubbles translated into architectural form. The design uses state-of-the-art technology and materials to create a building that is visually striking, energy efficient, and ecologically friendly.[2]

In traditional Chinese culture, square = earth; circle = heaven, or *gai tian*. The Beijing Olympic Park included an allusion to this pairing in the square shape of the Water Cube next to the 'Bird's Nest' National Stadium part-designed by Ai Wei Wei. That combination of ancient symbolism, aquatic sports, high-tech materials and international cooperation already make for quite a bit of 'foam', but that's only the start. More recently, the Water Cube has been refurbished as a public 'water park' and to serve as an Ice Cube for the 2022 Winter Olympics (Curling competition). The bubbles themselves have been appropriated as a 2013 art project, led by New York and Beijing-based artist Jennifer Wen Ma and lighting designer Zheng Jianwei. Ma again brought ancient tradition (the I Ching) into contact with the digital semiosphere (Weibo's microblogging platform). With data analytics (using the Berlin-based open-source *vvvv* platform), she was able to condense each day's emoticons from Weibo into a daily representation of 'the collective mood of the Chinese people', using it to drive a dynamic display of mood colours on the Water Cube's translucent surface. In this artwork (a.k.a. innovation experiment) the Cube itself becomes a 'netizen' of the digital semiosphere, in creative dialogue with ancient traditions and contemporary connections, combining cultural autocommunication with global, technological and artistic dialogue:

Ancient Chinese texts and social media meet in a new giant light show at the Beijing National Aquatics Center. Nature and Man in Rhapsody of Light at the Water Cube, an installation created by artist Jennifer Wen Ma and lighting designer Zheng Jianwei, uses a computer program to translate I Ching and the collective mood of the Chinese people into a stunning real-time light display on the building's exterior. (Ma and Zheng, interviewed in 2013)[3]

---

[2]http://www.ptw.com.au/ptw_project/watercube-national-swimming-centre/.
[3]See: https://www.littlemeat.net/water-cube; and an interview with Ma and Zheng: https://www.youtube.com/watch?v=9RS92_vnYpw. For *vvvv* see: https://vvvv.org/.

# Innovation systems

Powerful subsystems focus more on autocommunication; smaller and weaker ones focus on dialogue. The governance of contemporary society and economy requires an appropriate balance between dialogue and autocommunication. In this chapter, let us look at some of the core concepts and processes of such governance on a national level.

There is nothing new to the argument that it is good to link different economic sectors and industries, to facilitate knowledge exchange among different kinds of institutions. It has been evolving at least since Friedrich List and his *National System of Political Economy* (1841). The idea achieved new impetus with the articulation of 'national innovation systems' theory in the 1980s, in the works of Chris Freeman (1995), Bengt Åke Lundvall (1985) and many others. Indeed, the concept is now part of the innovation policies of most countries in Europe and elsewhere (OECD, 1997).

There is variation in how the concept is understood, but what all models of national innovation systems share, first, is that the growth and development of economic systems is conditioned by accumulation and growth of *knowledge* and, second, that growth of knowledge results from interactions, especially knowledge exchange between different kinds of *institutions* and their systems. Chaminade et al. (2018) have divided the approaches into two – the narrow and the broad. Narrow models focus on the interactions between research institutions and firms. The sequence of knowledge investments that in this tradition may bring growth has basic science first, then technical engineering and then markets. In contrast, broad models (Lundvall, 1992, 2010b; Potts, 2011) focus on all kinds of interactions that involve and result in cross-boundary learning and the emergence of new institutional constellations. For Lundvall, the concept of learning has been central: that is, knowledge-exchange and learning between those with diverse expertise or skills, learning between producers and users, and learning by interacting by using and by doing (Johnson, 2010; Lundvall, 1992). Factoring in learning in this way means that the analytic focus of innovation systems scholarship is divided between large-scale institutional settings and people's interpretative or cognitive capacities (Kull, 2018).

## Creative innovation and social network markets

Further, scholarship in the 'interactive learning' approach has notably emphasized the role of culture. Building on Commons' (1934) articulation of culture as 'collective control of individual action' and Veblen's writing on economic institutions as 'habits of use and wont' and 'habits of thought' (in Veblen, 2017), it has been accepted in evolutionary approaches to institutional economics that economic 'behaviour' is shaped by enculturation – that is, that culture conditions human actions (Johnson, 2010: 25).

However, Lundvall and others working within this tradition are concerned first and foremost with *national* systems of innovation. Therefore, they address the challenges that producers face owing to differences in national *cultures*. That is, 'culture' in their terms is a homogeneous national system (French, Chinese, etc.) that shapes the behavioural codes and norms structuring production processes of all kinds in those countries (likely making them opaque to foreign firms). They do not understand culture in Lotmanian terms – as an inherently heterogeneous system consisting of various kinds of more or less temporal subcultures or other systems of meaning, affecting production processes, forms of organization in industries and consumption processes alike. Also they ignore the role of cultural or creative industries or non-market production and the use of arts, media and leisure entertainment as an important constituent of national innovation systems.

This restriction of innovation to science, engineering and markets ignores the contemporary growth of the services economy, the substantial role of media and creative industries and the broader mediatization of social relations (Hepp, 2013; Hjarvard, 2013; Lundby, 2009). Analyses of these trends have found not only that the creative industries contribute usefully to national GDPs and are in a constant process of generating novelties (the variety that drives innovation) but also that creative innovation shapes technical innovation. For example, consumers' interest in cultural *content* drives the evolution of consumer electronics; their cultural practices condition the forms and affordances of these technologies.

The creative and cultural industries, their products, services and markets, have peculiarities that need to be taken into account when conceptualizing contemporary innovation systems, especially as they converge with other industries (Ibrus, 2019). The classic anomaly of creative products and services is that their use-value is unknown before the act of usage (you can't 'demand' artworks, music or other performances prior to they are 'supplied'), but it is usage that determines price (which may bear no relation to production costs). As cultural products are expected to provide, at a minimum, unique experiences, they must generate new meaning. These cannot, however, be experienced or deciphered beforehand. In this case, consumer choice cannot be 'rational' (based on price), as is presumed in neoclassical economics. It is instead mainly dependent on the choices of others ('influencers', fashion-leaders or prestige personnel in one's social network), such that choices are set by experiences and recommendations that reach consumers via their social networks ('word of mouth' for a film, for instance). It is for this reason that Potts et al. (2008) have proposed re-conceptualizing the creative industries as '*social network markets*' – markets where production and consumption decisions are based on the actions and signals of other agents in the social network, and prices are set by prestige, not cost or utility. This definition gives primacy to communicative actions in market dynamics and not to economic signals such as price or future gains. The anchor of neoclassical economics is *self-interested* choice, but social network markets trade in socially sanctioned choice (much as universities trade on prestige and credentialism, because a degree from a 'top' university is worth more in the jobs market than from an unknown one, no matter how well taught). That is, communication among market participants, increasingly organized into networks, determines how novelties emerge and whether they are adopted.

# Coordination mechanisms

Potts et al. (2008) also argue that such communications across social networks become the main means for innovation-system *coordination* in the contemporary mediatized service economy. Thence, Jason Potts (2011: 115) suggests, the creative and cultural industries become crucial players in contemporary innovation systems, because they facilitate and strengthen *social networks*. They ensure rapid adoption of new communication affordances, especially among desirable youth demographics, who act like a flash mob when they crowd into and then disperse from one preferred platform to the next: MySpace to Facebook to Instagram to Snapchat to TikTok.

The *social network market* reduces some of the uncertainties associated with consumption, as long as the way it works is understood:

- Supply precedes demand.
- Choices depend on the choices of others.
- Price is determined by prestige.
- Consumers may also be entrepreneurs, because consumption of creativity or fashion is also productive signalling to the social network market.
- All forms of media and culture can be used to process social information about new ideas, new phenomena, new possibilities and consequences, all judged on what peers and influencers are up to.

When it comes to how social network enterprises organize themselves, then, as with any novelties market, they keep organizing and reorganizing into complex value-chains where they sometimes compete, sometimes cooperate, sometimes fail and sometimes 'go viral'. It's a game of probabilities not predictable certainties, so good market information is crucial, which explains why data-mining and 'big data' play such a prominent role in social-network enterprises, which have created entirely new markets for 'big data' analytics.

## Creative firms

Creative and cultural industries are said to have an 'hourglass' structure with regard to the size of the companies, where at the top is a bulge, occupied by a small number of very large companies – tech giants, publishing groups or broadcasters. At the bottom is a bigger bulge, comprising the vast reservoir of very small companies, start-ups, sole-trader businesses and volunteers, who each employ only a handful of people. In between, where the 'hourglass' is cinched, there is a 'missing middle' of mid-sized industrial enterprises. Such a structure is hard to incorporate into existing policy frameworks. It combines incommensurate entities: monopolistic corporations at the 'top' and hyper-competitive micro-enterprises at the 'bottom'; it includes both public and private enterprises, and both a paid and a voluntary (or precarious) workforce. There is at the same time a dearth of mid-sized firms of the kind that, in an industrial structure, make significant contributions to employment, GDP, taxation (and industry-lobbies) and thence to public policy.

And yet, the structure makes sense in Lotman's terms. The large companies are the incumbent core and rule-makers of the creative-industries semiosphere. Myriad small firms spread outwards; some ultra-peripheral, others closer to the centre (indeed, a business plan of some small firms is to be brought out by one of the giants). Relationships among these small companies are in flux: competition is inevitable but, being small and vulnerable, they also need to cluster and cooperate. Small firms are often each other's customers and most immediate colleagues; they form social networks and complex, often reciprocal producer-user relationships.

Potts et al. (2008) suggest that such relationships facilitate the contemporary *growth of knowledge* and the emergence of new rules/ innovations for the economic semiosphere as a whole. They are the practical means for Lundvall's 'interactive learning'. Their innovations are incremental and artisanal (see Mokyr, 2009): the outcome of constant tinkering, iterations, modification, improvement or variation of emergent phenomena, whether platforms, products, services or textual forms. Sometimes they can lead to more radical or 'explosive' innovation. For instance, the early forms of self-publishing on YouTube evolved into a globally complex subindustry of 'multichannel networks' with its own genre systems, codes of conduct, business models, professional roles and so on: a social institution undermining the preceding structures of the audiovisual industries (Lobato,

2016; Vonderau, 2016; Burgess and Green, 2018). In this case the periphery is stabilizing, to become a new core.

## Overlapping systems

Those small creative-industries enterprises, mostly start-ups, are apt to link up and cluster with other sectors, such as tourism, education or health care (Ibrus, 2019). Another phenomenon in the broader semiosphere is 'system overlapping' – systems becoming intertwined, increasingly part of each other. Within the sphere of media and culture, important drivers have been cross-media strategies and transmedia storytelling.

What is the rationale of the institutions facilitating these hybrids, from the meso-perspective? On the one hand, we see that large enterprises, those owning a significant franchise or content brand and related intellectual property rights, seek to build on potential economies of scope and to develop related content for a variety of media and platforms. They need to do this because audiences are fragmented. Chasing audience maximization, social-media giants seek to reconnect audience segments that are dispersed among numerous different media and platforms. Smaller content or service companies – usually specialized on a certain modality or platform, say mobile game developers or animators – in turn seek to link to larger content brands and their network effects. However, this means that cross-media or transmedia strategies do not bring about full convergence or homogeneity, but linked difference, where autonomous (already autocommunicating) domains of culture establish dialogue, creating only relative coherence between them.

This is also why transmedia and cross-media practices and strategies are of societal importance. They bring about more intense intersemiotic translation and dialogue at various levels of culture. They contribute to interchange between different media, connect different kinds of institutions and users. They facilitate the emergence of socially pertinent representations and robust cultural heterogeneity, enabling social evolution (Ibrus and Ojamaa, 2018). While it can be argued that culture has always been a transmedia phenomenon (Scolari et al., 2014), intersemiotic intertwining is growing more elaborate, across more semiospheres and subsystems, which are in complex dialogue with each other, as well as with their own core/periphery relationship.

If we now return to the concept of innovation systems, a new question arises: how to facilitate those systems in the era of general mediatization? The question is justified, because a practical function of innovation systems thinking is to propose innovation policy improvements for countries or groups. To do that, the importance of media, communications, and other cultural industries, in facilitating knowledge-exchange needs to be recognized, along with the complex interactive learning processes in societies and among its different subsystems.

Then there is the question of what kinds of institutions are needed, especially in the sphere of media and culture, for such facilitation? As Cohendet and Llerena (1997: 227) put it, 'diversity drives evolution, and evolution generates diversity'. In other words, diversity is essential for well-functioning innovation systems. Johnson (2010: 39) has suggested that diversity in the institutional system is just as important for economic change as diversity in the production structure or in knowledge domains.

## Public and private

The system must include both public and private institutions. Public institutions are ready to invest in coordination activities that produce public value, developing knowledge resources (such as research and its results) for use by multiple parties. Public institutions extend to knowledge diffusion, such as public libraries or public broadcasting. Further, with their multiplicity of conflicting goals, public institutions bring alternative objectives to market-based systems (Gregersen, 2010: 136). They expand the potential range of innovation trajectories. Diversity in the system, involving both public and private institutions, is also important for the absorption of shocks. In the era of dynamic change, the system needs alternative operational models and objectives to alleviate risks and develop resilience.

With regard to creative and cultural industries, public service media institutions can operate as important coordinators of culture-oriented innovation systems because they invest in activities that create public value – such as investigative reporting, promoting alternative forms of culture, experimenting with new kinds of content formats, popularizing science and producing environmental programmes. These are either high-risk activities or programme formats without prior or known commercial value. But once public-service media have developed functional formats, created brand value for specific content or cultural forms, all kinds of other agents, including commercial firms, can build on this. The BBC was a decisive pioneer in the development of online platforms, saving itself from Thatcherite attack and technological irrelevance in the process. Its reinvented World Service performed the same trick for digital radio.[4] Bennett et al. (2012) report that when UK's public service broadcasters (BBC and Channel 4) started to commission new interactive formats from what were initially small independent digital content companies in the UK,

---

[4]Online story here: https://www.theregister.co.uk/2012/11/28/the_bbc_news_online_story/; digital radio here: https://www.telegraph.co.uk/culture/tvandradio/3562264/BBC-World-Service-a-digital-radio-pioneer.html.

it facilitated their subsequent development and growth. Working with large national broadcasters on their cross-media strategies and digital output gave these small companies the skills and experience to achieve international visibility, to develop novel products and services and eventually to achieve new international strategies and presence. Public media institutions are very much a part of innovation systems, although few of them were set up for that purpose. They produce 'public value' (Benington and Moore, 2011) that can then be utilized by a variety of parties, including commercial agencies.

The eventual focus of innovation-systems approaches on generating public value, on diversity and learning, has been controversial among policymakers. These functions undercut the neoliberal rationale for small government, deregulation and unfettered operation of market forces (Mazzucato, 2015). Innovation-systems thinking has provided new rationales for governments to intervene in and regulate markets. For instance, the global platformization of various service sectors may undermine the functioning of national/regional innovation systems, because privately owned global platforms rarely participate in these systems. For instance, global tourism platforms, such as Airbnb, Tripadvisor or Booking.com, overtook the market by offering local tourism operators ready-made communications tools (while keeping most of the user information to themselves). They demotivated these industries to work with the local media or ICT industries to develop relevant novel solutions. As an outcome, the locally relevant processes of 'interactive learning' are largely missing (Ibrus and Nani, 2019). Therefore, global platforms pose a variety of local risks (van Dijck et al., 2018), among which is a threat to national semiospheres when they undermine the readiness of national innovation systems to establish dialogic relationships among local firms, impeding the growth of integrating 'foam'.

# Foam

We have argued in this chapter that the governance of contemporary national innovation systems means the governance of 'foam' and care for its constant further bubbling – the coordination of dynamic multiplicity in social organization. Our second argument follows: the governance and regulation of contemporary creative media dynamics requires an understanding of the importance of culture in economics and of economics in culture, even though the economics *of* culture differs from the neoclassical model.

The natural born partners for nurturing this understanding are, on the one hand, innovation systems studies, based on various forms of institutional or evolutionary economics, and, on the other hand, cultural semiotics focused on systemic change in cultures, a.k.a. cultural science. Dialogue between economics and culture – between evolution and value – may seem far-fetched, since these are not adjacent intellectual domains, but that's why the encounter is so productive of new information and knowledge, arising from the mutual untranslatability and incommensurable calculations of the two approaches. The attempt is justified not because many of their premises may turn out to be similar, but because the digital semiosphere represents a qualitative change or in Lotman's terms an irreversible 'explosion', which is driving the continuing growth of the online service economy and the related mediatization or culturalization of most other leading sectors of the economy.

Mediatization of the economy not only means the multiplication of dialogue and 'interactive learning' between creative and other sectors, but also that these other sectors consequently become structurally similar. They fragment into smaller units, but these are more interconnected in complex ways. These units collaborate and compete, they learn from each other, adapt and modify each other's creations, such that the overall system grows and develops as an outcome collective and networked group action, not merely from aggregated individual behavioural choices.

Such population-based innovations accumulate incrementally, but their interactions accumulate across the whole of the system, which may, from time to time, lead to radical innovations. Such interactions and the evolution of relevant networks occur at different sites. Most often the cross-fertilization occurs in urban environments, cities being the crucible of the creative economy (Hartley, 2015a), but national cultures and economies are also important spaces for newness, and because legislative sovereignty is national (unlike global and digital media) these are the most comprehensively governed systems. This is why we have focused on national systems in this chapter. However, no country is an island, so in the next chapter we turn to the global digital semiosphere.

# PART FIVE

# Macro-scale: Global system

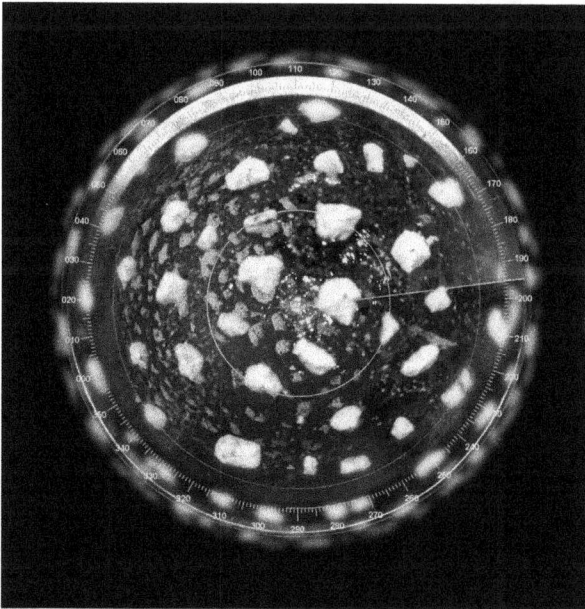

*Peeter Laurits, 'Atlas of Heavens 22' (2000), from* Atlas of Heavens
https://www.peeterlaurits.com/archive/atlas-of-heavens

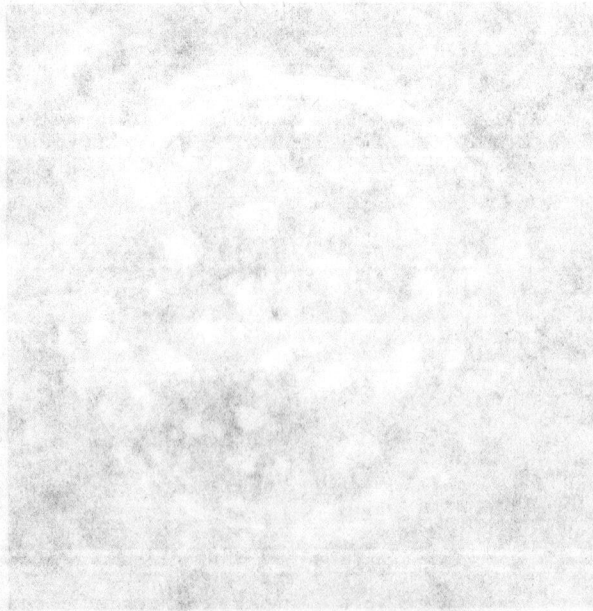

# 15

# Globe: Production of digital distinctions

*Is the world sleepwalking into a crisis?* Global risks are intensifying
but the collective will to tackle them appears to be lacking. *Instead,
divisions are hardening ... We are drifting deeper into global
problems from which we will struggle to extricate ourselves.*
(WORLD ECONOMIC FORUM, 2019: 9)

\* \* \*

## Scope and scale

We have mentioned the logic of economies of scope and scale (Chapter 12),
and their effects on media markets and industries, motivating convergence.
Scope and scale work because of their rationalities. In relation to *scope*, once
you own significant IPR (intellectual property rights), it makes economic
sense to use them on other platforms and in other modalities, either to
support and market the original product or to generate new ones. Similarly,
if you have built up a large production infrastructure – say a large newspaper
or a TV channel – it makes sense to use its outputs on a variety of media and
platforms. The cost of digital conversion and output is cheap compared with
the sunk capital already invested in machinery and production facilities.

With the broad digitization and 'mediatization of everything' in
contemporary culture, economies of *scale* have started to affect other
cultural industries as well as other economic sectors, especially all service
industries. It all starts with the *nonrival* nature of information products and

services – one can sell such products but continue owning these (enabled by international copyright agreements). Initial costs of media content production are often high, but the marginal cost of making digital copies is very low, so media industries always strive towards maximizing their audiences/customers, such that a multimillion-dollar movie or TV series can be watched by each consumer for a few dollars (or at no cost, in exchange for a subscription and eyeballs). Compared with start-ups and newcomers, it has proven easier for already-large media companies to hold on to a dominant position, once achieved, and to grow further, including internationally – hence the oligarchic trend among the bigger companies.

In the digital era this trend has been amplified by 'network effects'. These matter because they allow market leaders to grow even bigger. Network effects can be understood as 'demand-side' economies of scale. It is beneficial for people to use services that are used by a majority of others, even if they are not the most advanced. Skype, for example, may no longer be a superior service for internet-based calls, but it is still used by many, because 'everybody else' seems to be using it and therefore a call is easier to set up (this is a classic 'social network market' phenomenon). In the same way, YouTube is used for video-sharing, on the assumption that this is what everyone else does. However, this means that while classic economies of scale facilitated the emergence of *oligopolies*, digital-era network effects facilitate the evolution of internet *monopolies*. More important, these monopolies are not bounded by national boundaries: they are striving to be global.

The media and cultural industries that are most actively contributing to the production of the digital semiosphere are motivated by audience-maximization. Normally, they do not produce small sets of custom-made products with high margins. Instead, their operational models rely on high turnover and vast customer sets. In turn, this motivates them to internationalize their business, not to serve the national home market. Some do it regionally: Scandinavian enterprises consider the whole of Nordic and Baltic region as their 'home' turf and enter most of these neighbouring markets. Some, however, have global strategies. When it comes to more classical forms of media – especially publishing and broadcasting – the world has long been divided between five large media groups –Time-Warner, Disney, Viacom, News Corporation and Bertelsmann: four from the United States, one from Germany. There are also other large companies, but the big five tend to prevail in most regions of the world. They may not enter all countries, especially not the smallest ones, but they are represented in the larger markets.

# Sending and receiving

Ulrike Rohn (2010) has studied how large Western companies have (or have not) entered three largest, but very different, Asian economies – China, Japan and India. Two of these are elective democracies on the Western model; one is a People's Republic. China has been open to international cooperation, but it is protectionist, regulated and centrally controlled. There's a saying: 'If you want to succeed in China, make sure your company's goals line up with the government's'.[1] In other words, China is no push-over market. This means, for instance, collaborating with local partners in order to stimulate China's own domestic economy. The Japanese media market is fully saturated and dominated by strong local companies. India has been less saturated and open to Western media, but it is complex in terms of its own internal cultural diversity. In response to these differences, companies will struggle with legal, political or economic barriers, and in addition they will need to address various cultural barriers to Western content. Rohn has shown that companies use different strategies to overcome these barriers: buying a stake in established local companies, starting new ones (especially joint ventures), using intermediaries and so on. When it comes to cultural barriers, the big question is whether to provide culturally 'odourless' universal content or to adapt to local requirements. Rohn (2011) suggests that the success of either strategy depends on which phase a culture/media system is in – the 'receiving' or in the 'sending' phase (Lotman, 1990: 144–7). A culture's relative openness to international cultural trade changes from *receptive*, when foreign influence flows freely, to *resistant*, when the time comes – as it clearly has for China – to take over a 'sending' role. China's switch was signalled in its 'belt and road' initiative (from 2013 onwards).

The process of indigenizing cross-border trade and institutions like companies can itself be divided into five stages (see Chapters 5 and 9). A text or utterance, for example a foreign film, but also, as here, a foreign company or institution, is first received *as foreign*, its difference from the familiar being its value. Next, its semiotic load is transformed as it is repeated, imitated and copied along the cultural periphery of the receiving culture. Then, its *codes* are absorbed, abstracted, indigenized, remixed and recoded, bringing it towards the core of the receiving culture. New texts can then be generated, containing new ideas, which can then be exported back to the previously transmitting culture, turning it into the receiving one in turn.

The internationalization of firms in the digital semiosphere is a *translation* process. It occurs in these five phases, which are homologous with respect to both translation and textual communication, following a receiver/sender turn-taking logic:

---

[1]See for instance, the *quid pro quo* that China expects from Tesla: https://supchina.com/2020/01/16/how-china-is-using-elon-musk-to-further-its-ev-ambitions/.

- *Strangeness.* In the first stage of *exposure* to new texts or forms of foreign media, audiences value these as something exotic and interesting while viewing the media of their own culture as inferior. This was broadly the situation in the whole of Eastern Europe after the Iron Curtain collapsed at the end of the 1980s. It was also a time of opportunity for Western media conglomerates to reproduce themselves, without needing to borrow new clothes, and so to extend existing products in 'untranslated' form. Condé Nast (in the former Soviet and East European states) and Hachette (in China) were quick off the mark with *Vogue* and *Elle*, unapologetically reproducing their most provocatively Western styles, models, brands – and vision – and reaching new audiences eager to embrace the transformational promise of the foreign. As Gilles Lipovetsky (1991: 23) puts it, 'Fashion plays such a radical role in history because it institutes an essentially modern social system, freed from the grip of the past.'

- *Transformation.* The second stage could be characterized by gradual *adaptation or imitation* of imported media as local content producers learn how to create such different products. This is the phase that annoys copyright-holders and results in accusations of intellectual property theft, litigation and trade sanctions. But as commentators have pointed out, 'copying' can easily become 'innovation', creating more and different values from ideas, which is exactly what a Lotmanian approach reveals, and what China's 'tradition' of *shanzhai* copying and reverse-engineering relies on. IPR 'enforcement' is more about *protecting rents* than rewarding innovation (and it may be even more unethical than 'stealing' IP, as in the case of generic drugs).[2]

- *Abstraction.* In the third stage a perception emerges that these foreign *formats, elements and codes* could be improved if their concepts are used for local production, taking into account local cultural contexts, integrating locally relevant cultural conventions or references integrating. This occurs when TV channels produce new local formats, adapted from unique forms of foreign content or formats, or when a popular format like Wuxia (martial arts) films are produced *as Western* films and media, from Hong Kong Kung Fu movies to Hollywood mega-productions like Ang Lee's *Crouching*

---

[2]The debate continues. See: https://www.scmp.com/comment/opinion/article/3046129/us-targeting-china-intellectual-property-theft-fight-really-worth (from an innovation and ethical point of view), vs. https://foreignpolicy.com/2019/10/16/china-intellectual-property-theft-progress/ (from a strategic and diplomatic point of view).

*Tiger Hidden Dragon* (2001); or when Japanese anime comics
are Westernized as graphic novels, which are then established as a
previously unknown 'native' genre.

- *Productivity.* In the fourth stage, the previously foreign textual
elements have been dissolved entirely into the culture, meaning that
local companies now produce indigenously hybrid but innovative
formats: this is 'remix culture'. An example of this might be the
Korean film industry (as part of a larger *Hallyu* or Korean Wave
phenomenon), specifically the oeuvre of Bong Joon-Ho. This
culminated with Director Bong winning three Oscars in 2020 for
his film *Parasite* (best picture, best director, best original screenplay).
An avid fan of Hollywood cinema, Bong Joon-Ho had internalized
its blockbuster tropes and narrative structures but synthesized
these with Korea's local social circumstances and cultural milieu.
The outcome has been a new hybrid form, often seen to redefine,
even to save the classic Hollywood blockbuster. Similarly, the TV
series *Crash Landing on You* (16 episodes, 2020), was a top-10 hit
across Korea, China, Japan, and internationally via Netflix. It used
familiar melodrama/romcom tropes to tell a startlingly original story
about love across the boundary between North and South Korea,
humanizing the North in a drama that was essentially *about* the
productive process of translation between opposites.
- *Transmission.* In the fifth stage, the formerly receiving culture
becomes the sending culture, which now exports newly minted
unique and novel formats. Think here of Sweden as an exporter of
popular music. Having been for decades an open market for foreign
artists and their influences, starting from jazz, rock 'n' roll and beat
music, it learned from those, eventually to produce ABBA. This band
was its first vocal-heavy international outfit, which offered a unique
contrast to the bass- and drum-heavy styles popular in the dominant
Anglosphere markets. This early success was consolidated by the
rapid development of its own pop-music industry, culminating in
the emergence of Spotify, the new core of the global music industry
(Johansson, 2010), which eventually even Taylor Swift had to deal
with.

All this means that there are stages where countries are more receptive to
foreign investment, enterprises and media/cultural content, while during
other phases, they are not. For exporters, this means developing different
strategies: in the first case you can drop finished products into the market; in
other instances, you need to make appropriate local adaptations. Of course,
this is a game of trial and error, sometimes resulting in eye-watering losses
and sometimes untold profits.

# Media imperialism or spreading innovation?

To address the global dichotomies of sending and receiving countries versus unidirectional global cultural flows, there is a widely agreed change taking place. In the last quarter of the twentieth century, the concern of many media researchers and cultural policymakers around the world was with *unidirectional* flows of media out of the United States towards the rest of the world. Perhaps a landmark moment was Jeremy Tunstall's 1977 book *The Media Are American*. He argued that while mass media originated in Europe and elsewhere, the United States grew to dominate global media, because nearly every mass medium was *industrialized* within the United States, where media industries enjoyed a vast domestic market which was serviced almost entirely in English, whatever previous language immigrants spoke. That made exporting their products easier, because Anglophone markets were themselves international, following the colonial contours of the former British Empire, whose own imperial policies of trade and education had made English a lingua franca that many countries with their own national languages used for international communication (prior to the Industrial Revolution, the common language of world affairs had been French).

US production companies could earn back their initial investments in their home market, which was big enough to enable mass production, not only of consumer goods but also of media – comics, books, film, TV series and so on. All this enabled flexibility in export markets, both in pricing and in special offers and targeting of different national market segments. Exploitation of these advantages was vigorous, even ruthless, so that it became a common trope around the world after the 1970s to talk about America's 'cultural imperialism'.

The 'Global Village' that Marshall McLuhan foresaw in the 1960s, facilitated by the immediacy of the electronic broadcasting technologies and the uptake of US TV, film, radio and publishing around the world, can be understood as the first characterization of a truly global semiosphere. Yet, from the perspective of McLuhan's contemporaries, that semiosphere was homogenized by the American cultural industries and their global exporting power. The global village was *American*; decidedly not multicultural, multilingual or multivalent. For others, its motto of '*e pluribus unum*' (out of many, one) became all *unum*, no *pluribus*.

Nevertheless, no such power asymmetry can be absolute in the semiosphere. Despite the grim predictions at the time, despite also the advantages that American cultural industries enjoyed, and their heavy investment in global distribution settlements, nevertheless things changed over time, marked by Tunstall himself when thirty years later he published a new book called *The Media Were American* (Tunstall, 2008). This book made the case that instead of sole American control of world news flows and global entertainment markets, we now see global media comprising complex interlocking national, regional and cultural systems, corporations and forms.

How did that happen? A series of studies from around the world (for instance, Adamu, 2012; Kong, 2014; Kwon and Kim, 2014; Kawashima and Lee, 2018) suggests that local clusters of media and other creative companies, together with the 'interactive learning' processes among them, their modifications, incremental innovations and accumulating knowledge, lead eventually to them exporting their creations. Well-known examples here are Bollywood in India; Nollywood in Nigeria; South Korean *Hallyu* and K-Pop; TV and online enterprises in Brazil, Denmark and UK; video gaming industries in Finland and Sweden; and so on. And this is to say nothing of expertise used for international mischief: hacking, spamming, trolling and 'fake news', generated in industrial quantities out of countries whose own media are relatively unknown in the American sphere (e.g. Russia, Kosovo, China, Middle East countries).

Of these local industry clusters, some have evolved on their own – as for instance Bollywood and Nollywood – sustained by vast local or regional markets, as well as by flexible distribution networks adapted to local cultural, social and economic circumstances. The complex grass-roots distribution of Nollywood video films in Nigeria, Africa, and among African diasporas, could be seen as predicting the evolution of contemporary digital distribution and consumption (Lobato, 2010).

By contrast, in Europe and elsewhere, the emergence of creative industries clusters has often been driven by top-down policies. The development of such clusters has sometimes been criticized for constituting an uncritical Xeroxing of (British) policies across different countries and regions (Pratt, 2009), although it has also inspired progressive innovation policies for emergent economies and their indigenous cultures in diverse countries (Hartley, Wen and Li, 2015: 129–66; Crescenzi et al., 2019). Crescenzi and colleagues especially have demonstrated how the reception and adoption of such different models and how they affect innovation in different locations is deeply dependent on social and market structures, production efficiencies, forms of rent-seeking, competition and income distribution (Crescenzi et al., 2019: 29).

In the European context, however, the aggregate effects of EU-level sectoral regulations and local investments have produced results. European-level agreements and instruments to support more co-productions have precipitated an industry focus on films and TV series that can more easily travel across national boundaries. The EU's Audiovisual Media Services Directive (AVMSD) obliges European TV channels to fill 50 per cent of their programmes with European content. This too has motivated cross-border trade in European content and related investments in European audiovisual industries.

For example, look at Denmark, especially its leading production house Zentropa. This was founded in 1992 by Peter Aalbæk Jensen, Lars von Trier and Vibeke Windeløv (who was von Trier's producer until 2008). Since the late 1990s, Danish film policy has followed a straightforward transnational strategy. The very concept of what counts as a Danish film has changed significantly. Support has increasingly been given to films with an all-international cast and storylines (Bondebjerg, 2016). Zentropa, in turn, has been a shining example of how to build on those policy developments, both at national and at EU level, so much so that Mette Hjort has called their strategy 'opportunistic transnationalism' (Hjort, 2010). By 2019 the company had made more than 200 films, pursuing an explicit international network-building strategy from the beginning by working on co-production and establishing or partnering tens of subsidiaries across Europe.

The effectiveness of their strategy was recognized when Zentropa was named 'European Producer of the Year' in 2000, just as its distribution company, Trust Film Sales, won the Eurimages prize as 'European Exporter of the Year'. An important locally relevant step in their strategy has been the establishment of Filmbyen in 1999, a set of shooting studios and office space for film companies in Avedøre. Filmbyen has driven an internationally oriented audiovisual production cluster in Denmark. Such strategies have resulted in steady growth for the Danish film production sector, whose export revenues grew 400 per cent between 2009 and 2017. In 2019 the 'streaming wars' between the major VOD-platforms motivated even more international demand for Danish TV and film productions.

The spread of local industry strongholds has conditioned the development of what were previously known as 'counter-flows' – counter to American dominance, that is. Indeed, global exchanges in audiovisual content have become multidirectional. That is, there are many more of Lotman's 'sending' cultures around.

# Digital

What has been the role of digital culture and its networked infrastructures in this context? Online platforms have augmented or even accelerated the quick growth of clusters facilitating 'counter-flows', as for instance the case of *Hallyu*. The 'Korean Wave' of popular culture products dominates many Asian markets and beyond – as witness, among other phenomena, the conquest of the known world by Korean boy-band BTS, who nonetheless retain their 'Koreanness'.[3] The creative use of social media and video-sharing

---

[3]Korean writer Noah Yoo commented on the BTS 2018 tour of the US: 'At this point, it's well established that language and cultural barriers have virtually no bearing on K-pop's popularity ... Why that is remarkable is because BTS have retained a unique sense of their Koreanness, a culture that, unlike the British Invasion bands, doesn't share a language or Eurocentric musical traditions with American audiences.' https://pitchfork.com/thepitch/bts-how-the-biggest-boy-band-in-the-world-stays-radically-korean-citi-field-live-review/

platforms has contributed to their surge in popularity beyond culturally proxemic boundaries. Most recently, European and American Instagram influencers and YouTubers, always searching new trends, have discovered the entertaining nature of 'K-beauty', the latest and in many ways brightest materialisation of *Hallyu*. Face masks in bright-coloured milkshake cups, lids depicting baby faces, snail-slime facials and panda face masks have followed in the footsteps of K-pop.

While the global social media and streaming platforms have enabled the formation of various 'counter-flows', it needs to be noticed that the operational strategies of large international platforms (which are almost all American) have been notably different from the way that publishing or broadcasting media conglomerates expanded across the world last century. Apart from their interactions with China, US platforms are not really developing specific strategies to enter a new national market – say, via buying an existing media outlet or starting a new one and so on. Instead, these platforms just open their global service to certain territory. If it offers professionally produced content, as in case of Spotify or Netflix, it needs first to address the territorial rights for the particular country, but after that, especially in case of smaller countries, little effort is invested in servicing a specific market.

Here we can return to innovation systems theory, and particularly to Lundvall (2010: 67–9), who addressed the issue of multinational firms and their effects on national innovation systems. He suggested that their relative inflexibility in the markets in which they are present may undermine the functioning of those local innovation systems. That is, locally present multinational firms may simply be 'taking' the market and not participating effectively in the local 'interactive learning' processes. While Lundvall did not have the contemporary online service sector in mind, their effect to local cultural innovation processes is similarly limited. Platforms such as Amazon are providing services from a distance, without much of localization, apart from prestige projects designed to soften nationalist sentiment. For instance, the two-season thriller series *Marseille* (starring Gerard Depardieu), a locally made blockbuster series introduced that Netflix introduced in 2016. Netflix has later maintained its presence in France, opening a new Paris office in 2020 and announcing numerous new offerings, promising 'French series and films for French people' and at the same time promoting 'diversity in all its forms'.[4]

So, with Netflix we may be seeing a change. Their new strategy is to produce new locally relevant productions in local languages, although only in larger countries. TV series such as *Marseille* in France, *13%* in Brazil, *Dark* and *Dogs of Berlin* in Germany, *Suburra* in Italy, *1983* in Poland, *La Casa de Papel* in Spain, and several others are targeted to larger language

---

[4]See the company announcement: https://media.netflix.com/en/press-releases/netflix-opens-new-paris-office-and-increases-investment-in-france.

communities. While doing this, Netflix has been quick to emphasize that its 'foreign language' productions are being watched by users across the world. This has been confirmed by Straubhaar, who proposes that global taste patterns are becoming less dependent on the 'cultural proximity' of some kinds of content. This recognition is significant as it was Straubhaar once coined the 'cultural proximity' thesis and argued that audience's first preference is always content from own or neighbouring national culture (Straubhaar, 1991). Still, Netflix is nevertheless producing locally relevant series because of increasingly strident demand for them, coming especially from European countries and the EU in general, related to the fact that the catalogues of the dominant VOD services contain mostly American content (Grece et al., 2015). Demands to push back against this trend are increasingly encoded in official regulations – for instance, as part of European Union's Digital Single Market initiative, the newly updated AVMSD directive demands that at least 30 per cent of VOD catalogues must be of European origin.

Such policy positions and discourses indicate that while these countries are too small to resist being 'receiving cultures' in economic terms, in cultural terms they want to become sending cultures, too. Markets are regulated so that multinationals need to provide localizations, cooperating with local industries and in the process empowering them to become senders too. Many EU countries have developed a set of policy tools – international co-production funding, tax reliefs or cash rebates – aimed at attracting large foreign film or TV productions to their countries, so that local industries can cooperate with them, grow their own capabilities and capacity, acquire necessary skills and contacts and so on and become 'sender' cultures, too.

There are also risks in this strategy, especially for smaller and poorer countries. From the US perspective, the fact that films or TV series may be produced elsewhere is often addressed as a problem: that of 'runaway productions' (Elmer and Gasher, 2005; Johnson-Yale, 2008; Peltzman, 2012). Although it has been argued (Curtin and Sanson, 2016: 7) that from the global perspective such hunting for more favourable production sites contributes to a global 'race to the bottom' of prices for movie labour and services, on the local level working for such productions may well mean a rise in the prices of labour. An unforeseen consequence of that, as Primorac (2019) explains, is that the increased willingness of the workers to be employed by foreign-financed productions can reduce their availability for work in domestic film productions with much smaller budgets. Such a 'race to the sky' in the price of local film labour and services could affect local cultural production systems and so reduce cultural diversity (see also Szczepanik, 2013, 2015), even as 'local productions' made by the multinationals gain international visibility.

Taken together, however, all these conflicting dynamics accelerate 'cultural globalization'. This is because digitization and the internet have made copying and exporting easier, and media companies are motivated by international growth. But globalization is not a monolith: it has become multilinear and multidirectional, with increasing flows originating from new sites and distributed to new demographics. A truly global media-entertainment semiosphere is evolving, but like any semiosphere, it is inherently heterogeneous, and becoming more so. Paradoxically, the more autocommunicative subsystems there are within this global system, the more difference there is, promising a widening dialogue. These autocommunicating subsystems may include local production clusters or broader national media systems, the latter may increasingly include the contributions from localized-global platforms like Netflix, Amazon Prime, Stan and so on (until Disney+ comes along and tries to hoover everyone back into the American monoculture bag, that is).

If national cultural institutions digest the inflows and synthesize foreign elements with the local culture, they work autocommunicatively to re-produce their own culture, but in the process they may produce novelties that may have exporting potential. If countries or cities invest in local production infrastructures, facilitate local processes of 'interactive learning' or 'social network markets', then these too may facilitate locally relevant dialogic processes that on the higher level could be seen as broader autocommunicative processes, enabling a country's creative industries to develop new shared identities and approaches, and thence to offer the world new streams of cultural content.

The dynamics of the digital global semiosphere raises an important question of agency. It is split among different types of agents:

- Makers of content and the *owners* of intellectual property rights, who try to direct the distribution of their properties and their global afterlife.
- Since the emergence of the Web 2.0, internet *users* – individually and as populations or groups – exercise agency. They are significant in filtering and forwarding, in modifying, adapting and localizing various elements of internationally traded culture.
- With this activity has grown also the agency of *platforms*. They have their (usually US) origins, headquarters and outposts, and they provide services across many territories, often with different legal systems. Sometimes they choose to respect those systems and sometimes they ignore them. Sometimes territories resist and force them to change the models, and then platforms may threaten to leave – as, for instance Google has been promising to do in reaction to the European Union's copyright reform in 2019.

Sometimes platforms simply cannot enter a territory, as in case of some Western platforms in China. At first they could not do it without playing by the central government's strict rules for media oversight. But later this territory has become even harder for Western platforms, because China itself has grown their own and evermore powerful counterparts – Baidu, Alibaba and Tencent are by now among the ten biggest Internet companies globally. In their own account, Baidu out-competed Google China, just as Huawei is a competitive global player because its hardware is better than others. These companies are expanding beyond their home turf.

Somewhat similar developments are stirring in Russia, which has been building its own internet infrastructures, enabling it to cut the 'Russian Internet' off from the rest of the global internet infrastructures if it sees it necessary – as many authoritarian governments, in Turkey, Indian Kashmir and Ethiopia, already do – but in the Russian case imperceptibly, such that ordinary users don't notice.[5] The rush to control access to international cables, however, also indicates that Russia's digital creative industries have failed to build comparable market power to fend off Western or Chinese competitors.

Nevertheless, all this is about to condition the further evolution of global internet economies as it fragments into at least three increasingly distinct systems – the Chinese, the European and the American. It could be argued that after an expansive phase of centripetal movement, the new phase in the global digital semiosphere is the one of *centrifugal* dispersion in terms of Lotman – creation of difference as too much of universality was seen as not optimal from the perspective of different regions, their local cultures and governing systems. As for many observers the 'universality' of the internet has come to mean 'American' and the United States is seen as both an aggressive and a declining power, then the creation of difference becomes a priority, along with new concerns for autocommunicative rule-making and local cultural consolidation. What that will mean for the functioning of the overall global digital space, the semiosphere, we will soon find out.

In the context of the datafication of the 'everyday textures of our lives' (Silverstone, 1999; and see Schäfer and van Es, 2017), the three dominant regions with significant regulatory power – Europe, the United States and China – are already heading in different directions.

- Europe is moving towards the protection of personal data, possibly creating a new market for individuals trading their own data, with its 2018 data protection reform and further readiness to regulate the ways platforms collect and use data about their users.

- At the same time the US administration has been rolling back its net neutrality protections, empowering American telecommunications vendors and others to collect and trade relatively freely in data about different kinds of internet users.

---

[5] For how it's done, see: https://www.bbc.com/news/technology-50902496.

- In China, internet companies survey user data for government-led data analytics systems, usually referred to as the 'social credit system'.

These very different uses of social data in different parts of the world, together with trade in data among agencies with different affordances and the emergence of data use in modelling the social world by these institutions, could lead eventually to very different dynamics and forms of societal autocommunication for these increasingly distinct digital semiospheres.

Yet, autocommunication always conditions new dialogues. And dialogue in the digital world is not only multiple and growing but is also multimodal and unpredictable, varying with context and circumstance. Global dialogue can happen in YouTube or Facebook, but also through the adoption and modification of popular culture forms by media institutions, or through grassroots-level shaping of elements of modular technologies (solutions for the 'responsive web' emerged exactly in this way – see Chapter 11). The onward march of (Chinese-owned) TikTok as young demographics abandon (Facebook-owned) Instagram is a weathervane to show us which way the wind is blowing. It has also attracted predictable political pushback from the US government.

To understand further the global modelling of our planetary mash of technologies, communicative flows and systems of meaning, in the next chapter we take another step enabled by semiosphere analysis – to a macro-level view of the Earth system, as the semiosphere envelops it digitally.

# 16

# The Digital semiosphere and the technosphere

*How can a system develop and yet remain true to itself?*
(JURI LOTMAN, CULTURE & EXPLOSION, 2009)

\* \* \*

## Cultural, economic and technological co-evolution

Among many technologies that have evolved over deep time, technologies of communication are of special importance. But the study of the cultural forms and practices that emerge with them (reading, writing, creating, literacy, bureaucracy) and of the technologies themselves as a historical sequence is highly fragmented and entangled. Speech, writing, print, broadcasting, computation and the internet are studied in scattered departments, using incompatible methods ranging across humanities, social sciences and technology approaches. Too frequently, the 'digital' aspect appears to come from nowhere except the endless 'now' of marketing and the continuous present tense of behavioural sciences, where it is too easy to detach 'digital technologies' from the historical, economic, political and cultural context that might explain their particular forms, functions and connections.

Further, studying any new medium comes with evaluative baggage amounting to moral and reputational risk. The focus on popular culture and noncanonical entertainment (as opposed to canonical art) has never escaped moralistic suspicion of mediation in general, from Plato's 'shadow in the cave' to contemporary 'fake news'. Media *studies* (it's never attained the status of a self-named science) remains tainted by the popularity and ubiquity of its object of study. Disdain for media studies reaches into the very news media themselves (see Bennett and Kidd, 2017, for a systematic assessment), where academic subjects are still sorted by means of Veblenesque 'invidious comparison', where studying literature (i.e. writing and print media) is uplifting; studying movies and TV shows (i.e. audiovisual and electronic media) is degrading:

> Cambridge University called them a 'soft' option this week. John Humphrys [the BBC's highest-paid news presenter] thinks they're pointless … Until the late 1990s, seasoned journalists relished opportunities to rubbish media studies. It was the modern equivalent of 1960s sociology, a fool's paradise jammed full of bearded Marxists with 'sweetie mice for brains'. When Chris Woodhead, the former chief inspector of schools, condemned it as 'vacuous' and 'quasi-academic', there were cheers in newsrooms.[1]

Apparently, it's OK to study *residual* textual systems, like literature or philosophy, but not *emergent* ones with popular reach and importance. This is a repetitive trope, in fact, that has greeted each successive media technology as it gained ascendancy beyond the control of existing literate elites. Writing, print, the press, popular fiction, cinema, broadcasting, computation and the internet have all been accused of inauthenticity, duplicity and illusion, corrupting youth and truth, promoting bad behaviour, language, sexuality and riot. The more popular a new technology of communication becomes, the more it is denounced. It's a centuries-long tussle over control: those who control the means of communication seek to control the semiosphere, with economic and political as well as cultural consequences.

In this context, it's unwise to ignore the 'digital' aspect of the 'digital semiosphere'. We prefer to characterize digital media and mediation as part of the long history of communication and media technologies by claiming that this is *one* history, with one trajectory. It is not merely a history of technology: in the context of the semiosphere, it's a history of culture. Of course, culture must be understood as a general evolutionary process whereby knowledge is organized, grown, adapted and shared among increasingly large and abstract 'we'-groups (demes), and where it is controlled, contested, hidden or shaped to fit more or less powerful interests, ideologies and groups. At the same time, beyond the control of any agent, culture's own dynamism and contextuality means that the knowledge it supports changes gradually (and sometimes explosively) in line with developments in other domains, including technology.

---

[1]'What *is* the point of media studies?' By Tim Luckhurst. *The Independent*, 26 October 2006: https://www.independent.co.uk/news/media/what-is-the-point-of-media-studies-413472.html.

We are used to 'Moore's Law' in the field of technology. There are similar regularities in the long history of cultures and their knowledge systems. One such 'law' is that each successive stage in the technological evolution of media involves a further *decentralization* of media forms and users (and thus purposes). Each successively successful and dominant medium, from speech and song, via writing and print, to computation and the internet, further escapes the control of priests, kings and castes, provoking not just technological but also economic, social, political and moral disturbance. The ensuing moral consternation (among the incumbent powers) is a sure sign of just how disruptive these rule-breaking technologies can be to existing systems. They really are a threat; the more popular they are, the more incumbent powers want to own, control or direct them. But the trajectory prevails: decentralization and *self-organization* of the uses of media technologies are still the goal for users, who typically search for the most *transparent*, least 'mediated' media they can access.

It does seem that when communication technologies change in a decisive or in Lotman's terms an 'explosive' way, towards greater transparency, wider distribution and democratized use, the co-evolving systems of the economy, technology and social organization go through epochal change too. Here is distributed causation, each system affecting the others, with irreversible changes in an unbroken acceleration of communicative capability over several thousand years (Figure 16.1).

How all that can be explained requires a systematic and evolutionary rather than a piecemeal approach: one that accounts for these phenomena from the perspective of the planetary biosphere and global semiosphere, but which also explains the technological and 'digital' aspects. So it is these that we turn to first. How should cultural semiotics understand technology?

# Communication technosphere

In order to tackle these matters more systematically, we report here on a proposal for a new 'technosphere science'. It adds to Vernadsky (biosphere) and Lotman (semiosphere) by proposing that the *artefactual system* is also *autonomous* – technosphere science being the necessary response. The German evolutionary economist and sinologist Carsten Herrmann-Pillath (2018) has synthesized previous work on the 'technosphere' (e.g. Haff, 2014) to call for a new *technosphere science*. We want to add to the mix the proposition that confining 'technology' to tools – from pre-human stone axes to posthuman robots – misses the importance of *communication technologies*, possibly because all tools, from stone axes (Gintis, 2012; Gintis et al., 2019) to computers (Soukup, 2000), can be used to communicate, as needed. That is merely to recognize that both stone tools and computers need to be understood not as behavioural extensions of the will of individuals but as cultural artefacts, connecting at least two systems in dialogue.

If technology is dialogic and cultural, how then can it be autonomous? To tackle this question, we focus on communication technologies, by which we mean those that characterize certain types of society – oral, chirographic (writing), print-literate, electronic and networked (Ong, 2012) – in order to show that these fall into an evolutionary sequence. Further, *what* evolves with technologies is the *growth of knowledge* (Hayek, 1945) among humans over the extreme long haul (Hartley, 2020: 59–61). That process is uninterrupted throughout our species' history (despite the 'extinction' of most technologies, sooner or later), from the use of natural materials (stone, ochre, wood, bone, skin, plant and wool fibre, shell, feather), via coded writing (and mathematical symbols), to print (publishing and the press), then electronics (computation and broadcasting), to, most recently, the World Wide Web and the burgeoning 'dark' or private webs it sustains (Figure 16.1). Starting in the print era and continuing still, communication technologies eventually 'coded' the entire planet and have bound a majority of living humans into a dominant communicative network or deme. From this point on, 'the semiosphere' is no longer an ideal or abstract analytical concept, confined to the noosphere (sphere of thought), but an empirical entity, enveloping the Earth.

| ECONOMIC ERA | COMMUNICATION/KNOWLEDGE TECHNOLOGY | SOCIETAL SCALE |
|---|---|---|
| Mesolithic | *Natural:* Speech, Stone | Tribe |
| | Social forms: self-organized, scattered, competitive bands – ceremony, standing stones, pantheism | |
| Agricultural | *Manual:* Writing, Maths | Kingdom |
| | Social forms: states, monarchies, early empires – Pyramids, walled cities, monotheism | |
| Industrial | *Mechanical:* Print, Press | Nation |
| | Social forms: colonialism, modernity, imperialism, mass society, totalitarianism – science, the press, the novel, secularism | |
| Information | *Electronic:* Broadcast, Computer | Global |
| | Social forms: decolonization, postmodernity, globalization (trade/media), corporate managerialism – Hollywood, IBM, modernism | |
| Digital/Creative | *Networked:* Internet, Creative | Species/Planet |
| | Social forms: decentralization, autocommunication, staged conflict – platformization, datafication, multiculturalism, posthumanism | |

FIGURE 16.1 *Longue-durée economic/social organization, correlated with communication technology.*

Human sociality and culture are used for learning and transmitting knowledge to succeeding generations and to other groups:

- successive technologies (natural, manual, mechanical, electronic and networked) (Figure 16.1);
- carry increasingly abstract code among groups and spaces of increasing scale (tribe, kingdom, nation, globe, species);
- by means of and in turn stimulating the most efficient mode of economic production available at the time (Mesolithic, agricultural, industrial, information, digital-creative);
- such that the technologies themselves, together with the communication and knowledge 'load' that they carry, and the sociocultural relations they constitute and express, *co-evolve*. Change follows random variations in technologies and meaning-making, enabling social selection and system-wide retention under conditions of uncertainty.

This is the conclusion that Santa Fe scientist W. Brian Arthur comes to in his landmark theory of the evolution of technology (2009). Arthur argues that technology, like biological life, evolves from earlier forms, but it does so by what he calls 'combinatorial evolution' rather than 'natural selection', as described by Darwin. Any evolutionary adaptation of technology requires all its component parts to have been invented before they are combined in new ways to produce a new 'species' of technology. His prime example is the jet engine, which could not have been invented before its complex components had been developed, but which was then independently achieved (on both sides of the Second World War combatants) and rapidly adopted globally.

The same is true of communication technologies. Writing, for instance, required prior technologies (material on which and with which to inscribe), know-how (shared codes and skills) and organization (someone – trader or chief – to invest the necessary time, effort and labour) before anyone could take *this* clay, and *that* stylus, and prod *these* marks into the clay, to share information and instruction with others. Little did they know they had invented writing! And of course they hadn't, until uncounted random experiments or purposeless play had evolved, during which process prodding clay with sticks gave way to purposeful coded impressions made with reeds (which leave 'cuneiform' marks), and those marks were abstracted to signify words rather than objects, to be used for trade (e.g. numbers of animals or containers of grain), charms (e.g. to purify locusts from land) or royal boasting. This is the Western origin of writing, in Sumer, around 3100 BCE.[2]

---

[2]See the Sumerian stone tablet and texts in *The Sacred Books and Early Literature of the East* (1917), 34ff: http://www.billheidrick.com/Orpd/Sacr1917/Sacred_Books_1.pdf.

Chinese writing has an independent history, originating with 'oracle bones' rather than trading accounts (Keightley, 2014).

The same untidy process applies to the invention of print with moveable type. Already invented were printing with woodblocks, using dies to impress metal (for coins), applying pressure to a flat surface (to press vines for wine) and books (made of paper, vellum, etc.). It took Johannes Gutenberg (possibly copying an idea of a Dutch predecessor, Laurens Janszoon Coster around 1420–40) to put all that together in 1450 to make something robustly new: the printing press.

Like many inventors, he went broke, and *publishing* printed books – the meso-industry, not the micro-technology – fell to others, especially the firm founded by Gutenberg's financier Johan Fust (prototype of Faust) and his printer Peter Schöffer; a firm that outlived them all. Fust's capital (and Faustian ambition for knowledge), and Schöffer's craft and business skills, secured the wide dissemination of well-regarded books, leading to equally rapid copying and eventual global uptake. The same stories can be told about the invention of radio, cinema, TV, computation and the internet: no one individual can be held responsible for any of them, and none of them could precede their component parts. Everyone concerned tinkered with the possibilities of existing technology and of each other's ideas, and the eventual stabilization (law-formation) of a reproducible technology in each case required enterprise, capital, luck, distribution opportunities and sometimes war, as well as technological inventiveness or instrumental purposes, overlain by Faustian (or Schumpeterian) 'vaunting ambition' (with attendant risks and dangers).

# Autonomy of technosphere

This is the reason why Herrmann-Pillath and others call 'the technosphere' *autonomous*: it seems to evolve independently of individual human will or action. Starting from the concept of the biosphere, Herrmann-Pillath delineates a science that studies artefactual phenomena. This leads him to a stimulating discussion of where to set the boundary.

- Are dogs a technology, for example, because they are bred by humans?
- Is $CO_2$ an artefact, because it is emitted by industries?
- Are nuts artefacts, when they are no longer 'collected' from the wild but 'produced' by agribusiness?

- Are all farmed flora and fauna artefacts (Bar-On et al., 2018);[3] or only genetically modified ones, and then only if the modification is achieved by bioscience *in vitro*, rather than selective breeding, *in vivo*?
- Is the atmosphere now a 'hyper-object' and the Earth a 'hybrid' planet, given the changes wrought in both by technological means?

It is pretty clear that there is a difference between 'found' and 'made' objects, but equally clear that the boundary between 'nature' and 'technology' is fuzzy to say the least and is itself an artefact of knowledge and culture: for instance, fiercely policed distinctions between 'native' flora and 'invasive weeds', or edible and inedible foodstuffs; or the emergence of GM crops, patented genes, lab-grown meat and manufactured life (Porcar and Pereto, 2019).

Nevertheless, technology is not the same as culture, even though it is an open, human-made system, where 'human' includes technology-using ancestor species from *H. erectus* 'upright', up to 2 million years ago, including *H. habilis* 'handy', *H. ergaster* 'worker' and so on. Technology could be seen to evolve in a way similar to living matter: it produces 'technomass' in the way that the biosphere produces 'biomass'. First, both require external sources of energy. Although technology does not recycle itself, but rather sucks in energy from elsewhere (whether fossil fuels or solar panels), the same has to be said for the biosphere. As Herrmann-Pillath reminds us, it too relies on an external source of energy – the sun:

> The technosphere is an open, non-linear non-equilibrium system … this property is shared by the biosphere and the technosphere, and applies for the Earth system in general. This is based on the simple observation that these systems are thermodynamically open because they feed on external inflows of solar energy, which also directly explains that they are non-equilibrium systems.
>
> (26)

The biosphere and technosphere use external sources of energy (Vernadsky's 'free energy') to produce both 'mass' and *work*.

Even so, there is not complete overlap. Artefacts are produced by means of artefacts and humans are not artefacts. It is worth recalling here Julian Huxley's (1955) classification of cultural outputs into 'artifacts, mentifacts

---

[3]And see: https://www.zmescience.com/science/human-impact-biomass-043432/, which reports on Bar-On et al.'s findings, emphasizing the impact of agriculture on the biosphere: 'Humanity's biomass can grow to gargantuan proportions if you factor in our food: livestock. The researchers estimate that of all birds on the planet, 70% are farmed poultry, with just 30% being wild … 60% of all mammals on Earth are livestock, mostly cattle and pigs, 36% are the humans themselves, and a mere 4% are wild mammals.'

and sociofacts'. The suffix *-fact*, from L. *factum*, 'something made', makes clear that ideas (mentifacts) and structures and relationships (sociofacts) are *made*, like things (artefacts), but that *what* they make, including their own remains and the product of their work and waste, belongs also to other systems, as we humans are belatedly learning to acknowledge.

Herrmann-Pillath's conceptualization of the technosphere includes the necessity of *dialogue*. Interaction and communication are needed for novelties to emerge, just as is the case for the biosphere. This returns to the question of agency – who has made what – and to the relationship between the semiosphere and the technosphere. Herrmann-Pillath argues that the technosphere is autonomous from humans because technological agency proceeds from its own functions and not from human desires, needs or actions – although all of these are of course necessary inputs. For him there are two main reasons justifying the autonomy of the technosphere: first, '*unintended results* of human action are essential'; second, it includes 'causal interdependencies', which 'unfold autonomously, and feedback on human action, for instance by channelling further actions in a specific direction'. For example, humans produce $CO_2$ (an unintended consequence of creating free energy); $CO_2$ causes climate change; climate change forces human action; new sources of energy are developed (that is the model, anyway).

However, an autonomous technosphere process does not mean that technology is 'free' from human semiosis, agency and relationships. As we have argued, machines are imagined by people, designed by people, made by people, remade and adjusted by people, also ignored or rejected by people. Texts and technologies are often difficult to distinguish in the digital semiosphere. Machines and their operations are framed and guided by multiple layers of texts (programs, metadata schemas, standards, design forms, laws and regulations, etc.) that are written as well as read for meaning by both humans and machines. Humans design and/or operate machines because only they (so far) can process (interpret and make) meaning. In that they are, of course, increasingly channelled in technological path dependencies (David, 2000) or what Dosi (1982, 1984) called 'technological trajectories'.

As media archaeologists like to emphasize (Ernst, 2013), machines may process culture, may be made by humans, but they have their own operational logic that derives from their material nature and algorithmic design. As the technosphere grows, so its autonomous agency builds. The technosphere and its building process are difficult for any single group of humans to shape. It would need a conscious effort (action in the semiosphere) by the whole global population to shape the technosphere as whole, as is clearly demonstrated by both the demand for and the difficulty of achieving a concerted global response to climate emergency, for instance by shifting from carbon-based to alternative sources for energy generation.

All this means that while the semiosphere produced the technosphere, they are now destined to co-evolve, conditioning and shaping each other. Yet, as in any complex co-evolutionary process, no power, no asymmetry is absolute, just as no system or sphere is fully autonomous, independent of others. What distinguishes the technosphere from the semiosphere is that the semiosphere is made of semiosis (mentifacts) – signs, their process of making meaning and consequently thought, consciousness and human identity (Peirce, 1991: 84) – while the technosphere is made of artefacts – material tools, machines, structures and consequently 'technomass'. As thought shapes artefacts (one by one) so artefacts condition thought. They are co-evolutionary.

# Technology versus biology: one wastes, discards; the other connects, recycles

Just as the technosphere is not the same as the semiosphere, so it cannot be reduced to the biosphere, because its *outputs* are of a different order. The technosphere produces waste, pollution and irreversible changes in other systems. The biosphere, in contrast, produces 'biomass', using almost complete recycling, where life consumes life and every living organism is recycled. It is the fate of the mightiest whale, largest animal ever to have evolved, to be devoured by humble slaters (cousins of the woodlice familiar to gardeners).[4] The biosphere as a whole has evolved some astonishing systems that are only now being shown to communicate across boundaries previously thought to be incommensurable, where the forces of death and decay – fungi, bacteria, rot, mould and creepy-crawlies – turn out to play a vital role in the maintenance of life in interspecies/interphylum interaction networks, which some have gone so far as to compare with the internet – the 'wood wide web', as it were.

'Mycorrhizal' (fungus/root) association between plants and fungi has caused the biosciences to rethink the biosphere as a *communication sphere* (Martin et al., 2001; Bonfante and Anca, 2009; Kadowaki et al., 2018). Indeed, there are spores all over the zeitgeist. In *The Mushroom at the End of the World: On the Possibility of Life in Capitalist Ruins* (2015: 23), Anna Tsing extends these 'patterns of unintentional coordination' to human/nonhuman interactions, where human and nonhuman 'lifeways' are assembled through the worldbuilding efforts of multiple otherwise incommensurable species, in this case the matsutake mushroom, which will only grow in 'human-disturbed' media. These posthuman possibilities have of course led to several new 'species' of science/fiction: such as Richard

---

[4]See: http://museum.wa.gov.au/creature-feature-giant-marine-slater.

Powers's *The Overstory* (2019), Inga Simpson's *Understory* (2017) and Sue Burke's *Semiosis* (2018).[5] Peter McCoy's practical treatise *Radical Mycology* (2016) opens with a Vernadskian statement: 'All life is connected. This is the primary lesson that fungi teach.'[6]

# Mirrorworld (coming to a real world near you)

That primary lesson is of course replicated by technological means: all technology is connected. The internet, for example, can be seen as a human-made mirror-image of fungal networks. The internet may *operate* like a fungal or neural network, but it is *made* of technology, which is increasingly enveloping the world, starting from servers and undersea cables and ending with war drones or excavation robots. In the process, what Kevin Kelly (2019) and others are calling a 'Digital Twin' of the so-called real world is constructed – as a copy to be enhanced. This is the 'mirrorworld' (Gelernter, 1993), perhaps the most salient materialisation of a *technosphere as semiosphere*, which envelops the planet, together with its geosphere, biosphere and semiosphere.

A global digital network emerges when numerous ongoing and parallel technological developments are combined – in this case the internet of things, semantic web, augmented reality, 5G mobile connectivity, using more or less automated machinery. The mirrorworld comprises trillions of sensors and cameras that record the world and its every surface in three dimensions and from outer space. The behaviours and relationships of material objects, subjects and phenomena are recorded and measured in the mirrorworld, which augments their meanings, predicts and plans their behaviours, and manages their interactions. The mirrorworld is set to enable self-driving cars, smart cities, the gamification of space in the form of augmented reality, the automation of spatial management and control functions and so on. Mirrorworld's cameras will record the shapes of objects and their movements; sensors will track their movements, intentions, weather conditions, biometric data and so on; while semantic web solutions make meaningful connections among the objects, AI algorithms fill the gaps, predict behaviours and do the

---

[5] *Overstory*: https://wwnorton.co.uk/books/9780393635522-the-overstory; *Understory*: https://www.hachette.com.au/inga-simpson/understory; Radical Mycology: https://radicalmycology.com/.

[6] The 'intelligent plant' trope is taken further in Sue Burke's *Semiosis* (2018). Despite its name, this is a sci-fi novel, exploring posthuman interspecies trust. It pursues the idea that 'sentience takes many forms' on a planet where the sentient beings are plants, who have their own ideas about what to do with humans. The new colonizers learn that 'Only mutual communication can forge an alliance with the planet's sentient species and prove that humans are more than tools'. The wisest plant resembles a stand of bamboo (called Stevland). How to achieve interspecies communication and cohabitation with *that*?

heavy rendering of data and images. The emergent forms of augmented reality storytelling are used to model all this complexity in ways comprehensible and relevant to humans. That is, we have the complex mesh of culture and technology – multiple interrelated layers of data and metadata, texts and meta-texts and phases of modelling different realities.

Appropriately, Japanese architect Keisuke Toyoda, the head designer of Expo 2025 in Osaka, has given another name to the mirrorworld – 'the common ground' (Cotani, 2019). By this he refers to the meeting point of digital and physical worlds and, further, the meeting of game engines and the real world, games and the environment, fiction and space, culture and the environment. To explain his vision, he used the 'circular world' concept of Jakob von Uexküll (1909). As we have explained earlier, Uexküll's concept of Umwelt refers to the perceived, meaningful environment of every organism. These worlds can be quite different for different kinds of organisms. The 'circular world' function, then, is the process of semiosis, a feedback loop where the outside world and the internal world of the organism interact, interpret each other, adapt to and shape each other. Toyoda's argument is that the same will happen in 'the common ground' – where AI will perceive, learn about, adapt and shape its environment, both the biosphere and the semiosphere.

This is also about how humans use the affordances of game engines such as that of Unity, which is actively developing solutions and interfaces for augmented reality gamification and storytelling. Such engines could manipulate the real environment but also build new, fictional realities on top of the perceived real (or Umwelt). The mirrorworld as the 'common ground', both physical and virtual at the same time, constitutes a Lotmanian dialogic and translation space, facilitating mutual learning and adaptation, but also emergence of new forms of modelling, of new languages.

Then there is the economic dimension. As the 'common ground' will be the domain of digital service provision, it will unavoidably be structured by network effects. While in the mirrorworld the real world becomes the interface, it will thereafter be at risk of platformization (van Dijck et al., 2018). Increasing returns will accrue to the dominant solutions, and eventually the mirrorworld of planetary scale is in the risk to become dominated by one or two global platforms. This trajectory is presaged by Google's work on turning Toronto waterfront into a 'smart city', its involvement in the private development of New York City's Hudson Yards and Alibaba's experiment along the same lines in Hangzhou. In response to such potential centralization and platformization, Kelly (2019) suggests that it is imperative to turn the mirrorworld into a public and decentralized utility.[7] Around the world there are moves to use blockchain to keep this new space decentralized, because centralized rendering of holographic 3D

---

[7]For issues of data-privacy and surveillance at Hudson Yard, see: https://therealdeal. com/2019/03/15/hudson-yards-smart-city-or-surveillance-city/.

representations would be too heavy and unreliable. Decentralized regulation could set the mirrorworld/planetary mesh semiosphere/technosphere mesh onto a new evolutionary trajectory (Kawada, 2019).

# Technomass is inert matter

The sensors of the mirrorworld constitute 'technomass'. But in contrast to the biosphere, the technosphere does not recycle its own products to produce itself; nor do technological artefacts generally cooperate in an ecosphere, by any means. They are neither predator nor prey; not symbiotic or even communicative. In the long run, they are just rubbish, waste, pollution, ruins (humanity's most enduring 'artefact') and broken mirrors, in cumulative, archaeological strata of junk, plastic and garbage; and that is just from households, never mind the effluent of industry, tailings of mining and emissions of energy generation.[8] This is a fundamental difference between 'technology' (does not recycle itself) and 'nature' (recycles itself, using living matter for energy and recycling energy-making). Technomass (unlike biomass) is largely unbiodegradable, often toxic. Once discarded, technological artefacts belong at once to the geological category of 'inert matter': their communicative relations are dead.

There is widespread educated realization and scientific near-unanimity that global culture equals global warming and that the 'progressive' technosphere (modern, productive, expansive, democratizing, decentralizing, energy-guzzling) entails irrevocable change in the climate, biosphere and biogeochemical strata of the Earth system and needs to be upgraded from an 'exploitation' economy to a 'regeneration' economy.

This idea has aroused anxiety and fear (also manifest as denial), as well as calls for action and action itself among widely dispersed and multivalent groups, urging humans to tread more lightly upon the planet, to eat less, make less, use less, consume less, travel less, breed less (although in practice 'outsourcing' that requirement to less-favoured demographics, populations and regions). At the same time, others are experimenting with solutions based on renewable energy sources and recycling schemes. The ingenuity of human industriousness (a.k.a. the noosphere), in both the rhetorical and maker imagination, is applied to the task of making the technosphere more like, or better integrated into, the biosphere: fully recyclable and intercommunicative with other systems, not just productive but reproductive.

---

[8]For quantities of 'municipal solid waste' and recycling rates in the United States, see: https://www.epa.gov/sites/production/files/2019-03/documents/infographic_full-060513_v4.pdf.

# Agency and technosphere

Already, at least while in use, the technosphere as a system does exhibit one of the characteristics of life: it has agency, and it can do things. Where it differs from life is in the ability to reproduce, but it is not safe to say that while humans can make artefacts, artefacts cannot make humans. Technologies can indeed reproduce themselves; and they can make many human components, from *in-vitro* fertilization to 3D printing. The reproduction of techno-selves may be only a matter of timing: it is not possible *yet*. That it may be, and that this will pose moral, ethical and political dilemmas for ordinary suburban families as well as for the 'returning heroes' of archetypical narratives, is contemplated at length in the place reserved for such profound thinking: TV sci-fi series – in this instance Channel 4 UK's *Humans* (three seasons, 2015–18) (Hartley, 2020: 234–6).[9]

At present this can be done only in science fiction (where it seems equally desired and feared) and in the integrated cyborg transhumanism made famous by Donna Haraway (1985), where to be human includes *self-technologization*, using pharmaceuticals, diet, exercise, consumerism, screens and all the rest of our information-energy systems to *engineer* the contemporary body, not in the image of its ancestors, because it is possible to leave damaging or socially undesirable bits out. Like enclosed land, the privatized body can be 'improved' with capital investment and intensive methods. Crucially, the cyborg is a creation of information networks, not directly of technological components. In an interview with *Wired*, Haraway explained: cyborgs 'are information machines. They're embedded with circular causal systems, autonomous control mechanisms, information processing – automatons with built-in autonomy'. *Wired* took up the theme:

> Sociologists and academics from around the world have taken her lead and come to the same conclusion about themselves. In terms of the general shift from thinking of individuals as isolated from the 'world' to thinking of them as nodes on networks, the 1990s may well be remembered as the beginning of the cyborg era.
>
> (*Wired*, 1997)

---

[9]Based on the Swedish series *Real Humans*, *Humans* was made by Sam Vincent and Jonathan Brackley for Channel 4 UK and AMC (USA). During rehearsals, Gemma Chan (Anita/Mia) and her fellow 'synth' actors were sent to a 'synth school' run by the show's choreographer, Dan O'Neill, in a bid to rid themselves of human physical gestures and become convincing robots. 'It was about stripping back any physical tics you naturally incorporate into performance ... These things are ultimately machines and run on battery power, so every movement has to have an economy and a grace to it', Chan explains. https://web.archive.org/web/20150619011156/http://www.gloucestershireecho.co.uk/TV-Humans-Channel-4/story-26656706-detail/story.html.

# 'Hybrid planet'

Carsten Herrmann-Pillath explicitly locates his proposed 'technosphere science' in the tradition of Vernadsky's thought, and he comes to much the same conclusion as did the pioneering biogeochemist: that because of the 'maximum power' principle power (Odum, 1995),[10] *the technosphere governs the biosphere*:

> We need to reverse the relationship between the biosphere and the technosphere. This view stands in line with the original ideas in Earth system science about 'spheres', especially Vernadsky, in including the biosphere as a regulatory mechanism of the Earth system ... In this tradition, technosphere science would approach the technosphere as the overarching regulatory system of the Earth System in the Anthropocene ... Indeed ... the Earth might be conceived as a new type of 'hybrid planet', defined by the existence of the technosphere and the emergence of fundamentally new technological mechanisms of energetic transformations (moving from plant photosynthesis to photovoltaic technology).
>
> (9–10)

This is one of those discoveries discussed earlier in this book, where, as Mihhail Lotman put it, 'a situation can acquire the status of cause only after we know its effect' (M. Lotman, 2013: 274). Common sense (and its defenders in popular and quality press alike) may seem to position us to accept without question that causes must precede effects, that the biosphere takes priority over the semiosphere (life over communication), that action takes precedence over mediation (speech over writing) or that the biosphere comes before the technosphere (living energy transfer over artefactual energy transfer). Yet, we argue, following the lineage of thinkers noted above, it is just here where we need to exercise caution, in case reality – the arrow of causation – points the other way. The insistence of 'common sense' that one group should strut their supremacy while their challengers should be ashamed of themselves is all too familiar and might well be taken as evidence of ulterior motives, vested interests or rent-seeking behaviour. The precedence given to life, speech and natural processes over semiosis, mediation and technology – and, as an institutional or meso-level by-product, to the sciences over the humanities – may be seen as a Romantic

---

[10]Where 'power' is 'useful energy transformation'. 'The concept of maximum power can therefore be defined as the *maximum rate of useful energy transformation*. Hence the underlying philosophy aims to unify the theories and associated laws of electronic and thermodynamic systems with biological systems' [emphasis original] (https://en.wikipedia.org/wiki/Maximum_power_principle). The concept has been applied to living cells and to the economy.

gesture, allowing incumbents to claim an 'authenticity' that belies the new realities of our 'hybrid planet' and its Anthropocene geosphere. If semiosis, mediation and technology do play a role in regulating planetary processes, then 'we' had better get past a Romantic attachment to past realisms, to find out how the digital semiosphere works, and quickly.

Identifying the technosphere and distinguishing it from the biosphere draws attention to something that was previously impossible to observe in enough detail to measure and enough abstraction to model: that all types of technology or artifice, across all three of Julian Huxley's dimensions of cultural productivity – things (artefacts), ideas (mentifacts) and social organization (sociofacts) – function within an autonomous sphere, whose systemic complexity can now be traced more readily than was possible in the analogue world. Digital communication leaves traces that can be gathered, stored and mined as data. It was not in communication studies directly but in cybernetics, information-, web- and computer science that a new, networked-systems approach to communication emerged. Herrmann-Pillath synthesizes technological, biological and cultural-economic approaches by linking the agency of technological networks (systems) with physical work (thermodynamics):

> At this point, suffice to state that in this inclusion of thermodynamics, we finally end up with a synthesis between artefacts and biological entities in assigning agency to assemblages of artefacts, biological entities and human beings which process energy and information, hence 'autonomous agents'.
>
> (17)

The emergent concept of the technosphere, as a hybrid bio-techno assemblage, allows us to realize the importance of the *digital* semiosphere. It is not simply culture + tech, since there has never been a time when culture and technology were not connected – this mesh of textual matter and automated apparatus has evolved over a very long time. And it is not just a matter of digital culture being an updated version of popular culture. It goes beyond these cumulative notions to offer an overarching conceptualization of Earth system dynamics, in which thought, meaning and communications regain causal agency in planetary-scale processes. Once communication, culture, meaning and media have shed their metaphysical baggage and analytical exceptionalism, to be integrated into a biosphere-semiosphere-technosphere model, we can discern the workings of a distributed, interactive, networked, evolving but autonomous sphere where 'assemblages of artefacts, biological entities and human beings ... process energy and information' at accelerating rate. In short, we have a cultural science for the Anthropocene.

# 17

# Semiosis: Regulating politics and economics

*Everyone's so excited and having such a good time,*
the sort of time you have right before they invade Paris.
(PAUL FORD, BLOOMBERG BUSINESSWEEK)[1]

\*\*\*

In this chapter and the following ones in Part VI we apply a Lotmanian approach to the current era of global capitalism and trade (markets), to culture and conflict (politics) – and their human-induced consequences for the Earth environment, where the rubber of utopian intentions hits the road to dystopia. Here we bring the spotlight around to focus on the *regulatory* aspect of the digital semiosphere. In the biosciences, that is the least-discussed of the 'spheres' (compared with the biosphere and geosphere), but there is an argument for the semiosphere as the (or a) *regulatory mechanism for all Earth system spheres*, in the sense that what enables the energy, productivity and transformational capability of the biosphere is *communication* among incommensurable, untranslatable and competing systems, and thence their capacity to transform the Earth system and its subsystems (atmosphere, hydrosphere, lithosphere, etc.). Life and semiosis are one and the same; and Planet Earth is transformed into something cosmically rare if not unique (in the present state of knowledge) by its life systems.

Further, the *human* semiosphere is now having a discernible impact on all the other spheres and is itself *in need of regulatory attention* in order to navigate these transformational dynamics across systems that seem at

[1]Ford, P. (2018) 'Bitcoin Is Ridiculous. Blockchain Is Dangerous'. *Bloomberg Businessweek*, March 9: https://www.bloomberg.com/news/features/2018-03-09/bitcoin-is-ridiculous-blockchain-is-dangerous-paul-ford; DOI: https://doi.org/10.5334/csci.108.

first sight to have little to do with culture. This 'self-evident truth' has been impeded over decades by the joint lobbying power of 'Big Oil', 'Big Soda' and retail giants, who between them control the plastics industry, which is the source of 'planet plastic': 'Since 1950, the world has created 6.3 trillion kilograms of plastic waste – and 91 percent has never been recycled even once.' But now, even the perpetrators concede the need for 'management' (which they distinguish from 'regulation'): 'None of us want to have either the environmental or the legislative consequences of an unmanaged system'.[2]

As we have argued (Chapter 2), the global semiosphere as currently understood is as old as humanity and coterminous with it, although posthumanism has extended its boundaries beyond one species. Humanity has evolved piecemeal, in separate, contending, mutually incompatible (albeit overlapping and intertwined) national and imperial cultures that have proven to be inadequate to deal with the planet as a whole, either as an integrated 'single unit' (natural sciences, resources, markets) or differentiated 'complex system of systems' (politics, nationalism, difference, identity). Now, as cultural systems and national semiospheres intersect at accelerating rate, as different subcultures or professional domains are increasingly in dialogue, and as their emergent mixtures achieve global scale via the 'technosphere', we can see that previous, partial, adversarial conceptualizations of the cultural semiosphere are also inadequate:

- Practically, at global scale, such systems are part of the problem, not part of the solution.
- Theoretically, culture-based theory has not achieved a compelling model of the 'macro' spheres.
- The disciplinary complex of communication, culture and media studies has not been sufficiently 'literate' in planetary and techno-digital matters, owing to their neglect of evolutionary and systems approaches to culture, meaning and asymmetries of power.
- Knowledge systems based on culture are discounted in public policy, compared with those based on economy or technology, because they are regarded as unscientific and costly.
- Culture needs to be expanded to explain its role in constituting, coordinating and regulating other processes (including economic and political activities).

---

[2]Tim Dickinson (3 March 2020) 'Planet Plastic: How Big Oil and Big Soda Kept a Global Environmental Calamity a Secret for Decades.' *Rolling Stone*: 'The industry's voluntary actions to curb plastic pollution are driven by two clear motives: One is protecting the environment, the other is protecting profits from regulation. "None of us want to live in a world where waste is unmanaged," says Steve Russell of the American Chemistry Council. "None of us want to have either the environmental or the legislative consequences of an unmanaged system".' https://www.rollingstone.com/culture/culture-features/plastic-problem-recycling-myth-big-oil-950957/

*Semiotics*, as a 'regulatory' knowledge-system of the noosphere, needs to take this further step to be able to account for the digital semiosphere as a global phenomenon, one that is itself an evolved, species-specific form of a much deeper semiosphere, that of all-species life as a whole.

This means that 'regulation' of global digital technoculture is not just a matter of policing internet trolls at micro-scale and obliging tech-giants to behave themselves at meso-scale. Both of these are vital and progressive political activities. Nevertheless, if they are confined to human culture and horizons, they continue to miss the larger threat that lurks, Grendel-like, just outside the halls of human congress. Only in myth, fantasy and sci-fi, from ancient *Beowulf* to modern *Game of Thrones* or *Aliens*, do 'we' (humans) deal with planetary catastrophe, and only then by projecting our own fears onto monstrous others, without sufficiently recognizing that we are the principal villains in this long-imagined array of adversaries – from Grendel and Grendel's mother (*Beowulf*) to the Dragons and Mother of Dragons (*Game of Thrones*) – all of whom are personifications of *fighters*, reducing the non-human and post-human to a banal bar-room brawl (in Heorot Hall or at the Red Wedding), in which the only permitted outcome is that, eventually, 'we win'. Meanwhile, 'we' trash the planet, taking the 'others' with us. Sci-fi is our main guide to what happens next: the post-apocalyptic planet. Think of N. K. Jemisin's *Broken Earth* trilogy, Kim Stanley Robinson's *New York 2140* or Roger Levy's *The Rig*; not to mention entire genres of zombies, aliens, monsters and dystopias in transmedia games, movies, TV, graphic novels and fiction.

It is an axiom of evolutionary science that this process is not subject to regulation by the will of players within it, but nevertheless we can observe periodic mass extinctions, caused by climate change, vulcanism and now by human agency. Precisely because it is impossible to command or control the evolution of species or of the Earth system, we need to understand what does keep that system in poised and adaptive equilibrium, and on the basis of that understanding, to *imagine a better regulatory system* for human interactions with the planet. Equally, we need to institute regulatory understanding in the everyday world of the global digital semiosphere, where consciousness, knowledge, affinity and affect are created and circulated to keep groups viable. Such work is under way in the textual domain – in the relative peripheries of fantasy and sci-fi. As filmmaker Britt Marling (co-creator and star of *The OA*) put it in an opinion column for *The New York Times*:

> Excavating, teaching and celebrating the feminine through stories is, inside our climate emergency, a matter of human survival. The moment we start imagining a new world and sharing it with one another through story is the moment that new world may actually come.[3]

---

[3]Britt Marling, 7 February 2020, *New York Times*: https://www.nytimes.com/2020/02/07/opinion/sunday/brit-marling-women-movies.html.

And it is also under way in political peripheries – in activist organizations such as Extinction Rebellion or Greta Thunberg's FridaysForFuture. It has not yet achieved 'law-forming' status at the global political core of national legislatures and executive government, or among global corporations and their lobbyists. Even so, some supranational agencies and regulatory forums like the UN and its agencies (e.g. the World Health Organisation), or knowledge-brokering 'clubs' like the World Economic Forum (Davos),[4] are beginning to open their minds to the challenges of global regulation, even if some of the existing structures, for example the OECD, G7 (previously G8), G20, Shanghai Cooperation Organisation and so on seem designed to prevent or to dominate rather than to hasten it.

# Like-mindedness (across borders)

Just as mouse-sized mammals prevailed against monster-sized dinosaurs when environmental catastrophe forced evolutionary change, so the process of *innovation at the peripheries* should alert us to take seriously the insignificant, contemptible, marginal underground upstart and not to rely on the impressive scale and scary demeanour of incumbents, just when Vernadskian 'change and energy transfer' are darkening the sky. In keeping with our focus on the macro-scale, where we have worked from the biosphere (Vernadsky), through the semiosphere (Lotman), to the technosphere (Herrmann-Pillath), we want now to push through to something that applies each to the other, such that the planetary scope is maintained as we observe emergent phenomena and new chains of *causation, regulation* and *coordination* in the digital semiosphere, including some that look suspiciously insignificant, contemptible and marginal just now, 'unworthy adversaries' perhaps, but perhaps not adversaries at all, simply future systems in process of construction.

At the same time, we pursue the realization that just as every existential threat is not reducible to a fist-fight (because 'picking winners' is a mug's game if you are a dinosaur or a dragon), so the 'arrow of causation' may point in the opposite direction to the 'arrow of common sense'. It may seem obvious that the biosphere is primary, semiosphere secondary, technosphere tertiary, and certainly that is the order in which they were identified and characterized in scholarly history. But this may not be the way that causation works in these interconnected planetary systems. It may be that the latest, apparently least significant or least noticed development will exert a disproportionate and *regulatory* effect on its more prominent predecessors.

---

[4]The times may be changing: Davos 2020 focused on climate change and witnessed speeches by Greta Thunberg as well as the usual 'world leaders': https://www.weforum.org/events/world-economic-forum-annual-meeting-2020.

# Deliberation (debate), decision (voting), markets (exchange)

Because markets (the subject of economics), decision (the subject of political science) and deliberation (the subject of media studies) are now fully interoperative, it is no longer sufficient to study them as separate systems. In this chapter and the next we seek to connect and contrast *politics* (understood as social processes for deliberation and decision) with *markets* (systems of exchange). This combination adds up, we are told by economists Ole Jann and Christoph Schottmüller (2018: 32), to 'debates, votes, markets' – the 'three main mechanisms to aggregate information' in 'modern democratic societies'. In other words, there are mechanisms for linking micro-, meso- and macro-levels of political and economic subsystems. However, these mechanisms are not simply 'aggregates' of individual behaviour (arguing, voting, exchanging). They are both formal (legal) and informal (cultural) mechanisms, which *organize*, *regulate* and *coordinate* what individuals do and are likely or able to do.

In contemporary social media, as well as in countries characterized as 'trading democracies' and 'emergent economies', politics and markets are co-present and can be hard to distinguish: debate, decision and exchange are integrated mechanisms. Citizens and lobbyists alike are by now well aware that other users (including corporate or partisan organizations) may conceal hidden or duplicitous motives, based on in-group rather than whole-community needs; but at the same time communitarian or public-service initiatives may come from companies as well as from public-sector or community bodies.

Either way, political *deliberation* is decentralizing via such commercial platforms as Twitter, Facebook, WeChat, WhatsApp, Instagram and the like. With that process, *trust* of others is at a low ebb and declining, especially in societal discourses of news and public affairs, doubtless partly because formal political *decision* is increasingly abstracted from everyday life and voting is in decline, facing disillusion and discouragement as the old anarchist quip gains force: 'it doesn't matter who you vote for, the government gets in'. Political action is now a specialist profession, managed and foot-soldiered by lobbyists, lawyers, media and ideologues, who manoeuvre to disenfranchise awkward groups (including activists, whistleblowers and investigative journalists), to roll back democratic accountability in increasingly authoritarian states, and to enable runaway corporations to evade civic responsibility. As a result, *decision* and *markets* are withdrawing from public scrutiny, just as *deliberation* is converted into mass entertainment with little regulatory force.

As 'mechanisms' to 'aggregate' deliberation, digital social-media platforms have no precedent, but the trustworthiness of any information they distribute is not easily verifiable by users, whose deliberations may be swayed by populism, short-term trends or captured by activist groupuscules (Griffin, 2003) and concerted marketing campaigns, both political and commercial. Not surprisingly, in response, users tend spontaneously to cluster into like-minded and autocommunicative (self-regulating) groups – misleadingly called 'filter bubbles' or 'echo chambers' by some (Bruns, 2019), or 'knowledge clubs' (Hartley, 2015c; Neylon, 2015; Potts et al., 2017; Hartley et al., 2019) – where a level of trust is pre-coded into the 'preferences' that individuals bring to a semiotic encounter. As Jann and Schottmüller have argued, on the basis of a game analysis of Twitter users:

> if people have different preferences as well as different information, segregation into like-minded, homogeneous groups can be individually rational and Pareto-efficient … But even more importantly, we have shown that … the existence of echo chambers is the consequence of differences in preferences, and of uncertainty and mistrust about other people's motives.
>
> (Jann and Schottmüller, 2018: 32)

In other words, group allegiances are primary, and people use culturally created (learned) preferences to decide whom to trust (Gintis et al., 2019). *Culture-made groups* or demes take precedence over both individuals (other users) and information (true or false? – real or fake?) in the aggregation of knowledge, and in turn decide what kinds of information a particular user is going to trust. This means that individuals do not trust *themselves* any more than they do others: they need the assurance of social *like-mindedness*. People seek 'our language' groups *first*; and only then are they willing to concede trust to others and to information distributed electronically. Knowledge itself is a product of demes, not directly of individual knowing subjects (Hartley and Potts, 2014).

# Knowledge clubs

Because they are primary, demes are not just received from the past (heritable through language, custom, code, culture) but are also in constant process of adaptation, selection, remaking and renewal. We can observe their formation on the fly, in the situation analysed by Jann and Schottmüller. Twitter users are in principle individuals, although not all of them are 'natural persons', since meso-level political and marketing institutions 'impersonate' micro-level agents. However, the primary 'individual' action is to cluster into groups, and to learn from or to create knowledge – efficiently, according to this research. The concept of 'knowledge clubs' links culture and economics:

knowledge is not a public or a private good; it is a *club good* (Neylon, 2015), using 'club' in the economic sense originated by James Buchanan (1965). People make *political* clubs: more or less Jacobin; more or less liberal; more or less fascist (el-Ojeili, 2020;), and it is these that connect with each other online and contend with authorities in the streets (Tufekci, 2017). Often they wear a rhetorical garb that identifies their 'knowledge club', which in turn is mocked by opponents, as in the alt-right taunt of 'virtue-signalling' to belittle activist deliberation; or they parade in the 'uniform' of some other social movement (gender politics, football, 'freedom') in order to recruit new members.

Lotmanian semiotics takes this insight to higher levels of scale and aggregation than informal clusters in the Twittersphere. Lotman conceives of the semiosphere as a whole as an aggregation of *groups* (rather than individuals or information), which are *identified* internally by autocommunication and *differentiated* externally by language. 'We' speak like this and can be trusted; 'they' speak like that and are 'the other'. However, as we know, Lotman does not leave it at that. Instead, he argues that no single language – no *one* 'we' – can 'embrace the world' external to it, and that this is foundational to language (semiosis) as a whole, requiring in turn the existence of an 'open number of diverse languages' and a perceived necessity to constantly create new and 'better' ones in different contexts. Each of these different languages or modes of communication is reciprocally dependent on the other, owing to the 'incapacity of each to express the world independently' (Lotman, 2009: 2) and to the fact that different cultural spaces, and therefore also their modelling systems and modes of communication, are inextricably intertwined. The semiosphere *necessitates* other languages, other versions of the real and the true, other like-minded groups, to 'embrace' the external world differently. A single semiotic unit, independent of others, cannot grasp the world because no such unit can exist. As we have stressed throughout, any language necessarily needs to be functionally preceded by other languages in the semiosphere, and it needs to be immersed in semiotic space. Any semiotic unit exercises both *memory* and *learning*, meaning that it makes itself up out of elements from the past and from outside, such that both *identity* (autocommunication) and innovation (anomaly, change, adaptation) are driven by *other* semiospheres and other approximations of the world.

For Lotman, it is not simply the case that each language promotes trust among speakers and distrust of those who speak in other tongues, and not only that many languages (in other words, a global semiosphere) are needed to align the 'extra-semiotic object' of the Earth system with semiosis, but also that this higher level of adjustment to the real can only take place *between* languages, in translation of the untranslatable, which impasse forces 'adjustment' (innovation). That is, it is unavoidably necessary that autocommunicative regulation and gradually homogenizing cultural 'bubbles' are 'blown' from time to time. Hence, 'culture' and 'explosion' are coeval processes (Lotman, 2009).

This happens not just because the internal adequacy of a semiotic system must be maintained (regulated; updated) diachronically, over time, in order to guarantee its effectivity in the world, but also because dialogue and translation among incommensurate systems is needed synchronically, right now, to provoke new ideas, new truths, new languages and new subsystems within the semiosphere. One striking example is the extent to which polarized groups poach concepts from their opponents (past and present), not to reproduce an idea but in translation to invert it: for instance the 'men's movement' as a 'countermovement' to feminism (Blais and Dupuis-Déri, 2011); or 'white victimhood' among alt-right groups (Berbrier, 2000); or Trump as the 'anti-Obama' president.[5]

In social life, the same model applies to:

- groups cluster around shared code (semiosphere);
- form into coherent identities that supply individuals with 'preferences' and knowledge (rules; autocommunication);
- interact across borders of untranslatability (translation); and
- adjust – as groups, not as individuals – to new realities (creation) or new groups to constitute those realities (memory).

# Politics + markets: brokering untranslatable difference

The two semiotic systems for brokering untranslatable difference between social groups, where partisan truths give way to mutual adjustment, are *politics* and *markets*.

Both politics and markets involve ways to *connect* parties with different interests. Think of the space required for them to meet as a combination of theatre or dance floor (Athenian *Pnyx* or amphitheatre) and bazaar (Athenian *Agora* or town square). As Richard Sennett has noted, the *Pnyx* requires ritual, concentration and rules, while the *Agora* thrives on mixture and dispersion of attention (Sennett, 2016). These are both 'spaces for democracy' but the marketplace, in Sennett's words, is a space of 'difference' and 'diversity'; the dance-ground or corroboree (Haebich and Taylor, 2007)

---

[5] Far-right slogans – such as 'white lives matter' and 'It's OK to be white' – are in turn available to do mischief in the chambers of representative politics. See: https://www.theguardian.com/commentisfree/2018/oct/16/its-ok-to-be-white-is-not-a-joke-its-careless-politicians-helping-the-far-right; and see: https://www.sbs.com.au/nitv/article/2017/11/02/backlash-against-black-lives-matter-just-more-evidence-injustice. For 'the anti-Obama' see: https://www.theguardian.com/us-news/2018/may/11/donald-trump-barack-obama-legacy.

is a space of 'discipline' and 'concentration', as well as diplomacy, delight and desire. In Lotman's terms, the ideal Aristotelian city (Eusunoptos – 'taken in at a single glance') is recast as a semiosphere in which core and periphery, law-forming repetition and anomalous newness, are both separated and linked (Figure 17.1).

In the *digital* semiosphere, there is even more potential for overlap between the two types, although 'spaces' emerge in the form of different platforms, apps, genres and preferences. For instance, Amazon and Alibaba are closer to the 'Agora' side; Netflix (movies and TV) and Tencent (games) are closer to the 'discipline' side (because audiences have to concentrate, work within genre-rules and develop skills). In relation to news and journalism, you might say that clickbait news and 'fake news' cluster in the 'Agora'; investigative and in-depth coverage (including drama-documentary hybrids like *Chernobyl*)[6] cluster at the Pnyx. But both sides are needed for an ideal or a 'synoptic' city (polity) to emerge.

At present, although social media and online affordances play a prominent role as both marketplaces and places for debate, there is a crucial element missing, at least in person, and that's the citizen, either grouped in ordered tribes (Pnyx) or assembled in multivalent mixture (Agora). Aristotle for one (*Politics*, Bk VII) had firm views on the need for cities and citizens to be visible to one another (Janssens, 2010), arguing that collective action, law and politics all required speakers and voters, magistrates and jurors, to be able to scrutinize and test each other eyeball-to-eyeball, so that the ideal city should be '*eusunoptos*' or 'easily taken in at a glance' (Figure 17.1).

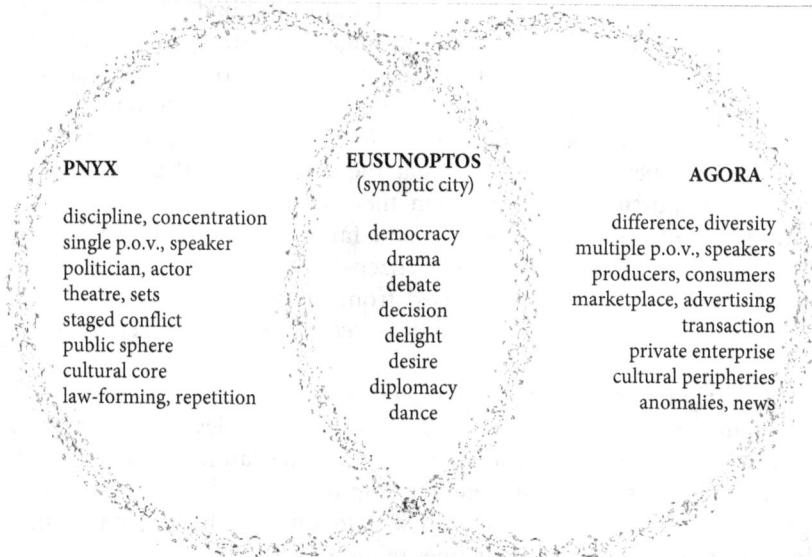

| PNYX | EUSUNOPTOS (synoptic city) | AGORA |
|---|---|---|
| discipline, concentration | democracy | difference, diversity |
| single p.o.v., speaker | drama | multiple p.o.v., speakers |
| politician, actor | debate | producers, consumers |
| theatre, sets | decision | marketplace, advertising |
| staged conflict | delight | transaction |
| public sphere | desire | private enterprise |
| cultural core | diplomacy | cultural peripheries |
| law-forming, repetition | dance | anomalies, news |

FIGURE 17.1 *Public space in the ideal (Aristotelian) city: both Pnyx and Agora.*

---

[6]TV-miniseries, created by Craig Mazin, produced by HBO and Sky UK, screened in 2019.

Athens was already too big for this even in ancient times, and Rome much more so (up to a million inhabitants in the 100s CE), so Aristotle identifies a problem in Classical political theory rather than a solution. His 'synoptic city' is one ideal that did not survive into democratic modernity. 'Representative' democracy took over from direct participation in decision-making; and state-surveillance took over from mutual scrutiny. The 'labour' of deliberation and decision (politics) was divided between the two functions, so that 'deliberation' became a spectator sport and mass entertainment (think Colosseum rather than Pnyx), while 'decision' was specialized into oligarchical bureaucracies dominated by elite families (and their armies) that monopolized elective offices and judicial governance as well as public administration. 'Senatus Populusque Romanus' (SPQR, or 'Senate and People of Rome') became an imperial fiction.

Modern representative democracy maintains something very much like this fiction. Political 'participation' is conducted *on behalf* of citizens, not by them; and decisions are taken in lobbies (out of sight), not forums (theatrical cockpits). Similarly, the Agora split into specialist markets (for slaves, cattle, vegetables, fish, etc.) but Senatorial and Equestrian (military) ranked families were (officially at least) barred from trade, so markets in Rome tended to be staffed by plebeians, freedmen/women or slaves. The Agora did not survive as a cross-section of the population; the function of markets remained with the populace, while their betters got on with running the empire – in other words, performing a coordinating function at macro-level, not just a productive one at meso-level.

Come the digital world, there was good news and bad news. The good news was that the relationship between looking and bodies was abstracted and multiplied without limit, to allow single gatherings, performances or events to be seen by billions of eyeballs on millions of screens, making it possible for 'numberless infinities of souls' (as John Donne put it) to co-scrutinize theatrical, spectacular and political events. The Colosseum went viral. The bad news was not just that the co-presence of citizens proved physically impossible, but now even their status as citizens has eroded, because of course the digital semiosphere far exceeds the 'view' of any one nation or polity. Many users and 'netizens' are inactive politically, either disenchanted with or disenfranchised from the political deliberation that governs them. Participation in politics is *delegated*, indirect, representative and opaque to the common view.

The digital semiosphere, then, *represents* populations (of citizens and of institutions, of transactions) at the highest level of aggregation and abstraction, using narratives employing the latest technologies and computational networks, allowing a group or knowledge club ('we') to be represented to itself as universal (with a claim on all), while remaining often adversarial in attitude and sometimes miniscule in fact.

Indeed, a new problem is not that the digital 'polity' is too big but that it is all too easy to be 'taken in at a glance', because the apparently limitless horizons of the internet are just the place for the *smallest* 'groupuscules' to hang out and act out, pretending they speak for all. For example extreme-right activists: the internet assumes a 'particular significance' for them, because:

> It allows the creation of a 'virtual community' of activists ... This virtual community can avoid any sort of 'reality check', cocooning its members against contacts with the outside world ... In particular, by sparing extremists the need to debate with opponents or lecture to small gatherings of the faithful ... [it] enables its protagonists to indulge in an utterly illusory sense of the potential of the extreme right for realizing utopias of alternative world orders.
>
> (Griffin, 2003: 45–6)

Video game researchers have found that young people are recruited to this 'virtual community' via video games and associated chatrooms and livestreams. A report on US NPR featured an Antifa organization Free Radicals, run by 'reformed skinhead' Christian Picciolini, who said:

> 'Thirty years ago, when I was involved in the white supremacist movement, it was very much a face to face interaction,' he says. 'You know, you had to meet somebody to be recruited, or you had a pamphlet or a flyer put on your car.' But today, he says, it's much more common for extremists to initially reach out online. And that includes over kids' headsets during video games.[7]

The news item noted the planetary extent and scale of the digital semiosphere in which gamers operate:

> But it's a daunting technical challenge. The three biggest video game platforms – Microsoft, PlayStation and Steam – host 48 million, 70 million and 130 million monthly active players respectively, Boyd says. 'That's the populations of Spain, France and Russia. And then imagine that you're monitoring all of their text chat ... all of their voice chat, in literally every language, dialect, and subdialect spoken in the world.'[8]

---

[7] Anya Kamenetz, 'Right-Wing Hate Groups Are Recruiting Video Gamers'. NPR *All Things Considered*, 5 November 2018: https://www.npr.org/2018/11/05/660642531/right-wing-hate-groups-are-recruiting-video-gamers.

[8] Source as at previous note. The internal quotation is from Greg Boyd, who represents video game companies for the law firm Frankfurt Kurnit.

Politics and markets are the coordination mechanisms for what Hartley (1996) has called the 'twin energies of modernity', namely, the pursuit of *freedom* (democratizing and technically sophisticated representative deliberation and governance) and its twin, the pursuit of *comfort* (family and material well-being, ensured by market economics, industrialization and accelerating technological change). Both politics and markets are 'realisms', not justified by premodern religious faith or monarchical fantasy; they function to achieve *truth in decisions*: one for group or collective action, the other for transactions. Both have evolved as mechanisms to maximize *individual* autonomy within *group* systems, while at the same time allowing the giant *scale* of modern associated life to bring efficiencies without snuffing out individual choice. In other words, politics and markets both *mediate* individuality in *systems*. Both can be analysed as models, seeking rules for right action (protocols). Both are mediated in turn by knowledge-sharing arrangements that coordinate groups of strangers, who do not know each other but whose identity is shared in culture, language, codes, customs and commitments.

# Journalism and groupuscules

Journalism is a chief means by which both politics and markets have connected with populations. As the 'textual system of modernity' (Hartley, 1996), journalism has served to *coordinate* knowledge ('truth in decisions'), distributing the terms of conflict and state of play of contending forces across disparate groups and agencies (producers/consumers, owners/users, regulators/citizens, creatives/audiences), to construct and communicate what counts as a 'we' community and why intrusive anomalies should worry it.

In the era of 'the press', journalism thrived for many decades on centralized print-industrial production, on hierarchical power (politics) and mass organization (markets). However, as screen media, postmodern thought and digital-computational technologies emerged and consolidated, journalism suffered transformational changes, wherein its coordination role was put in crisis, while its 'users', once seen as homogenous classes or consumers – demes if not nations – dissolved into multiple identities ('echo-chambers') that struggle for coherence as groups (identity politics). Mainstream journalism has still to come up with a viable response to these developments, with the continuing mass extinction of mastheads, corporations, occupations and jobs, as news has migrated to social media and the ability of media to mobilize those it sought to 'represent' has dissipated.

The result are 'groupuscules' (apparently insignificant in size but transformational in effect), as they are suggestively named by Roger Griffin on a Deleuzian model of cells. A groupuscule forms as a 'cellular, centreless and leaderless network with ill-defined boundaries and no formal hierarchy or internal organizational structure to give it a unified intelligence' (2003: 34). Griffin characterizes groupuscules as:

> fully developed, highly specialized and largely autonomous grouplets that simultaneously form the constituents of an amorphous, leaderless and centreless cellular network of political ideology, organization and activism ... As such, these 'groupuscules' are to be seen as the product of a sophisticated process of evolutionary adaptation to post-1945 realities that allows extreme variants of revolutionary nationalism to survive in the 'post-fascist' age in a form that is largely resistant to attempts to suppress them.
>
> (Griffin, 2003: 27)

Griffin's own research is exclusively concerned with what he calls 'the groupuscular right' (fascist groups), but his insight that political organization has undergone 'evolutionary adaptation' from the industrial-hierarchical class-based form to the 'amorphous, leaderless and centreless cellular networks' associated with the alt-right (*avant la lettre*) is both compelling and applicable beyond the right.

The important general insight we can draw from his analysis is that *'politics' takes the form of its constituent organizational units and is known via the media affordances of the time*. In the present circumstances, this means that the model of journalism that many (including journalists and politicians) carry around in their heads is dangerously outdated, leaving both producers and readers floundering when new kinds of energy are released into political conflict by these means, as witness the rise of 'tribal' (ultra-nationalist) politics and the alt-right across many countries, including both the United States and Russia. In response, the stability of liberal democracy is shaken, and commentators are at a loss to explain it or to counter it. Griffin observes:

> As if to consolidate its place within modern politics, two further factors then emerged in the course of the 1990s that made the groupuscule in perfect tune with the dominant Zeitgeist in the West: the growing public perception of an all-pervasive cultural globalization, and the capillary penetration into the nervous system of planetary society of the World Wide Web. Together they guaranteed that each groupuscule, no matter how small, could act as a nodal point in a vast, constantly evolving network of extremist organizations of far greater significance than the sum of its parts: the groupuscular right.
>
> (Griffin, 2003: 40)

Griffin names Russia as a fertile international breeding ground for the groupuscular right: the combination of globalization, the World Wide Web and the need to operate outside mass political party systems enabled 'highly specialized variants of fascism to rush into some of the gaps that had so dramatically opened up in Russia's political system [post-1991] and into the spaces ... that had become available in its society for both civil and uncivil forms of cultural and ideological production' (2003: 40).

Writing more than a decade before the intervention of Russian hackers and of the alt-right in the American electoral process during the Trump election of 2016, Griffin predicted just such an outcome: 'the groupuscular right could come to be looked on in future studies of extremism, not as the inconsequential afterlife of classical fascism, but rather more as the intangible, diaphanous shape of extremist things to come in the age of high modernity' (2003: 49). It is beyond time to take notice.

# PART SIX

# Cultural science for the Anthropocene

*Peeter Laurits, 'Down the Stream' (2003) from* Dining with Worms
https://www.peeterlaurits.com/archive/dining-with-worms

# 18

## Staged conflict:
## New demes and classes

*A snake sheds its skin when it grows. This is a perfect symbolic expression of scholarly process. In order to stay true to itself, the process of cultural development should change sharply in its own time ... All that remains is to hope that the snake, having shed its skin, changed its color, and increased in size, will preserve the very unity of itself.*

(JURI LOTMAN, 2014: 79)

\* \* \*

### 'Useless bums' of the world, unite!

Politics and markets are historical rather than strictly conceptual phenomena; and in some respects, they have started to pull in different directions, away from the congruent modernizing energies identified by economic historians Deirdre McCloskey (2006, 2010, 2016) and Joel Mokyr (2009). Now, politics trends towards increasing conflict among proliferating groupuscules of unskilled thinkers; markets towards increased abstraction, automation and data-based, computational, communications technologies, where all the world's corporate giants, American and Chinese, are now intensively clustered.

This shift from industrial manufacturing to information creativity has also decimated the skilled working class or exported it to emergent countries in the global South. As more types of repetitive work are automated, fears are growing that large numbers of people – those masses that capitalism has long relied upon as markets as well as workers – will become a new 'unworking class', leading to the overpolicing of 'surplus populations', likely by the very AI and robots (drones) that have replaced them (Davis, 2019). This machine-blaming trope has its forebears in the Luddite, Captain Swing and Rebecca riots, the unrest that accompanied the mechanization of agriculture in the first Industrial Revolution in the UK and elsewhere. But this time it has been given an extra kick because it is now possible to imagine a form of capitalism that not only finds 'productive workers' unnecessary but doesn't even need consumers or audiences either. Historian Yuval Noah Harari is a prominent proponent of that scenario (Harari, 2018), summing up in a 2017 TED Talk the connection between 'computer games' and 'unnecessary people' by envisaging a future in which the very lives of 'useless bums' are no longer 'sacred' (see also Wang, 2018):

> The coming technological bonanza will probably make it feasible to feed and support people even without any effort from their side. But what will keep them occupied and content? One answer might be drugs and computer games. Unnecessary people might spend increasing amounts of time within 3D virtual-reality worlds that would provide them with far more excitement and emotional engagement than the drab reality outside. Yet such a development would deal a mortal blow to the liberal belief in the sacredness of human life and of human experiences.[1]

Harari asks the awkward question about 'unnecessary people' – unnecessary to technolibertarians and libertarian transhumanists, that is: '*What's so sacred about useless bums who pass their days devouring artificial experiences?*' There's not much left here of the convivial bazaar and Aristotelian Agora or town square, in corporate strategy anyway, although these are now re-emerging at community-level as self-organized markets both physical and online: farmers' and makers' markets, pop-up shops and 'renewal' schemes (Westbury, 2015).

At the same time, a larger-scale *political* response has emerged globally, in the form of street demonstrations, strikes and protest movements, provoked by youth-led popular impatience with gridlock government, populist authoritarianism and policies dictated by the energy and gun lobbies. Protest has crystalized around climate change, environmental and wildlife activism. In contrast to established activist organizations like Greenpeace or Amnesty, new activist movements like Extinction Rebellion (Hallam, 2019) and #FridaysForFuture (Thunberg, 2019) are not centrally organized and

---

[1]https://ideas.ted.com/the-rise-of-the-useless-class/.

led, but made up of self-organized local groupuscules, linked by activism strategies and social media across the world, and making creative use of social media across the digital semiosphere (Tufekci, 2017). Much more important, they reject conventional politics altogether, reserving a particular contempt for 'business as usual' rhetoric. As Greta Thunberg, founder of #FridaysForFuture, put it at the UN: 'You have stolen my dreams and my childhood with your empty words ... We are in the beginning of a mass extinction, and all you can talk about is money and fairy tales of eternal economic growth. How dare you!' (23 September 2019). These words soon resonated around the world – in her own voice, and also remixed in various musical mashups that took her message to venues far from politics-as-usual.[2] At the turn of 2020 it seemed the message was getting through: the 'useless bums' were no longer mere docile 'bums on seats'. Starting from one autistic teenager sitting on a cold street in Stockholm,[3] by 2019 there had been documented FridaysForFuture action in 228 countries, 7,000 cities, with 86,000 strike events involving 13,000,000 strikers (Figure 18.1). It was more a case of 'Useless bums of the world, unite!' And it needed the digital semiosphere for that to happen.

Not least because new social media create new types of group and affordances – new classes and institutions – the stakes of this type of political activism are much higher than anything representative politics-as-usual seems able to mobilize. In a perceptive review of Greta Thunberg's published speeches (Thunberg, 2019), Lucy Diavolo wrote:

Like a biblical flood, the impending doom of climate crisis is a threat with the power of an angry god. And just as Greta's advocacy for scientific consensus and immediate action says 'no gods' can save us from this threat, her rhetoric says 'no masters' to the people running the world. If it's a question of saving the world or the status quo, it's obvious where Greta's loyalty lies ... 'Everything needs to change. And

---

[2]Transcript here: https://asia.nikkei.com/Spotlight/Environment/How-dare-you-Transcript-of-Greta-Thunberg-s-UN-climate-speech. This remarkable speech was soon remixed as Swedish Black Metal, by Indonesian thrash band Suaka's John Mollusc, here: https://www.youtube.com/watch?v=CLxpgRqxtEA); as mood music by Australians Megan Washington and Robert Davidson, here: (https://www.theguardian.com/environment/video/2019/dec/09/greta-thunbergs-how-dare-you-speech-performed-by-megan-washington-and-robert-davidson-video), and as a dance mash-up by UK DJ Fatboy Slim, here: (https://www.theguardian.com/global/video/2019/oct/09/fatboy-slim-samples-greta-thunbergs-speech-to-the-un-during-uk-concert-video). Each of these was well received, with YouTube views in the millions, and fully integrated into youth-oriented live events.
[3]For 'autistic teenager' see Steve Silberman (author of *NeuroTribes*) in *Vox*: https://www.vox.com/first-person/2019/5/6/18531551/greta-thunberg-autism-aspergers.

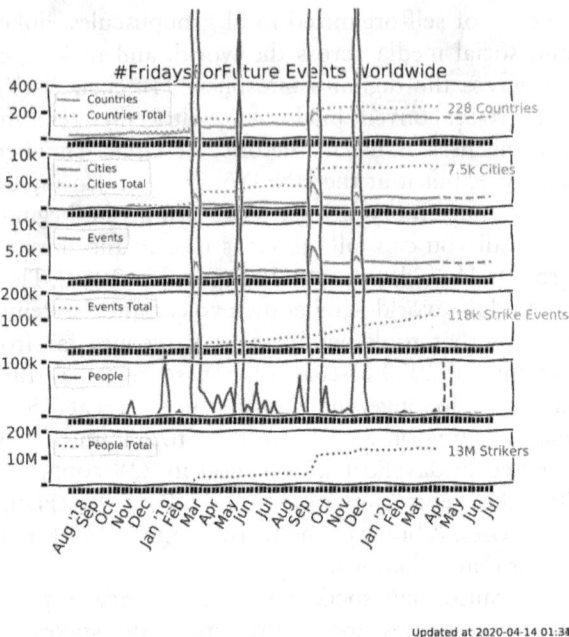

**FIGURE 18.1** *Coordinating rebellion:* FridaysForFuture *cuts through where representative politics doesn't.*[4]
*Source: FridaysForFuture.org: https://www.fridaysforfuture.org/statistics/graph.*

it has to start today', Greta told the crowd. 'So everyone out there: It is not time for civil disobedience. It is time to rebel'. (*Teen Vogue*, 12 November 2019)[5]

As one of Extinction Rebellion's recommended chants puts it: 'System Change, not Climate Change!'[6] There's an echo here of the fundamental antagonism between capitalism and socialism that characterized the political choices of the twentieth century, up to 1989, when history was

---

[4]*Original caption*: 'The dotted lines in countries and cities are the total number of countries and cities that had ever participated so far at the given date. For people, the dotted blue line is simply the sum of all strikers each week. Many of them will be the same week after week, but we don't track people individually, so that's what it has to be.' *Source*: FridaysForFuture.org: https://www.fridaysforfuture.org/statistics/graph. Updated January 2020.

[5]'Greta Thunberg's Book *No One Is Too Small to Make a Difference* Is a Clarion Call for Climate Rebellion'. *Teen Vogue* (12 November 2019): https://www.teenvogue.com/story/greta-thunberg-book-review-no-one-is-too-small-to-make-a-difference-climate-rebellion.

[6]An existing eco-slogan (e.g. https://theecologist.org/2016/jun/16/change-system-not-climate) that was widely noticed by observers of climate action rallies in September 2019, from the *Financial Times* to *Dissent Magazine*. It's also a resource website: https://systemchangenotclimatechange.org/.

proclaimed to be over. Since then, liberal democracy, neoliberal economics and authoritarian populism have vied with each other to *manage* the system, believing it to be an achieved global reality, rather than to overthrow the lot and install a quite different system.

However, such ambitions do still motivate radical movements and activists who have spent the intervening decades on the fringes of political deliberation and decision. Here, 'politics' bifurcates into two very different crews (currently, they're passing ships in the night, not gladiatorial combatants jousting eyeball to eyeball), not really opposites because the 'two sides' are looking at different problems for different solutions to be achieved by different means and different agents.

On the one hand, there is nationalist populism, which has made a big comeback in mainstream governing parties in the United States, the United Kingdom, Turkey, China, Brazil, Hungary and elsewhere, which has successfully caused 'globalization' and 'nationalism' to seem to represent opposite values, where 'nationalism' is the (currently betrayed, they say) preference of 'we' groups, and 'globalization' is the ideology of 'them' – rootless cosmopolitans, elites, scientists and immigrants who owe no allegiance to 'our values'. Such politics pay no attention to the global interdependency of all advanced economies and results in real-world initiatives like Brexit, Trump's wall and the US trade war with China. Whether these policies stick around or not, the ground has shifted away from welcoming globalization to making it the latest hate-object for online trolls and actual extremists, especially the alt-right and white supremacists, who see globalization as a conspiracy against themselves.

On the other hand, there is the alternative envisioned by climate activists. Lucy Diavolo lets Greta Thunberg explain:

> Addressing the notion that [Greta Thunberg] and youth climate activists are not providing answers, she laid out a trio of cutting-edge solutions, saying, 'We start talking about a circular economy and rewilding nature and the need for a just transition.' But she was aware even in mentioning these policy ideas that politicians 'don't understand what we're talking about.'
>
> (*Teen Vogue*, 12 November 2019)

So what are they talking about?

- A 'circular economy' is one that recycles what it produces, on the model of the biosphere: also known as the regeneration economy.[7]

---

[7]For the circular or regenerative economy, see: https://www.ellenmacarthurfoundation.org/circular-economy/concept; https://www.sciencealert.com/can-we-build-a-circular-economy-to-save-the-planet; https://medium.com/activate-the-future/a-glossary-of-regenerative-culture-c6107a8a93cd.

- 'Rewilding nature' is conservation biology turned to agricultural policy: reducing active management (by land-clearing, ploughing, fertilizer, pest control, irrigation) of field, farm, forest and water, in favour of natural regeneration processes and production aligned with those.[8]
- The 'need for a just transition' is what many call 'climate justice'. With its roots among labour unions who sought a way for workers in extractive and polluting industries to transition into new jobs, it expanded to include the rights of all those involved: the land of Indigenous groups, the poverty and exploitative working conditions of people of colour in low-paid and offshore workforces and the rights of children to a safe and ethical future. Any affiliate group commits to:
  - ○ work to keep global warming below 1.5 degrees;
  - ○ advocate for just and sustainable solutions to the climate crisis; and
  - ○ take leadership from, and work together to build the power of, those most affected by the climate crisis.[9]

This 'justice' aspect of climate activism bemuses some observers. For instance, Amazon's 'most helpful' customer review of *This Is Not a Drill: An Extinction Rebellion Handbook* (2019) gives it one star and complains: 'None of this has anything to do with climate change. The majority of the book is dedicated to fighting sexism, racism, colonialism, inequality, the 1%, capitalism in general, and the mistreatment of indigenous people' (Amazon. com website). The reviewer concludes:

> The battle against global warming is not about «having fun» or feeling radical, it is about tough choices and facing reality, first and foremost that acting like a clown only hurts whatever cause you join.
>
> (Amazon.com website)

Grumpy bemusement is a sure sign that there's an elephant in the room. 'Politics' in the digital semiosphere has transitioned to a whole different scale: that of the planet as a whole (*everywhere*), people as a species (*everyone*) and it's not just about the economy as we know it but about *everything*. Hartley et al. (2015) call these 'the three bigs'. Of course they are stalked by the equally large-scale 'three buts' – *control* of freedom (technical, political and commercial), *sustainability* of comfort (wasted words, wasted people, wasted planet) and *divisions* of knowledge (economic, political, cultural-creative) – where contemporary politics is actually practised.

---

[8]For rewilding, see: https://rewildingeurope.com/what-is-rewilding/; http://rewildaustralia.org/.
[9]For climate justice, see: https://climatejusticealliance.org/just-transition/; Australian group: https://www.aycc.org.au/climate_justice.

# Creative industries:
# anomalous or law-forming?

The colliding and sometimes explosive 'tectonic plates' of global politics, trade, communication and technology are subject to the most accelerated, intense and/or sudden change where political-economic-semiotic subduction (one side goes over, the other goes under) grinds along their mutual borders, which is also where the most 'explosive' (in Lotman's sense) new meanings are created (Hartley and Potts, 2014). In the process, the 'anomalous' peripheral edges of economic-political and market-media semiospheres bring new energies and ideas in towards the familiar, repetitive 'law-forming' core of the cultural semiosphere (Lotman, 1979b [*Poetics Today*]).

To see how the '*digital* semiosphere' works, and to identify what's important about it at planetary scale, we can now focus on two of their latest and most controversial forms: one 'explosive' – '*staged conflict*' (Hartley, 2018); and the other 'law-forming' – *blockchain* or distributed ledgers (Casey and Vigna, 2018; Potts and Hartley, 2018; Rennie et al., 2019). These phenomena – one a political-semiotic form or genre, the other a market-based technological application – are 'native' to the digital/global semiosphere. Connecting them is of analytic value, as a way to make the overall semiosphere *strange* (Shklovsky/Berlina, 2015). To defamiliarize them further, we do not analyse them on their own home ground, that is 'politics' as decision-reaching, blockchain as mostly used as a financial technology or 'fintech' (e.g. Bitcoin), although platforms like Vitalik Buterin's Ethereum (founded 2014) go further: Ethereum announces itself as 'a public, open-source, Blockchain based distributed software platform that allows developers to build and deploy decentralised applications'. We argue that both 'staged conflict' (politics) and blockchain (distributed-ledger markets, using decentralized apps or 'Dapps')[10] are *creative industries* (Potts and Hartley, 2018).

## Blockchain

The idea of blockchain as a creative industry is counterintuitive if all you've heard about is Bitcoin, but if you consider its uses – those 'dapps' – it makes more sense, following an intriguing suggestion by Jason Potts and Ellie Rennie (2019):[11]

---

[10]See a curated list of dapps under these categories: Games, Gambling, Social, Finance, High risk, Exchanges, Development, Media, Wallet, Marketplaces, Security, Property, Governance, Storage, Identity, Energy, Health, Insurance, at: https://www.stateofthedapps.com/.

[11]Potts and Rennie first broached this topic in 2017 with a paper on SSRN:, Blockchains and Creative Industries (https://ssrn.com/abstract=3072129). The two quotations here (from Potts and Hartley (2018) summarize their ideas.

Arguably, the single most significant new creative industry sector to emerge in the past two decades is, on the face of it, one of the weirdest and most unlikely: namely digital private money, or cryptocurrencies, and the engine behind this, which is blockchain (also known as distributed ledger technology, which can be defined as multi-organisational databases with a super audit trail and some embedded code).

Potts and Rennie characterize blockchain in the language of creative industries, to find that this particular cap fits perfectly:

> Blockchain is a pure creative industry ... It is a designed, creative product, made of software. Furthermore, it came from the deepest, purest sources of open source software culture, and spread through the internet, largely through amateur, outsider and hacker channels. Blockchain emerged from the cultural margins of the informal economy, and continues to grow and thrive there, while being rapidly co-opted into the corporate and government mainstream.

They go on to note that many of blockchain's (currently lesser-known) applications are sourced from the creative industries, for instance music industry (e.g. Ujo Music, musicNow), audiovisual production and distribution (Cinezen, FilmChain) in visual arts (e.g. Dada.nyc) and in collective storytelling (e.g. Cellarius). Blockchain brings digital capabilities to finance and trade, and at the same time brings new finance and trade options to creative practice:

> It would be remiss of us not to point out that blockchain is itself a creative industry, the most newly formed protean landmass to erupt from the deep digital oceans of the internet. And while new species of blockchain platforms and applications continue to develop in the finance and trade sectors of the economy, a significant range are also emerging from the creative industries.

The promise of blockchain for datafied culture is in it being an autonomous technology enabling data markets that are free of large-scale institutional intermediation – that is, data become resistant to the network effects of platforms and the habit of the latter to extract value from creations of others (Mazzucato, 2018). The core affordance of blockchains for cultural data management is transparent accountability – any digitally produced piece of content can be written to a blockchain, establishing a secure verifiable record of creation that can subsequently be tracked, traded, licensed, verified and so on, promoting networked trust, as it were. The distinct qualities that a ledger possesses are clarity (for legibility), consistency and consensus as a factual and agreed-upon recording of the basic datum of an economy: of identity, property, contract and value (Potts and Rennie, 2018; O'Dair, 2019).

Markets rely on the ability of agents to validate identity, in order to enter into contracts or to contract within blockchain-based organizational forms, without needing to share private information. This means overcoming the trust problems characteristic of internet-based cooperation and trade (Potts and Hartley, 2018; Dopfer and Potts, 2019). Blockchains can enable creative labour to be traced across a supply chain – who produced or repurposed what would become a public record. This could change public perception of the role of labour in value creation and, more specifically, in public value creation (Benington and Moore, 2011; Mazzucato, 2018). It might also circumvent the kind of dispute between creative artists and distribution networks that was personified by Taylor Swift's boycott of Spotify (2014–17) and her subsequent return.[12]

The question is how a data management technology could bring about a new form of coordination where cultural labour becomes publicly visible and can start influencing value perceptions. This relates to John Locke's concept of 'just deserts' – an economic system in which individual labour is important and possible to identify. In contemporary digital culture, which celebrates remix, mashups, collage, pastiche/homage, memes and combinations, and where incremental innovations accumulate to precipitate radical change, individual labour contributions have been paradoxically impossible to identify. This has encouraged what Nobel Prize winner Herbert Simon (2000) has pointed out – that any one inventor or investor builds on a vast store of collectively produced intellectual capital, yet each feel justified in earning a much higher proportion of rewards than their own contribution warrants. In response, as a complementary technology to open-data provision by governments, blockchain could enable users to trace how value is built when some of its 'particles' are, for instance, publicly contributed forms of content and data, or collaboratively developed novel cultural forms or insights. Governments could set up blockchain-based registries of digital infrastructure, to underpin cultural production ecosystems. These would enable identity management, data security, asset provenance, contracting and value-transfer (Potts and Rennie, 2018). The aim would then be to make creative labour visible and identifiable and thereby to redistribute wealth proportionally back to the creators of new meanings/public value and not to let it accumulate on the accounts of the vast platform companies (Mazzucato, 2018).

# Anger or antagonism?

To the extent that blockchain has become a creative industry – and not just a novelty fintech fad – it has become at the same time a topic of

---

[12]See *NME*, April 2018: https://www.nme.com/news/music/spotify-boss-daniel-ek-talks-taylor-swift-streaming-return-2280169.

debate and contestation across the digital semiosphere. For devotees, it is a libertarian wonder, presaging a new era of decentralized governance that will remove the need for any kind of intermediaries, not just rent-seeking platforms but also the public sector, cities, government and so on. Why do 'we' need government if all kinds of social interaction can be trusted using technology? Why can't 'we' manage cities via private corporations? Who needs passports when migration could be marketized? For opponents, blockchain equals fascism; and indeed, connections are there. For instance, the leader of the far-right German AfD party, Alice Weidel, is, among other things, a bitcoin entrepreneur and trained follower of Austrian economics. But does that make her a Nazi? As a sympathetic news site, in a 2018 profile of Weidel, put it:

> And with that background, we won't believe a lesbian is a nazi. Nor will we believe someone who quotes Hayek is an authoritarian … But our preferred way to see the bigger picture, from which we think everything else derives, is Hayek vs Keynes. The former stands for decisions at the most local level, the latter stands for redistribution of wealth. The former argues for no barriers to the free market, not even to currencies, the latter would rather use money as a means of wealth distribution.[13]

Support for a single market is one thing; support for a single currency is another, it seems. The EU becomes a fight between Keynes (Merkel, Macron) and Hayek (AfD, Brexit). For others, unsurprisingly, 'Blockchain isn't about democracy and decentralisation – it's about greed':

> No serious institution would ever allow its transactions to be verified by an anonymous cartel operating from the shadows of the world's authoritarian kleptocracies. So it is no surprise that whenever 'blockchain' has been piloted in a traditional setting, it has either been thrown in the trash bin or turned into a private permissioned database that is nothing more than an Excel spreadsheet or a database with a misleading name.[14]

In Audrey Watters's list of 'The 100 Worst Ed-Tech Debacles of the Decade', memorably filed under 'what a shitshow' on her blog (31 December 2019, as listed in Chapter 13), Blockchain comes in at #13 (with links to relevant news items):

---

[13]https://www.trustnodes.com/2018/02/24/alice-weidel-leader-alternative-germany-launch-bitcoin-startup.
[14]Nouriel Roubini (15 October 2018): https://www.theguardian.com/technology/2018/oct/15/blockchain-democracy-decentralisation-bitcoin-price-cryptocurrencies. And see Bruce Schneier in Wired: https://www.wired.com/story/theres-no-good-reason-to-trust-blockchain-technology/.

Blockchain Anything

There is no good reason to use Blockchain technologies – in education or otherwise. The Blockchain will not prevent cheating. It will not stop people from lying on their resumé. It will not make it easier for students to request a copy of their school transcripts. It will not improve college retention rates. It would not have prevented the 'college admissions scandal.'

Stop it.[15]

This kind of antagonism doesn't look like individualist emotion (angry Audrey); it looks like class antagonism (*cui bono?*). And certainly, antagonism is a built-in feature of contemporary creative industries.

# Staged Conflict

Blockchain is not the only new form currently erupting from the internet's digital ocean. Just as important, and equally hard to identify as a 'creative industry' until you look more closely, is *politics*. Politics has emerged, similarly, as a new creative industry, in the form of what we can call '*staged conflict*', which exactly follows the delineation drawn by Potts and Rennie for blockchain:

- It is a product of the internet (digital semiosphere), although, like anything else in that environment, it has its origins in previous media technologies, for example the popular press and broadcasting, and predecessor cultural forms, for example 'politics as spectator sport'. This was conducted in the press via the kind of rhetorical adversarialism that might boost circulation or bring down the government. In broadcasting, its extremist tendencies could mature into what Raymond Williams called terrorism as a 'spectator sport', where 'an arranged version' of the world (the 1972 Olympic Games) was invaded by what parts of the world are 'actually like' (Palestinian hostage-takers), resulting in 'a battle of political wills', with multiple fatalities, played out live in front of up to a third of the world's population (Williams, 1989: 21–4).
- It is designed, creative, made of software, amateur, outsider-centric, hacker-made, at the cultural margins but available for co-option into government and the corporate mainstream.

---

[15]http://hackeducation.com/2019/12/31/what-a-shitshow.

Observers may not like what they see but can agree that contemporary politics is influenced by groups, discourses and action that circulate from the outer margins towards the political core. Thus, Breitbart → Bannon → Trump: 'Perhaps the most vocal online support for Trump was channelled through websites like Reddit, 4chan, and 8chan' (Heikkilä, 2017). In turn, the alt-right, white supremacist and Nazi extreme is but one heartbeat away from Utøya, Norway; Christchurch, NZ; or El Paso, TX; with lethal outcomes and tragic legacies. But the body count is 'staged' conflict nonetheless, where both perpetrator's motivation for action and the distribution of 'broadcast' communication (including self-filmed video of atrocities themselves) are and are meant to be amplified through digital channels.

The terrorist extreme does not place 'staged conflict' beyond the pale of politics but right at its populist heart. Staged conflict – without terrorism but quite often with the underlying threat of violence – has restored popular politics to the boisterous status it enjoyed in the era of the 'Virgin Vote' in the United States (Grinspan, 2016) or the 'pauper press' in the UK (Williams, 1978). To cut a long story short, modern democratic politics was founded on sanguinary excess (a.k.a. modernising revolutions), and equally on spectacle and entertainment, emblematized by the *'tricoteuse'*, who knitted liberty caps while watching the guillotining of aristos in Revolutionary Paris,[16] sex and scandal (Hartley, 1996), where boxing (sport) and street-fighting (riot), drama (Shakespeare) and bearbaiting (same theatre) were not separate from political deliberation and decision but on a gradient within it. Political 'argy-bargy'[17] is 'normal', and the theatrical component of 'we'-group intimidation of opponents (also called 'shirtfronting')[18] goes back to the early days of US democratic politics, when, to mobilize the 'virgin vote', as Jon Grinspan shows, 'parents trained their children to be "violent little partisans".' Rallies sought to create like-mindedness among youth, migrants and newly

---

[16]The *tricoteuse* was immortalized by Charles Dickens in *A Tale of Two Cities*. See: https://timeline.com/tricoteuse-french-revolution-b9887af073f4.

[17]'Argy-bargy' is an Anglo-Australian term for the push and shove of political disputation. It made international headlines when Australian prime minister Kevin Rudd explained it to the world's media during the Global Financial Crisis (2009): '"What I sense across most of my counterparts across the G20 is a strong sense of emerging consensus on most of those questions," Mr Rudd said. "There's always going to be, and let me use a technical Australian term for you, argy bargy, that's short for argument ... Mr Rudd repeated his warning that talks next week will be tough and hard ... "I think we should not be distracted by what I'd describe as disagreements at the margins"' (https://www.news.com.au/finance/business/plenty-of-argy-bargy-at-g20-rudd/news-story/9214e04bbcf1b1653f487c2718433efb). The 'technical Australian' term is also used in the UK parliament, e.g.: https://www.independent.co.uk/news/uk/politics/this-isnt-about-the-normal-argy-bargy-of-politics-it-is-about-13000-civilian-deaths-756017.html.

[18]Shirtfronting: https://www.macquariedictionary.com.au/blog/article/200/.

industrialized citizens, whose allegiances were interpellated as much by the opportunity for exploit and contest (in the manner of spectacular youth subcultures) as by rousing ideological rhetoric, with the added attraction of meeting compatible others and, maybe, romantic partners among a population of strangers at rallies and conventions (Grinspan, 2016).

In this early era of staged conflict, theatre was a potent political force in its own right. It was identified by no less an observer than Alexis de Tocqueville as the likely venue for popular revolt against established elites: a revolt that duly occurred in the 'Shakespeare Riots' of 1849 in New York City (Hartley, 2020: 173–8), which resulted in a truly Shakespearean tragedy: dozens dead, hundreds injured and a new alignment of adversarial groups identified. Fast forward to the era of the Trump rally, where:

> According to a new study reported by *The Washington Post*, counties that hosted political rallies with Donald Trump as the headliner in 2016 saw a 226 percent increase in hate crimes over comparable counties that did not host such a rally in subsequent months.[19]

Although of course it has a long history and wider application (Hartley, 2018), 'staged conflict' may be understood for present purposes to refer to the contemporary amalgam of:

- authoritarian, anti-immigration populist tribalism (Trump, Brexit, etc.);

- online hate speech, trolling, misogyny, cyberbullying and so on (e.g. Gamergate) (Jane, 2017);

- commercialization of the groupuscular right: a 'new social network market' (Potts et al., 2008) developed by upstart or *soi-disant* 'outsider' organizations, from libertarian think tanks (many funded by the US Koch brothers) to Breitbart and the alt-right, picked up for commercial exploitation, notably by Rupert Murdoch's Fox News; and

- capitalization of surveillance data and psychometric profiles that identify which groupuscule, 'echo chamber' or knowledge club suits you, based on your responses to online stimuli, and adjusts advertising feeds accordingly; for which the 'poster-organization' is Cambridge Analytica, also held responsible for helping to elect the forty-fifth US president.[20]

---

[19] *Vox* (March 2019): https://www.vox.com/2019/3/24/18279807/trump-hate-crimes-study-white-nationalism. See also: https://www.washingtonpost.com/politics/2019/03/22/trumps-rhetoric-does-inspire-more-hate-crimes/.

[20] Here: https://www.theguardian.com/news/2018/mar/17/cambridge-analytica-facebook-influence-us-election?CMP=share_btn_tw.

All this may be a case of 'beware what you wish for', if your interest in the creative industries was sparked by the early utopian potential of digital culture and the World Wide Web, combined with the 'bottom-up' activism of maker culture, DIY creative enterprise and community-level arts practice, across neglected or marginal identities and demographics. The combination of new forms of organization enabled by digital connectivity, and new possibilities for ideas, enterprise and exploit to come from anywhere in the system, not just from institutional incumbents, opens the creative door to unwelcome visitors even as advocates hold it open for their affinity groups. It has not taken long for the romantic-libertarian optimism of 'living on thin air' (Leadbeater, 1999) to give way to the grimmer realities of climate change, the Anthropocene, surveillance culture, carceral capitalism (Wang, 2018) and the Trump era, with what we might call its 'mirror sites' in Egypt, Turkey, Hungary, Poland, the Philippines and the fringes of mainstream politics in Australia, UK, France, Spain, Germany, Estonia, Sweden, Finland and so on.

Creativity like politics turns on contestation, and political contestation has gone creative, matching (as opponents) global movements such as #MeToo with the 'alt-lite' antics of *conflict entrepreneurs* such as Milo Yiannopoulos. It is no longer a matter of conflict leading to resolution via political compromise, but of push and push back as a new (or perhaps newly re-costumed) participant- and spectator-sport, where the performance of difference and opposition becomes an end in itself, like the hard Mod/rude-boy/skinhead subcultures of the 1970s: one that has spawned creative industriousness on a scale that is transforming media organizations, platforms and protocols as well as representative politics. Politics is not conducted – if it ever was – in a neutral 'public sphere', defining the regulatory space of cities or nations, but via celebrities, stories, stunts and spectacle in entertainment formats, technological affordances and digital affinity-groups, spilling across news feeds not to inform but to provoke those who differ.

Journalism was made respectable as a *coordinating* mechanism for modern social difference at city or national scale. Journalists were able, like the detective and the prostitute in fiction, to talk and act across class, gender, regional, sectarian and other borders within a polity – and, unlike them, to report what they found through popular media. Now, where it is not used for exposing data-leaks, journalism is a mechanism for *exacerbating* social difference well past the point of enmity; or, it is *taken to be* such a mechanism by opponents:

> The FAKE NEWS media (failing @nytimes, @NBCNews, @ABC, @CBS, @CNN) is not my enemy, it is the enemy of the American People!
> (Donald J. Trump @*realDonaldTrump*: Twitter, 17 February 2017)[21]

---

[21]Source: https://twitter.com/realDonaldTrump/status/832708293516632065. (This tweet has over 150,000 likes – October 2018.)

Since the 2010s, this slide to foe-creation in public colloquy has become a commonplace of political talk in many countries, and no amount of comment and opinion has seemed to come close to fixing it. But, as far as we know, it has not been analysed in terms of the creative industries or economy (or cognates: the knowledge economy, smart economy, quaternary economy). Nor has sufficient attention been paid to the long history of spectacular urban subcultures, going back at least to those Shakespeare Riots of 1849, which were provoked in part by the 'Bowery Boys' (Adams, 2005), who:

> dressed in outlandish manner, with slicked-down forelocks, gaudily colored suits, expensive walking sticks, high working boots, and tall beaver hats set at a jaunty, defiant angle. Avid drinkers, carousers, and battlers with rival gangs, the Bowery toughs comically asserted their place in the urban landscape, with stage plays devoted to their exploits and their aggressive aping of their betters.
>
> (Zecker, 2008: 25–6)

Like later such groups, these were *insurgent* as well as insolent; '*dangerous*' in the way that Milo Yiannopoulous means when he claims, in an eponymous book, that he is 'loved' for his 'humor, mischief, and sex appeal'. According to reviews, '"Be Dangerous" is the Yiannopoulos war cry, along with "Stay Humble," "Seek Attention," and "Be Hot".'[22]

Meanwhile, 'critical' attention has focused on *conducting* the argument, not on elucidating how that argument has become institutionalized and industrialized, translated into a popular idiom and played out globally. The old strictures apply: 'follow the money'; '*cui bono*' (who benefits?). It is a business, stupid. Here is where pursuing the idea of 'staged conflict' *as* a creative industry may join hands with political critique, to identify new trends in political action at global scale.

---

[22]Source: *Dangerous*, by Milo Yiannopoulos. Dangerous Books, ISBN 978-0-692-89344-9: https://www.publishersweekly.com/9780692893449.

# 19

# Populations of rules: The constitution and coordination of media-made groups

*Be fruitful, multiply, and fill the earth,*
*Subdue it, and throughout dominion hold … But of the Tree,*
*Which tasted works knowledge of good and evil,* Thou may'st not.

(JOHN MILTON, *PARADISE LOST*, VII, 531–2; 542–4)[1]

Milton's *Paradise Lost* (1674), an epic poem of Homeric stature, expresses the early modern European cosmology in which individual 'free will' (appetite), tempered by 'reason' (obedience), offers 'dominion' (freedom to expropriate) over the biosphere, construed as a divine 'gift' (how fortunate for *us*!). Knowledge, on the other hand, yields only death. Having said that, Milton 'was a true Poet and of the Devil's party without knowing it' (as William Blake memorably put it). Milton's cosmology assigned sovereignty, governance and regulation to the biblical God. But the times assigned them to *knowledge* (see Chapter 4), and so did Milton's poetry. The energy, passion and desire of the poem makes reason 'of the Devil's party', in a Faustian agonism where knowledge and death, freedom and obedience, desire and control contend for 'dominion' over the world, natural and social.

Secular modernity is still troubled by an unsatisfactory 'macro' model of regulation; there are vestiges, surrogates and stand-ins for the god-function wherever you turn: the true 'ghost in the machine' of synthesizing macro-level thought. Human 'dominion' over the 'fish of the sea, and fowl of the air, And every living thing that moves on the earth' (*Paradise Lost*, VII, 533–

---

[1]Source: https://www.bartleby.com/4/407.html.

4) is said to be motivated by individual will: it is a micro-scale arrangement. However, in conditions of increasing secularism, during the long history of exploration, empire and the capitalist world system (Wallerstein, 2004), there is still no population-wide agreement on the existence or nature of a macro-level governance regulator. For four hundred years, modernity and individualism have let 'dominion' mean 'infinite exponential growth', of both knowledge and wealth (McCloskey's trilogy), by whatever means – not just at individual but also at corporate and state scale. Without governance at macro-scale, there is no restraining model or mechanism, no compelling agent, to enforce the 'Thou may'st not' rule, to temper self-interest with responsibility for planetary sustainability under accelerating growth and change. Even libertarian theorists have begun to think about the role of the state in their political creed; see especially Tyler Cowen's model of 'State Capacity Libertarianism' (2020) (and see Quiggin, 2001; Dincecco, 2017).

# Macro-regulation for secular modernity

We argue – using Popper's scientific protocol of 'bold conjecture' – that only *the semiosphere* can take up the role of integrated regulator across these incommensurate and contending systems. Why? Because it sets the rules by which rules are set, it distributes knowledge of those rules, their meanings across whole populations, and it binds those populations into knowledge-making/sharing groups of varying scale, from 'knowledge clubs' and commons to nations and species. It is not just the product or producer of global systems but their *coordinating mechanism*.

We move on to the current era of global capitalism and trade, culture and conflict, and to their human-induced consequences for the Earth environment. In particular, we focus on the regulatory aspect of the digital semiosphere. What is 'action' in this context? It is *transformation*, not individual *doings* but collective agency that results in *changing systems*. This kind of action is not subject to individual will, even though it emerges from Schumpeterian creative and enterprising actions among myriad individuals. Each individual may be seeking to exploit uncertainty, but none is in control of the general, distributed, systematic consequences of their actions. How does that tangle of contending and collective wills and works result in coherent systems at larger scale?

For Dopfer et al. (2004), in an evolutionary approach to macroeconomics, the 'central insight is that an economic system is a population of rules'. A network effect, therefore, is where rules are changed by population-scale *social action* (Hayek, 2012); a 'user' effect rather than one resulting from those who control the 'producer' end of the value chain.

To understand such processes we need to investigate the overall output of human actions rather than the input of divine purposes. In other words, the explanation of world systems does not come from the *content* of a particular rule ('Thou may'st not'). Systematic change is effected when a 'population of rules' is disrupted. That is where creativity and innovation (culture as well as technology) come together: they are bold, rule-breaking actions at system scale. To understand how systems work, therefore, we need to make room for peripheries in Lotman's terms, and for *rule-breakers* operating in them, and to look for them among a population of users, disrupting incumbent hierarchies.

The peripheries of the semiosphere, its spaces conditioned for dialogue with the Other and for searching new solutions for apparent changes in the semiotics milieu – including the arts – are the spaces for bold, rule-breaking experimentation (a.k.a. youthful 'exploit'). The benefits (or dangers) of their probable outcomes need to be *imagined*. 'Movers and shakers' trouble the system in which their 'irritations' (Hutter, 2015) might provoke more general changes and transformations; they are themselves a risk element for existing users and makers. Rule-breakers are nevertheless highly valued in various overlapping but distinct semiospheres: the Trickster in myth (Hyde, 1998), modernist artists (Hutter, 2015), Schumpeterian entrepreneurs (Swedberg, 2006) and sci-fi and fantasy fiction (Merrick, 2009).

# Users: a new class?

In the digital semiosphere, such innovator-disruptors have been hailed as a new *class* – in the Marxist sense – by McKenzie Wark (2004): the hacker class. Wark contrasts the many groups (writers, artists, biotechnologists, software programmers) who use the rules to break the rules (those who *produce* IP) with the classes that seek to impose or retain control (those who *own* IP), enforcing self-made rules (copyright; rent). Wark's model thereby recasts the classic Marxist antagonism between the 'labouring' or 'productive' classes and the 'rent-seeking' or 'capitalist' classes. She models a structural antagonism between *open* systems of the 'hacker class', where the transformations are at the scale of ideas and meanings, and *closed* systems, controlled by ownership, contract and market dominance (organized scale), where the 'transformation' is at market scale (my company outcompetes yours). This is a classical Lotmanian opposition of the dialogic periphery and the autocommunicating and therefore inflexible core. It can be suggested, therefore, that the *digital* semiosphere is largely a matter of the antagonism between these two 'classes'.

The so-called labouring classes got organized on a grand scale in the nineteenth century, not only through industrial trades unions and political Labour Parties (and other mass parties) but also through community-based organizations – the Co-operative movement, smallholdings, Workers'

Education Associations and welfare groups (including sanatoria and rest homes for workers). Compared with these national-scale institutions, the institutions supporting the hacker class seem much less solid: think of WikiLeaks. But this is not necessarily a failure to 'organize' at sufficient scale or with sufficient energy and will. It may have more to do with the *media through which organization is achieved*. In a Facebook post, Wark has observed:

> The history of the labour movement is a history of forms of organisation which can be understood in terms of the affordances of media.
>
> (FB 9 March 2018)

In this instance, Wark is discussing a teachers' strike in West Virginia (USA), particularly its coverage in *The New York Times* as a 'Crowd-Sourced Strike' (*NYT* March 8 2018). Her point is that the *actions* and also internal *structures* of labour organizations are shaped by the contemporary 'affordances' of *media*. The labour movement of the early industrial age was shaped by the press ('mass' media), that of the broadcasting era by radio and television (identity and popular representative democratic politics) and now by digital media (open source systems, 'crowd-sourced' action and hacker platforms), making what once would have been called 'mass action' into what might now be called a 'flash mob' or a 'viral' video event. These tactics have been adopted by both the alt-right (Griffin, 2003)[2] and the Antifa left, from the Arab Spring to global 'networked protest' (Tufekci, 2017). Activists and academic researchers alike (e.g. Fenton, 2016; Gregg, 2018) have taken up the challenge of the very different modes of politics needed in the digital era (and among the 'millennial' generation) to reconfigure the labour movement itself as one that *begins* from the centrality of digital networks to contemporary global capitalism: not from mass workforces and emphysema.

This is a specific instance of something that we want to model at a more general level: that the mode, means and 'affordances' of media shape not only individual behaviour (what a person says) or action (what they do) but also organizational (system-level and institutional) arrangements, purposes and actions; not only meanings (how a text can signify) but also how social institutions and organizations emerge and self-organize around the capabilities available or makeable at the time to call the desired group into being.

In short, how organized associations *mediate* is how they are *constituted*. A class is organized around its means of mediation (as well as production).

---

[2]One of the most astute observers of which has been *Guardian* journalist Jason Wilson: https://www.theguardian.com/profile/wilson-jason.

This means that in the digital era classes are not organized in the same way as industrial classes were. As collective agents, classes are responsible for transmitting new forms of consciousness, politics and thence action throughout larger populations in a process that revolutionaries used to call 'agit-prop'. That means in turn that groups previously regarded as non-political actors may turn out to be more militant than expected and may even go unrecognized by activists trained in 'legacy' forms of class-mediation. Thus it may be that what are now called 'influencers' are a source of class-consciousness for internet users, especially among intersectional groups who have been systematically absented from class-based organizations in the past. It may have come as a surprise to veteran activists to find the global movement for climate justice led by school-age girls (Neubauer and Repenning, 2019; Thunberg, 2019; Jeffrey, 2020).[3] But that's how future-facing *demes* are formed and how they share knowledge-action suited to new times and technologies, although some commentators remain sceptical.[4]

The semiosphere, what its texts are like, sets the rules. Here it is important to re-stress that the semiosphere's rules – unlike abstract laws – are strongly context-dependent and feature exceptions, which means that change is already written into the system. Rules that become rigid and in relation to the surrounding context become outdated. Setting rules inevitably generates new conflicts and, in the digitally connected era, the easiness and speed of conflict-escalation underlines once more the need to understand the semiotic mechanisms governing conflicts. This could help us learn ways to cope when a local conflict 'goes nuclear' with potentially lethal consequences.

However, here, as elsewhere, antagonism is not simply a personal emotion or individualist behaviour but a *class relation*, in the classical Marxist sense of two or more fundamentally opposing classes, which itself is already a 'Lotmanian' conceptualization of how systems work. Times have changed since Marx, and so has the process of creating classes (a class 'in itself') and of a class self-identifying, autocommunicating (class consciousness or a class 'for itself' in Marxist terminology), developing relations with other classes including relations of conflict (class struggle) and thence acting upon the world. Now, it is not sufficient to identify a tripartite producer-object-user model based on commodity production and to allocate 'class formation' only to the 'producer' side, that is, in the labour process. For as Wark has demonstrated, class formation and class consciousness infuse, as it were, the user side.

---

[3]And see: https://www.vox.com/identities/2019/10/11/20904791/young-climate-activists-of-color; https://www.youtube.com/watch?v=Ie9cACQnqew (Luisa Neubauer's TED talk, 'Why you should be a climate activist', Munich, 2019).

[4]See for instance Penny Andrews in the UK *Independent* (22 June 2020): https://www.independent.co.uk/voices/trump-rally-kpop-tiktok-aoc-turnout-coronavirus-tulsa-ok-a9579976.html; and Rebecca Jennings in *Vox* (30 June 2020): https://www.vox.com/the-goods/2020/6/30/21307564/tiktok-trump-rally-tulsa-teens-k-pop.

It suffuses too the very object of information capitalism, as for example Sebastian Sevignani (2017) has argued. Sevignani cleverly adds 'classification' to class theory, arguing that:

> classification processes are element of surveillance in the context of the growing relevance of (online) markets in information and the blurring line between production and consumption in current informational capitalist societies.
>
> (Sevignani, 2017: 77)

Analysing social media and the internet, Sevignani argues that 'a (revised) notion of exploitation and antagonistic social relations should not be omitted from theorizing the information economy. Exploitation establishes an antagonism between all Internet users and the owners of the means of communication, surveillance, and classification' (Sevignani, 2017: 77). A 'self-regulating' system still generates class antagonism, not just between labour and capital but also between users and capital, and furthermore there is a class struggle involved in the very process of classifying the content and uses of the 'information' (semiosis) that we would identify as 'text'. Class struggle is *distributed* across producer, object and user, resulting in some counterintuitive notions of class.

Wark's equation of 'the affordances of media' and the 'forms of organization' of 'the labour movement' is insightful and accurate, but it needs to be extended, because 'labour' now includes the practices of what used to be dismissed as passive consumers, i.e. users of social media and the internet. The emergence of girls as just such a class has been a marked trend of the social-media era (Hartley, 2020: 239–69), first in the process of 'class formation' or *attention* as users and consumers; then in the rise of *action*, via both internet 'influencers' (Abidin, 2018) and internet activists, that is, market personifications and political personifications, respectively. Those who put their heads up immediately attract class antagonism for their trouble (e.g. Gamergate) or, as *Buzzfeed News* put it, 'A new movement of teenage climate activists – most of whom are girls – are getting dragged, doxed, hacked, and harassed online.'[5] Similarly, Eve Andrews has written in *Grist*:

> A high school girl has a uniquely precarious place in American society. She doesn't have a voice in the political system, but she's depended upon heavily as a consumer ... She knows how to use social media to be heard, but she can also be tortured by it. And maybe most overwhelmingly of all, she knows that the world she's going to grow up in is going to be

---

[5]Zahra Hirji (25 September 2019), 'Teenage Girls Are Leading the Climate Movement – and Getting Attacked for It': https://www.buzzfeednews.com/article/zahrahirji/greta-thunberg-climate-teen-activist-harassment.

much more chaotic than the one her parents expected, and she had no role in making it that way.[6]

She comments: 'They have demanded to be seen, heard, and heeded, and they've at least gotten their way with the first two ... But it's that third item on their wish list, that pesky "heeded" part, that remains elusive.' The translation of class formation and leadership into action is clearly occurring, although the outcomes remain uncertain. Daisy Jeffrey, an Australian school-student leader of the Global Climate Strike of September 2019, was bowled over by the scale:

There was a lot of panic. Then the realisation that we'd hit 80,000 people in Sydney, then a lot of joy, then the realisation we'd hit 330,000 nationwide, then six million worldwide. We'd just done the impossible. What would we do next? (Jeffrey, 2020)[7]

Good question. As *Vox* reported when Greta Thunberg was named *Time* magazine's youngest-ever 'person of the year' (2019).

Today, Thunberg and other young female activists finally have the world's attention. But as Thunberg herself has pointed out, hearing these voices is only part of the battle – whether people in power actually do something in response to their words remains to be seen.[8]

# Regulatory mechanisms

*Action* is always *performative*, in two senses: first, action *performs to* an audience, which the performance calls into being (say, a march, or demonstration; or the readership of a journal); and second, in the sense advanced by Carsten Herrmann-Pillath (2018a), where he identifies as *performative* those contemporary social sciences that *constitute their object of study in the process of studying it*. In other words, knowledge is not just abstract rules but also a mode of action in the world.

---

[6]Source: E. Andrews (1 January 2020), 'Teen Girls Took Over the Climate Movement. What Happens Next?' *Grist*: https://grist.org/climate/teen-girls-took-over-the-climate-movement-what-happens-next/.
[7]Jeffreys's book was excerpted in Australian *Vogue*, April 2020, 170–1, under the headline 'Action Hero'.
[8]Anna North (11 December 2019), 'Young Female Activists Like Greta Thunberg Have the World's Attention. Will People in Power Take Action?': https://www.vox.com/2019/12/11/21010936/greta-thunberg-time-magazine-cover-person-year.

Both cultural studies and economics are in this category. They do not study already-constituted matter-energy from the outside, but model what culture and the economy are, in the act of describing them. Knowledge is an act that uses the resources it seeks to explain and – in the case of economics – it may alter the reality that the model seeks to describe. The act of bringing an object into knowledge is also the act of creating and changing that object. This reflexive, self-creating and autocommunicative aspect of knowledge in performative disciplines is a long way from Newtonian physics (although perhaps not so far from quantum physics); it uses the system-level relations of causation, action and change that are at work in the biosphere and biosciences: it belongs to the semiosphere, not to inert matter.

Now we can return with new insight to Carsten Herrmann-Pillath's challenging remark about the *regulation* of the spheres under consideration. He proposes (2018a: 10, quoted above) that the technosphere – not the

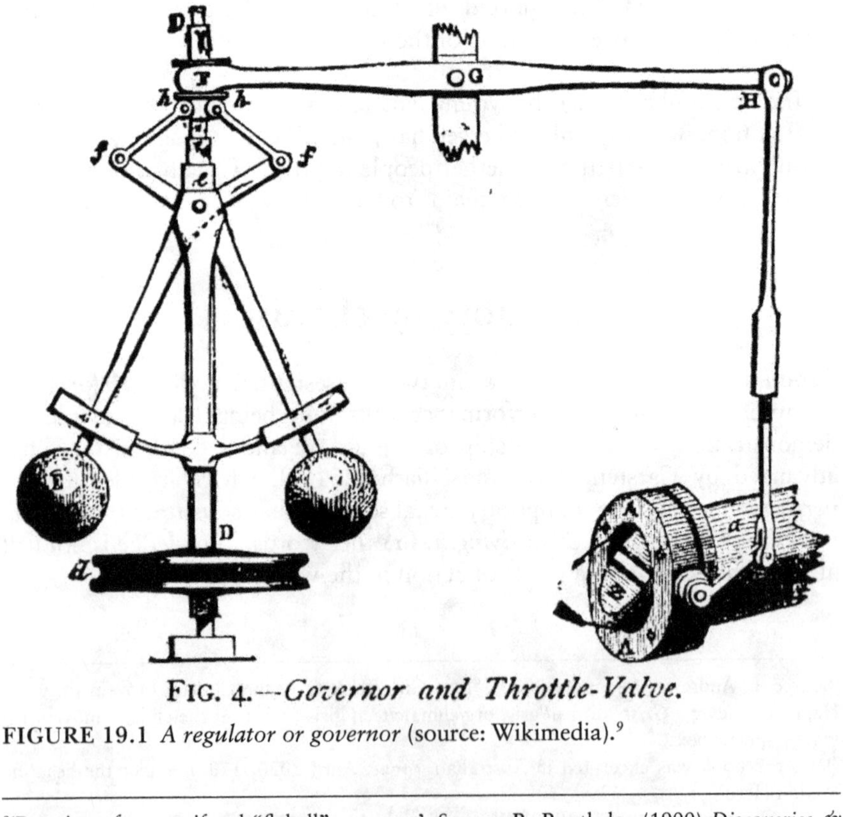

FIG. 4.—*Governor and Throttle-Valve.*

FIGURE 19.1 *A regulator or governor* (source: Wikimedia).[9]

[9]"Drawing of a centrifugal "flyball" governor'. Source: R. Routledge (1900) *Discoveries & Inventions of the Nineteenth Century*, 13th edn. Public domain: https://en.wikipedia.org/wiki/Centrifugal_governor#/media/File:Centrifugal_governor.png.

biosphere – is the 'overarching regulatory system of the Earth System in the Anthropocene'. Here, Herrmann-Pillath is making the same move that the Lotmans (*père et fils*) made: reversing inter-sphere relationships, such that for him the technosphere exercises 'overarching regulatory' status, while for the Lotmans, it is the semiosphere that does that. It may not be necessary to resolve or erase this difference, in fact, as both the semiosphere and the technosphere are co-dependent and co-evolutionary; increasingly they condition each other: it may be more correct to say that between them, they make a 'regulating mechanism' (Figure 19.1), where systemic communication requires accelerating energy and artefactual coordination.

'Regulation' is itself transitioning from engineering, where it describes the control of mechanical speed, to the cultural world of politics and semiosis, where it applies to explicit rules for conduct among and between groups, and on to the digital world of global economics and culture, where it functions both to stabilize dynamic systems and to broker inter-system interactions (technical interoperability or political antagonism), which may take cultural form (from dance to diplomacy) or technological form ('maintaining a range of values in a machine').[10]

# Aristotle versus blockchain

To make a startling and thereby more informative contrast, we return to compare the founding text of politics in the Western tradition with digitally distributed regulation in the global era: that is, to compare Aristotle's *Politics* with techno-marketing's blockchain, since we have cast 'staged conflict' (politics) along with blockchain (markets) as emblematic 'creative industries' of the digital era (Chapter 17).

Both, in fact, are in search of ways to *represent* populations (of citizens; contracts/transactions) at the highest level (of integration, aggregation, abstraction), using latest technologies (then, philosophy; now, computation); both want to achieve truth-in-decisions; both want to maximize *individual* autonomy within *group* systems (cities, cultures; markets); and so they can both be analysed as models, seeking rules for right action (protocols).

It is a commonplace observation that politics – the study of it – commenced with Aristotle, who wrote his *Politics* (7 volumes) in about 350 BCE. He maintained that a state (by which he meant the Ancient Greek city-state, comprising free adult men, no women, no children, no slaves, no

---

[10]https://en.wikipedia.org/wiki/Regulator_(automatic_control): a regulator is a device that 'performs the activity of managing or maintaining a range of values in a machine'. Note that 'regulators' are also called 'controllers' and 'governors'. It is worth bearing their engineering provenance in mind when observing human cultures.

foreigners) is a 'sort of partnership' that subsumes all other levels of human partnership, thereby aiming 'at the most supreme of all goods', the state or 'political association'.

> Every state is as we see a sort of partnership, and every partnership is formed with a view to some good ... It is therefore evident that, while all partnerships aim at some good the partnership that is the most supreme of all and includes all the others does so most of all, and aims at the most supreme of all goods; and this is the partnership entitled the state, the political association. (Bk 1)[11]

His prescription for the ideal size of a 'polity' was that of a population whose members could see, hear and recognize one another (self-surveillance) and that the size of a city-state should be limited by *communication*:

> It is clear therefore that the best limiting principle for a state is the largest expansion of the population, with a view to self-sufficiency that can well be taken in at one view ... The same thing holds good of the territory that we said about the size of the population – it must be well able to be taken in at one view, and that means being a country easy for military defence ... The city must be in communication with all parts of the territory for the purpose of sending out military assistance. (Aristotle, *Politics*, Bk 7)[12]

Although political science has moved on quite a bit since Aristotle (see Cowen, 2020), it is valuable to remind ourselves that this founding text of political philosophy was dedicated to the right understanding, conduct and education of *self-in-group*, not to specifying control mechanisms for 'superintendence' by government:

> And inasmuch as the end for the whole state is one, it is manifest that education also must necessarily be one and the same for all and that the superintendence of this must be public, and not on private lines ... Matters of public interest ought to be under public supervision; at the same time we ought not to think that any of the citizens belongs to himself, but that all belong to the state, for each is a part of the state, and it is natural for the superintendence of the several parts to have regard to the superintendence of the whole. (Bk 8)[13]

---

[11]See: http://www.perseus.tufts.edu/hopper/text?doc=Perseus:abo:tlg,0086,035:1:1252a.
[12]See: http://www.perseus.tufts.edu/hopper/text?doc=Perseus%3Atext%3A1999.01.0058%3Abook%3D7%3Asection%3D1326b.
[13]See: http://www.perseus.tufts.edu/hopper/text?doc=Perseus%3Atext%3A1999.01.0058%3Abook%3D8%3Asection%3D1337a.

Aristotle's politics is the very opposite of individualist. It is founded on the idea of partnership for mutual good within a group that is bound by mutuality and communication. Interestingly, so is the blockchain. But before we get to that, we need to consider further how groups act: in the context of group-made association, what is action?

## Regulation of conflict and trust

The questions that remain open are whether 'staged conflict' or blockchain are candidates for user-led transformations of networked systems and whether they offer the right kind of regulatory apparatus for the digital semiosphere, maximizing group formation (knowledge clubs), cross-border semiosis (knowledge commons) and flexible adoption of 'newness' at macro-scale, while minimizing ungoverned individualism, aggression, duplicity, intercommunal violence and waste at micro-scale. The 'meso-scale' *institutions* required to broker these extremes are not 'institutions' in the marble-clad sense but in the sense that has been developed in evolutionary/ institutional economics (and see Chapter 3). Here, 'institutions' are 'populations of rules'. An early statement of this idea is from Jason Potts (2003), taking up a theoretical thread from Veblen (1898), Hayek (1945), North (1990), Ostrom (1990), Loasby (1999). For evolutionary economists in general (see Nelson and Winter 1982; Freeman and Louçã 2001; Dopfer, Foster and Potts, 2004; Hodgson, 2006; Lundvall 2010), knowledge rather than 'scarce resources' is the substance of the economy and subject of economics:

> And knowledge is what the economic system is made of. In an evolutionary economic process, it is knowledge that evolves. Capital is knowledge in an operational form. Labour is knowledge in an active form. Money, as a store of value, is unspecified knowledge potential. Knowledge is subject to selection, variation, and replication. These evolutionary mechanisms operate over systems and populations of rules (that is, institutions) to produce the growth of knowledge process known as economic evolution. It is the growth of knowledge that ultimately underpins the wealth of nations ... Wealth is ultimately a product of specialised and integrated knowledge, which is to say as an ongoing product of all people, and not just elites.
>
> (Potts, 2003: 5–6, 13)

'Populations of rules' are inherently unstable over evolutionary time; they change, and they are changed, both gradually (via culture, as its incremental innovations) and suddenly or irreversibly (via explosion) (Lotman, 2009). Further, they characterize groups ('populations') not individuals, and hence the rules themselves, the differences between one subpopulation of rules and another and the changes wrought in any one rule set over time are all group-scale (meso) or institutional phenomena. The same applies to knowledge, as the product of systems and populations of rules. However, the *interactions among* these systems, institutions and groups belong to the *semiosphere* at macro-scale (which is a global population of these interactions – that is, of communications that exist in the form of texts governed by rules of their composition). It is here that *regulation* becomes a pivotal issue, for the macro-system will determine the limits of scale, textual forms as well as forms of use of both knowledge itself and of its institutional producers. 'Staged conflict' is a mediatized mechanism for regulating conflict across institutional boundaries, and, for instance, blockchain is a technological protocol for brokering (regulating) trust across the same boundaries. At this scale, it is possible to identify *classes* of rules. Georg Blind (2017) summarizes:

> The rule-based approach proposes a taxonomy of four classes of rules: cognitive, behavioural, social and technical. As a mutually exclusive and collectively exhaustive concept, this taxonomy allows for fully capturing the diversity of economic phenomena and helps to resolve definitional issues.
>
> (Blind, 2017: 148)

The different terminology used by different writers can be integrated: *cognitive rules* encompass 'mental habits', 'decision rules' and the distinction between strategies and rules. 'Organizational routines', 'control mechanisms' and 'information rules' are all *social rules*. 'Internalized norms' correspond to *behavioural rules* (Blind, 2017: 148). *Technical rules* cover for instance the difference between platforms and protocols. You will note that no cultural or semiotic rules are mentioned, partly for reasons of disciplinary blindness, but also because semiosis operates at both a much smaller and much larger scale than that of institutions: it integrates that meso-level with micro-scale signification rules and macro-scale semiosphere rules. Recognizing cognitive, behavioural, social and technical *classes* of rules is to recognize that these are all *cultural* phenomena.

# Truth machines?

While 'staged conflict' seems at first sight an unlikely regulatory mechanism, its *causal impetus* as a rule-breaker is having a transformative effect on existing political and cultural systems, making it an example of the 'explosion' component of semiosphere evolution (Lotman, 2009), whereas blockchain is of the 'gradual' type. It is not that 'staged conflict' *verifies* what is true but *changes* it.

In relation to blockchain, Michael Casey and Paul Vigna, in *The Truth Machine* (2018), argue for the application of the blockchain to journalism, to fix the trust-deficit the traditional news media have suffered (Casey is a senior columnist and Vigna a financial blogger for the *Wall Street Journal*). They define 'truth' as 'consensus': the more who agree, the truer the statement or document.

This is a Latourian position.[14] In an interview with *The New York Times* in 2018, this story is used to sum up Bruno Latour's discovery:

> At a meeting between French industrialists and a climatologist a few years ago, Latour was struck when he heard the scientist defend his results not on the basis of the unimpeachable authority of science but by laying out to his audience his manufacturing secrets: 'the large number of researchers involved in climate analysis, the complex system for verifying data, the articles and reports, the principle of peer evaluation, the vast network of weather stations, floating weather buoys, satellites and computers that ensure the flow of information.' The climate denialists, by contrast, the scientist said, had none of this institutional architecture. Latour realized he was witnessing the beginnings a seismic rhetorical shift: from scientists appealing to transcendent, capital-T Truth to touting the robust networks through which truth is, and has always been, established. (*NYT*, 25 October 2018)[15]

Truth changes from an absolute value, arbitrated by priesthood or expert, or even an 'objective' property of external things, to a self-organizing effect of 'robust networks', where the more users there are, the more certitude there should be: a logic also used by Lotman (2009) to conceptualize the in-principle requirement for a multiplicity of languages to model the extra-semiotic world. That which users accept as true becomes a guarantor of decentralized trust in user-centric networks, as long as transactions can be verified. If this works, then truth is something that can be 'agreed' via tamperproof blockchain protocols. Such a model can be applied to any truth discourse based on evidence and documents, including journalism and a self-correcting system like science, where there is a premium on improving accuracy iteratively among an attentive throng.

---

[14]See: https://www.nytimes.com/2018/10/25/magazine/bruno-latour-post-truth-philosopher-science.html.

[15]'Bruno Latour, the post-truth philosopher, mounts a defence of science: He spent decades deconstructing the ways that scientists claim their authority. Can his ideas help them regain that authority today?' https://www.nytimes.com/2018/10/25/magazine/bruno-latour-post-truth-philosopher-science.html.

If so, then truth, as consensually agreed *accuracy*, becomes a value that can be tokenized and rewarded, thereby providing an 'incentive' for more truth, as it were. Tokens can be monetized, and so to market. Such a postmodern, decentralized system could bypass the incumbent media giants, who all operate on a centralized, intermediation (external governance) model of trust, where a statement is judged by the masthead (*Economist* = high-trust; Fox News = low trust). Casey argues that what is needed instead of proprietary platforms, such as CNN or Murdoch, is a *neutral platform* – something more like the World Wide Web. On a neutral platform, transaction or exchange is between content-creator and user-attention directly, not the intermediated nexus between publisher/advertiser and consumer. The logic is that there is no such thing as 'publishing' once the platform works; creators and users interact directly but through a decentralized system, where the ledger, not the masthead, is the guarantor of accuracy. We leave the 'mediasphere' (Hartley, 1996) and enter the 'ledgersphere' – it's 'ledgers, all the way down' (Berg et al., 2017).

Meanwhile, other experiments are at proof-of-concept stage (Potts and Rennie, 2019), including blockchain for science,[16] blockchain for storytelling (Cellarius),[17] blockchain for music industry payments and licensing (O'Dair, 2019) and so on. In other words, the DIY-user-hacker class, already fully immersed in the creative and digital economies, is turning to blockchain as a *rule-changing apparatus* that they can make for themselves, with the added benefit of building not only tamperproof transaction ledgers but also a common pool resource or innovation commons (Potts, 2019). As musician Imogen Heap put it, in relation to her Ethereum-based venture to publish her own music, Mycelia (using the Ujo open source platform):

> It needs to be truly open and perhaps a combination of both decentralised and centralised, built on the work of lots of people coming together to make this accessible to everyone. There are many different people working towards realising parts of this – building databases, payment and storage systems … I'm … interested … in seeing the ethical, commercial and technical standards come to life for a fair trading and bustling creative music industry ecosystem to grow around … This will only happen if everyone … musicians, technologists, lawyers, policy people, services – big and small – can work together, pooling resources toward a common goal.[18]

---

[16]See: 'Blockchain solutions for scientific publishing' by Evgeniia Filippova: https://medium.com/crypto3conomics/blockchain-solutions-for-scientific-publishing-ef4b4e79ae2; and the International Society of Blockchain for Science: https://www.blockchainforscience.com/ibfs-international-society-blockchain-science/.

[17]See: https://cellarius.network/.

[18]See: http://myceliaformusic.org/2016/03/21/what-blockchain-can-do-for-the-music-industry/; and see: https://blog.ujomusic.com/the-ujo-platform-a-decentralized-music-ecosystem-e530c31b62bc.

The hope among blockchain advocates is that the distributed ledger can take the place of any centralized or authority-brokering institution, from news media to governments. This is a digital utopia, relying on hacker-made hacker-proof systems logic to imagine new ways in which citizens and organized groups can conduct their affairs and test their truths. Inevitably, there are impediments to the practical realization of this revolutionary reality, although – as ever – blockchain enthusiasts are confident of eventual success.

# Who will regulate the regulator: Blockchain (tech) or semiosphere (culture)?

This brings us to an unsettling conclusion about the contrast between blockchain, on the one hand, and staged conflict, on the other. We have floated the idea that these are both creative industries, and so they are, but there is a further implication of the analysis that can't go unremarked, which is that they are *both* marked by populism. Indeed, Asress Adimi Gikay and Catalin Gabriel Stanescu (2019) have coined the term 'technological populism' to identify the nub of the problem. They open with a powerful conjecture:

> Technological populism as reflected by blockchain platforms exploits the rhetoric of empowering the disenfranchised through decentralized decision-making process, enabling anonymity of transactions, dehumanizing trust (promoting trust in computation rather than trust in humans and institutions) as well as breaking the monopoly in the financial system and money supply. The rhetoric of empowering the disenfranchised against financial elites is not only propaganda but also a method of accumulating wealth for technocratic elites.
>
> (Gikay and Stanescu, 2019: 66)

In other words, it is not the technological specification of blockchain or distributed Digital Ledger Technology (DLT) that needs critique, but the hype surrounding it, which is manifest in tech-journalism and policy forums, industry conferences and government documents, academic papers and research-funding institutions. Gikay and Stanescu conclude by calling for 'technological populism consciousness', starting with 'acknowledging the existence of the problem. Such first step should enable regulators and policymakers to quit their self-induced denial and regulatory stupor and act, not just react' (2019: 109).

> Technological populism as reflected by blockchain platforms exploits the rhetoric of empowering the disenfranchised through decentralized decision-making process, enabling anonymity of transactions,

dehumanizing trust (promoting trust in computation rather than trust in humans and institutions) as well as breaking the monopoly in the financial system and money supply. The rhetoric of empowering the disenfranchised against financial elites is not only propaganda but also a method of accumulating wealth for technocratic elites.

(Gikay and Stanescu, 2019: 103)

The populist argument in both cases – 'staged conflict' in the political sphere and blockchain (standing for libertarian techno-fix solutionism more generally) in the economic/technosphere – is directed against *regulation*. They want to 'disrupt' the establishment and its minders (the 'elites'), they want to 'empower' the disenfranchised (who, however, are not present or welcome in their forums), they want 'decentralization' as rhetoric (delivering it in fact proves not to be real, feasible or desirable) and they want to replace trust in people (micro) and institutions (meso) with trust in computation (macro) (as long as they control the algorithms). Gikay and Stanescu direct their critique at a wide range of agents – 'entrepreneurs, industry experts, advocates, intellectuals, and the media' – and among the promises made, they note claims that 'blockchain could revolutionize finance, could help in fighting against poverty, could be used to safeguard the environment and combat climate change' (2019: 67).

But they can't (as we have noted in Chapter 13, via Audrey Watters), because that's not in fact what they are purposed to do. Instead, and in reality, the spate of 'blockchain manifestos' are directed towards *regulating the semiosphere*, thereby producing polarized communities upon whose behalf the communicators can legislate and execute their own agenda:

Our research revealed that blockchain manifestos are neither technological, nor programmatic documents, but mere communication strategies resembling populist speeches, meant to attract supporters and create polarization.

(Gikay and Stanescu, 2019: 108)

We should point out that the use of the word 'mere'– as in 'mere communication strategies' –is ill-advised here, since our own argument is that 'communication strategies' rule the roost in the world of semiosis. Control of the political sphere and of the technosphere by populists does not seem likely to produce what they promise, namely 'to safeguard the environment and combat climate change'. For that, it seems we will need quite different kinds of activism, agency and regulatory systems for the digital semiosphere.

# 20

# Where to now, planet?

*We need these people, especially now, when we need to change things and we can't see it just from where we are.* We need to see it from a bigger perspective and from outside our current systems ... That's why people who are different are so necessary: *because they contribute so much. Therefore we need to really look after the people who are different and who may not be heard.* We need to listen to those and to look after each other.

(GRETA THUNBERG)[1]

\* \* \*

## Uncertain future-sphere

We leave the digital semiosphere poised between the techno-fix 'solutionism' (Morozov, 2014) of blockchain and the explosive, social-insurgency model of the hacker class, both seeking new models for trust and organization in the digital semiosphere. That is, lurking in the political undergrowth are those who seek to govern the internet, from ultra-right groupuscules to blockchain libertarians. Yet, systemic autopoiesis, autocommunication and the sustainability of poised systems all require that regulation is self-organized, by the system itself, and this can only be the semiosphere. Instead of continuing with the rules set by the long human history of mutual fear

---

[1]Lucy Diavolo (16 September 2019) 'Greta Thunberg Wants You – Yes, You – to Join the Climate Strike'. *Teen Vogue*: https://www.teenvogue.com/story/greta-thunberg-climate-strike-teen-vogue-special-issue-cover.

and competitiveness among scattered groups, 'the semiosphere' needs to adapt to planetary scale and one-species problem-solving as one 'we'-group, preferably without making an adversary out of the environment, and certainly in dialogue with other species. The biosphere clearly did not agree to the bargain where a human fiction (a.k.a. god) granted 'dominion' over it to two fictional ancestors. Instead, the semiosphere and its digital overlay need to interact in a regenerative way with the environment, taking seriously the integrated commonalty of semiosis and life, and the life-support systems of energy transfer and change between the biosphere and the geosphere, because the species has yet to face the truly planetary challenges of *regulating* the unfolding Anthropocene era. Among these challenges is the obvious problem of disarray within the semiosphere about who takes responsibility for collective actions. Despite previous attempts at supranational 'government' (the League of Nations, UN, Warsaw Pact, NATO, EU, APEC and Shanghai Cooperation Organisation), humanity has not yet managed to consolidate itself beyond a premodern 'two camps' model of mutually hostile competitors: East and West, North and South, capitalist and communist, rich and poor, owners and workers. At the same time, no one has come up with a viable way to interact with nature that does not involve colonizing and exploiting it.

In practice, the immediate geopolitical challenge to globalization comes from 'the other direction', coordinated not by American tech firms but by China and its rapidly proliferating lines of interconnection with like-minded countries – Russia, India and the countries in Africa and Asia, along its rapidly expanding 'belt and road' – which is re-bordering the 'tectonic plates' of the global geostrategic semiosphere, and where the writ of the Euro-American corporate-regulatory system does not run. On the environmental front, the challenge of climate change, pollution, waste and the human species' slash-and-burn attitude to resources, which are already, it seems, beyond the control of human systems, semiotic or technological, shows that the geosphere cannot be taken for granted: it too is a player in the changes wrought upon it.

This separation of tectonic plates is complicated by a multiplicity of cultural flows and these are facilitated by local/national institutional networks – 'innovation systems' that work autocommunicatively, as we discussed in 'Globe' (Chapter 15). The opposition of China (and its allies) versus America (and its allies) can be observed in action in apparently commercial (rather than directly political) globalized trade, for example the long-running political tussle about Huawei's involvement in the installation of 5G networks in numerous countries. At stake is who will control the IoT-AR-5G- Semantic Web mirrorworld that we discussed in Chapter 16 – the physical-digital technosphere covering, automating and augmenting every inch of the material world.

It is globalization among these incommensurate and conflicting systems (not the kind based on the internationalization of existing trade hierarchies) that will require the fullest understanding of how the biosphere, semiosphere and technosphere interact, for which purpose, the application of Lotmanian cultural science to the digital semiosphere of the Anthropocene is offered as a future-facing conceptual model.

# Action versus studies?

In recent years, it has become clear that the utopian promise of the internet is tempered by dystopian disruption, coming from both the 'post-fascist' right and a 'new communism' of the left (el-Ojeili, 2020) as well as non-Western interruptions to the smooth narrative of modern progress, whether from 'Russian hackers', 'Chinese crackdown' or territorially unglued religious extremist groups. Does – or *how does* – freedom to communicate have to live with online extremism or fake news? Does libertarian decentralization lead inevitably to corporate monopoly? Does individualist emancipation entail planetary environmental destruction? Or can these polar extremes be avoided, and if so, how do we find the sweet spot between them to achieve optimum dynamism and sustainability: Kauffman's (1991) 'poised system'? To change the system from the 'staged conflict' of adversarial-exploitative history to regenerative futures, first there must be a reconfiguration of what is meant by 'we'. That work is well under way on social media.

New players in semiosis-organizing enterprises are finding new ways to bring activism, mediation and policy practice together. Indeed, many observers propose that activists are – or should be – the new leaders of new 'we' movements in the semiosphere. To take one example from our own specialist field, a recent 'companion' to global television featured more than forty chapters (including by one of the present authors), but only one chapter even mentions the environment (Shimpach, 2020: 9–11 and Chapter 7). That chapter is by long-term ecocritic of media Toby Miller (Maxwell and Miller, 2012), who suggests that 'advocacy is crucial in one sphere where television really does have a dire influence on the world ... The truly negative effect of television is not to do with violence or education ... For the real damage done by TV is material'.

> Cathode Ray Tubes are made of zinc, copper, cesium, cadmium, silver, and lead. Major environmental problems occur both when they are made and when they are thrown away. Componentry seeps into underground water, leaving a legacy of heavy metals and toxic chemicals.
>
> (Miller, 2020: 91)

For Miller, the salient issue is that 'Workers, activists, and scientists are aware of the issues. TV studies is not. Again, activists lead the way for us to follow' (91). He concludes: 'In short, TV should be understood in terms of its labour process, environmental impact, and textual pleasure' (93). But he makes clear that by 'labour process' and 'textual pleasure' he *also* means advocacy: in terms of labour process, 'the forceful feminist desire to participate in, govern, and consume genres is transformative' (90), and in relation to textual pleasure, despite reference to his 'toddling daughter's demands', he finds that 'the key lesson … is the need to construct new gender and racial relations' (92).

This intellectually driven agenda to promote an advocacy-led field of study and action is very much in tune with the times and with our own survey of the digital semiosphere. Miller's impatience with the 'rhetoric of celebration grounded in populist fandom', however, leads him to overstate the claim that TV's 'truly negative effect is not to do with violence or education' (i.e. what's *on* television screens) but only on the 'legacy of heavy metals and toxic chemicals' (what's *in* television sets). This is to exclude semiosis itself from analysis altogether and to retreat to an old-fashioned sociological positivism that won't study textuality because it's immaterial, and therefore cannot concede that media studies has played or can play any role in 'forceful feminism' as well as 'populist fandom'.

We would argue for integration and synthesis of approaches, not for evaluative inclusion or exclusion. Media studies must certainly take account of the 'labour process, environmental impact, and textual pleasure' of semiosis in the media, in digital communications and in the semiosphere generally, but it only works when you bring all three together and do not reserve agency only to the 'producers' (be they workers or capitalists). We do this by means of the micro (textual), meso (labour/corporate) and macro (environmental) approach we've adopted in this book, and through which we are able to identify not only new forms of class consciousness, for instance among girls and young women, but also new forms of class exploitation, as alerted by Sevignani:

> classification and surveillance reinforce exploitation in contemporary informational capitalism and [this paper has reminded readers] of the important other side of the story of social inequality that goes beyond market mechanisms, i.e. the problem of social sorting, individual attribution, and opportunity hoarding.
>
> (2017: 96)

# Advocacy: *Il n'y a pas de hors-semiosphere!*

We are convinced by the need for advocacy and activism (leadership) within the same process by which we create and distribute knowledge – in selves, communities, industries and policy forums, and in relation to environmental contexts, as well as in critical and disciplinary work. Some of that activism can be built into the enterprises and corporate structures that coordinate the media and the digital semiosphere, while some of it is much better suited to direct activism at street level.

One example of enterprise-based activism comes from Katherine Keating. As the daughter of former Australian prime minister Paul Keating, this New York resident has been familiar with intermediation at societal scale all her life. As an executive with millennial media enterprises like *Vice*, *Vice Impact* and *Matters Journal* and the Los Angeles–based entertainment-management company Maverick, she has sought to put such communicative reach to work, not as a 'regulator' on the old 'enforcer' model but as a synthesizer and integrator for groups, 'driving' (as she puts it, in the language of start-ups) both activist 'knowledge clubs' and social-network demes, such that their efforts are coordinated, and effective, in the context of the digital semiosphere:

> My experience in government and the nonprofit sector has taught me that you can't steer meaningful change if there is no communication between policy-makers trying to push legislation, traditional media reporting on the issues, and foundations and grassroots organisations trying to advocate for their cause … With VICE Impact, we have built a platform grounded in VICE's content which we have married with policy and advocacy expertise … Wary of the complexity of the issues we are tackling, we are forging partnerships with respected NGOs, local organisations, foundations, activists, and companies to conceive and roll out these campaigns. Through this process, we hope to advance the role that companies and organisations should and can play in driving change via our platform. (Keating, 2019)[2]

Digital and media literacy cannot be confined to technical skills alone. There is also a need for collaboration among three sets of agencies: *policymakers* who legislate for productivity, growth and change in a competitive but open society; *media companies* raising and reporting issues for the public (in both factual and fictional forms); and *advocates* for change (including philanthropic and activist agencies) (Keating, 2019). Working together, these three partners can not only increase awareness and understanding using digital media and connectivity; they can also accomplish real change to improve the lives of citizens in an uncertain world.

However, often they don't. That's where direct action comes in, sometimes to explosive effect (in Lotman's terms). The recent history of climate activism,

---

[2]And see: https://www.afr.com/world/north-america/inside-the-high-altitude-world-of-katherine-keating-20190821-p52jcl.

linked with 'climate justice' across the spectrum of identity and difference in a digital world, has proven to be a case study in how new players can precipitate general and irreversible change in a short time.

The global action associated with Greta Thunberg and the organizations with which she is connected is the obvious case in point, not least because the 'effect' of one autistic child at planetary scale is itself a *textual dynamic* that changes institutional communication and even provokes adjustments to the self-organizing mechanisms of large-scale institutions and systems. Thunberg appeared from the very periphery of the digital semiosphere and shook it to the core within a single year. The only 'technology' she 'invented' was her familiar placard (Skolstreijk för Klimatet); it was the digital semiosphere itself that amplified and distributed the message.

Along the way, Greta Thunberg herself became an 'institution' (Figure 20.1).[3] She was obliged to warn against 'imposters', to register her own name, #FridaysForFuture and '*Skolstreijk för Klimatet*' as trademarks, and to set up a family foundation to handle 'royalties, donations, prize money' in a transparent way. She wrote to her 10 million Instagram followers about 'imposters, trademarks, commercial interests, royalties and foundation', remarking that 'the foundation's aim will be to promote ecological, climatic and social sustainability as well as mental health. Love/Greta' (Instagram, 30 January 2020): not the usual Insta fare for a schoolgirl, even a '17 year old climate and environmental activist with Asberger's'.

In short, even personal activism of the most individual and vulnerable kind is at the same time institutional and global and must get organized accordingly, to take account of trolls, trade and trouble in the 'labour process, environmental impact, and textual pleasure', in Toby Miller's formula (2020), of activism itself. There is no outside to the semiosphere! *Il n'y a pas de hors-semiosphere!* (Deutsche, 2014).

The ethics and uncertainties involved in our increasing interaction with nonhuman agents, from animals to algorithms to robots, poses practical problems for internet workers, health professionals, public servants and activists alike. Similarly, the challenges of climate change, sustainability and waste in the era of globalized media require a coordinated response from many different cultural contexts and political jurisdictions. How to accommodate diversity and difference while addressing global issues in turn requires new kinds of media literacy and new understandings of democratic resilience that reach across existing boundaries. Our research agenda helps users, makers and regulators to navigate the environment of risk, contestation and change. This requires working with community, corporate and government partners to connect *knowledge, communication* and *action* in a changing world. Or else:

---

[3]See: https://www.bloomberg.com/news/articles/2020-01-29/greta-thunberg-seeks-trademarks-to-prevent-commercial-misuse.

FIGURE 20.1 *Greta Thunberg: instituting action. Picture credit: Anders Hellberg.*[4]

---

[4]Original caption: 'In August 2018, outside the Swedish parliament building, Greta Thunberg started a school strike for the climate. Her sign reads, "Skolstrejk för klimatet," meaning, "school strike for climate"' (27 August 2018). Picture credit: Anders Hellberg. Wikimedia Commons. Image at: https://upload.wikimedia.org/wikipedia/commons/c/cd/Greta_Thunberg_4.jpg.

The world was all before them...
They, hand in hand, with wandering steps and slow,
*Through Eden took their solitary way.*
(John Milton, *Paradise Lost*, XII, 644–8; see Figure 20.2)[5]

\*\*\*

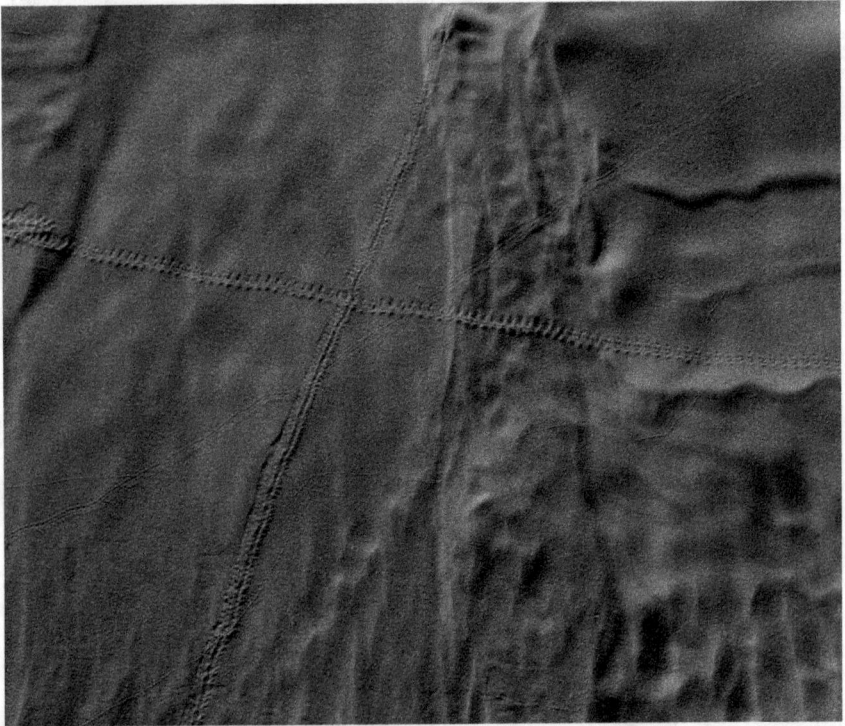

**FIGURE 20.2** *'Through Eden took their solitary way': Where to Now, Planet?*
*Peeter Laurits 'New Earth 2' (2010) from* Tuareg Dreams. https://www.peeterlaurits.
com/archive/tuareg-dreams

---

[5]So ends *Paradise Lost*, with the *Götterdämmerung* scenario (Hartley, 2020: 162–3): the gods
are gone; the cosmos is sublunary and secular. You, alone and together, are responsible for the
Earth system: Source: https://www.bartleby.com/4/412.html.

# ACKNOWLEDGEMENTS

We're very glad we got together to plan this book (as you can see in the accompanying authors' photograph), albeit only once. Despite the intervening 13,000 kilometres, and various life events for all of us since then, we completed the manuscript almost exactly two years later. It was an act of faith throughout, as we relied entirely on the digital semiosphere to keep in touch and only secured a contract for the project after it was completed. We thank each other for the trust and for a wonderfully enlightening experience, from which we all learnt so much along the way.

We are grateful to Peeter Laurits, who has generously allowed us to use his artwork to illustrate successive parts of this book, as well as for the cover image. You can follow Laurits's work here: https://www.peeterlaurits.com/.

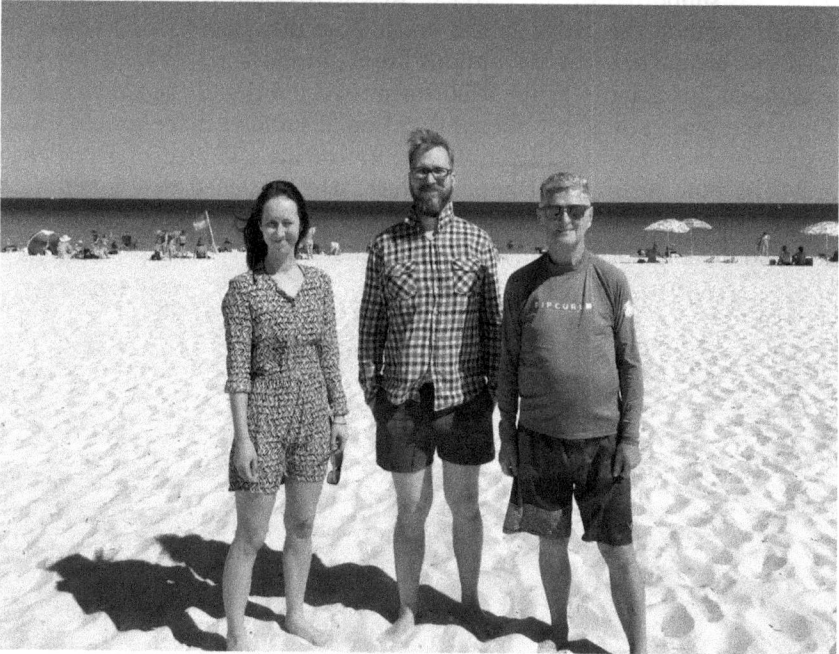

*The authors get together to ponder the semiosphere, Leighton Beach, Fremantle, March 2018.* Photo credit: T. Horton

He is represented by VAAL gallery, Tartu maantee 80D, Tallinn, Estonia (+372 681 0871), galerii@vaal.ee.

We thank Katie Gallof of Bloomsbury for continuing to support the 'cultural science' adventure – of which this is 'volume three' – and for guiding this book throughout the publication process.

*John:* This book was conceived when I was a professional academic researcher and completed after I'd unexpectedly quit all that but still found myself pondering the semiosphere. For that, I'm grateful to many people: I thank Tina Horton, for introducing me to *The Structure of the Artistic Text*; the late Tom O'Regan, for introducing me to *Universe of the Mind*; co-authors Indrek and Maarja, for introducing me to so much more; as well as Kalevi Kull, Peeter Torop, Ulrike Rohn, Rein Raud, Piret Peiker, Marek Tamm and all who welcomed me to the land of semiosis itself. Throughout, my chief support and inspiration have come from my family.

*Indrek:* This book completes much of the work I have done since 2001, when I started working on my master's thesis on how to use cultural semiotics for making sense of digital culture and innovation. Therefore I thank all my advisors during the early stages of this work: Gunnar Liestøl, Robin Mansell, Sonia Livingstone, as well as several colleagues later on for their advice (John and Maarja being first among many!). My work towards this book was supported by the Estonian Research Council (grant PUT1176). Most important, this work gained much from the empathy and advice of Ulrike Rohn and 'creative disruptions' from our kids.

*Maarja:* I'm grateful to the department of semiotics at the University of Tartu, the place where my thought and understanding have grown most. I am also thankful to MEDIT, Tallinn University's Centre of Excellence in Media Innovation and Digital Culture, which opened new intellectual avenues during my postdoctoral studies. And my biggest thank-you goes to Pärt and the kids for making the world wonderful.

# REFERENCES

Abernathy, W. and J. Utterback (1978) 'Patterns of Industrial Innovation'. *Technology Review*, 80(7), 41–7.

Abidin, C. (2018) *Internet Celebrity: Understanding Fame Online*. Bingley: Emerald Publishing.

Adams, P. (2005) *The Bowery Boys: Street Corner Radicals and the Politics of Rebellion*. Westport, CT: Praeger.

Adamu, A. U. (2012) 'Transnational Media Flows and Contra-Flows: Shifting Paradigms in South-South Entertainment Flows'. *Hemispheres. Studies on Cultures and Societies* (27), 63–90.

Ahmed, A. K. (2018) 'Human Rights and the Non-Human Black Body'. *HRLR Online*, 3(2), 1–17: http://hrlr.law.columbia.edu/files/2018/11/Ahmed_Human-Rights-and-the-Non-Human-Black-Body_HRLR-Online-3.2.pdf.

Ahn, J. (2011) 'The effect of social network sites on adolescents' social and academic development: Current theories and controversies'. *Journal of the American Society for Information Science and Technology*, 62(8), 1435–45.

Alexander, B. (2011) *The New Digital Storytelling: Creating Narratives with New Media*. Santa Barbara: Praeger.

Alvaredo, F., L. Chancel, T. Piketty, E. Saez and G. Zucman (eds) (2018) *World Inequality Report 2018*. Cambridge, MA: Harvard University Press.

Andersen, N. Å. (2003) *Discursive Analytical Strategies. Understanding Foucault, Koselleck, Laclau, Luhmann*. Bristol: Policy Press.

Anderson, B. (2006, first edn 1983) *Imagined Communities: Reflections on the Origin and Spread of Nationalism*, Revised edn. London: Verso. http://art.yale.edu/file_columns/0000/8647/anderson.pdf.

Andrews, E. (2003) *Conversations with Lotman: Cultural Semiotics in Language, Literature, and Cognition*. Toronto: University of Toronto Press.

Aristotle (n.d.) *Politics, Book VII*. Online: http://www.perseus.tufts.edu/hopper/text?doc=Perseus:abo:tlg,0086,035:7.

Arthur, W. B. (2009) *The Nature of Technology: What It Is and How It Evolves*. New York: Free Press.

Atterton, P. (1994) Power's Blind Struggle for Existence: Foucault, Geneaology and Darwinism. *History of the Human Sciences*, 7(4), 1–20.

Ballantyne, A. and A. Law (2011) *Tudoresque: In Pursuit of the Ideal Home*. London: Reaktion Books.

Barnet, B. (2013) *Memory Machines: The Evolution of Hypertext*. London and New York: Anthem Press.

Bar-On, Y., R. Phillips and R. Milo (2018) 'The Biomass Distribution on Earth'. *PNAS* (published ahead of print): https://doi.org/10.1073/pnas.1711842115.

Baron, J. (2014) *The Archive Effect: Found Footage and the Audiovisual Experience History*. London: Routledge.

Barthes, R. (1977) 'From Work to Text'. In *Image, Music, Text*. New York: Hill and Wang, 155–64.

Barthes, R. (2010 [1964]) 'Elements of Semiology'. In *Writing Degree Zero & Elements of Semiology*. London: Vintage Books.

Baudrillard, J. (1983) *Simulations*. New York: Semiotext(e).

Bawden, D. (2008) 'Origins and Concepts of Digital Literacy'. In M. Knobel and C. Lankshear (eds), *Digital Literacies: Concepts, Policies and Practices*. New York: Peter Lang, 16–32.

Bender, J. and D. Wellbery (eds) (1990) *The Ends of Rhetoric: History, Theory, Practice*. Stanford, CA: Stanford University Press.

Benington, J. and M. Moore (eds) (2011) *Public Value: Theory and Practice*. London: Palgrave Macmillan.

Bennett, J., N. Strange, P. Kerr and A. Medrado (2012) *Multiplatforming Public Service Broadcasting: The Economic and Cultural Role of UK Digital and TV Independents*. London: Royal Holloway, University of Sussex, London Metropolitan University.

Bennett, L. and J. Kidd (2017) 'Myths about Media Studies: The Construction of Media Studies Education in the British Press'. *Continuum*, 31(2), 163–76. DOI: 10.1080/10304312.2016.1265096.

Berbrier, M. (2000) 'The Victim Ideology of White Supremacists and White Separatists in the US'. *Sociological Focus*, 33(2), 175–91.

Berg, C., S. Davidson and J. Potts (2017) 'The Blockchain Economy: A Beginner's Guide to Institutional Cryptoeconomics'. *Medium*: https://medium.com/cryptoeconomics-australia/the-blockchain-economy-a-beginners-guide-to-institutional-cryptoeconomics-64bf2f2beec4.

Bernardo, N. (2011) *The Producer's Guide to Transmedia: How to Develop, Fund, Produce and Distribute Compelling Stories across Multiple Platforms*. Lisbon: beActive books.

Berry, T. B. (2015) *The Film of Tomorrow: A Cultural History of Videoblogging*. A University of Sussex DPhil thesis: http://sro.sussex.ac.uk/id/eprint/53713/1/Berry%2C_Trine_Bj%C3%B8rkmann.pdf.

Berry, T. B. (2018) 'Videoblogging before YouTube'. *Theory on Demand* 27. Amsterdam: Institute of Network Cultures.

Beyer, S. and L. Gorris (2009) *Spiegel* Interview with Umberto Eco: 'We Like Lists Because We Don't Want to Die'. *SPIEGEL*, 11 November: https://www.spiegel.de/international/zeitgeist/spiegel-interview-with-umberto-eco-we-like-lists-because-we-don-t-want-to-die-a-659577.html.

Bilton, C. (2017) *The Disappearing Product: Marketing and Markets in the Creative Industries*. Cheltenham: Edward Elgar.

Björnberg, K., M. Karlsson, M. Gilek and S. Hansson (2017) 'Climate and Environmental Science Denial: A Review of the Scientific Literature Published in 1990–2015'. *Journal of Cleaner Production*, 167, 229–41.

Blaim, A. (1992a) 'Constructivist Aspects of Cultural Semiotics'. In J. Andrew (ed.), *Poetics of the Text*. Amsterdam and Atlanta, GA: Rodopi, 17–27.

Blaim, A. (1992b) 'The Twain Shall Meet? Some Observations on Soviet Cultural Semiotics and Empirical Study of Literature and the Media'. *Poetics: Journal of Empirical Research on Literature, the Media and the Arts*, 21, 33–44.

Blaim, A. (1998) 'Lotman in the West: An Ambiguous Complaint'. In J. Andrew and R. Reid (eds), *Neo-Formalist Papers*. Amsterdam and Atlanta GA: Rodopi, 329–37.

Blais, M. and F. Dupuis-Déri (2011) 'Masculinism and the Antifeminist Countermovement'. *Social Movement Studies*, 11(1), 21–39.

Blanco Rivero, J. J. (2019) 'Mediality, Temporality, Social Cognition, and Evolution'. *Philosophies* 4(44). https://doi.org/10.3390/philosophies4030044.

Blind, G. (2017) 'Behavioural Rules: Veblen, Nelson-Winter, Ostrom and Beyond'. In R. Frantz, S.-H. Chen, K. Dopfer, F. Heukelom and S. Mousavi (eds), *Routledge Handbook of Behavioural Economics*. London: Routledge, 139–51. DOI: 10.4324/9781315743479.

Boden, M. (1990) *The Creative Mind: Myths and Mechanisms*. London: Weidenfeld and Nicolson.

Boden, M. (2016) *AI: Its Nature and Future*. Oxford: Oxford University Press.

Bolter, J. and R. Grusin (1998) *Remediation: Understanding New Media*. Cambridge, MA: MIT Press.

Bondebjerg, I. (2016) 'Regional and Global Dimensions of Danish Film Culture and Film Policy'. In M. Hjort and U. Lindqvist (eds), *A Companion to Nordic Cinema*. Oxford: Wiley Blackwell.

Bonfante, P. and I. Anca (2009) 'Plants, Mycorrhizal Fungi, and Bacteria: A Network of Interactions'. *Annual Review of Microbiology*, 63, 363–83: https://www.annualreviews.org/doi/10.1146/annurev.micro.091208.073504.

Boudana, S., P. Frosh and A. Cohen (2017) 'Reviving Icons to Death: When Historic Photographs Become Digital Memes'. *Media, Culture & Society*, 39(8): 1210–30.

Bouvier, G. (2015) 'What Is a Discourse Approach to Twitter, Facebook, YouTube and other Social Media: Connecting with Other Academic Fields'. *Journal of Multicultural Discourses*, 10(2), 149–62.

Braidotti, R. (2018) 'Posthuman Critical Theory'. In R. Braidotti and M. Hlavajova (eds), *Posthuman Glossary*. London: Bloomsbury, 339–42.

Bratton, B. (2016) *The Stack: On Software and Sovereignty*. Cambridge MA: MIT Press.

Brier, S. (2006) 'Biosemiotics'. *Encyclopaedia of Language and Linguistics*, 2nd edn. Elsevier, Vol. 2, 31–40.

Brier, S. (2010) 'Cybersemiotics: An Evolutionary World View Going beyond Entropy and Information into the Question of Meaning'. *Entropy*, 12(8), 1902–20: (https://doi.org/10.3390/e12081902); https://www.mdpi.com/1099-4300/12/8/1902/htm.

Brinkerink, M. (2014) *Europeana Sounds Milestone 7: End-user Contributions Defined v1.0*: https://pro.europeana.eu/files/Europeana_Professional/Projects/Project_list/Europeana_Sounds/Milestones/EuropeanaSounds-MS7-End-user-contributions-defined.pdf.

Brodbeck, F. (2011) *Cinemetrics*. KABK [Royal Academy of Arts]. Den Haag: http://cinemetrics.fredericbrodbeck.de/.

Broms, H. and H. Gahmberg (1983) 'Communication to Self in Organizations and Cultures'. *Administrative Science Quarterly*, 28(3), 482–95.

Brown, J. S. and P. Duguid (1996) 'Keeping It Simple'. In T. Winograd (ed.), *Bringing Design to Software*. Reading MA: Addison Wesley: https://hci.stanford.edu/publications/bds/7-brown.html.

Bruns, A. (2008) *Blogs, Wikipedia, Second Life, and Beyond: From Production to Produsage*. New York: Peter Lang.

Bruns, A. (2019) *Are Filter Bubbles Real?* Cambridge: Polity.

Bruns, A. and B. Moon (2019) 'One Day in the Life of a N. Twittersphere'.
   *Nordicom Review*, 40(s1), 11–30: https://doi.org/10.2478/nor-2019-0011.

Bruns, A. and J. Burgess (2012) 'Researching News Discussion on Twitter'.
   *Journalism Studies*, 13(5–6), 801–14. DOI: 10.1080/1461670X.2012.664428.

Buchanan, J. (1965) 'An Economic Theory of Clubs'. *Economica NS*, 32(125) 1–14.

Burgess, J. (2006) 'Hearing Ordinary Voices: Cultural Studies, Vernacular
   Creativity and Digital Storytelling'. *Continuum: Journal of Media and Cultural
   Studies*, 20(2), 201–14.

Burgess, J. and J. Green (2018) *YouTube: Online Video and Participatory Culture*,
   2nd edn. Cambridge: Polity Press.

Callicott, J. B. (2013) *Thinking Like a Planet: The Land Ethic and the Earth Ethic*.
   Oxford: Oxford University Press.

Cannizzaro, S. (2016) 'Internet Memes as Internet Signs: A Semiotic View of Digital
   Culture'. *Sign Systems Studies* 44(4), 562–86.

Castells, M. (2001) *The Internet Galaxy: Reflections on the Internet, Business, and
   Society*. Oxford, New York: Oxford University Press.

Castells, M. and G. Cardoso (eds) (2005) *The Network Society: From Knowledge
   to Policy*. Washington, DC: Johns Hopkins Center for Transatlantic
   Relations: https://www.researchgate.net/profile/Gustavo_Cardoso5/
   publication/265108845.

Casey, M. and P. Vigna (2018) *The Truth Machine: The Blockchain and the
   Future of Everything*. New York: St. Martin's Press (https://us.macmillan.com/
   books/9781250114570).

Chakrabarty, D. (2008) *Provincializing Europe: Postcolonial Thought and
   Historical Difference*. Princeton, NJ: Princeton University Press.

Chaminade, C., B-Å Lundvall and S. Haneef (2018) *Advanced Introduction to
   National Innovation Systems*. Cheltenham: Edward Elgar.

Chandler, D. (2017) *Semiotics: The Basics*, 3rd edn. London: Routledge.

Chandrashekar, A., F. Amat, J. Basilico and T. Jebara (2017) 'Artwork
   Personalization at Netflix'. *Netflix TechBlog*: https://medium.com/netflix-
   techblog/artwork-personalization-c589f074ad76.

Cheney, G. and L. T. Christensen (2001) 'Organizational identity: Linkages between
   internal and external communication'. In F. Jablin and L. Putnam (eds), *The
   New Handbook of Organizational Communication: Advances in Theory,
   Research, and Methods*. Thousand Oakes, CA: Sage Publications.

Christensen, L. T. (1997) 'Marketing as Auto-Communication'. *Consumption,
   Markets and Culture*, 1(3), 197–227.

Chua, E-J. (2011) 'A Minoritarian Digital Poetics of YouTube'. *Screening the Past*
   32: http://www.screeningthepast.com/2011/11/a-minoritarian-digital-poetics-of-
   youtube/.

Chun, W. H-K. (2008) 'The Enduring Ephemeral, or the Future Is a Memory'.
   *Critical Inquiry* 35(1), 148–71.

Citton, Y. (2012) 'From Theory to Bricolage: Indiscipline and the Exemplary
   Gestures of Interpretation'. *International Social Science Journal*, 63(207–8),
   53–66: https://hal.archives-ouvertes.fr/hal-01373204/document.

Cohendet, P. and P. Llerena (1997) Learning, Technical Change, and Public Policy:
   How to Create and Exploit Diversity. In C. Edquist (ed.), *Systems of Innovation:
   Technologies, Institutions and Organizations*. Abingdon: Routledge.

Colebrook, C. and J. Weinstein (2015) 'Anthropocene Feminisms: Rethinking the Unthinkable'. *philoSOPHIA*, 5(2), 167–78: https://www.muse.jhu.edu/article/608466.

Colleoni, E., A. Rozza and A. Arvidsson (2014) 'Echo Chamber or Public Sphere? Predicting Political Orientation and Measuring Political Homophily in Twitter Using Big Data'. *Journal of Communication* 64(2), 317–32.

Commons, J. (1934) *Institutional Economics: Its Place in Political Economy*. New York: Macmillan.

Coppins, M. (2020) 'The 2020 Disinformation War'. *The Atlantic*, March: https://www.theatlantic.com/magazine/archive/2020/03/the-2020-disinformation-war/605530/.

Cotani, T. (2019) 'Common Ground Awakens'. *Wired Japan*, 33, 58–75.

Couldry, N. and U. Mejias (2019) *The Costs of Connection: How Data Is Colonizing Human Life and Appropriating for Capitalism*. Stanford: Stanford University Press.

Cowen, T. (2020) 'What Libertarianism Has Become and Will Become – State Capacity Libertarianism'. *Marginal Revolution*, 1 January: https://marginalrevolution.com/marginalrevolution/2020/01/what-libertarianism-has-become-and-will-become-state-capacity-libertarianism.html.

Crescenzi, R. S. I., C. Ioramashvili, A. Rodríguez-Pose and M. Storper (2019, November) *The Geography of Innovation: Local Hotspots and Global Innovation Networks*. London: WIPO: https://www.wipo.int/edocs/pubdocs/en/wipo_pub_econstat_wp_57.pdf.

Cunningham, H. (2005) *Children and Childhood in Western Society since 1500*, 2nd edn. Harlow: Pearson Longman.

Curtin, M. and K. Sanson (2016) *Precarious Creativity: Global Media, Local Labor*. Oakland: University of California Press.

Cusumano, M. (2011) 'Platform Wars Come to Social Media'. *Communications of the ACM*, 54(4), 31–3.

Danesi, M. (2016) *The Semiotics of Emoji: The Rise of Visual Language on the Internet*. London: Bloomsbury.

David, P. (1995) 'Standardization Policies for Network Technologies: The Flux between Freedom and Order Revisited'. In R. Hawkins, R. Mansell and J. Skea (eds), *Standards, Innovation and Competitiveness: The Politics and Economics of Standards in Natural and Technical Environments*. Cheltenham: Edward Elgar, 15–35.

David, P. A. (2000) Path Dependence, Its Critics and the Quest for 'Historical Economics'. In P. Garrouste and S. Ioannides (eds), *Evolution and Path Dependence in Economic Ideas: Past and Present*. Cheltenham: Edward Elgar, 15–39.

David, P. and S. Greenstein (1990) 'The Economics of Compatibility Standards: An Introduction to Recent Research'. *Economics of Innovation and New Technology*, 1(1–2): 3–41.

Davis, O. (2019) 'Theorising the Advent of Weaponized Drones as Techniques of Domestic Paramilitary Policing'. *Security Dialogue*, 50, 4 (August), 344–60.

Dawkins, R. (2006 [1976]) *The Selfish Gene*. Oxford: Oxford University Press.

Deleuze, G. and F. Guattari (1987) *A Thousand Plateaus: Capitalism and Schizophrenia*. Minneapolis, MN: University of Minnesota Press.

Derrida, J. (1967 [2016]) *Of Grammatology* (Trans. G. Spivak). Baltimore, MD: Johns Hopkins University Press.

Deutsche, M. (2014) '"Il n'y a pas de hors-texte" – Once More'. *Australasian Continental Philosophy*, 18(2), 98–124: https://researchers.mq.edu.au/en/publications/il-ny-a-pas-de-hors-texte-once-more.

Dijck, J. V. (2007) *Mediated Memories in the Digital Age*. Stanford, CA: Stanford University Press.

Dijck, J. V. (2014) 'Datafication, Dataism and Dataveillance: Big Data between Scientific Paradigm and Ideology'. *Surveillance & Society*, 12(2), 197–208.

Dijck, J. V., T. Poell and M. de Waal (2018) *The Platform Society: Public Values in a Connective World*. New York: Oxford University Press.

DiMaggio, P. and J. Cohen (2005) 'Information Inequality and Network Externalities: A Comparative Study of the Diffusion of Television and the Internet'. In V. Nee and R. Swedberg (eds), *The Economic Sociology of Capitalism*. Princeton, NJ: Princeton University Press, 227–67.

Dincecco, M. (2017) *State Capacity and Economic Development: Present and Past*. Cambridge: Cambridge Elements in Political Economy: DOI: 10.1017/9781108539913.

Dlakavu, S., S. Ndelu and M. Matandela (2017) 'Writing and Rioting: Black Womxn in the Time of Fallism'. *Agenda*, 31(3–4), 105–9. DOI: 10.1080/10130950.2017.1392163

Dopfer, K. and J. Potts (2008) *The General Theory of Economic Evolution*. New York: Routledge.

Dopfer, K., J. Foster and J. Potts (2004) 'Micro–Meso–Macro'. *Journal of Evolutionary Economics*, 14(3), 263–79.

Dosi, G. (1982) 'Technological Paradigms and Technological Trajectories: A Suggested Interpretation of the Determinants and Directions of Technical Change'. *Research Policy*, 11(3), 147–62.

Dosi, G. (1984) *Technical Change and Industrial Transformation – The Theory and an Application to the Semiconductor Industry*. London: Macmillan.

Dowd, T., M. Niederman, M. Fry and J. Steiff (2013) *Storytelling across Worlds: Transmedia for Creatives and Producers*. Boston: Focal Press.

du Sautoy, M. (2019) *The Creativity Code: How AI Is Learning to Write, Paint and Think*. London: Fourth Estate

Dutton, W., B. Reisdorf, E. Dubois and G. Blank (2017) 'Social Shaping of the Politics of Internet Search and Networking: Moving beyond Filter Bubbles, Echo Chambers, and Fake News'. *Quello Center Working Papers*, no. 2944191. Lansing MI: Michigan State University.

Eco, U. (1977) *A Theory of Semiotics*. Bloomington, IN: Indiana University Press.

Eco, U. (1979) *The Role of the Reader: Explorations in the Semiotics of Texts*. Bloomington IN: Indiana University Press.

Eco, U. (1984) *Semiotics and the Philosophy of Language*. Bloomington, IN: Indiana University Press.

Eco, U. (2009) *The Infinity of Lists: From Homer to Joyce*. London: MacLehose.

el-Ojeili, C. (2020) *The Utopian Constellation. Future-Oriented Social and Political Thought Today*. London: Palgrave Pivot.

Elias, N. (1978) *What Is Sociology?* London: Hutchinson.

Elmer, G. and M. Gasher (2005) *Contracting Out Hollywood: Runaway Productions and Foreign Location Shooting*. Lanham, MD: Rowman & Littlefield.

Enzensberger, H. M. (1982) 'The Industrialization of the Mind'. In R. Grimm and B. Armstrong (eds), *Hans Magnus Enzensberger: Critical Essays*. New York: Continuum Publishing Co, 3–14. Reissued by Bloomsbury, 1997.

Epstein, M. (2018) 'Lotman, Yuri'. In A. DeBlasio and M. Epstein (eds), *Filosofia: An Encyclopedia of Russian Thought*. Online: http://filosofia.dickinson.edu/encyclopedia/lotman-yuri/.

Erlich, V. (1981) *Russian Formalism: History and Doctrine*, 3rd edn. New Haven CT: Yale University Press.

Erll, A. (2011) *Memory in Culture*. Basingstoke, NY: Palgrave Macmillan.

Ernst, W. (2013). *Digital Memory and the Archive* (ed. J. Parikka). Minneapolis, MN: University of Minnesota Press.

Favareau, D., K. Kull, G. Ostdiek, T. Maran, L. Westling, P. Cobley, F. Stjernfelt, M. Anderson, M. Tønnessen and W. Wheeler (2017) 'How Can the Study of the Humanities Inform the Study of Biosemiotics?' *Biosemiotics* 10(1), 9–31.

Fenton, N. (2016) *Digital, Political, Radical*. Cambridge, UK: Polity Press.

Foerster, H. von (1992) 'Ethics and second-order cybernetics'. *Cybernetics & Human Knowing*, 1(1), 9–19.

Follett, J. (2019) 'How 22 Years of AI Superiority Changed Chess: Notes from the Frontiers of Machine Perfection'. *Towards Data Science*: https://towardsdatascience.com/how-22-years-of-ai-superiority-changed-chess-76eddd061cb0.

Foster, J., R. McChesney and R. Jamil Jonna (2011) 'The Global Reserve Army of Labor and the New Imperialism'. *Monthly Review*, 63(6), November: https://monthlyreview.org/2011/11/01/the-global-reserve-army-of-labor-and-the-new-imperialism/.

Foucault, M. (1982) 'The Subject and Power'. *Critical Inquiry* 8(4), 777–95.

Foucault, M. (1990) *The History of Sexuality, vol. 1*. New York: Vintage Books.

Foucault, M. (2002a) *Power. The Essential Works of Foucault 1954–1984*. London: Penguin.

Foucault, M. (2002b) *The Archaeology of Knowledge*. London and New York: Routledge.

Freeman, C. (1992) *Economics of Hope*. London: Pinter.

Freeman, C. (1995) 'The "National System of Innovation" in Historical Perspective'. *Cambridge Journal of Economics*, 19 (1), 5–24. https://doi.org/10.1093/oxfordjournals.cje.a035309

Freeman, C. and F. Louçã (2001) *As Time Goes By: From the Industrial Revolutions to the Information Revolution*. Oxford: Oxford University Press.

Freeman, C. and C. Perez (1988) 'Structural Crises of Adjustment, Business Cycles and Investment Behaviour'. In G. Dosi, C. Freeman, R. R. Nelson, G. Silverberg and L. Soete (eds), *Technical Change and Economic Theory*. London: Pinter, 656.

Frosh, P. (2018) *The Poetics of Digital Media*. Cambridge: Polity.

Funk, J. (2001) *The Mobile Internet: How Japan Dialed Up and the West Disconnected*. New York: ISI Publications.

Galloway, A. R. (2004) *Protocol: How Control Exists after Decentralization*. Cambridge, MA: MIT Press.

Garde-Hansen, J., A. Hoskins and A. Reading (eds) (2009) *Save As … Digital Memories*. London: Palgrave Macmillan.

Gelernter, D. (1993) *Mirror Worlds: Or the Day Software Puts the Universe in a Shoebox. How It Will Happen and What It Will Mean*. Oxford: Oxford University Press.

Genette, G. (1997 [1987]) *Paratexts: Thresholds of Interpretation*. Cambridge: Cambridge University Press.

Georgakopoulou, A. (2014) 'Small Stories Transposition and Social Media: A Micro-Perspective on the "Greek Crisis"'. *Discourse & Society*, 25(4), 519–39.

Ghenawat, P. (2012) *World 3.0: Global Prosperity and How to Achieve It*. Cambridge MA: Harvard Business Review Press. https://eic.cfainstitute.org/2012/10/26/pankaj-ghemawat-globalisation-or-globaloney/.

Gevinson, T. (2019) 'Who Would I Be without Instagram? An Investigation'. *The Cut (New York Magazine)*: https://www.thecut.com/2019/09/who-would-tavi-gevinson-be-without-instagram.html?utm_source=tw.

Gikay, A. and C. Stanescu (2019) 'Technological Populism and Its Archetypes: Blockchain and Cryptocurrencies'. *Nordic Journal of Commercial Law*, 2019(2), 66–109. SSRN: https://ssrn.com/abstract=3379756. DOI: http://dx.doi.org/10.2139/ssrn.3379756.

Gilster, P. (1997) *Digital Literacy*. New York: Wiley.

Gintis, H. (2012) 'Human Evolution: A Behavioral Synthesis'. *Santa Fe Institute*: https://pdfs.semanticscholar.org/96d3/83f95118075d7a3e4fe7fb3def0161d4c023.pdf.

Gintis, H., C. van Schaik and C. Boehm (2019) 'Zoon Politikon: The Evolutionary Origins of Human Socio-Political Systems'. *Behavioural Processes*, 161, April, 17–30: https://doi.org/10.1016/j.beproc.2018.01.007.

Gollop, A. (2016) *Introduction to Traffic Signals: An Introduction to Signalised Junctions and Crossing Facilities in the UK*. Online: CreateSpace.

Gough, N. (2002) 'Thinking/Acting Locally/Globally: Western Science and Environmental Education in a Global Knowledge Economy'. *International Journal of Science Education*, 24(11), 1217–37.

Gray, J. (2010) *Show Sold Separately: Promos, Spoilers, and Other Media Paratexts*. New York: New York Times Press.

Grece, C., A. Lange, A. Schneeberger and S. Valais (2015) *The Development of the European Market for On-Demand Audiovisual Services*. Strasbourg: European Audiovisual Observatory: https://rm.coe.int/1680788974.

Gregersen, B. (2010) 'The Public Sector as a Pacer in National Systems of Innovation'. In B. Lundvall (ed.), *National Systems of Innovation: Toward a Theory of Innovation and Interactive Learning*. London: Anthem Press, 133–50.

Gregg, M. (2018) *Counterproductive: Time Management in the Knowledge Economy*. Durham, NC: Duke University Press.

Griffin, R. (2003) 'From Slime Mould to Rhizome: An Introduction to the Groupuscular Right'. *Patterns of Prejudice*, 37(1), 27–50. DOI: 10.1080/0031322022000054321.

Grinspan, J. (2016) *The Virgin Vote: How Young Americans Made Democracy Social, Politics Personal, and Voting Popular in the Nineteenth Century*. Chapel Hill, NC: University of North Carolina Press.

Grosz, E. (2011) *Becoming Undone*. Durham, NC: Duke University Press.

Grusin, R. (ed.) (2017) *Anthropocene Feminism*. Minneapolis: University of Minneapolis Press.

Gullström, B. (n.d.) 'Snacking at the Digital Museum'. *Artworks*: https://artworksapp.com/articles/snacking-at-the-digital-museum

Haase, D. (2000) 'Feminist Fairy-Tale Scholarship: A Critical Survey and Bibliography'. *Marvels & Tales: Journal of Fairy-Tale Studies*, 14(1), 15–63.

Haebich, A. and J. Taylor (2007) 'Modern Primitives Leaping and Stomping the Earth: From Ballet to Bush Doofs'. *Aboriginal History*, 31, 63–84: http://press-files.anu.edu.au/downloads/press/p74151/pdf/ch0454.pdf.

Haff, P. (2014) 'Humans and Technology in the Anthropocene: Six Rules'. *The Anthropocene Review*, 1(2), 126–36.

Hall, S. (2001) 'Foucault: Power, Knowledge and Discourse'. In M. Wetherell, S. Taylor and S. Yates (eds), *Discourse, Theory and Practice*. London: Open University/Sage Publications, 71–82.

Hall, S. (2006) 'Stuart Hall and Cultural Studies: Decoding Cultural Oppression'. https://www.corwin.com/sites/default/files/upm-binaries/13286_Chapter_2_Web_Byte__Stuart_Hall.pdf.

Hallam, R. (2019) 'The Civil Resistance Model'. In *This Is Not a Drill: An Extinction Rebellion Handbook*. London: Penguin Books, 99–105.

Harari, Y. N. (2015) *Sapiens*. London: Harvill Secker.

Harari, Y. N. (2018) *21 Lessons for the 21st Century*. New York: Vintage.

Haraway, D. (1985) 'A Cyborg Manifesto'. Republished in D. Haraway, *Manifestly Haraway* (ed. C. Wolfe). Minneapolis, MN: University of Minnesota Press, 2016.

Haraway, D. (1991) 'A Cyborg Manifesto: Science, Technology, and Socialist-Feminism in the Late Twentieth Century'. In *Simians, Cyborgs and Women: The Reinvention of Nature*. New York: Routledge, 149–81: https://web.archive.org/web/20120214194015/; http://www.stanford.edu/dept/HPS/Haraway/CyborgManifesto.html

Hartley, J. (1992) *The Politics of Pictures: The Creation of the Public in the Age of Popular Media*. London: Routledge.

Hartley, J. (1996) *Popular Reality: Journalism, Modernity, Popular Culture*. London: Arnold [Bloomsbury].

Hartley, J. (2002) *A Short History of Cultural Studies*. London: Sage Publications.

Hartley, J. (2004) 'The "Value Chain of Meaning" and the New Economy'. *International Journal of Cultural Studies* 7(1), 129–41.

Hartley, J. (2008) *Television Truths: Forms of Knowledge in Popular Culture*. Malden, MA: Wiley-Blackwell.

Hartley, J. (2009) *The Uses of Digital Literacy*. St. Lucia: University of Queensland Press (published in the US by Transaction, now Routledge, 2010).

Hartley, J. (2012) *Digital Futures for Cultural and Media Studies*. Malden MA and Oxford: Wiley-Blackwell.

Hartley, J. (2015a) 'Urban Semiosis: Creative Industries and the Clash of Systems'. *International Journal of Cultural Studies*, 18(1), 79–101.

Hartley, J. (2015b) 'Stories Tell Us? Political Narrative, Demes, and the Transmission of Knowledge through Culture'. *Communication Research and Practice*, 1(1), 5–31. DOI: 10.1080/22041451.2015.1042424.

Hartley, J. (2015c) 'Public Intellectuals: *La lutte Continue?*' *Media International Australia*, 156, 108–22.

Hartley, J. (2018) 'What Hope for Open Knowledge? Productive (Armed) *vs.* Connective (Tribal) Knowledge and Staged Conflict'. *Cultural Science Journal*, 10(1), 27–41. DOI: http://doi.org/10.5334/csci.107.

Hartley, J. (2020) *How We Use Stories and Why That Matters: Cultural Science in Action*. New York: Bloomsbury.

Hartley, J. and K. McWilliam (eds) (2009). *Story Circle: Digital Storytelling Around the World*. Malden, MA: Wiley-Blackwell.

Hartley, J. and J. Potts (2014) *Cultural Science: A Natural History of Stories, Demes, Knowledge and Innovation*. London: Bloomsbury.

Hartley, J., W. Wen and H. S. Li (2015) *Creative Economy and Culture: Challenges, Changes and Futures for the Creative Industries*. London: Sage Publications.

Hartley, J., J. Potts, M. Montgomery, E. Rennie and C. Neylon (2019) 'Do We Need to Move from Communication Technology to User Community? A New Economic Model of the Journal as a Club'. *Learned Publishing*, 32, 27–35.

Harvey, D. (1991) *The Condition of Postmodernity: An Enquiry into the Origins of Cultural Change*. Oxford: Wiley-Blackwell.

Hawkes, T. (1977) *Structuralism and Semiotics*. London: Routledge.

Hayek, F. (1945) 'The Use of Knowledge in Society'. *American Economic Review* 35, 519–30.

Hayek, F. (2012) *Law, Legislation and Liberty: A New Statement of the Liberal Principles of Justice and Political Economy, Volume 1: Rules and Order*, Revised edn. London: Routledge.

Heikkilä, N. (2017) 'Online Antagonism of the Alt-Right in the 2016 Election'. *European Journal of American Studies*, 12(2), Online: https://journals. openedition.org/ejas/12140.

Helyar, V. (2001) 'Usability of Portable Devices: The Case of WAP'. In B. Brown, N. Green and R. Harper (eds), *Wireless World: Social and Interactional Aspects of the Mobile Age*. London: Springer.

Hepp, A. (2013) *Cultures of Mediatization*. Cambridge: Polity.

Hepp, A. and U. Hasebrink (2014) 'Human Interaction and Communicative Figurations: The Transformation of Mediatized Cultures and Societies'. In K. Lundby (ed.), *Mediatization of Communication*. Berlin and New York: de Gruyter, 249–72.

Hepp, A. and U. Hasebrink (2018) 'Researching Transforming Communications in Times of Deep Mediatization: A Figurational Approach'. In A. Hepp, A. Breiter and U. Hasebrink (eds), *Communicative Figurations: Transforming Communications in Times of Deep Mediatization*. Cham: Palgrave Macmillan.

Hepp, A. and F. Krotz (eds) (2014) *Mediatized Worlds: Culture and Society in a Media Age*. London: Palgrave Macmillan.

Herrmann-Pillath, C. (2018) 'The Case for a New Discipline: Technosphere Science'. *Ecological Economics*, 149(July), 212–25.

Herrmann-Pillath, C. (2018a) 'Dilthey and Darwin Combined? 19th Century Geisteswissenschaft for 21st Century Cultural Science'. *Cultural Science Journal*, 10.

Herrmann-Pillath, C. (2020) 'The Art of Co-creation: An Intervention in the Philosophy of Ecological Economics'. *Ecological Economics*, 169(March): https://doi.org/10.1016/j.ecolecon.2019.106526.

Hjarvard, S. (2013) *The Mediatization of Culture and Society*. Oxon: Routledge.

Hjort, M. (2010) 'Affinitive and Milieu-building Transnationalism: The Advance Party Initiative'. In D. Iordanova, D. Martin-Jones and B. Vidal (eds), *Cinema at the Periphery*. Detroit IL: Wayne State University Press, 46–66.

Hodgson, G. M. (2006) 'What Are Institutions?' *Journal of Economic Issues*, 40(1), 1–25.

Hodgson, G. M. (2007) 'Evolutionary and Institutional Economics as the New Mainstream?' *Evolutionary and Institutional Economics Review*, 4(1), 7–25.

Hoffmeyer, J. and C. Emmeche (1991) 'Code-duality and the Semiotics of Nature'. In M. Anderson and F. Merrell (eds), *Semiotic Modeling*. New York: Mouton de Gruyter, 117–66.

Honko, L. (2000) *Thick Corpus, Organic Variation and Textuality in Oral Tradition*. Helsinki: Finnish Literature Society, 3–28.

Hoskins, A. (2001) 'New Memory: Mediating History'. *Historical Journal of Film, Radio and Television*, 21(4), 333–46.

Huhtamo, E. (1994) 'From Kaleidoscomaniac to Cybernerd: Towards an Archaeology of the Media'. In M. Tarkka (ed.), *ISEA '94 Catalogue*. Helsinki: The University of Art and Design, 130–5.

Huhtamo, E. (1995) Resurrecting the Technological Past: An Introduction to the Archeology of Media Art. *InterCommunication*, 14.

Huhtamo, E. (2011) 'Pockets of Plenty. An Archaeology of Mobile Media'. In M. Rieser (ed.), *The Mobile Audience: Media Art and Mobile Technologies*. Amsterdam/New York: Rodopi, 23–38.

Huntington, S. (1996) *The Clash of Civilizations and the Remaking of World Order*, New York: Simon & Schuster.

Hutter, M. (2015) *The Rise of the Joyful Economy: Artistic Invention and Economic Growth from Brunelleschi to Murakami*. London and New York: Routledge.

Huxley, J. (1942) *Evolution: The Modern Synthesis*. London: George Allen and Unwin: https://ia801600.us.archive.org/28/items/in.ernet.dli.2015.218848/2015.218848.Evolution-The.pdf.

Huxley, J. (1955) 'Guest Editorial: Evolution, Cultural and Biological'. *Yearbook of Anthropology*, 2–25.

Hyde, L. (1998) *Trickster Makes This World: How Disruptive Imagination Makes Culture*. Edinburgh: Canongate.

Ibrus, I. (2010) *Evolutionary Dynamics of New Media Forms: The Case of the Open Mobile Web*. London: LSE PhD theses: http://etheses.lse.ac.uk/53/.

Ibrus, I. (2012) 'The AV Industry's Microcompanies Encounter Multiplatform Production'. In I. Ibrus and C. A. Scolari (eds), *Crossmedia Innovations: Texts, Markets, Institutions*. Frankfurt: Peter Lang.

Ibrus, I. (2013a) 'Evolutionary Dynamics of the Mobile Web'. In J. Hartley, A. Bruns and J. Burgess (eds), *A Companion to New Media Dynamics*. Oxford: Wiley Blackwell.

Ibrus, I. (2013b) 'Evolutionary Dynamics of Media Convergence: Early Mobile Web and Its Standardisation at W3C'. *Telematics and Informatics*, 30(2), 66–73.

Ibrus, I. (2014) 'Path Dependencies in Media Design: Evolutionary Dynamics of Early Mobile Web and Its Textual Forms'. *Social Semiotics*, 24(2), 191–208. DOI: 10.1080/10350330.2013.859479.

Ibrus, I. (2015a) 'Histories of Ubiquitous Web Standardization'. In A. Bechmann and S. Lomborg (eds), *The Ubiquitous Internet: User and Industry Perspectives*. London: Routledge.

Ibrus, I. (2015b) 'Dialogic Control: Power in Media Evolution'. *International Journal of Cultural Studies*, 18(1), 43–59. DOI:10.1177/1367877914528117

Ibrus, I. (ed.) (2019) *Emergence of Cross-innovation Systems: Audiovisual Industries Co-innovating with Education, Health Care and Tourism*. Bingley: Emerald.

Ibrus, I. and M. Ojamaa (2014) What Is the Cultural Function and Value of European Transmedia Independents?' *International Journal of Communication* 8, 2283–300.

Ibrus, I. and M. Ojamaa (2018) 'Newsreels versus Newspapers versus Metadata – A Comparative Study of Metadata Modelling the 1930s in Estonia'. *VIEW Journal of European Television History and Culture*, 7(14), 123–37.

Ibrus, I. and M. Ojamaa (2020) 'The Creativity of Digital (Audiovisual) Archives: A Dialogue between Media Archaeology and Cultural Semiotics'. *Theory, Culture & Society*, 37(3), 49–70.

Ibrus, I. and S. Lassur (2019) 'Conclusions: Cross-innovations between Audiovisual and Tourism Sectors'. In I. Ibrus (ed.), *Emergence of Cross-innovation Systems*. London: Emerald Publishing Ltd, 201–6. https://doi.org/10.1108/978-1-78769-977-920191021.

Ibrus, I. and A. Nanì (2019) 'Cross-innovation, Is It a Thing?' In I. Indrek (ed.), *Emergence of Cross-innovation Systems: Audiovisual Industries Co-innovating with Education, Health Care and Tourism*. Bingley: Emerald.

Ibrus, I. and K. Tafel-Viia (2019) 'Conclusions: Cross-innovations between Audiovisual and Health Sectors'. In I. Ibrus (ed.), *Emergence of Cross-innovation Systems: Audiovisual Industries Co-innovating with Education, Health Care and Tourism*. Bingley: Emerald.

Ibrus, I. and M. Rajahonka (2019) 'Conclusions: Cross-innovations between Audiovisual and Education Sectors'. In *Emergence of Cross- innovation Systems: Audiovisual Industries Co-innovating with Education, Health Care and Tourism*. Bingley: Emerald, 105–11.

Ings, S. (2016) *Stalin and the Scientists: A History of Triumph and Tragedy 1905–1953*. London: Faber and Faber.

IRMA [Information Management Research Association] (2019) *Digital Curation: Breakthroughs in Research and Practice*. Hershey PA: IGI Global. DOI: 10.4018/978-1-5225-6921-3.

Ivanov, V. V. (1998) Избранные труды по семиотике и истории культуры: язык, семиотика, культура. *[Selected works on semiotics and cultural history: language, semiotics, culture]*, Vol VII. Moscow: Школа Языки Русской Культуры [Institute of Russian Language and Culture]. ISBN 5785900734; 9785785900738.

Иванов, В. В. [Ivanov, V. V.] et al. (1987) 'Об итогах и проблемах семиотических исследований'. [On the results and problems of semiotic studies] *Труды по знаковым системам [Sign System Studies]*, 20, 3–17.

Jakobson, R. (1971 [1959]) 'On Linguistic Aspects of Translation'. In *Selected Writings II, Word and Language*. The Hague, Paris: Mouton, 260–6.

Jakobson, R. (1985) *Selected Writings VII*. Berlin: Mouton.

Jane, E. A. (2017) 'Systemic Misogyny Exposed: Translating Rapeglish from the Manosphere with a Random Rape Threat Generator'. *International Journal of Cultural Studies*. https://doi.org/10.1177/1367877917734042.

Jane, E. and C. Fleming (2014) *Modern Conspiracy: The Importance of Being Paranoid*. London: Bloomsbury.

Jann, O. and C. Schottmüller (2018) 'Why Echo Chambers Are Useful'. Online: http://olejann.net/wp-content/uploads/echo_chambers.pdf.

Janssens, D. (2010) 'Easily, at a Glance': Aristotle's Political Optics'. *The Review of Politics*, 72, 385–408.

Jauss, H. (1982) *Toward an Aesthetic of Reception*. Minneapolis: University of Minnesota Press.

Jeffrey, D. (2020) *On Hope*. Sydney: Hachette Australia: ISBN: 9780733644665.

Jenkins, H. (2006) *Convergence Culture: Where Old and New Media Collide*. New York: NYU Press.

Jenkins, H. (2006b) *Fans, Bloggers, and Gamers: Exploring Participatory Culture*. New York: NYU Press.

Jenkins, H. (2011) 'Transmedia 202: Further Reflections'. In *Confessions of an Aca-Fan*: http://henryjenkins.org/blog/2011/08/defining_transmedia_further_re.html

Jenkins, H. (2019) '"Art Happens Not in Isolation, but in Community": The Collective Literacies of Media Fandom'. *Cultural Science Journal*, 11(1), 78–88. DOI: http://doi.org/10.5334/csci.125.

Jenkins, H., S. Ford and J. Green (2013) *Spreadable Media: Creating Meaning and Value in a Networked Culture*. New York: New York University Press.

Jenkins, H., S. Shresthova, L. Gamber-Thompson, N. Kligler-Vilenchik and A. Zimmerman (2016) *By Any Media Necessary: The New Youth Activism*. New York: NYU Press.

Jensen, K. B. (2013) 'Definitive and Sensitizing Conceptualizations of Mediatization'. *Communication Theory* 23(3), 203–22.

Johansson, O. (2010) Beyond ABBA: The Globalization of Swedish Popular Music. *Focus on Geography*, 53(4), 134–9.

Johnson, B. (2010) 'Institutional Learning'. In B. Lundvall (ed.), *National Systems of Innovation: Toward a Theory of Innovation and Interactive Learning*. London: Anthem Press.

Johnson-Yale, C. (2008) 'So-Called Runaway Film Production: Countering Hollywood's Outsourcing Narrative in the Canadian Press'. *Critical Studies in Media Communication*, 25(2), 113–34. DOI: 10.1080/15295030802032259.

Kadowaki, K., S. Yamamoto, H. Sato, A. Tanabe, A. Hidaka and H. Toju (2018) 'Mycorrhizal fungi Mediate the Direction and Strength of Plant – Soil Feedbacks Differently between Arbuscular Mycorrhizal and Ectomycorrhizal Communities'. *Nature – Communications Biology*, 196, DOI: 10.1038/s42003-018-0201-9. https://rdcu.be/bO7mK.

Kasparov, G. (2017) *Deep Thinking: Where Machine Intelligence Ends and Human Creativity Begins*. London: John Murray.

Katz, M. and C. Shapiro (1986) 'Technology Adoption in the Presence of Network Externalities'. *Journal of Political Economy*, 94(4), 822–41.

Kauffman, S. (1991) 'Antichaos and adaptation'. *Scientific American*, 265(2), 78–84.

Kawada, T. (2019) 'Life in the Mirror World'. *Wired Japan*, 33, 76–85.

Kawashima, N. and H-K. Lee (2018) *Asian Cultural Flows: Cultural Policies, Creative Industries, and Media Consumers*. Singapore: Springer.

Kean, H. and P. Howell (eds) (2018) *The Routledge Companion to Animal-Human History*. London: Routledge.

Keating, K. (2019) 'Driving Advocacy and Action'. *Matters Journal*, 29 May: https://mattersjournal.com/stories/katherinekeating.

Keightley, D. (2014) *These Bones Shall Rise Again: Selected Writings on Early China*. New York: Press.

Kelly, K. (2019) 'AR Will Spark the Next Big Tech Platform. Call It Mirrorworld'. *Wired*, 3.

Kinder, M. (2002) 'Narrative Equivocations between Movies and Games'. In D. Harries (ed.), *The New Media Book*. London: British Film Institute, 119–32.

Kinder, M. (2003) 'Uncanny Visions of History: Two Experimental Documentaries from Transnational Spain – *Asaltar los cielos* and *Tren de sombras*'. *Film Quarterly*, 56(3), 12–24.

Kittler, F. A. (1990) *Discourse Networks 1800/1900*. Stanford: Stanford University Press.

Kittler, F. A. (1994) 'Wenn die Freiheit wirklich existiert, dann soll sie doch ausbrechen. Discussion with Rudolf Maresch'. In R. Maresch (ed.), *Am Ende Vorbei*. Wien: Gespräche, 95–129.

Kittler, F. A. (1999) *Gramophone, Film, Typewriter*. Stanford: Stanford University Press.

Kittler, F. A. (2009) *Optical Media*. London: Polity Press.

Klastrup, L. and S. Tosca (2004) *Transmedial Worlds – Rethinking Cyber-world Design*: www.itu.dk/people/klastrup/klastruptosca_transworlds.pdf

Kondratieff, N. (1984) *Long Wave Cycle* (Trans. G. Daniels). New York: E P Dutton.

Kong, L. (2014) 'Transnational Mobilities and the Making of Creative Cities'. *Theory, Culture & Society*, 31(7–8), 273–89. DOI: 10.1177/0263276414549329.

Koskimaa, R. (2018) 'Management Skills'. In C. Scolari (ed.), *Teens, Media and Collaborative Cultures: Exploiting Teens' Transmedia Skills in the Classroom*. Barcelona: Universitat Pompeu Fabra, 33–43.

Kosnik, A. D., L. El Ghaoui, V. Cuntz-Leng, A. Godbehere, A. Horbinski, A. Hutz, R. Pastel and V. Pham (2015) 'Watching, Creating, and Archiving: Observations on the Quantity and Temporality of Fannish Productivity in Online Fan Fiction Archives'. *Convergence*, 21(1), 145–64.

Kotov, K. (2002) 'Semiosphere: A Chemistry of Being'. *Sign System Studies*, 30(1), 41–56.

Kress, G. (2003) *Literacy in the New Media Age*. London: Routledge.

Kress, G. (2010) *Multimodality. A Social Semiotic Approach to Contemporary Communication*. London: Routledge.

Kress, G. and T. van Leeuwen (2001) *Multimodal Discourse*. London: Arnold.

Krippendorff, K. (1995) 'Redesigning Design: An Invitation to a Responsible Future'. In P. Tahkokallio and S. Vihma (eds), *Design – Pleasure or Responsibility*, Helsinki: Helsinki University of Art and Design, 138–62.

Krippendorff, K. (1995) 'Undoing Power'. *Critical Studies in Mass Communication*, 12(2), 101–32.

Krippendorff, K. (2008) *Reconciling Radical Constructivism with Social Organisations as Networks of Conversations and of Stakeholders*. Paper presented at the American Society for Cybernetics 2008 Conference, Urbana, IL.

Krotz, F. (2007) 'The Meta-Process of Mediatization as a Conceptual Frame'. *Global Media and Communication*, 3(3), 256–60.

Krotz, F. and A. Hepp (2013) 'A Concretization of Mediatization: How Mediatization Works and Why "Mediatized Worlds" Are a Helpful Concept for Empirical Mediatization Research'. *Empedocles. European Journal for the Philosophy of Communication*, 3(2), 119–34.

Kull, K. (1998a) 'Organism as a Self-Reading Text: Anticipation and Semiosis'. *International Journal of Computing Anticipatory Systems*, 1, 93–104.

Kull, K. (1998b) 'On Semiosis, Umwelt, and Semiosphere'. *Semiotica*, 120, 299–310.

Kull, K. (1999) 'Towards Biosemiotics with Yuri Lotman'. *Semiotica*, 127(1/4), 115–31.

Kull, K. (2005) 'Semiosphere and a Dual Ecology: Paradoxes of Communication'. *Sign Systems Studies* 33(1): 175–89.

Kull, K. (2010) 'Umwelt'. In P. Cobley (ed.), *The Routledge Companion to Semiotics*. London: Routledge, 348–9.

Kull, K. (2015) 'A Semiotic Theory of Life: Lotman's Principles of the Universe of the Mind'. *Green Letters: Studies in Ecocriticism*, 19(3), 255–66.

Kull, K. (2018) 'Choosing and Learning: Semiosis Means Choice'. *Sign Systems Studies*, 46(4), 452–66.

Kull, K. and M. Lotman (2012) 'Semiotica Tartuensis: Jakob von Uexküll and Juri Lotman'. *Chinese Semiotic Studies*, 6(1), 312–23.

Kumar, V. S. P. and D. Agrawal (2003) 'WAP: Present and Future'. *IEEE Pervasive Computing*, 2(1), 79–83.

Küng [or Kueng], L. (2017) *Strategic Management in the Media: Theory to Practice*, 2nd edn. London: Sage Publications.

Kwon, K. (2011) *A Network Approach to Web 2.0 Social Influence: The Influentials, Word-of-mouth Effect, and the Emergence of Social Network on Facebook*. Buffalo: SUNY.

Kwon, S-H. and J. Kim (2014) 'The Cultural Industry Policies of the Korean Government and the Korean Wave'. *International Journal of Cultural Policy*, 20(4), 422–39. DOI: 10.1080/10286632.2013.829052.

Laclau, E. and C. Mouffe (1991) *Hegemony and Socialist Strategy: Towards a Radical Democratic Politics*, 2nd edn. London: Verso.

Lambert, J. (2013) *Digital Storytelling: Capturing Lives, Creating Community*, 4th edn. New York: Routledge.

Lampert, A. (2019) 'Over-Exploitation of Natural Resources Is Followed by Inevitable Declines in Economic Growth and Discount Rate'. *Nature Communications*, 10, 1419. https://doi.org/10.1038/s41467-019-09246-2.

Leach, E. (1976) *Culture and Communication: The Logic by Which Symbols Are Connected*. Cambridge: Cambridge University Press.

Leadbeater, C. (1999) *Living on Thin Air – The New Economy*. London: Penguin Books.

Leaver, T., T. Highfield and C. Abidin (2020) *Instagram: Visual Social Media Cultures*. Cambridge: Polity Press.

Legg, C. (2013) 'Peirce, Meaning, and the Semantic Web'. *Semiotica*, 193, 119–43.

Lesage, F. (2016) 'Reviewing Photoshop: Mediating Cultural Subjectivities for Application Software'. *Convergence: The International Journal of Research into New Media Technologies*, 22(2), 215–29.

Lesage, F. (2017) 'Popular Digital Imaging: Photoshop as Middlebroware'. In A. Malinowska and K. Lebek (eds), *Materiality and Popular Culture: The Popular Life of Things*. London: Routledge, 76–87.

Licoppe, C. (2004) '"Connected" Presence: The Emergence of a New Repertoire for Managing Social Relationships in a Changing Communication Technospace'. *Environment and Planning D: Society and Space* 22(1), 135–56.

Lindmark, S., E. Bohlin and E. Andersson (2004) 'Japan's Mobile Internet Success Story – Facts, Myths, Lessons and Implications'. *info*, 6(6), 348–58.

Lipovetsky, G. (1991) *The Empire of Fashion: Dressing Modern Democracy* (Trans. C. Porter). Princeton: Princeton University Press.

List, F. (1841), *The National System of Political Economy*. Accessible at: https://oll.libertyfund.org/titles/list-the-national-system-of-political-economy

Livingstone, S. (2004) 'Media Literacy and the Challenge of New Information and Communication Technologies'. *The Communication Review*, 7(1), 3–14.

Loasby, B. (1999) *Knowledge, Institutions and Evolution in Economics*. London: Routledge.

Lobato, R. (2010) 'Creative Industries and Informal Economies: Lessons from Nollywood'. *International Journal of Cultural Studies*, 13(4), 337–54. DOI: 10.1177/1367877910369971.

Lobato, R. (2016) 'The Cultural Logic of Digital Intermediaries: YouTube Multichannel Networks'. *Convergence*, 22(4), 348–60. DOI: 10.1177/1354856516641628

Lotman, J. (1977 [1970]) *The Structure of the Artistic Text*. Ann Arbor, MI: University of Michigan Press: https://monoskop.org/images/3/3e/Lotman_Jurij_The_Structure_of_the_Artistic_Text_1977.pdf.

Lotman, J. (1979a) 'The Future for Structural Poetics'. *Poetics*, 8, 501–7.

Lotman, J. (1979b) 'The Origin of Plot in the Light of Typology'. *Poetics Today*, 1(1/2), 161–84. DOI: 10.2307/1772046. http://www.zbi.ee/~kalevi/LotmanPlot.htm.

Lotman, J. (1988a [1981]) 'The Semiotics of Culture and the Concept of a Text'. *Soviet Psychology*, 26(3), 52–8. DOI: 10.2753/RPO1061-0405260352

Lotman, Y. (1988b) 'Text within a Text'. *Soviet Psychology*, 26(3), 32–51. DOI: 10.2753/RPO1061-0405260332.

Lotman, J. (1990) *Universe of the Mind: A Semiotic Theory of Culture*. London and New York: I.B. Tauris.

Lotman, J. (1994 [1981]) 'The Text within the Text'. *PMLA*, 109(3), 377–84

Lotman, Y. (1988) 'Text within a Text'. *Soviet Psychology*, 26(3), 32–51, DOI: 10.2753/RPO1061-0405260332.

Lotman, J. (1997 [1989]) 'Culture as a Subject and an Object in Itself'. Trames: A Journal of the Humanities and Social Sciences, 1(1), 7–16.

Lotman, J. (2005 [1984]) 'On the Semiosphere'. *Sign Systems Studies*, 33(1), 205–29.

Lotman, J. (2009 [1992]) *Culture and Explosion*. Berlin: Mouton de Gruyter.

Lotman, J. (2011 [1967]) 'The Place of Art among Other Modelling Systems'. *Sign Systems Studies*, 39(2/4), 249–70.

Lotman, J. (2012 [1992]) 'Text and Cultural Polyglotism'. In *Abstracts of the International Congress on Cultural Polyglotism Dedicated to the Anniversary of Juri Lotman's 90th Birthday*. Tartu, 9–14.

Lotman, J. (2014) *Non-Memoirs*. Champaign, IL: Dalkey Archive Press.

Lotman, M. (2013) *The Unpredictable Workings of Culture*. Tallinn: Tallinn University Press.

Лотман, Ю. М. (1974) 'О соотношении первичного и вторичного в коммуникативно-модели-рующих системах'. *Материалы Всесоюзного симпозиума по вторичным моделирующим системам I (5)*. Тарту: Тартуский государственный университет, 224–8.

Лотман, Ю. М. (1981) 'Мозг – текст – культура – искусственный интеллект'. *Семиотика и информатика*, 17, 3–17.

Лотман, Ю. М. (2000 [1989]) 'Культура как субъект и сама-себе объект'. *О семиосфере. Культура и взрыв. Внутри мыслящих миров. Статьи. Исследования. Заметки*. Санкт-Петербург: Искусство-СПБ, 639–47.

Лотман, Ю. М. (2000 [1986]) 'Память культуры'. *О семиосфере. Культура и взрыв. Внутри мыслящих миров. Статьи. Исследования. Заметки*. Санкт-Петербург: Искусство-СПБ, 614–21.

Лотман, Ю. М. (2000 [1985]) 'Память в культурологическом освещении'. *О семиосфере. Культура и взрыв. Внутри мыслящих миров. Статьи. Исследования. Заметки*. Санкт-Петербург: Искусство-СПБ, 673–6.

Лотман, Ю. М. И. З. Г. М. [J. Lotman and Z. Mints] (1981) 'Литература и мифология' [Literature and Mythology]. *Труды по знаковым системам [Sign System Studies]*, 13, 35–55.

Lotman, J. M., B. A. Uspensky and G. Mihaychuk (1978) 'On the Semiotic Mechanism of Culture'. *New Literary History*, 9(2), 211–32.

Lotman, J. M., V. V. Ivanov, A. M. Pjatigorskij, V. N. Toporov and B. A. Uspenskij (2013 [1973]) 'Theses on the Semiotic Study of Cultures (as Applied to Slavic Texts)'. In S. Salupere, P. Torop and K. Kull (eds), *Beginnings of the Semiotics of Culture*. Tartu: University of Tartu Press, 51–77.

Lotman, M. (2013) 'Afterword: Semiotics and Unpredictability'. In J. Lotman (ed.), *The Unpredictable Workings of Culture*. Tallinn: TLU Press, 239–74.

Luhmann, N. (1995) *Social Systems*. Stanford: Stanford University Press.

Lundby, K. (ed.) (2008) *Digital Storytelling, Mediatized Stories: Self-Representations in New Media*. New York: Peter Lang.

Lundby, K. (2009) *Mediatization: Concept, Changes, Consequences*. New York: Peter Lang.

Lundgren, A. (1991) *Technological Innovation and Industrial Evolution: The Emergence of Industrial Networks*. Stockholm: Akademisk Avhandling.

Lundvall, B. (1992) *National Innovation Systems: Towards a Theory of Innovation and Interactive Learning*. London: Pinter.

Lundvall, B. (ed.) (2010) *National Systems of Innovation: Toward a Theory of Innovation and Interactive Learning*. London: Anthem Press.

Lundvall, B. (2010) 'User-Producer Relationships, National Systems of Innovation and Internationalisation'. In B. Lundvall (ed.), *National Systems of Innovation: Toward a Theory of Innovation and Interactive Learning*. London: Anthem Press.

Madisson, M-L. (2014) 'The Semiotic Logic of Signification of Conspiracy Theories'. *Semiotica*, 202, 273–300.

Madisson, M-L. and A. Ventsel (2016) 'Autocommunicative Meaning-Making in Online Communication of the Estonian Extreme Right'. *Signs Systems Studies* 44(3), 326–54.

MacGregor, N. (2018) *Living with the Gods: On Beliefs and Peoples*. London: Allen Lane.

Madrigal, A. (2014) 'How Netflix Reverse Engineered Hollywood'. *The Atlantic*, 2 January.

Mandoki, K. (2004) Power and Semiosis. *Semiotica*, 151(1/4), 97–114.

Manovich, L. (2001) *The Language of New Media*. Cambridge, MA: MIT Press.

Manovich, L. (2017a) *Instagram and Contemporary Image*. Online: http:// manovich.net/index.php/projects/instagram-and-contemporary-image.

Манович, Л. (2017b) *Теории софт-культуры*. Нижний Новгород: Красная ласточка. [Manovich, L. (2017b) *Theories of Soft Culture*. Nizhny Novgorod: Red Swallow].

Mansell, J. (2017) *The Age of Noise in Britain: Hearing Modernity*. Urbana, IL: University of Illinois Press.

Mansell, R. (2012) *Imagining the Internet: Communication, Innovation, and Governance*. Oxford: Oxford University Press.

Mansell, R. and E. Berdou (2009) Political Economy, the Internet and Free/Open Source Software Development. In J. Hunsinger, M. Allen and L. Klastrup (eds), *International Handbook of Internet Research*. Amsterdam: Springer.

Mansell, R. and R. Silverstone (1996) 'Introduction'. In R. S. Robin Mansell (ed.), *Communication by Design: The Politics of Information and Communication Technologies*. Oxford: Oxford University Press, 1–14.

Martin, F., S. Duplessis, F. Ditengou, H. Lagrange, C. Voiblet and F. Lapeyrie (2001) 'Developmental Cross-Talking in the Ectomycorrhizal Symbiosis: Signals and Communication Genes'. *New Phytologist*, 151 (issue on *Signalling in Plants*), 145–54: https://nph.onlinelibrary.wiley.com/doi/pdf/10.1046/j.1469-8137.2001.00169.x.

Maturana, H. and F. Varela (1980) *Autopoiesis and Cognition: The Realization of the Living*. Dordrecht: Reidel; Boston, MA: Kluwer.

Maxwell, R. and T. Miller (2012) *Greening the Media*. New York: Oxford University Press.

Maxwell, R., J. Raundalen and N. Vestberg (eds) (2014) *Media and the Ecological Crisis*. New York: Routledge.

Mazzucato, M. (2015) 'Innovation Systems: From Fixing Market Failures to Creating Markets'. *Intereconomics*, 50(3), 120–5: https://www.researchgate.net/publication/310465935_Innovation_Systems_From_Fixing_Market_Failures_to_Creating_Markets.

Mazzucato, M. (2018) *The Value of Everything: Making and Taking in the Global Economy*. Milton Keynes: Allen Lane.

McAfee, A. and E. Brynjolfsson (2017) *Machine, Platform, Crowd: Harnessing Our Digital Future*. New York: W. W. Norton.

McCloskey, D. (2006) *The Bourgeois Virtues: Ethics for an Age of Commerce*. Chicago: University of Chicago Press.

McCloskey, D. (2010) *Bourgeois Dignity: Why Economics Can't Explain the Modern World*. Chicago: University of Chicago Press.

McCloskey, D. (2016) *Bourgeois Equality: How Ideas, Not Capital or Institutions, Enriched the World*. Chicago: University of Chicago Press.

McCoy, P. (2016) *Radical Mycology: A Treatise on Seeing and Working with Fungi*. Portland, OR: Chthaeus Press: https://chthaeus.com/collections/books-1/products/radical-mycology-a-treatise-on-seeing-working-with-fungi.

McKinsey (2016) *Digital Globalization: The New Era of Global Flows*. McKinsey Global Institute, February: https://www.mckinsey.com/business-functions/mckinsey-digital/our-insights/digital-globalization-the-new-era-of-global-flows.

McLuhan, M. (1964) *Understanding Media: The Extensions of Man*. New York: McGraw-Hill.

Merrick, H. (2009) *The Secret Feminist Cabal: A Cultural History of Science Fiction Feminisms*. Seattle, WA: Aqueduct Press.

Mesoudi, A. (2011) *Cultural Evolution: How Darwinian Theory Can Explain Human Culture and Synthesize the Social Sciences*. Chicago: Chicago University Press.

Miller, T. (2020) 'Future Perfect TV – and TV Studies'. In S. Shimpach (ed.), *The Routledge Companion to Global Television*. New York and London: Routledge, 84–96.

Miller, V. (2008) 'New Media, Networking and Phatic Culture'. *Convergence*, 14(4), 387–400.

Mitchell, W. J. T. (2005) 'There Are No Visual Media'. *Journal of Visual Culture*, 4(2), 257–66.

Mokyr, J. (2009) *The Enlightened Economy: An Economic History of Britain 1700–1850*. New Haven, CT: Yale University Press.

Monticelli, D. (2016) 'Critique of Ideology or/and Analysis of Culture? Barthes and Lotman on Secondary Semiotic Systems'. *Signs Systems Studies*, 44(3), 432–51.

Moore, P. (2015) *The Weather Experiment: The Pioneers Who Sought to See the Future*. New York: Farrar, Straus & Giroux.

Moore, T., M. Gibson and C. Lumby (2017) 'Recovering the Australian Working Class'. In D. O'Neill and M. Wayne (eds), *Considering Class: Theory, Culture and the Media in the 21st Century*. The Netherlands: Brill, 217–34.

Morgan, S. (2006) *The Feminist History Reader*. London: Routledge.

Morozov, E. (2014) *To Save Everything, Click Here: The Folly of Technological Solutionism*. USA: PublicAffairs.

Morsing, M. (2006) 'Corporate Social Responsibility as Strategic Auto-Communication: On the Role of External Stakeholders for Member Identification'. *Business Ethics: A European Review*, 15(2), 171–82.

Needham, J. (1954) *Science and Civilisation in China, Vol. 1*. Cambridge: Cambridge University Press: https://monoskop.org/images/3/30/Needham_Joseph_Science_and_Civilisation_in_China_Vol_1_Introductory_Orientations.pdf.

Nelson, C. (2010) *Representing the Black Female Subject in Western Art*. New York: Routledge.

Nelson, R. and S. Winter (1982) *An Evolutionary Theory of Economic Change*. Cambridge, MA: Harvard University Press.

Nelson, T. (1965) 'A File Structure for the Complex, the Changing and the Indeterminate'. In *Proceedings of the ACM 20th National Conference*. New York: ACM Press, 84–100.

Nelson, T. (2010) *Possiplex: Movies, Intellect, Creative Control, My Computer Life and the Fight for Civilization: An Autobiography of Ted Nelson*. Hackettstown NJ: Mindful Press.

Neubauer, L. and A. Repenning: (2019) *Vom Ende der Klimakrise – Eine Geschichte unserer Zukunft*. Stuttgart: Tropen Verlag, ISBN 978-3-608-50455-2

Neylon, C. (2015) 'The Limits on "Open": Why Knowledge Is not a Public Good and What to Do about It'. *Science in the Open*, 22 October: http://cameronneylon.net/blog/the-limits-on-open-why-knowledge-is-not-a-public-good-and-what-to-do-about-it/.

North, D. C. (1990) *Institutions, Institutional Change and Economic Performance*. Cambridge: Cambridge University Press.

Nöth, W. (2006) 'Yuri Lotman on Metaphors and Culture as Self-Referential Semiospheres'. *Semiotica*, 161(1/4), 249–63. DOI: 10.1515/SEM.2006.065: https://philarchive.org/archive/NTHYLOv1.

Nöth, W. (2015) 'The Topography of Yuri Lotman's Semiosphere'. *International Journal of Cultural Studies*, 18(1), 11–26. DOI: https://doi.org/10.1177/1367877914528114.

Nunes, M. (2019) 'Memory of the Future, Explosion, Panchronism: The Semiotics of Lotman and Studies of Memory and Time in Juvenile Theatricalities'. *Bakhtiniana, Rev. Estud. Discurso*, 14(4), São Paulo: http://www.scielo.br/scielo.php?pid=S2176-45732019000400192&script=sci_arttext&tlng=en.

O'Dair, M. (2019) *Distributed Creativity: How Blockchain Technology Will Transform the Creative Economy*. London: Palgrave Macmillan.

Odum, H. (1995) 'Self-Organization and Maximum Empower'. In C. Hall (ed.), *Maximum Power: The Ideas and Applications of H.T. Odum*. Colorado: Colorado University Press.

OECD (1997) *National Innovation Systems*. Paris (France): https://www.oecd.org/science/inno/2101733.pdf.

Ong, W. J. (2012) *Orality and Literacy: The Technologizing of the Word*. 30th Anniversary Edition with additional chapters by John Hartley. London: Routledge.

O'Regan, T. (1996) *Australian National Cinema*. London: Routledge.

Ostrom, E. (1990) *Governing the Commons: The Evolution of Institutions for Collective Action*. New York: Cambridge University Press.

Papacharissi, Z. (2009) 'The Virtual Sphere 2.0: The Internet, the Public Sphere, and Beyond'. In A. Chadwick and P. Howard (eds), *Routledge Handbook of Internet Politics*. London and New York: Routledge, 230–45.

Papacharissi, Z. (2010) *A Private Sphere: Democracy in a Digital Age*. Cambridge: Polity Press.

Parikka, J. (2013) Archival Media Theory: An Introduction to Wolfgang Ernst's Media Archaeology. In J. Parikka (ed.), *Digital Memory and the Archive*. Minneapolis and London: University of Minnesota Press, 1–22.

Parikka, J. (2014) *The Anthrobscene*. Minneapolis: University of Minnesota Press.

Parikka, J. (2015) *A Geology of Media*. Minneapolis: University of Minnesota Press.

Pariser, E. (2011) *The Filter Bubble: What the Internet Is Hiding from You*. London: Penguin Books.

Peirce, C. S. (1988) 'Pragmatism as the Logic of Abduction'. In *The Essential Peirce: Selected Philosophical Writings, 1893–1913*. Bloomington: Indiana University Press.

Peirce, C. S. (1991) *Peirce on Signs: Writings on Semiotic by Charles Sanders Peirce* (ed. J. Hoopes). Chapel Hill, NC: University of North Carolina Press.

Peltzman, D. (2012) 'The Impact of Runaway Productions on Hollywood Labor Organizations'. *InMedia*, 1. https://journals.openedition.org/inmedia/123.

Perez, C. (2009) 'Technological Revolutions and Techno-Economic Paradigms'. *Working Papers in Technology Governance and Economic Dynamics*, no. 20. http://hum.ttu.ee/wp/paper20.pdf.

Peters, J. D. (1999) *Speaking into the Air: A History of the Idea of Communication*. Chicago, IL: University of Chicago Press.

Phillips, A. (2012) *A Creator's Guide to Transmedia Storytelling: How to Captivate and Engage Audiences across Multiple Platforms*. New York: McGraw-Hill.

Phillips, W. and R. Milner (2017) *The Ambivalent Internet: Mischief, Oddity, and Antagonism Online*. Cambridge: Polity Press.

Pias, C. (ed.) (2016) *The Macy Conferences 1946–1953. The Complete Transactions*. Chicago, IL: University of Chicago Press.

Pilshchikov, I. and M. Trunin (2016) 'The Tartu-Moscow School of Semiotics: A Transnational Perspective'. *Sign Systems Studies*, 44(3), 368–401. http://dx.doi.org/10.12697/SSS.2016.44.3.04.

Pomerantz, J. (2015) *Metadata*. Cambridge, MA: MIT Press.

Porcar, M. and J. Peretó (2019) 'Manufactured Life: The Scientific and Social Challenges of Synthetic Biology'. *Mètode Science Studies Journal – Annual Review*. DOI: http://dx.doi.org/10.7203/metode.10.13229.

Pottage, A. (1998) 'Power as an Art of Contingency: Luhmann, Deleuze, Foucault'. *Economy and Society*, 27(1), 1–27.

Potts, J. (2003) 'Evolutionary Economics: An Introduction to the Foundation of Liberal Economic Philosophy'. *University of Queensland*: School of Economics Discussion Paper No 324: http://www.uq.edu.au/economics/abstract/324.pdf.

Potts, J. (2011) *Creative Industries and Economic Evolution*. Cheltenham: Edward Elgar.

Potts, J. (2019) *Innovation Commons*. Oxford: Oxford University Press.

Potts, J. and J. Hartley (2018) 'Two New Creative Industries: Blockchain and Staged Conflict'. *Medium*: https://medium.com/@jason.potts/two-new-creative-industries-blockchain-and-staged-conflict-830c2e9a5c24.

Potts, J. and E. Rennie (2019) 'Web3 for Creative Industries: How Blockchain Is Reshaping Business Models'. In S. Cunningham and T. Flew (eds), *A Research Agenda for the Creative Industries*. Cheltenham: Edward Elgar, 93–111.

Potts, J., S. Cunningham, J. Hartley and P. Ormerod (2008) 'Social Network Markets: A New Definition of the Creative Industries'. *Journal of Cultural Economy*, 32, 167–85.

Potts, J., J. Hartley, L. Montgomery, C. Neylon and E. Rennie (2017) 'A Journal Is a Club: A New Economic Model for Scholarly Publishing'. *Prometheus: Critical Studies in Innovation*, 35(1), 75–92. DOI: 10.1080/08109028.2017.1386949.

Pratt, A. (2009) 'Policy Transfer and the Field of the Cultural and Creative Industries: What Can Be Learned from Europe?' In L. Kong and J. O'Connor (eds), *Creative Economies, Creative Cities: Asian-European Perspectives*. Dordrecht: Springer Netherlands, 9–23.

Pratten, R. (2011) *Getting Started in Transmedia Storytelling: A Practical Guide for Beginners*. San Francisco: CreateSpace.

Prigogine, I. and I. Stengers (1984; new edn 2018) *Order Out of Chaos: Man's New Dialogue with Nature*. London: Verso.

Primorac, J. (2019) 'The Impact of Global Film Productions on the Local Audio-Visual Labour Market'. *Paper Presented at the Annual Conference of International Association of Media and Communication Research*, Madrid.

Propp, V. (1968/1928) *Morphology of the Folktale*. Austin, TX: University of Texas Press.

Quiggin, J. (2001) 'Globalization and Economic Sovereignty'. *Journal of Political Philosophy*, 9(1), 56–80. https://doi.org/10.1111/1467-9760.00118.

Ravelli, L. and T. van Leeuwen (2018) 'Modality in the Digital Age'. *Visual Communication*, 17(3), 277–97.

Reading, A. (2011) 'Memory and Digital Media: Six Dynamics of the Globital Memory Field'. In M. Neiger, O. Meyers and E. Zandberg (eds), *On Media Memory: Collective Memory in a New Media Age*. London: Palgrave Macmillan, 241–52.

Reed, D. (2001) 'The Law of the Pack'. *Harvard Business Review*, February, 23–4.

Rennie, E., J. Potts and A. Pochesneva (2019) *Blockchain and the Creative Industries: Provocation Paper*. Melbourne: RMIT Analysis and Policy Observatory. DOI: 10.25916/5dc8a108dc471.

Rigney, A. (2005). 'Plenitude, Scarcity and the Circulation of Cultural Memory'. *Journal of European Studies*, 35(1), 11–28. DOI: https://doi.org/10.1177/0047244105051158.

Riley, M., L. Machado, B. Roussabrov, T. Branyen, P. Bhawalkar, E. Jin and A. Kansara (2018) 'AVA: The Art and Science of Image Discovery at Netflix'. *Netflix TechBlog*: https://medium.com/netflix-techblog/ava-the-art-and-science-of-image-discovery-at-netflix-a442f163af6

Rivett, M. (2000) 'Approaches to Analysing the Web Text: A Consideration of the Web Site as an Emergent Cultural Form'. *Convergence*, 6(3), 34–56.

Rohn, U. (2010) *Cultural Barriers to the Success of Foreign Media Content: Western Media in China, India, and Japan*. Frankfurt: Peter Lang.

Rohn, U. (2011) 'Lacuna or Universal?: Introducing a New Model for Understanding Cross-Cultural Audience Demand'. *Media, Culture & Society*, 33(4), 631–41.

Romer, J. (2012) *A History of Ancient Egypt: From the First Farmers to the Great Pyramid*. London: Allen Lane.

Rose, N. (1999) *Governing the Soul: The Shaping of the Private Self*. London, New York: Free Association Books.

Roulstone, I. (2015) 'The Impact of Mathematics on Meteorology and Weather Prediction'. *London Mathematical Society Impact150 Stories* (ed. J. Greenlees), Ch1, 1–8: DOI: 10.1112/i150lms/t.0001.

Roy, R. D. (2018) 'Decolonise Science – Time to End Another Imperial Era'. *The Conversation*, 5 April: https://theconversation.com/decolonise-science-time-to-end-another-imperial-era-89189.

Rühse, V. (2017) 'The Digital Collection of the Rijksmuseum: Open Content and the Commercialization of a National Museum'. In O. Grau (ed.), *Museum and Archive on the Move: Changing Cultural Institutions in the Digital Era*. Berlin: de Gruyter, 37–56.

Salthe, S. (2007) 'Meaning in Nature: Placing Biosemiotics in Pansemiotics'. In M. Barbieri (ed.), *Biosemiotics: Information, Codes and Signs in Living Systems*. New York: Nova Publishers. Chapter 10.

Salupere, S. (2015) 'The Cybernetic Layer of Juri Lotman's Metalanguage'. *Recherches sémiotiques/Semiotic Inquiry*, 35(1), 63–84.

Salupere, S., P. Torop and K. Kull (eds) (2013) *Beginnings of the Semiotics of Culture*. Tartu: University of Tartu Press.

Saussure, F. D. (1974) *Course in General Linguistics*. London: Fontana.

Sawhney, H. and S. Lee (2005) 'Arenas of Innovation: Understanding New Configural Potentialities of Communication Technologies'. *Media, Culture & Society*, 27(3), 391–414.

Schäfer, M. K. and K. van Es (eds) (2017) *The Datafied Society: Studying Culture through Data*. Amsterdam: Amsterdam University Press.

Schich, M. et al. (2014) 'A Network Framework of Cultural History'. *Science*, 345(6196), 558–62.

Schneiderman, J. (2015) 'Naming the Anthropocene'. *philoSOPHIA*, 5(2), 179–201: https://muse.jhu.edu/article/608467.

Schönle, A. (2001) 'Social Power and Individual Agency: The Self in Greenblatt and Lotman'. *The Slavic and East European Journal*, 45(1), 61–79.

Schönle, A. (2003) 'Lotman and Cultural Studies: The Case for Cross-fertilization'. *Sign System Studies*, 30(2), 429–40.

Schönle, A. and J. Shine (2006) 'Introduction'. In A. Schönle (ed.), *Lotman and Cultural Studies: Encounters and Extensions*. Madison, WI: University of Wisconsin Press, 3–35.

Schulz, W. (2004) 'Reconstructing Mediatization as an Analytical Concept'. *European Journal of Communication*, 1(19), 87–101.

Schumpeter, J. (1939) *Business Cycles: A Theoretical, Historical and Statistical Analysis of the Capitalist Process*. New York and London: McGraw-Hill.

Scolari, C. (2013) 'Lostology: Transmedia Storytelling and Expansion/Compression Strategies'. *Semiotica*, 195, 45–68.

Scolari, C., P. Bertetti and M. Freeman (2014) *Transmedia Archaeology: Storytelling in the Borderlines of Science Fiction, Comics and Pulp Magazines*. London: Palgrave Macmillan.

Scolari, C., M.-J. Masanet, M. Guerrero-Pico and M.-J. Establés (2018) 'Transmedia Literacy in the New Media Ecology: Teens' Transmedia Skills and Informal Learning Strategies'. *El profesional de la información*, 27(4), 801–12.

Sebeok, T. (2001) *Global Semiotics*. Bloomington IN: Indiana University Press.

Sebeok, T. and M. Danesi (2000) *The Forms of Meaning: Modeling Systems Theory and Semiotic Analysis*. Berlin: Mouton de Gruyter.

Senft, T. and N. Baym (2015) 'What Does the Selfie Say? Investigating a Global Phenomenon. Introduction to a Special Section on the Selfie'. *International Journal of Communication*, 9, 1588–606.

Sennett, R. (2016) 'The Pnyx and the Agora'. *Reading Design*: https://www.readingdesign.org/the-pnyx-and-the-agora. http://eprints.lse.ac.uk/68075/, pdf: 6-9.

Sevignani, S. (2017) 'Surveillance, Classification, and Social Inequality in Informational Capitalism: The Relevance of Exploitation in the Context of Markets in Information'. *Historical Social Research/Historische Sozialforschung*, 42(1) (159), 77–102.

Shannon, C. and W. Weaver (1949) *The Mathematical Theory of Communication*. Urbana: The University of Illinois Press.

Sharma, C. and Y. Nakamura (2003) *Wireless Data Services*. Cambridge: Cambridge University Press.

Shimpach, S. (ed.) (2020) *The Routledge Companion to Global Television*. New York and London: Routledge.

Shklovsky, V. (2015) 'Art, as Device'. Translated with an introduction by A. Berlina (first published in 1919). *Poetics Today*, 36, 3, 151–74: https://warwick.ac.uk/ fac/arts/english/currentstudents/undergraduate/modules/fulllist/first/en122/ lecturelist2017-18/art_as_device_2015.pdf.

Silverstone, R. (1999) *Why Study the Media?* London: Sage Publications.

Silverstone, R. (2007) *Media and Morality: On the Rise of the Mediapolis*. Cambridge: Polity.

Sigurdson, J. (2001) *WAP OFF – Origin, Failure and Future* (Vol. 135). Stockholm: Stockholm School of Economics.

Simon, H. (2000) 'Public Administration in Today's World of Organizations and Markets'. *PS: Political Science and Politics*, 33(4), 749–56.

Sloterdijk, P. (2011) *Bubbles. Spheres Volume I: Microspherology*. Pasadena, CA: Semiotext(e).

Sloterdijk, P. (2014) *Globes. Vol II of Spheres: Macrospherology*. Pasadena, CA: Semiotext(e).

Sloterdijk, P. (2016) *Foams. Spheres Volume III: Plural Spherology*. Pasadena, CA: Semiotext(e).

Sorkin, M. (2016) 'Parametrics and Power: How the Social, Economic, and Political Forces that Impact Architecture are Moving to Shape the Future'. *Architectural Record*, September: https://www.architecturalrecord.com/ articles/11850-parametrics-and-power.

Soukup, C. (2000) 'Building a Theory of Multi-media CMC: An Analysis, Critique and Integration of Computer-Mediated Communication Theory and Research'. *New Media and Society*, 2(4), 407–25: https://shareok.org/bitstream/ handle/11244/25374/10.1177.1461444800002004002.pdf.

Sperling, A. (2019) 'Anthropocene'. In R. T. Goodman (ed.), *The Bloomsbury Handbook of 21st-Century Feminist Theory*. London: Bloomsbury, 311–24.

Srnicek, N. (2016) *Platform Capitalism*. Cambridge: Polity Press.

Steedman, M. (2006) 'State Power, Hegemony, and Memory: Lotman and Gramsci'. In A. Schönle (ed.), *Lotman and Cultural Studies: Encounters and Extensions* Madison, WI: University of Wisconsin Press, 136–58.

Steele, E., et al. (2018) 'Cause of Cambrian Explosion – Terrestrial or Cosmic?' *Progress in Biophysics and Molecular Biology*. Online: https://www. sciencedirect.com/science/article/pii/S0079610718300798.

Steinbock, D. (2003) *Wireless Horizon: Strategy and Competition in the Worldwide Mobile Marketplace*. New York: AMACOM.

Straubhaar, J. (1991) 'Beyond Media Imperialism: Asymmetrical Interdependence and Cultural Proximity'. *Critical Studies in Mass Communication*, 8(1), 39–59. DOI: 10.1080/15295039109366779.

Straubhaar, J. (2018) 'Netflix and the Rise of Transverse, Transnational Flows'. Tallinn: Tallinn University: https://www.youtube.com/ watch?v=jHeHP3zk6FM&t=545s.

Strauven, W. (2011) 'The Observer's Dilemma: To Touch or Not to Touch'. In E. Huhtamo and J. Parikka (eds), *Media Archaeology: Approaches, Applications, and Implications*. Berkeley: University of California Press, 148–63.

Swedberg, R. (2006) 'The Cultural Entrepreneur and the Creative Industries'. *Journal of Cultural Economics*, 30(4), 243–61.

Szczepanik, P. (2013) 'Globalization through the Eyes of Runners: Student Interns as Ethnographers on Runaway Productions in Prague'. *Media Industries Journal* 1(1), 56–61.

Szczepanik, P. (2015) 'Transnational Crews and the Post-socialist Precarity: Globalizing Screen Media Labor in Prague'. In M. Curtin and K. Sanson (eds), *Precarious Creativity: Global Media, Local Labor*. Oakland, CA: University of California Press, 88–103.

Tee, R. (2005) 'Different Directions in the Mobile Internet: Analysing Mobile Internet Services in Japan and Europe'. In A. Zerdick, A. Picot, K. Schrape, J. C. Burgelman, R. Silverstone, V. Feldmann, C. Wernick and C. Wolff (eds), *E-merging Media: Communication and the Media Economy of the Future*. Berlin: Springer, 143–59.

Thompson, C. (2019) 'Code Space'. *Wired*, 6, 26–31.

Thumim, N. (2012) *Self-Representation and Digital Culture*. London: Palgrave Macmillan.

Thunberg, G. (2019) *No One Is Too Small to Make a Difference*. London: Penguin Books.

Tomasello, M. (2000) 'First Steps toward a Usage-Based Theory of Language Acquisition'. *Cognitive Linguistics*, 11(1/2), 61–82.

Tomasello, M. (2014) *A Natural History of Human Thinking*. Cambridge, MA: Harvard University Press.

Torlasco, D. (2013) *The Heretical Archive: Digital Memory at the End of Film*. Minneapolis: University of Minnesota Press.

Torop, P. (2004) 'Semiospherical Understanding: Textuality'. *Signs Systems Studies*, 31(2), 323–39.

Torop, P. (2005) 'Semiosphere and/as the Research Object of Semiotics of Culture'. *Sign Systems Studies*, 33, 169–83.

Torop, P. (2008) 'Translation as Communication and auto-Communication'. *Sign Systems Studies*, 36(2), 375–97.

Torop, P. (2009) 'Foreword: Lotmanian Explosion'. In J. Lotman, *Culture and Explosion*. Berlin: Mouton de Gruyter, xxvii–xxxix.

Torop, P. (2017) 'Semiotics of Cultural History'. *Sign Systems Studies*, 45(3/4), 317–34.

Tsing, A. L. (2015) *The Mushroom at the End of the World: On the Possibility of Life in Capitalist Ruins*. Princeton, NJ: Princeton University Press.

Tufekci, Z. (2017) *Twitter and Tear Gas: The Power and Fragility of Networked Protest*. New Haven, CT: Tale University Press.

Tunstall, J. (1977) *The Media Are American: Anglo-American Media in the World*. New York: Columbia University Press.

Tunstall, J. (2008) *The Media Were American: US Mass Media in Decline*. New York: Oxford University Press.

Uexküll, J. V. (1909) *Umwelt und Innenwelt der Tiere*. Berlin: J. Springer.

Uexküll, J. von (1957) 'A Stroll through the Worlds of Animals and Men: A Picture Book of Invisible Worlds' (1934). In C. H. Schiller (ed.), *Instinctive Behavior: The Development of a Modern Concept*. New York: International Universities Press, 5–80.

Vaan, M. de, B. Vedres and D. Stark (2015) 'Game Changer: The Topology of Creativity'. *American Journal of Sociology*, 120(4), 1144–94.

Västrik, E-H. (2015) 'In Search of Genuine Religion: The Contemporary Estonian Maausulised Movement and National Discourse'. In K. Rountree (ed.), *Contemporary Pagan and Native Faith Movements in Europe: Colonialist and Nationalist Impulses*. Oxford: Berghahn, 130–53.

Veblen, T. (1898, July) 'Why Is Economics Not an Evolutionary Science?' *The Quarterly Journal of Economics*, 12(4), 373–97.

Veblen, T. (2017) *The Place of Science in Modern Civilization*. New York: Routledge.

*Vernadsky, V. I. (1925) 'Human Autotrophy'. Republished *in 21st Century Science & Technology*, Fall-Winter 2013, 13–22. http://21sci-tech.com/Articles_2013/Fall-Winter_2013/Human_Autotrophy.pdf

*Vernadsky, V. I. (1938a) 'The Transition from the Biosphere to the Noösphere'. Excerpts from *Scientific Thought as a Planetary Phenomenon*. Republished in *21st Century*, Spring–Summer 2012, 10–31. http://21sci-tech.com/Articles_2012/Spring-Summer_2012/04_Biospere_Noosphere.pdf.

*Vernadsky, V. I. (1938b) 'On Some Fundamental Problems of Biogeochemistry: In Connection with the Work of the Laboratory of Biogeochemistry of the Academy of Sciences of the USSR'. Republished in *21st Century*, Winter 2005-2006, 39–49. http://21sci-tech.com/2006_articles/Biogeochemistry.pdf.

*Vernadsky, V. I. (1943) 'Some Words about the Noösphere'. Republished in *21st Century*, Spring 2005, 16–21. http://21sci-tech.com/translations/The_Noosphere.pdf.

Vernadsky, V. I. (1998, first published in Russian, 1926) *The Biosphere*. New York: Copernicus (Springer: https://www.springer.com/us/book/9780387982687).

Visionmobile (2011) 'Developer Economics 2011'. Online: https://www.slashdata.co/blog/developer-economics-2011-winners-and-losers-in-the-platform-race. And see: https://www.slideshare.net/andreasc/mobile-megatrends-2011-visionmobile.

Voigts, E. (2017) 'Memes and Recombinant Appropriation: Remix, Mashup, Parody'. In T. Leitch (ed.), *The Oxford Handbook of Adaptation Studies*. Oxford: Oxford University Press, 285–302.

Vološinov, V. (1973) *Marxism and the Philosophy of Language*. New York & London: Seminar Press.Von Hippel, E. (2005) *Democratizing Innovation*. Cambridge MA: MIT Press.

Von Hippel, E. (2005) *Democratizing Innovation*. Cambridge MA: MIT Press.

Vonderau, P. (2016) 'The Video Bubble: Multi-Channel Networks and the Transformation of YouTube'. *Convergence*, 22(3).

Wallerstein, I. (2004) *World System Analysis: An Introduction*. Durham, NC: Duke University Press.

Wang, J. (2018) *Carceral Capitalism*. Cambridge, MA: Semiotext(e), MIT Press.

Wark, M. (2004) *A Hacker Manifesto*. Cambridge, MA: Harvard University Press.

Weber, S. (2004) *The Success of Open Source*. Cambridge, MA and London: Harvard University Press.

Westbury, M. (2015) *Creating Cities*. Australia: Niche Press.

Wildfeuer, J., E. Adami, M. Boeriis, L. Ravelli and F. Veloso (2018) 'Analysing Digitized Visual Culture (Editorial)'. *Visual Communication*, 17(3), 271–5.

Williams, R. (1961) *The Long Revolution*. London: Chatto and Windus.

Williams, R. (1978) 'The Press and Popular Culture: An Historical Perspective'. In G. Boyce, J. Curran and P. Wingate (eds), *Newspaper History: From the Seventeenth Century to the Present Day*. London: Constable, 41–50.

Williams, R. (1989) *Raymond Williams on Television: Selected Writings* (ed. A. O'Connor). London: Routledge, reissued 2011.

Winthrop-Young, G. (2000) 'Silicon Sociology, or, Two Kings on Hegel's Throne? Kittler, Luhmann, and Posthuman Merger of German Media Theory'. *The Yale Journal of Criticism*, 13(2), 391–420.

*Wired* (1997) 'You Are Cyborg' (by Hari Kunzru). *Wired*, February 2, 1997: https://www.wired.com/1997/02/ffharaway/.

Forum, W. E. (2019) *The Global Risks Report 2019, 14th Edition*. http://www3.weforum.org/docs/WEF_Global_Risks_Report_2019.pdf

Wiggins, B. E. (2019) *The Discursive Power of Memes in Digital Culture Ideology, Semiotics, and Intertextuality*. New York: Routledge.

Wolfe, C. (2010) *What Is Posthumanism?* Minneapolis, MN: University of Minnesota Press.

Wolfe, C. (2018) 'Posthumanism'. In R. Braidotti and M. Hlavajova (eds), *Posthuman Glossary*. London: Bloomsbury.

Wolfe, T. (1968) *The Pump House Gang*. New York NY: Bantam Books.

Yudell, M. and R. DeSalle (2000) 'Essay Review: *Sociobiology*: Twenty-Five Years Later'. *Journal of the History of Biology* 33, 577–84.

Zecker, R. (2008) *Metropolis: The American City in Popular Culture*. Westport, CT: Praeger.

Zittrain, J. (2008) *The Future of the Internet and How to Stop It*. New Haven, CT: Yale University Press. Open Access at: https://dash.harvard.edu/bitstream/handle/1/4455262/Zittrain_Future+of+the+Internet.pdf.

Zylko, B. (2001) 'Culture and Semiotics: Notes on Lotman's Conception of Culture'. *New Literary History*, 32, 391–408.

\* \* \*

\* The Vernadsky papers cited, and other translated excerpts from his work, can be found here: https://larouchepac.com/vernadsky.

# INDEX

*1983* 233

ABBA 229
Abernathy, W. and J. Utterback 188
Acerbi, A. 33
Adams, P. 285
Adamu, A. 231
affect 33, 37, 257
agora (Athens) 262–4, 272
Ahmed, A. 30
Ahn, J. 197
AI (artificial intelligence) 7, 8, 36, 40,
    60, 74, 159–61, 248–9, 272
Ai, Wei Wei 44
Akhenaten (pharaoh) 23
Alexander, B. 189
Alibaba 45, 197, 236, 249, 263
AlphaGo (Google) 160, 162
alternate reality games 139
Alvaredo, F. et al. 8
*Amélie* 127
Amnesty 272
analogue 5
    code 81, 87, 124, 133–4, 253
    era 7, 45
Anderson, B. 178, 192
Andrews, Edna 94, 98, 112
Andrews, Eve 292–3
Andrews, P. 291 n. 4
Ang, I. 106
Anglosphere 69, 101, 105, 178, 229
Anthropocene
    era 6, 11, 21–2, 32, 33, 36, 57, 64,
        304
    geosphere 253
AO3 (Archive of Our Own) 140
Apple 45, 102, 183, 187, 197, 210
    Apple Lisa 88, 191
    iOS 102, 191–2

Archimedes lever 5–6, 104
Aristotle 263–4, 295, 296
    Aristotelian 263, 272
Arthur, W. B. 160, 243
Ashby, R. 113
Atlas (titan) 50
atmosphere 13, 20, 24, 26, 38–41, 63,
    245, 255
Atterton, P. 107
audiovisual
    affordances 179
    culture 92
    media 240
    production 92, 200, 217–18, 232,
        278
    recaps 140, 141
    storytelling 128, 206
    text 123, 141, 167, 172
Audiovisual Media Services Directive
    (EU) 231, 234
augmented reality (AR) 187, 209–10,
    248–9
automation 7, 8, 60, 202, 248,
    271
    of translation 87
autopoiesis 32, 113, 173, 303

Bagge, P. 128
Baidu 45, 197, 236
Bakhtin, M. 58, 104, 110
    Bakhtinian 154
Ballantyne, A. and A. Law 89 n. 3
Banksy, 123 n. 1, 149
Bannon, S. 42, 282
Bar-On, Y. et al. 21, 245
Baron, J. 141, 167, 172
Barthes, R. 78, 104, 122
Bateson, G. 113
Baudrillard, J. 97

BBC (British Broadcasting
    Corporation) 101, 219
*Before Sunrise* 124
'belt and road' initiative (China) 37,
    227, 304
Benington, J. and M. Moore 220, 279,
    314
Bennett, J. et al. 219–20
Bennett, L. and J. Kidd 240
*Beowulf* 257
Berbrier, M. 262
Bernardo, N. 189
Berners-Lee, T. 45, 64, 180
Berry, B. 152
Bertalanfy, L. von 113
Bertelsmann 226
Beyer, S. and L. Gorris 117
Beyoncé and Jay Z ('Apeshit') 156
Bilton, C. 143
biomass 21, 24, 245, 247, 250
*Birth of Venus* 151, 153
Björnberg, K. et al. 44
*Black Mirror: Bandersnatch* 139
Blaim, A. 56
Blais, M. and F. Dupuis-Déri 262
Blind, G. 298
blockchain 5, 249, 303
    applications 300–1
    Aristotle and 295–7
    as creative industry 277–9
    critique of 280–1
    regulation of 301–2
    as rule-changing apparatus 300
    and trust 298–300
Boden, M. 159–60
Bollywood 231
Bolt 197
Bolter, J. and R. Grusin 77, 99, 172,
    191
Bond (franchise) 179
Bondebjerg, I. 232
Bonfante, P. and I. Anca 247
Bong, J-H. 229
Boudana, S. et al. 149
Bourdieu, P. 109
Bouvier, G. 156
Boyd, B. 33
Boyd, G. 265
Braidotti, R. 111

Bratton, B. 38
Brexit 44, 275, 280
bricolage 151, 165
Brier, S. 18–19, 31
Brinkerink, M. 130
British 86, 231
    empire 230
    Film Institute (BFI) 133, 193
    invasion (pop) 232
    Library 141
*Broken Earth* trilogy 257
Brodbeck, F. 133
Broms, H. and H. Gahmberg 80, 186
Brown, J. and P. Duguid 191
Bruns, A. 61, 142, 156, 185–6, 193,
    260
    and J. Burgess 138
BTS 232
Buchanan, J. 261
Burgess, J. 148
    and J. Green 75, 132, 157, 218
Buzzfeed 83, 292

Callicott, J. B. 22
Cannizzaro, S. 148
Casey, M. and P. Vigna 277, 299–300
Castells, M. 94
    and G. Cordoso 19
Chakrabarty, D. 36–7
Chaminade, C. et al. 214
Chan, G. 251 n. 9
Chandler, D. 25, 73, 104, 105
Chandrashekar, A. et al. 140
Channel 4 (UK) 219, 251
Cheney, G. and L. Christensen 186
*Chernobyl* 263
Chomsky, N. 58
Christian, D. 28
Christensen, L. 186
Chua, E-J. 118
Chun, W. 160
circular
    causation 251
    economy 275
    re-emergence 152
    world 249
citizen 9, 32, 199, 206, 259, 263, 264,
    266, 295, 301, 307
    Aristotle on 296

citizenship 45
industrial 283
world 45, 29
Citton, Y. 151
climate justice 5, 276, 291, 308
Cohendet, P. and P. Llerena 219
Colebrook, C. and J. Weinstein 6
collective action 5, 15, 36, 263, 266
Colleoni, E. et al. 156
Columbus, C. 50
Commons, J. 214
Continental philosophy 56
convergence. See also Jenkins, H.
AR/VR 187
and divergence 91–3
economic 225
historical/evolutionary dynamics 17
institutional 181–2
media 45, 97, 178, 180, 184, 196, 218
semiotic 77
convergent
domains 182
forms 54
identity 208
industries 189
languages 77, 108
pricing 181
subsystems 77, 92
Coppins, M. 8
coronavirus 4, 7, 291 n. 4
COVID-19 4
Pandemic 5, 36
Coster, L. J. 244
cosmopolitans 45, 275
anti- 44
cosmos 67, 310 n. 5
cosmic origins 22–3
Cotani, T. 249
Couldry, N. 106, 109
and U. Mejias 38
Cowen, T. 288, 296
CNN 284, 300
Craith (Hidden) 101
Crash Landing on You 229
Crescenzi, R. et al. 317
Cribb, J. 177

Crouching Tiger Hidden Dragon 228–9
cultural science 31–3, 103, 106, 114, 220, 253, 305
cultural studies 15, 27, 33, 37, 72, 94, 96, 103–6, 294
culture snacker 130–1
Cunningham, H. 168
Curtin, M. and K. Sanson 234
Cusumano, M. 197
cybernetics 6, 27, 56, 58, 78, 103, 106, 113, 143, 253
cyborg 251

Danesi, M. 78, 130
Dark 233
Dark Knight 140
Darwin, C. 40, 112, 243
data. See also metadata
analytics 92, 106, 186, 190, 213, 217, 237
big 6, 39, 41, 106, 114, 122, 217
datafication 55, 205, 236, 242
database 87, 119, 130, 135, 161, 193, 280, 300
blockchain as 278
culture 190
digital 118, 134, 157
narratives 167–8
object 135
online 167
practices 119
David, P. 188, 193–4, 246
and S. Greenstein 196
Dawkins, R. 147–8
decoding 61, 76, 122, 154
dual coding 76
deconstruction 87, 105, 299 n. 15
Deep Blue (IBM) 161–2
defamiliarisation 99, 107, 206, 277
Deleuze, G. and F. Guattari 112
demes 13, 32, 178, 192, 240, 242, 260, 266, 291, 307
Derrida, J. 97, 104–5
Deutsche, M. 308
diachrony 20, 61, 72, 77, 81, 99, 100, 106, 108, 120, 139, 166, 167, 172, 173, 262. See also panchrony, synchrony

Diavolo, L. 273, 275, 303 n. 1
*Dick Tracy* 179
Dickens, C. 282 n. 16
digital storytelling 168–70
Dijck, J. van 55, 168
  et al. 38, 55, 197, 205, 220, 249
DiMaggio, P. and J. Cohen 196
Dincecco, M. 288
discretization 134
Disney 102, 142, 226
  Disney+ 235
  Disneyfication 131, 132
Dlakavu, S. et al. 30
*Dogs of Berlin* 233
Donne, J. 50–1, 264
Dopfer, K. et al. 124, 288, 297
  and Potts, 210, 279
Dor, D. 33
Dosi, G. 195, 246
Dowd, T. et al. 189
Drake, F. 43, 46
Dutton, W. et al. 193
dystopia 4, 38, 45, 52, 255, 305
  digital 7 n. 3, 8
  in games 257

Earth system 5, 7, 10–11, 17, 24, 27,
    31, 35, 38, 60, 67, 237, 245,
    255, 257, 261, 295, 310 n. 5
  dynamics 253
  semiotic 13, 48
  science 252
  strata 14, 250
  theory 15
echo chamber 156, 192, 260, 266, 283
Eco, U. 60, 76–7, 104, 117, 172, 188,
    189
*Economist* 46 n. 15, 300
ecosphere 74, 250
*Edge, The* 22 n. 13, 25 n. 18
EdTech 201–2, 205–6, 280
Eisenstein, S. 58
Elias, N. 109, 110
*Elle* 228
Elmer, G. and M. Gasher 234
el-Ojeili, C. 38, 261
Enzensberger, H. M. 16–17, 27, 36
Epstein, M. 80, 90,

Erlich, V. 58
Ernst, W. 142, 193, 246
Estonia/n 9, 56–7, 112, 152–3, 170,
    197, 284
  film 149
  language 128
  *maausk* 170
  president 152–3
Ethereum 276, 300
*Europeana* 136–7, 200
Eusunoptos (ideal city) 263
Evans, N. 33
exceptionalism
  analytical 253
  human 111–12
extinction 23, 36, 42, 81, 99, 165, 257,
    273
  of media 266
  of technologies 242
  of texts 81–2
Extinction Rebellion 38, 258, 272,
    276
  *Handbook* 276

Facebook 74, 128, 138, 146, 155 n. 9,
    200, 216, 237
fake news 44, 231, 239, 263, 284, 305
*Falling for Hamlet* 162
fallism 30
fan fiction (fanfic) 140–1
fandom 110, 141, 306
*Farewell to Arms* 129
Faust/ian 287, 244
Favareau, D. et al. 148
feminism 44, 56, 155, 262, 306
Fenton, N. 290
Filmbyen 232
filter bubbles 156, 185, 192, 260
*Final Fantasy* 79
Fitzroy, R. 40–1
Fleischfresser, S. 22
Florenski, P. 58
Foerster, H. von 56
Follett, J. 162
food, as 'thinking world' 68
Forbidden City (Beijing) 131–2
Ford, P. 155
Fornäs, J. 106

Foster, J. R. McChesney and R. J.
    Jonna 8
Foucault, M. 94–6, 104, 106, 208–9
    governmentality 95
Fox News 283, 300
'free energy' (Vernadsky) 15, 17, 21,
    25, 36, 245, 246
Freeman, C. 98–9, 214
    and Louçã 98, 297
    and Perez 98
Freud, L. 151
Fridays for Future 38, 272–3, 274, 308
Frosh, P. 118
Frost, A. 199
Four Corners (ABC-TV) 51
Funk, J. 179
Fust, J. and P. Schöffer 244

Galloway, A. 55
Game of Thrones 257
Garde-Hansen, J. et al. 168
Garrouste, P. and S. Ioannides 194
Gelernter, D. 248
generativity 109
Genette, G. 140
Georgakopoulou, A. 156
Gevinson, T. 85
Gibson, M. 103
Gikay, A. and C. Stanescu 301–2
Gintis, H. 241, 260
global consciousness 36, 42, 43, 46
global digital
    capitalism 9
    culture 6, 9, 56, 118
    data 43
    media 13, 56, 111
    network 248
    power 9
    semiosphere 9, 210, 221, 326, 257
    social media 42
    technoculture 257
global village 55, 230
'globaloney' 46 n. 15
Globe (theatre) 46, 50
Gollop, A. 128
Google Arts & Culture 136, 141
Gough, N. 37
Gray, J. 137, 139–40, 141

Gregg, M. 290
Greenpeace 272
Grece, C. 234
Gregersen, B. 219
Griffin, R. 260, 265, 266–8, 290
Grinspan, J. 282, 283
Grist 292–3, 293 n. 6
Grosz, E. 112
groupuscules 260, 265, 266–8, 271,
    273, 283, 303
Grusin, R. 6
Guild Wars 79
Gullström, B. 130
Gutenberg, J. 244
    era 120
Gwyll (Hinterland) 101

Haase, D. 155
Haebich, A. and J. Taylor 262–3
Haff, P. 241
Hall, S. 84, 105
Hallam, R. 272
Hallyu 229, 231, 232, 233
Hamlet 156, 162
Harari, Y. N. 8, 49, 272
Haraway, D. 67, 251
Harry Potter: A History of Magic
    141–2
Harvey, D. 118
hate
    crimes 283
    groups 265 n. 7
    speech 44, 155, 283
    object 275
Hawkes, T. 58, 107
Hayek, F. 242, 280, 288, 297
Heap, I. 300
hegemony 105
    discourses 78
    unity 96
Heikkilä, N. 282
Helyar, V. 179
Hemingway, E. 129
Hepp, A. 108, 109, 215
    and U. Hasebrink 109, 110
Herrmann-Pillath, C. 13, 145, 241,
    244–6, 252–3, 258, 293–5
Hjarvard, S. 109, 110, 215

Hjelmslev, L. 58
Hjort, M. 232
Hodgson, G. 185, 297
Hoffmeyer, J. 31
    and C. Emmeche 129
Honko, L. 171
Hoskins, A. 168
Huawei 45, 178, 197, 236
Huhtamo, E. 106–7, 152, 179
*Humans* (C4 TV) 251
Huntington, S. 53
Hutter, M. 289
Huxley, J. 19, 245, 253
Hyde, L. 289
hypertext 134, 171

Ilves, T. H. 152–3
imperialism 30, 242
    American 230
    European 37
    Roman 264
Industrial Revolution 42, 98–9, 230,
    272
influencers 8, 46, 169, 196–7, 215,
    216, 233
information theory 27, 61, 143
Ings, S. 15–16
Instagram 124, 126, 237, 259, 308
    influencers 196, 197, 233
    Instagrammability 133
    network effect 197
    photos 70, 79, 137–8, 139
    platform 128, 138, 216
    stories 138
intellectual property
    and creativity 121
    human rights as 16
    law 178
    rights (IPR) 218, 225, 228, 235
    theft 228
*International Journal of Cultural
    Studies* 106
intersemiotic translation (Jakobson)
    88, 120, 145, 166–7, 168, 172,
    218
isomorphism 118, 120, 124, 130,
    70
    repetition 69

relations 79
systems 125
IRMA (Information Management
    Research Association) 142
Ivanov, V. 58, 74, 124

Jakobson, R. 58, 88, 104, 145, 172
Jane, E. A. 44, 283
    and C. Fleming 169
Jann, O. and C. Schottmüller 259–60
Janssens, D. 263
Jauss, H. 191
Jeffrey, D. 291, 293
Jenkins, H. 38, 45, 77, 91, 110, 128,
    140, 157, 189
Jensen, K. B. 109
Jensen, P. A. 232
Johansson, O. 229
Johnson, B. 214–15, 219
Johnson-Yale, C. 234
journalism 83, 263, 266–7, 284
    and blockchain 299
    as coordination mechanism 266, 284
    post-truth 44
    tech- 301

K-beauty 233
K-pop 111, 231, 232 n. 3, 233
Kasparov, G. 161–2
Katz, M. and C. Schapiro 196
Kauffman, S. 93, 100, 305
Kawada, T. 250
Kawashima, N. and H-K. Lee 231
Kean, H. and P. Howell 168
Keating, K. 307
Keating, P. 307
Keightley, D. 244
Kelly, K. 210, 248–9
Kinder, M. 168
Kipling, R. 127
Kittler, F. 72, 107
Klastrup, L. and S. Tosca 157
Kondratieff, N. 195
Kong, L. 231
Korea/n 229
    Koreanness 232
    North 45, 229
    South 229, 231

Koskimaa, R. 132
Kosnik, A de et al. 140, 141
Kotov, K. 97
knowledge
  club 201, 206, 208, 260–2, 264,
    283, 288, 297, 307
  growth of 143, 158, 201, 214, 217,
    242, 297
Kress, G. 78, 132
  and T. van Leeuwen 133, 188–9
Krippendorff, K. 77, 96
Krotz, F. 108
Kuhn, T. 57
Kull, K. 31, 70, 74, 82, 89, 112–13,
    118, 129, 148, 162–3, 173, 214,
    312
Kumar, V. S. P. and D. Agrawal 180
Küng, L. 207
Kwon, K. 197
Kwon, S-H. and J. Kim 231

La Casa de Papel 233
Laclau, E. and C. Mouffe 46
Lambert, J. 168
Lampert, A. 8
language functions (Jakobson) 125–6
Latour, B. 299
Laurits, P. 1, 65, 115, 175, 223, 269,
    310, 311
Leach, E. 134, 154
Leadbeater, C. 284
ledger 278, 300. See also blockchain
  digital ledger technology (DLT) 301
  distributed 277, 278, 301
  ledgersphere 300
Legg, C. 152
Lesage, F. 161
Lévi-Strauss, C. 58, 104, 151
Licoppe, C. 126
Lindmark, S. et al. 179
Lipovetsky, G 228
List, F. 214
literacy 121, 149, 239
  digital 121, 307
  information 136
  media 122, 307, 308
  transmedia 121, 132
  visual 135

Loasby, B. 297
Lobato, R. 217–18, 231
Locke, J. 279
Lord of the Rings (game) 157
Lotman, M. 27–9, 112–13
Lovelace test 159, 160
Luhmann, N. 33, 94–5, 96, 97, 107
Luhrmann, B. 80
Lumby, C. 103
Lundby, K. 109, 168, 215
Lundgren, A. 194
Lundvall, B. 109, 196, 198, 214–15,
    233, 297

McAfee, A. and E. Brynjolfsson 38
McCloskey, D. 42, 271, 288
MacGregor, N. 36
McKinsey Global Institute 7, 44
McLuhan, M. 31. 23, 81, 88–9, 230
McWhorter, J. 86 n. 2
Ma, J. W. and J. Zheng 213
Madisson, M-L. 169
  and A. Ventsel 126
Madrigal, A. 190
Malinowski, B. 58
Mandoki, K., 96
Manovich, L. 79, 122, 135, 168, 188,
    190
  Cultural Analytics Lab 133
Mansell, J. 170
Mansell, R. 209, 312
  and E. Berdou 94
  and R. Silverstone 96
Marling, B. 257
Marseille 233
Martin, F. et al. 247
Marx, K. 51–2, 291
  Marxist 56, 289, 291
Matrix 91, 128
Matters Journal 307
Maturana, H. 56
  and F. Varela 173
maximum power principle 252
Maxwell, R. 38
  and T. Miller 305
Mazzucato, M. 211, 220, 278, 279
media
  archaeology 81, 103, 106–8

studies 9, 27, 104, 239–40, 256, 259, 306
mediality 81–82
mediapolis 54
mediatization 103, 108–11, 215, 218, 221
of everything 225
memes 122, 147–52, 279
Cigar Guy 148–9
*Downfall* 149, 151
Grumpy Cat 147–8
Mercator 43 n. 12, 46, 51
Merrick, H. 289
Mesoudi, A. 27
mental text 170–1
metadata 60, 87–8, 135–6, 142, 167, 189–90, 193, 210, 249
as 'devil's work' 4
schema 92, 135–6, 160, 189, 190, 193–4, 246
systems 146, 190
usage 157
meteorology 33, 39, 41, 63
Miller, T. 305–6
Miller, V. 126, 160
Milton, J. 287, 310
Mints, Z. 57, 169
'Mirrorworld' 210, 248–50, 304
misogyny 44, 283
Mitchell, W. J. T. 76
mnemonic
collection 170
community 173
device 166
field 174
function 62, 129, 167
logic 120
program 166
modality 131, 133–4, 208, 218. *See also* multimodal/ity
affordances 78
modalities 70, 76, 79, 109, 119, 121, 132, 133, 151, 186, 225
variables 133
modelling system/s 113, 143, 145, 172, 261
complex 41

languages and 77–9, *see also* secondary modelling
Mokyr, J. 98, 217, 271
*Mona Lisa* 156, 166
megamonalisa.com 166
monad, semiotic 77, 119
Monticelli, D. 78
Moore, P. 39, 40
Moore, T. 103
Moore's Law 241
Morozov, E. 303
Morsing, M. 186
multimodal/ity 119, 136, 149, 237

National Stadium (Beijing) 213
Needham, J. 29–30, 40
Nelson, C. 151
Nelson, T. 133–4, 171
Nelson, T. and S. Winter 297
Netflix 92–3, 119, 200, 229, 233, 263
algorithms of 190, 193
interactive titles 139
local production 233–4, 235
recommendations by 160
network effects 102, 196–8, 200, 218, 226, 249, 278, 288
Neubauer, L. and A. Reppening 291
Neumann, J. von 113
neural network 87, 160, 248
*New York 2140* 257
*New York Times* 83, 148, 257–8, 290, 299
News Corporation
Neylon, C. 260, 261
Nintendo 139, 190
Nollywood 231
Nordic Noir 101
North, D. C. 297
Nöth, W. 72, 78, 87
Nunes, M. R. F. 165

OA 257
observation (science) 38, 52, 60
observation–calculation–communication (as method) 33, 39, 40, 41
O'Dair, M. 278, 300
Odum, H. 252

OECD (Organisation for Economic Cooperation and Development) 214, 258
Ong. W. J. 13, 171, 242
O'Regan, T. 105, 312
Ostrom, E. 297
*Overstory* 248

Palace Museum (Beijing) 131–2
panchrony 172. *See also* diachrony, synchrony
Papacharissi, Z. 10, 158
*Paradise Lost* 287, 310
*Parasite* 229
paratext 139–40
Parikka, J. 38, 108
Pariser, E. 192
Peele, G. 129
Peirce, C. S. 19, 104, 147, 152, 247
Peltzman, D. 234
Perez, C. 195–6
Peters, J. D. 39
phatic 125–6, 160
Phillips, A. 189
Phillips, W. and R. Milner 156
Pinterest 130, 157, 167
Pjatigorskij, A. 58
plastic, planet 256
platformization 38, 55, 197, 205, 220, 242, 249
Plato's shadow in the cave 50, 239
Playstation 190, 265
pnyx (Athens) 262–4
Pomerantz, J. 189
Popper, K. 17, 288
populism 260, 301
    authoritarian 42, 48, 56, 275
    nationalist 275
    technological 301–2
posthuman 31, 36, 74, 111–14, 241, 247, 248 n. 6
    posthumanism 48, 111–14, 242, 256
postmodern/ity 56, 118, 130, 266, 300
    postmodernism 27, 105, 151, 167
post-truth 44, 67 n. 1, 299 n. 14–15
Pottage, A. 95, 208
Potts, J. 178, 214, 297, 300

and Rennie 277–9, 281, 300
    et al. (2008) 109, 194, 215–17, 283
    et al. (2017) 201, 206, 215–17, 260
Pratt, A. 231
Pratten, R. 189
probability 28, 29, 201
    archive 142–3
Pronk, M. 130
protocol/s 55, 266, 284, 295, 298
    blockchain 298, 299
    internet 197
    machine-readable 194
    meteorological 33
    scientific 288
precarious (labour) 8, 217, 292, 291, 292
Prigogine, I. and I. Stengers 28
Propp, V. 10, 58
public sphere 263, 284
Putin, V. 71 n. 2, 100

Quiggin, J. 288

*Radical Mycology* 248
Ravelli, L. and T. van Leeuwen 133
rearviewmirrorism 89, 151–2
Reddit 147, 282
Reed, D. 197
regeneration economy 5, 250, 275–6, 304–5
relational stratification 78–9
Rennie, E. 277
rewilding 275, 276
*The Rig* 257
Rigney, A. 81
Rijksmuseum (Amsterdam) 130–1
*Rijksstudio* 130–2
Riley, M. et al. 140
Rivero, B. 81
Rivett, M. 189
Robinson, K. S. 117, 257
Rohn, U. 157, 227, 312
*Romeo and Juliet* 80–1, 115
Romer, J. 23
Roulstone, I. 39
Rousseau, J-J. 97
Roy, R. D. 30

Rühse, V. 131–2
Russian Formalism 58, 99, 104, 107, 206

Salthe, S. 31
Salupere, S. 58, 67, 117, 121, 143
Saussure, F. de 56, 72–3, 104–5
  Saussurian 74, 104–5, 154
Sautoy, M. du 159–61
Sawhney, H. and S. Lee 94
Schäfer, M. and K. van Es 236
Schich, M. 133
Schneiderman, J. 6
Schönle, A. 94
  and J. Shine 94, 96, 197
School Strike for Climate 38, 308, 309 n. 4
Schumpeter, J. A. 99–100, 195, 199
Scolari, C. 33, 86, 121, 140–1, 189, 218
Sebeok, T. 104
secondary modelling 135–7
  as euphemism for semiotics 78, 79
semantic web 152, 161, 193, 210, 248, 304
Semiosis (novel) 248
semiotic space 11, 28, 53, 73, 261
  extra-semiotic space 89
Senft, T. and N. Baym 152
Sennett, R. 262
Sevignani, S. 292, 306
Shakespeare, W. 46, 50, 80, 282
  Riots (NYC) 283, 285
Shannon, C. and W. Weaver 125
Sharma, C. and Y. Nakamura 179
Shetland 101
Shimpach, S. 305
Shklovsky, V. 99, 104, 107, 206, 277
Sign Systems Studies 58
Sigurdson, J. 179
Simon, H. 279
Silva, A. 168
Silverstone, R. 54, 236
Skolstreijk för Klimatet. See School Strike for Climate
Skype 200, 226
Sloterdijk, P. 50, 186, 211
smart city 4, 5, 248, 249

Snapchat 128, 138, 196, 216
social network market/s 194, 214–17, 226, 235, 283
Sorkin, M. 3–5
Soukup, C. 241
Soviet Union 15, 16, 94, 170, 228
  army 57
  authorities 78
  leaders 71–2
  linguistics 58
  post- 90
  regime 162
  science 15
  Sovietism 56
Sperling, A. 6
Spotify 72, 119, 137, 190, 193, 229, 233, 279
Srnicek, N. 38
staged conflict 242, 277, 281–5, 295, 297–8, 298–9, 301–2, 305
  entrepreneurs of 284
Star Wars 102
  fandom 110, 142
Steam (platform) 190–1, 265
steampunk 165
Steele, E. et al. 22
Steinbock, D. 180
stereoscopy (semiotic) 121, 136, 158
Straubhaar, J. 234
Strauven, W. 139
structuralism 56, 57, 58, 75, 89, 105, 122
  post- 58, 59, 94, 105
Suburra 233
Super Carlin Brothers 141–2
Supernova 149, 150
supranational agencies 36, 258
  government 304
Swedberg, R. 289
Swift, T. 229, 279
Swinney, J. T. 129
synchrony 20, 72, 77, 81, 89, 99, 108, 120, 166, 167, 172, 173, 262.
  See also diachrony, panchrony
  asynchrony 98
  synchronisation 98
Szczepanik, P. 234

Tartu-Moscow School (cultural semiotics) 55–8, 61, 78, 104, 137, 143
technosphere 11, 13, 31, 239–53, 256, 258, 305
  agency 251
  autonomy 244–7
  biology and 247–8
  consciousness and 113
  digital 74, 304
  economic 301
  hybridity 252–3
  regulatory system 294–5
  science 241
  technomass 250
Tee, R. 179
*Teen Vogue* 274, 275, 303 n. 1
Tencent 45, 197, 236
  games 263
Thumim, N. 169
Thunberg, G. 42, 258, 272, 275, 291, 293, 303, 308–9
  as 'institution' 308
  speeches 273
TikTok 126, 169, 216, 237
*Time* 293
Time-Warner 226
Tomasello, M. 54, 72–3
Toporov, V. 58
Topotheque 133
Torlasco, D. 141, 172
Torop, P. 58, 73, 113, 117, 129, 147, 152, 157, 170–1, 173, 312
translatability 32, 86, 87, 147. *See also* intersemiotic translation
translation, five stages of 100–1, 227–9
transmedia 73, 189, 218, 257
  fandom 110
  literacy 121, 132
  producer 189
  recursivity 81
  stories 120
  storytelling 77, 86, 91, 128, 139, 157, 185, 189, 218
  storyworld 79, 102, 140
  strategies 140, 218
  system 124

tribal/ism 23, 44, 53, 267
Tripadvisor 72, 220
Trivago 72
Trump, D. 5, 44, 262, 282, 283
  era 284
  presidency 3, 268
Tsing, A. 247
Tufekci, Z. 261, 273, 290
Turchin, P. 33
Tunstall, J. 230–1
Turing test 159
Twitter 70, 126, 138, 146, 186, 259, 260
  Twittersphere 261
  tweets 61, 126, 284
Tynianov, Y. 104

Uber 197, 207
  'for education' 204
Uexküll, J. von 31, 74, 112–13, 173, 249
Ujo 278, 300
umwelt 32, 74, 112–14, 173, 249
*Un Bore Mercher* (*Keeping Faith*) 101
United Nations (UN) 36
*Understory* 248
untranslatability 32, 61, 85, 86, 120, 130, 146, 206, 221, 262. *See also* translatability
  systems 85, 86, 88, 119
'us' vs 'them' 53, 62, 82, 201, 275. *See also* 'we'-groups
useless (class) 271–3
  uselessness 8
Uspenskij/Uspensky, B. 58, 117, 148, 165
*ustrojstvo* (semiotic device) 121, 143
Ut, N. 148–9
utopia/n 38, 45, 54, 255, 284, 301, 305

Vaan, M. de, B. Vedres and D. Stark 206
Västrik, E-H. 170
*VKontakte* (*ВКонтáкте*) 200
Veblen, T. 214, 297
Veblenesque 240
*Venus of Willendorf* 151

*Vera* 101
Vernadsky, V. I. 11–19, 21–4, 26, 35,
    63, 252
  humanistic sciences 17
  Lotman's use of 19–20, 23, 52, 112,
    241, 258
  vitalism 23–4
Viacom 226
*Vice* 83, 307
*Vice Impact* 307
video on demand (VOD) 92, 234
videogames 61, 62, 102, 157, 179, 187,
    190–1, 202, 265
Vimeo 92, 158
virtual reality (VR) 167, 206, 272, 249
  community 5, 265
  health 206
  museum 141
*Vogue* 228, 293 n. 7
Vološinov, V. 104
Von Hippel, E. 179
Vonderau, P. 92, 218
Vygotsky, L. 58

Wales 10 n. 4, 47, 89 n. 3
  Welsh globe 47
  Welsh language 47, 101
  Welsh Noir 101
Wallerstein, I. 98, 288
Wang, J. 8, 56, 272, 284
Wark, McK. 289–90, 291
Water Cube (Beijing) 211–13
Watters, A. 202–5, 280–1, 302
'we'-groups 178, 240
  'wedom' 53, 178
Weber, S. 94
Weidel, A. 280
Westbury, M. 272
WhatsApp 110, 128, 200, 259
white supremacist/s 45, 265, 275, 282
Wiener, N. 58, 113
Wiggins, B. 149

Wikipedia 77
Williams, R. 170, 281, 282
Winthrop-Young, G. 107
Wireless Application Protocol (WAP)
    179–81, 184
Wolfe, C. 111, 113–14
Wolfe, T. 31 n. 23
Woo, B. 106
Woods, T. 148
World Economic Forum 225, 258
world languages 47
*World of Warcraft* 79
World Wide Web 45, 64, 180, 242,
    267–8, 284, 300
  Consortium (W3C) 180–4, 193
  wood wide web 247
writing 97, 171, 239–44
wrong-way-round discovery 11, 48
wuxia films 228

xenophobia 44

Yiannopoulos, M. 284, 285
YouTube 92–3, 119, 140, 142, 169,
    217, 237
  algorithms of 137
  compilation videos 172
  poetics of 118
  recommendations of 160
  as search engine 132
  as social network market 226
  as text 72, 76, 81
  as traffic 102
Yudell, M. and R. DeSalle 19

Zecker, R. 285
Zentropa 232
Zhou, Enlai 16
Zimmer, B. 152 n. 8
Žirmunskij, V. 58
Zittrain, J. 102
Zylko, B. 98

www.ingramcontent.com/pod-product-compliance
Lightning Source LLC
Chambersburg PA
CBHW060139280326
41932CB00012B/1565